# Just War or Just Peace?

## *Humanitarian intervention and international law*

SIMON CHESTERMAN

OXFORD

UNIVERSITY PRESS

# OXFORD

UNIVERSITY PRESS

Great Clarendon Street, Oxford OX2 6DP

Oxford University Press is a department of the University of Oxford.
It furthers the University's objective of excellence in research, scholarship,
and education by publishing worldwide in

Oxford New York

Auckland Bangkok Buenos Aires Cape Town Chennai
Dar es Salaam Delhi Hong Kong Istanbul Karachi Kolkata
Kuala Lumpur Madrid Melbourne Mexico City Mumbai Nairobi
São Paulo Shanghai Singapore Taipei Tokyo Toronto

Oxford is a registered trade mark of Oxford University Press
in the UK and in certain other countries

Published in the United States
by Oxford University Press Inc., New York

First published 2001
First published new in paperback 2002

British Library Cataloguing in Publication Data

Data available

Library of Congress Cataloging in Publication Data
Chesterman, Simon.
Just war or just peace?: humanitarian intervention and
international law / Simon Chesterman.
p. cm.—(Oxford monographs in international law)
Includes bibliographical references.
1. Humanitarian intervention.   2. Intervention (International law).
I. Title.   II. Series.
JZ6369.C48   2001   341.5'84—dc21   00–053033
ISBN 0–19–924337–9
ISBN 0–19–925799–X (pbk)

Typeset by Hope Services (Abingdon) Ltd.
Printed in Great Britain
on acid-free paper by
Biddles Ltd.,
Guildford and King's Lynn

# JUST WAR OR JUST PEACE?

WITHDRÁWN

# Editor's Preface

This study constitutes a significant addition to the abundant literature on the use of force by States. A comprehensive account is given of the numerous episodes which are concerned with humanitarian intervention, or which are assumed by the commentators to be related to the topic. Careful account is taken both of the policy considerations and of the political or moral ideas lying behind the identification of rules or emergent principles.

A particular virtue of the work is the access which Dr Chesterman gives to the documents and to the facts. The result is a text of considerable value to lawyers, historians, and students of international affairs.

Blackstone Chambers                                                    IAN BROWNLIE QC

# Acknowledgements

Writing a doctoral thesis may well be a solitary task, but it is rarely completed alone. I have many people to thank.

Professor Ian Brownlie, my supervisor, inspired and challenged me throughout this endeavour. Having written the leading text and acted in the major cases on international law and the use of force by states, he nevertheless had the wisdom and patience to let me find my own feet in this area. He made time for me in his extraordinary schedule, and continued to supervise my work after his retirement from Oxford (though hardly from professional life, as a glance at the docket of the International Court of Justice will show). As one of his last doctoral students, I consider myself privileged indeed.

Many other people took the time to discuss or correspond with me on the question of humanitarian intervention, of whom I can only identify a handful. I note my thanks to Professors Guy Goodwin-Gill, Vaughan Lowe, and Adam Roberts of the University of Oxford; Dr Christine Gray of the University of Cambridge; Dr Chaloka Beyani of the London School of Economics; Professor Louis Henkin of Columbia University; Professor Noam Chomsky of the Michigan Institute of Technology; and Commander Doug Denneny of the United States Navy. Professor Michael Byers of Duke University helped me to develop my ideas; together we co-authored two pieces that bear on the issues considered at greater length here. Friends and colleagues helped in various capacities, particularly in the final stages of the thesis. My thanks go to Michael Fullilove, Jéan Meiring, and Patricia Shuming Tan. Robert Dann and Sven Koopmans in particular were painstaking and thorough proofreaders.

My time at Oxford was funded by the Rhodes Trust, ably managed by Warden Sir Anthony Kenny and his successor Dr John Rowett. The Trustees contributed more directly to the content of this work by funding trips to, among other places, Rwanda and the former Yugoslavia. The text was completed within the walls of Magdalen College, Oxford, an institution to which I quickly developed strong ties. I wish to note my sincere thanks to President Anthony Smith, the Fellows, staff, and students of the College for making these years so rewarding.

My warmest thanks are reserved for my family: to my parents, Shirley and Peter, and to my brothers Michael, John, and Andrew for supporting me in all the ways that matter.

Some parts of the present work develop material first published elsewhere. Sections of Chapter 3 have appeared in Michael Byers and Simon Chesterman, '"You, the People": Pro-Democratic Intervention in International Law', in Gregory H Fox & Brad R Roth (eds), *Democratic Governance and International Law* (Cambridge University Press, 2000) 259. The first half of Chapter 5 draws on my 'Passing the Baton: The Delegation of Security Council Enforcement Powers from Kuwait to Kosovo', in Wang Tieya and Sienho Yee (eds), *International Law in the Post-Cold War World: Essays in Memory of Li Haopei* (Routledge, forthcoming). Some early thoughts on Panama appear in 'Rethinking Panama: International Law and the US Invasion of Panama, 1989', in Guy S Goodwin-Gill and Stefan A Talmon (eds), *The Reality of International Law: Essays in Honour of Ian Brownlie* (Oxford University Press, 1999) 57. Permission to reprint the relevant passages is gratefully acknowledged.

# Chapter Outline

# Contents

Contents                                                   xiii

# Table of Cases

*Table of Cases*

# Table of Treaties and UN Resolutions

## SECURITY COUNCIL RESOLUTIONS

## GENERAL ASSEMBLY RESOLUTIONS

# Abbreviations

| | |
|---|---|
| *African JICL* | *African Journal of International and Comparative Law* |
| *AJIL* | *American Journal of International Law* |
| *American University JILP* | *American University Journal of International Law and Policy* |
| *ASIL Proc* | *Proceedings of the American Society of International Law* |
| *Austrian JPIL* | *Austrian Journal of Public International Law* |
| *British YBIL* | *British Yearbook of International Law* |
| *Bush Papers* | *Public Papers of the Presidents of the United States: George Bush* (4 vols; Washington, DC: US Govt Printing Office, 1990–93) |
| BVerfGE | Entscheidungen des Bundesverfassungsgerichts |
| *California Western ILJ* | *California Western International Law Journal* |
| CAR | Central African Republic |
| *Columbia JTL* | *Columbia Journal of Transnational Law* |
| *Cornell LJ* | *Cornell Law Journal* |
| CSCE | Conference on Security and Cooperation in Europe |
| CTS | Consolidated Treaty Series |
| *Denver JILP* | *Denver Journal of International Law and Policy* |
| *Denver LJ* | *Denver Law Journal* |
| *Dept of State Bull* | *USA Department of State Bulletin* |
| DOMREP | Mission of the Special Representative of the Secretary-General in the Dominician Republic |
| *Duke JCIL* | *Duke Journal of Comparative and International Law* |
| Duvergier | J B Duvergier (ed), *Lois, décrets, ordonnances, réglemens, avis du conseil d'état* (Paris: Guyot, 1834-1858) |
| EC | European Community |
| ECOMOG | ECOWAS Cease-fire Monitoring Group |
| ECOWAS | Economic Community of West African States |
| EU | European Union |
| *European JIL* | *European Journal of International Law* |
| FBIS | Foreign Broadcast Information Service |
| *Fordham ILJ* | *Fordham International Law Journal* |

| | |
|---|---|
| FRY | Federal Republic of Yugoslavia |
| *Georgia JICL* | *Georgia Journal of International and Comparative Law* |
| *Harvard ILJ* | *Harvard International Law Journal* |
| *Houston JIL* | *Houston Journal of International Law* |
| ICJ | International Court of Justice |
| *ICLQ* | *International and Comparative Law Quarterly* |
| ICRC | International Committee of the Red Cross |
| ICTR | International Criminal Tribunal for Rwanda |
| ICTY | International Criminal Tribunal for the Former Yugoslavia |
| IFOR | NATO-led Implementation Force in Bosnia and Herzegovina |
| *IHT* | *International Herald Tribune* |
| ILC | International Law Commission |
| *ILC YB* | *Yearbook of the International Law Commission* |
| ILR | International Law Reports |
| *Indiana LJ* | *Indiana Law Journal* |
| INTERFET | International Force in East Timor |
| *Johnson Papers* | *Public Papers of the Presidents of the United States: Lyndon B Johnson* (10 vols; Washington, DC: US Govt Printing Office, 1965–70) |
| *Keesing's* | *Keesing's Contemporary Archives: Record of World Events*, vol 1 (1932)—vol 32 (1986) and *Keesing's Record of World Events* vol 33 (1987)— |
| KFOR | NATO Kosovo Force |
| KLA/UÇK | Kosovo Liberation Army |
| *Loyola of Los Angeles ICLJ* | *Loyola of Los Angeles International and Comparative Law Journal* |
| *McGill LJ* | *McGill Law Journal* |
| *Michigan JIL* | *Michigan Journal of International Law* |
| MICIVIH | International Civilian Mission in Haiti |
| MINURCA | UN Mission in the Central African Republic |
| MISAB | Inter-African Mission to Monitor the Implementation of the Bangui Agreements |
| MSC | Military Staff Committee |
| NATO | North Atlantic Treaty Organization |
| *Netherlands ILR* | *Netherlands International Law Review* |
| *New York Law School JICL* | *New York Law School Journal of International and Comparative Law* |

| | |
|---|---|
| *NYT* | *New York Times* |
| *NYUJILP* | *New York University Journal of International Law and Politics* |
| OAS | Organization of American States |
| OAU | Organization of African Unity |
| OECS | Organization of Eastern Caribbean States |
| ONUC | UN Operation in the Congo |
| ONUCA | UN Observer Group in Central America |
| OSCE | Organization for Security and Cooperation in Europe |
| *RCADI* | *Recueil des cours de l'académie de droit international* |
| *Reagan Papers* | *Public Papers of the Presidents of the United States: Ronald Reagan* (15 vols; Washington, DC: US Govt Printing Office, 1982–91) |
| *RGDIP* | *Revue générale de droit international public* |
| RP | Repertory of the Practice of United Nations Organs |
| RPF | Rwandan Patriotic Front |
| SFOR | NATO-led Stabilization Force in Bosnia and Herzegovina |
| *Stanford JIL* | *Stanford Journal of International Law* |
| *Syracuse JILC* | *Syracuse Journal of International Law and Commerce* |
| *Texas ILJ* | *Texas International Law Journal* |
| *Tulane JICL* | *Tulane Journal of International and Comparative Law* |
| UNAMET | UN Mission in East Timor |
| UNAMIR | UN Assistance Mission in Rwanda |
| UNAMSIL | UN Mission in Sierra Leone |
| UNAVEM I | UN Angola Verification Mission I |
| UNAVEM II | UN Angola Verification Mission II |
| UNCIO | United Nations, Documents of the United Nations Conference on International Organization, San Francisco 1945 (21 vols; New York: United Nations, 1945–55) |
| UNDOF | UN Disengagement Observer Force |
| UNEF I | First UN Emergency Force |
| UNEF II | Second UN Emergency Force |
| UNFICYP | UN Peace-Keeping Force in Cyprus |
| UNGOMAP | UN Good Offices Mission in Afghanistan and Pakistan |

| | |
|---|---|
| UNHCHR | UN High Commissioner for Human Rights |
| UNHCR | UN High Commissioner for Refugees |
| UNIFIL | UN Interim Force in Lebanon |
| UNIIMOG | UN Iran-Iraq Military Observer Group |
| UNIKOM | UN Iraq-Kuwait Observation Mission |
| UNIPOM | UN India-Pakistan Observation Mission |
| UNITA | National Union for the Total Independence of Angola |
| UNITAF | United Task Force |
| UNMIH | UN Mission in Haiti |
| UNMOGIP | UN Military Observer Group in India and Pakistan |
| UNOGIL | UN Observation Group In Lebanon |
| UNOMSIL | UN Observer Mission in Sierra Leone |
| UNOSOM I | UN Operation in Somalia I |
| UNOSOM II | UN Operation in Somalia II |
| UNPREDEP | UN Preventive Deployment Force |
| UNPROFOR | UN Protection Force |
| UNSCOM | UN Special Commission |
| UNSF | UN Security Force in West New Guinea (West Irian) |
| UNTAET | UN Transitional Administration in East Timor |
| UNTAG | UN Transition Assistance Group |
| UNTSO | UN Truce Supervision Organization |
| *UNYB* | *Yearbook of the United Nations* |
| UNYOM | UN Yemen Observation Mission |
| USSR | Union of Soviet Socialist Republics |
| *Vanderbilt JTL* | *Vanderbilt Journal of Transnational Law* |
| *Virginia JIL* | *Virginia Journal of International Law* |
| *Yale JIL* | *Yale Journal of International Law* |
| *Yale LJ* | *Yale Law Journal* |

# Abstract

## Just War or Just Peace?
## Humanitarian intervention and international law

The question of the legality of humanitarian intervention is, at first blush, a simple one. The Charter of the United Nations clearly prohibits the use of force, with the only exceptions being self-defence and enforcement actions authorized by the Security Council. There are, however, long-standing arguments that a right of unilateral intervention pre-existed the Charter. This book begins with an examination of the genealogy of this right, and arguments that it may have survived the passage of the Charter, either through a loophole in Article 2(4) or as part of customary international law. It has also been argued that certain 'illegitimate' regimes lose the attributes of sovereignty and thereby the protection given by the prohibition of the use of force. None of these arguments is found to have merit, either in principle or in the practice of states.

A common justification for a right of unilateral humanitarian intervention concerns the failure of the collective security mechanism created after the Second World War. Chapters 4 and 5 therefore examine Security Council activism in the 1990s, notable for the plasticity of the circumstances in which the Council was prepared to assert its primary responsibility for international peace and security, and the contingency of its actions on the willingness of states to carry them out. This reduction of the Council's role from substantive to formal partly explains the recourse to unilateralism in that decade, most spectacularly in relation to the situation in Kosovo. Crucially, the book argues that such unilateral enforcement is not a substitute for but the opposite of collective action. Though often presented as the only alternative to inaction, incorporating a 'right' of intervention would lead to more such interventions being undertaken in bad faith, it would be incoherent as a principle, and it would be inimical to the emergence of an international rule of law.

# Introduction

There are few questions in the whole range of International Law more difficult than those connected with the legality of intervention, and few have
been treated in a more unsatisfactory manner by the bulk of writers on the
subject. . . . Yet this deficiency in the treatment of a great subject is hardly to
be wondered at. We can generally deduce the rules of International Law
from the practice of states; but in this case it is impossible to do anything of
the kind. Not only have different states acted on different principles, but the
action of the same state at one time has been irreconcilable with its action at
another. On this subject history speaks with a medley of discordant voices,
and the facts of international intercourse give no clue to the rules of
International Law.

T J Lawrence, 1895[1]

On 24 March 1999 the North Atlantic Treaty Organization (NATO) commenced air strikes against the Federal Republic of Yugoslavia (FRY). Various
reasons were given for the action. NATO Secretary-General Javier Solana
stated that the military alliance acted because the FRY had refused to comply
with the demands of the international community in relation to actions in the
Serbian province of Kosovo; US President Bill Clinton emphasized the
potential for a wider war if action were not taken, and the humanitarian concerns that led the allies to act; UK Prime Minister Tony Blair argued that the
choice was to do something or do nothing.[2]

On the face of it, international law is clear on the legal status of such an
action. Article 2(4) of the UN Charter establishes a broad prohibition of the
use of force, subject to two exceptions: self-defence and actions authorized by
the UN Security Council. Operation Allied Force against the FRY manifestly
did not fall within either exception. There has, however, been a long-running
debate that an additional exception may allow for humanitarian intervention,
defined by Ian Brownlie as 'the threat or use of armed force by a state, a belligerent community, or an international organization, with the object of protecting human rights'.[3] It was striking that, although this doctrine was cited

---

[1] T J Lawrence, *The Principles of International Law* (London: Macmillan, 1895) 116–17.
[2] See Ch 5, Sect 4.2.
[3] Ian Brownlie, 'Humanitarian Intervention', in John N Moore (ed), *Law and Civil War in the
Modern World* (Baltimore, Maryland: Johns Hopkins University Press, 1974) 217. Other definitions include Ellery C Stowell, *Intervention in International Law* (Washington, DC: John Byrne
& Co, 1921) 53: 'the reliance upon force for the justifiable purpose of protecting the inhabitants
of another state from treatment which is so arbitrary and persistently abusive as to exceed the
limits of that authority within which the sovereign is presumed to act with reason and justice.'
    Fernando R Tesón, *Humanitarian Intervention: An Inquiry into Law and Morality* (Dobbs
Ferry, NY: Transnational, 1988) 1: 'the proportionate transboundary help, including forcible

by many commentators during and after the operation, the acting states themselves showed great reluctance to rely upon it—indeed, one of the conditions for the conclusion of hostilities was the passage of a Security Council resolution granting legitimacy to the eventual settlement.

As the quote from Lawrence indicates, such discordant voices on the question of intervention are not a novelty. Indeed, the relative enthusiasm of publicists to embrace a doctrine of humanitarian intervention has long contrasted with the reticence of states to do the same, perhaps wary of creating a normative rod for their own backs. The resulting uncertainty as to the status of the doctrine is expressed in the following terms in the ninth edition of *Oppenheim*:

[W]hen a state commits cruelties against and persecution of its nationals in such a way as to deny their fundamental human rights and to shock the conscience of mankind, the matter ceases to be of sole concern to that state and *even* intervention in the interest of humanity *might* be legally permissible.[4]

The UK Foreign and Commonwealth Office used similarly tortured language in a 1984 internal document on intervention, when it concluded that the best case that can be made in support of humanitarian intervention is that 'it cannot be said to be unambiguously illegal'.[5]

This book explores the doctrine of humanitarian intervention in its historical and political context. The debate surrounding it encapsulates crucial tensions in the international legal order between sovereignty and human rights, between the prohibition of the use of force and the protection of human dignity. At the same time, it raises questions of evidence and motive in the formation of international law, as humanitarian justifications may be used in practice to cloak less altruistic foreign-policy objectives in the robes of dubious legality. As a legal concept it will be argued that humanitarian intervention is incoherent—any 'right' of humanitarian intervention amounts not to an asserted exception to the prohibition of the use of force, but to a lacuna in the enforceable content of international law. An examination of the doctrine of humanitarian intervention must therefore consider not merely the law concerning the use of force by states, but the status of an international rule of law more generally.

---

help, provided by governments to individuals in another state who are being denied basic human rights and who themselves would be rationally willing to revolt against their oppressors.'

Adam Roberts, *Humanitarian Action in War: Aid Protection and Implementation in a Police Vacuum* (Adelphi Paper 305; London: IISS, 1996) 19: 'military intervention in a state without the approval of its authorities, and with the purpose of preventing widespread suffering or death among the inhabitants.'

[4] Lassa Francis Lawrence Oppenheim, *International Law* (Robert Jennings and Arthur Watts (eds); 9th edn; London: Longman, 1996) 442 (emphasis added).

[5] Planning Staff of the Foreign and Commonwealth Office, 'Is Intervention Ever Justified?' (internal document 1984), released as Foreign Policy Document No 148, excerpted in (1986) 57 *British YBIL* 614, 619.

A preliminary distinction must be drawn between humanitarian intervention and other putative legal bases for actions that may include a humanitarian component. In addition to self-defence and Security Council authorized
enforcement actions, these include claims of protection of nationals abroad
(arguably a species of self-defence), consent of the target state, and authorization by treaty. It is also necessary to make clear that the doctrine of
humanitarian intervention as considered here concerns the threat or use of
*force*—over the 1990s the term has sometimes been used to refer to less-
intrusive actions, such as the provision of food, medicine, and shelter.[6] The
term 'humanitarian *assistance*' will be used for such non-forcible actions.[7]

As most arguments for a right of humanitarian intervention presume that
this right pre-existed the UN Charter, it will first be necessary to examine its
genealogy. Chapter 1 considers the emergence of a doctrine of the just war in
the Middle Ages, and the competing principle of non-intervention that arose
as a corollary of sovereignty. This was not simply a precursor to the contemporary tension between human rights and sovereignty, however: the principle
of non-intervention must be seen as linked also to the displacement of
scholasticism by positivism in international law in eighteenth-century
Europe, and the political transformations taking place at the same time. The
term 'humanitarian intervention' only emerged in the nineteenth century as a
possible exception to this rule of non-intervention, but its meaning was far
from clear: some writers held it to be a legal right; others confidently rejected
it; a third group held that international law could or should have little to say
about the matter. Neither the writings of publicists nor state practice establishes any coherent meaning of this 'right'; at best it existed as a lacuna in a
period in which international law did not prohibit recourse to war.

The renunciation of war was central to the proceedings that led to the
creation of the United Nations, and Chapters 2 and 3 examine whether a right
of humanitarian intervention can exist under the UN Charter. Chapter 2 discusses the prohibition of the use of force and arguments that a right of
humanitarian intervention is not incompatible with the Charter provisions.
These arguments fall broadly into two schools. First, it has been argued that
humanitarian intervention might not contravene the Charter prohibition if it
does not violate the 'territorial integrity or political independence'[8] of the target state. As Oscar Schachter has observed, this demands an Orwellian construction of those terms.[9] Secondly, it has been argued that humanitarian
intervention may be justified where the appropriate international organ (the

---

[6] Adam Roberts, 'Humanitarian War: Military Intervention and Human Rights' (1993) 69
*International Affairs* 429, 445. See, eg, Nirmala Chadrahasan, 'Use of Force to Ensure
Humanitarian Relief—A South Asian Precedent Examined' (1993) 42 *ICLQ* 664 (discussing
Indian air drop of goods in Sri Lanka).

[7] Cf *Nicaragua* (*Merits*) [1986] ICJ Rep 14, 114 para 242.     [8] UN Charter, art 2(4).

[9] Oscar Schachter, 'The Legality of Pro-Democratic Invasion' (1984) 78 *AJIL* 645, 649.

Security Council) is unwilling or unable to act to prevent atrocities. This argument presumes a more general customary right of forcible self-help that is incompatible with fundamental precepts of the international legal order.

An alternative argument for the legality of humanitarian intervention is the subject matter of Chapter 3: that humanitarian intervention may be justified not as a valid use of force against a sovereign state, but because certain actions by a governing regime may *invalidate* that state's sovereignty. This conception of sovereignty as defeasible is said to create a legal vacuum into which any state may step. At its most extreme, this has been said to apply to non-democratic states, allowing other states to intervene in support of democratic reform. More commonly, the argument has been used to discredit a regime and justify intervention on the grounds that the impugned government does not speak for the people it represents. Sometimes characterized as a 'sovereignty of the people', this approach has been said to present a challenge to the traditional understanding of sovereignty as absolute. As in the case of a right of self-help, the legal form that such a normative order would take is a reversion to the pre-Charter position of debating the relative merits of wars that were not, in themselves, prohibited.

Chapters 4 and 5 turn to enforcement actions authorized by the Security Council for humanitarian reasons, sometimes called 'collective humanitarian intervention'. An irony of collective security in the 1990s is that just when it was said that the end of the Cold War would allow a more unified and active Security Council to fulfil its primary responsibility for the maintenance of international peace and security, the same period saw a blurring of the circumstances and the manner in which it could exercise that responsibility. Crucially, the definition of a threat to international peace and security—the trigger for Security Council enforcement actions—underwent a remarkable transformation. This is the subject matter of Chapter 4. Amid euphoric talk of a 'new world order' after the expulsion of Iraq from Kuwait, the Council declared in its January 1992 summit that instability in the economic, social, humanitarian, and ecological fields could also constitute threats falling within its purview.[10] This followed actions in Iraq and the former Yugoslavia that appeared to relate primarily to internal strife; two years later, after problematic operations in Somalia and Rwanda, it authorized an intervention to address the 'threat' posed by refugees and the obstruction of democratic rule in Haiti. By 1995 the International Criminal Tribunal for the Former Yugoslavia was able to assert that it was 'settled practice' that Chapter VII powers could be invoked to address purely internal armed conflicts as a species of 'threats to the peace'.[11]

---

[10] Security Council Summit Statement Concerning the Council's Responsibility in the Maintenance of International Peace and Security, UN Doc S/23500 (1992), [1992] *UN YB* 33.

[11] *Prosecutor v Tadic*, IT-94-1-AR72, Interlocutory Appeal on Jurisdiction (1995) para 30.

At the same time, however, the absence of international institutions capable of dealing with this increased responsibility led to a reliance on delegation. Security Council enforcement actions were thus limited to situations where acting states had the political will to bear the financial and human costs of such measures; this in turn raised concerns about the use of Council authority to give legitimacy to the foreign-policy objectives of certain states. The result has been a series of ambiguous resolutions and conflicting interpretations of the extent and duration of the authority conferred by the Council, most notably in the ongoing operations against Iraq throughout the 1990s. Chapter 5 argues that the weakening of these formal requirements has affected the substantive provisions of the collective security system established by the Charter, leading to actions in advance of Council authorization as epitomized by Operation Allied Force in Kosovo.

The structure of the book assumes the continued relevance of a distinction between a unilateral 'right' of humanitarian intervention and enforcement action duly authorized by the Security Council under Chapter VII of the UN Charter. For many years this distinction was regarded as fundamental,[12] but the nature of the enforcement actions undertaken in the 1990s has led some commentators to merge the categories.[13] Michael Reisman, for example, adopts a broader definition of humanitarian intervention that encompasses interventions under the auspices of the United Nations.[14] Similarly, Fernando Tesón has attempted to invoke Security Council authorized actions as evidence of a customary international law norm sanctioning *unilateral* intervention.[15] In light of the loose way in which such authorizations have been granted and interpreted, such a conflation of categories is revealing of the manner in which Security Council 'authorization' came to be deployed as a political rather than a legal justification for military action.[16]

Far from realizing the hitherto untapped potential of the Charter's collective security system, the practice of the Security Council in the 1990s more closely resembles the model of the League of Nations. The Covenant of the League only gave its Council the power to advise Members of the League on

---

[12] See, eg, John P Humphrey, 'Foreword', in Richard B Lillich (ed), *Humanitaran Intervention and the United Nations* (Charlottesville: University Press of Virginia, 1973) vii, viii; Dino Kritsiotis, 'Reappraising Policy Objections to Humanitarian Intervention' (1998) 19 *Michigan JIL* 1005 n 1.

[13] See, eg, Sean D Murphy, *Humanitarian Intervention: The United Nations in an Evolving World Order* (Philadelphia: University of Pennsylvania Press, 1996) 11–12.

[14] W Michael Reisman, 'Hollow Victory: Humanitarian Intervention and Protection of Minorities' (1997) 91 *ASIL Proc* 431.

[15] Fernando R Tesón, *Humanitarian Intervention: An Inquiry into Law and Morality* (2nd edn; Dobbs Ferry, NY: Transnational Publishers, 1997) 234.

[16] Cf the Sept 1999 speech by Secretary-General Kofi Annan to the UN General Assembly, in which he said that 'it is important to define intervention as broadly as possible, to include actions along a wide continuum from the most pacific to the most coercive': UN Press Release SG/SM/7136 (20 Sept 1999). This, presumably intentionally, muddied the normative question of whether such coercive interventions were legal without the authorization of the Council.

matters of collective security—the decision to act on any such advice lay ultimately with the states themselves.[17] Similarly, the arguments considered in Chapters 2 and 3 may be understood as a reversion to a pre-Charter regime in which the prohibition of the use of force is considerably weakened. Proponents of a right of humanitarian intervention argue, by contrast, that the emergence of such a doctrine is a defining feature of a new international order in which sovereignty is not absolute, and in which teeth are given to the corpus of human rights law that has developed since the Charter was written. These themes are brought together in Chapter 6, which evaluates the political, legal, and jurisprudential implications of the preparedness to use force to promote humanitarian ends.

The purpose of this book then, *pace* Lawrence, is not to adduce rules of international law so much as to use humanitarian intervention to reflect on the manner in which international law deals with a 'hard case' such as this. Humanitarian intervention brings into question not merely the substance but the moral foundations of international law; the question of whether there is or is not such a 'right' is of secondary importance to the implications that these arguments have for world order and international morality. Crucially, the book argues that such unilateral enforcement is not a substitute for but the opposite of collective action. Though often presented as the only alternative to inaction, incorporating a 'right' of intervention would lead to more such interventions being undertaken in bad faith, it would be incoherent as a principle, and it would be inimical to the emergence of an international rule of law.

---

[17] Covenant of the League of Nations, art 10.

# 1

# The Just War

## *The origins of humanitarian intervention*

The subject of intervention is one of the vaguest branches of international law. We are told that intervention is a right; that it is a crime; that it is the rule; that it is the exception; that it is never permissible at all. A reader, after perusing Phillimore's chapter upon intervention, might close the book with the impression that intervention may be anything from a speech of Lord Palmerston's in the House of Commons to the partition of Poland.

P H Winfield, 1922[1]

Much of the historical analysis of humanitarian intervention suffers from a lack of precision as to what that term embraces. On the one hand, early commentators failed to distinguish between limited intervention for a specific purpose and all-out war;[2] on the other, subsequent publicists conflated intervention premised on the threat or use of force (sometimes termed 'dictatorial interference'[3]) with purely diplomatic intercession.[4]

This Chapter argues that these semantic difficulties reflect a more basic contradiction in the genealogy of humanitarian intervention. For its origins must be seen in the tension between the belief in the justice of a war waged against an immoral enemy and the emerging principle of non-intervention as the corollary of sovereignty. It is misleading to regard this simply as a precursor to the contemporary tension between human rights and sovereignty, however. Analysis of the early international law writings of the scholastics, natural law theorists, and positivists discloses that its moral and legal heritage lies in the earlier conflict between the moral impetus to war over religious differences and the legal restraints that came to be placed on states entering into a society of equals.

In the classical texts, this came to be mediated by recognizing the capacity of one sovereign to wage war on behalf of a people unjustly oppressed by another

---

[1] P H Winfield, 'The History of Intervention in International Law' (1922) 3 *British YBIL* 130.
[2] See below nn 5–11 and accompanying text.
[3] See, eg, Lassa Francis Lawrence Oppenheim, *International Law* (New York: Longmans Green & Co, 1905) vol 1, 182; Amos S Hershey, *The Essentials of International Public Law* (New York: Macmillan, 1918) 148; J L Brierly, *The Law of Nations* (C H M Waldock (ed); 6th edn; Oxford: Oxford University Press, 1963) 402.
[4] Relatively modern examples include Roland R Foulke, *A Treatise on International Law* (Philadelphia: John C Winston, 1920) vol 2, 63–4; Ellery C Stowell, *Intervention in International Law* (Washington, DC: John Byrne & Co, 1921) *passim*.

sovereign. This is the subject matter of Section 1 of this Chapter. Section 2 considers the opposing doctrine of non-intervention (or non-interference), which arose during the eighteenth century, connected with the rise of positivism in international law and the political transformations in Europe in that and the following century. Partly in response to this, it was only in the nineteenth century that humanitarian intervention emerged as a coherent term, broadly recognized by publicists as a politically unavoidable—if not strictly legal—exception to the general principle of non-intervention. Section 3 analyses state practice of the era, focusing on the few incidents that are usually cited as evidence of a customary international law right of humanitarian intervention. Section 4 critically reviews the writings of publicists on the subject.

The result is a far more complex picture of pre-Charter international law than that presented in subsequent writings. Many of the debates that arose after the enactment of the UN Charter had been rehearsed long before: the tension between moral and legal rights, politics and law, was already an established part of the discourse on this issue and establishes the context within which contemporary approaches must be considered.

## 1. CLASSICAL PRECURSORS TO HUMANITARIAN INTERVENTION

International law did not proscribe unilateral resort to war as a means of settling disputes between states until the twentieth century.[5] It is therefore not surprising that prior to this time there was little agreement on the principles regulating less extreme circumstances involving the threat or use of force.[6] In any event, such a distinction was not often made. Grotius, for example, defined war as the state or condition of parties contending by force as such,[7] elsewhere citing Cicero to the effect that between war and peace there is no medium.[8] This encompassed even single combats, which he regarded as a form of private war.[9] The term 'intervention' came into use over the course of the nineteenth century, but its meaning remained imprecise. Moreover, in the absence of a clear distinction between intervention and war[10] any regulation of the former could be circumvented by resort to the latter. Thus when the United States objected to measures that Great Britain and Germany pro-

---

[5] See Ian Brownlie, *International Law and the Use of Force by States* (Oxford: Clarendon Press, 1963).

[6] J L Brierly, *The Law of Nations: An Introduction into the International Law of Peace* (Oxford: Clarendon Press, 1928) 155–6. On the emergence of norms governing hostile measures short of war, see Brownlie, above n 5, 45–6.

[7] Hugo Grotius, *De jure belli ac pacis libri tres* ([1646] Classics of International Law; Kelsey trans; Oxford: Clarendon Press, 1925) I, i, § 2(1).

[8] Ibid III, xxi, §1(1).                    [9] Ibid I, i, § 2(1).

[10] See, eg, Fanciscus de Victoria, *De Indis et jure belli relectiones* ([1557] Classics of International Law; Washington, DC: Carnegie Institution, 1917) *De Indis*, Sect 3, § 12.

posed to take against Venezuela in 1902 in the form of a pacific blockade, the European powers simply acknowledged a state of war to exist.[11]

It is nevertheless important to distinguish the origins of humanitarian intervention from other justifications for recourse to the threat or use of force. Intervention to protect nationals, for example, has been variously regarded as the exercise of the right of self-preservation, of self-defence, or as justified by necessity.[12] Intervention with the consent of the target state and in accordance with treaty obligations also have discrete legal pedigrees, though in practice all may be invoked in circumstances also claimed as warranting intervention on humanitarian grounds. The relationship with such interventions will be considered in Chapter 2.

The classical origins of what became known as humanitarian intervention lie in the emergence of a substantive doctrine of the just war in the Middle Ages.[13] This was developed in large part by the scholastics, but achieved its most comprehensive and widely publicized form in the work of the Protestant Hollander Hugo Grotius (1583–1645). International law as originally conceived by the man sometimes labelled its father[14] was based less in legal doctrine than it was in a body of principles rooted in the laws of nature. His seminal text, *De jure belli ac pacis*, presented for the first time a systematization of practice and authorities on the *jus belli*. Though he drew heavily on the work of earlier theorists,[15] the intellectual heritage of Grotius, and in particular the idea of the 'international society' that he described, continue to inform our understanding of the law of nations.[16] This conception of what Hedley Bull came to term the 'anarchical society'[17] of states provided an alternative world view to both the entirely chaotic state of nature as described

---

[11] J L Brierly, *The Law of Nations: An Introduction into the International Law of Peace* (4th edn; Oxford: Clarendon Press, 1949) 285; John Basset Moore, *A Digest of International Law* (Washington, DC: Government Printing Office, 1906) vol 7, 140–1.

[12] See Brownlie, above n 5, 289.

[13] The *justum bellum* of the Roman empire was construed largely in formal terms, though notions of equity had been introduced by pagan moralists such as Plato and the Stoics, Cicero and Seneca, who condemned unjust war: see Brownlie, above n 5, 4; John Eppstein, *The Catholic Tradition of the Law of Nations* (London: Burns Oates & Washbourne, 1935) 80; Joachim von Elbe, 'The Evolution of the Concept of the Just War in International Law' (1939) 33 *AJIL* 665, 667–70.

[14] See, eg, Sylvester John Hemleben, *Plans for World Peace Through Six Centuries* (Chicago: University of Chicago Press, 1943) 42–4.

[15] See Coleman Phillipson, 'Introduction', in Alberico Gentili, *De jure belli* ([1612] Classics of International Law; Rolfe trans; Oxford: Clarendon Press, 1933) vol 2, 9*a*, 12*a*.

[16] Unlike Hobbes, who grounded law and morality on the mutual fear of men, Grotius based his conception on the social impulses of the human animal: Grotius, above n 7, Prolegomena, §8; ibid I, i, §10. This international society centred around the understanding that states and their rulers are bound by rules and form a society or community with one another, of however rudimentary a kind: Hedley Bull, 'The Importance of Grotius in the Study of International Relations', in Hedley Bull, Benedict Kingsbury, and Adam Roberts (eds), *Hugo Grotius and International Relations* (Oxford: Clarendon Press, 1990) 65, 71.

[17] See generally Hedley Bull, *The Anarchical Society: A Study of Order in World Politics* (London: Macmillan, 1977).

by Machiavelli and later Hobbes,[18] and the attempts to bring this chaos under centralized control by restoring the institutions of Latin Christendom,[19] or through the construction of new institutions seeking a perpetual peace through human progress as ultimately articulated by Immanuel Kant (1724–1804).[20]

Grotius raises issues relevant to the emergence of a doctrine of humanitarian intervention in two sections of Book II of *De jure belli ac pacis*: the quasi-judicial police measure of war against the immoral,[21] and the waging of war on behalf of others.[22] These will be considered in turn.

## 1.1. War as punishment

Justification for taking up arms against the wicked can be found in the writings and practice of most religions and those empires styling themselves as civilized.[23] In Europe of the sixteenth and seventeenth centuries, wars and interventions over religious differences were frequent[24] and many writers continued to accept such wars as just, either in themselves or insofar as they were undertaken on the orders of God.[25] (It took a rare writer such as Alberico

[18] See, eg, Michael Walzer, 'On the Role of Symbolism in Political Thought' (1967) 82 *Political Science Quarterly* 191, 203; and see generally C B Macpherson, *The Policital Theory of Possessive Individualism: Hobbes to Locke* (Oxford: Clarendon Press, 1962). Hobbes' thought in particular remains the intellectual foundation of the dominant Realist (and 'Neo-Realist') school of international relations.

[19] One issue on which both Hobbes and Grotius were as one was the authority of the state over the Church: Bull, above n 17, 77. See also Grotius, above n 7, Prolegomena §11 (natural law would exist even on the assumption that God did not), discussed below n 47.

[20] See Immanuel Kant, 'Toward Perpetual Peace', in Immanuel Kant, *Practical Philosophy* ([1795] Gregor trans; Cambridge: Cambridge University Press, 1996) 311. For a modern articulation of Kantian international legal theory, see Fernando R Tesón, 'The Kantian Theory of International Law' (1992) 92 *Columbia Law Review* 53.

[21] Grotius, above n 7, II, xx: 'On Punishment'.

[22] Ibid II, xxv: 'On Undertaking War on Behalf of Others'.

[23] On Christianity in particular, see Thomas Aquinas, *Summa theologica*, II, ii, Question 40; Augustine, *Questions on the Heptateuch, On Joshua*, Question 10; Alphonsus de Castro, *De justa hæreticorum punitione*, ii, 14; Francisco Suárez, *The Three Theological Virtues: On Charity* (1612), 'Disp XIII: On War', in Francisco Suárez, *Selections from Three Works* (Oxford: Clarendon Press, 1944) §5(5) [trans 824]; Grotius, above n 7, II, i and xx; Emmerich de Vattel, *The Law of Nations: Principles of the Law of Nature, Applied to the Conduct and Affairs of Nations and Sovereign* ([1758] Classics of International Law; Fenwick trans; Washington, DC: Carnegie Institution, 1916) II, iv. See generally Eppstein, above n 3, 66–7. On Islam and the doctrine of *jihad*, see Majid Khadduri, *War and Peace in the Law of Islamd* (Baltimore: Johns Hopkins, 1955) 51–73.

[24] Arthur Nussbaum, *A Concise History of the Law of Nations* (rev edn; New York: Macmillan, 1962) 69.

[25] Phillipson, above n 15, 34a, lists Bartolus, Baldus, Joannes da Lignano [Giovanni de Legnano], John Wycliffe, Domingo Soto, Covarruvias, and Ayala. See, eg, Giovanni da Legnano, *Tractatus de bello, de represaliis et de duello* ([1447] Classics of International Law; Brierly trans; Washington, DC: Carnegie Institution, 1917) x–xi [trans 224–31]. Balthazar Ayala, *De jure et officiis bellicis et disciplina militari libri III* ([1582] Classics of International Law; Bate

Gentili (1552–1608) to observe that not merely Jews and Christians, but Ethiopians, Spartans, Turks, and Persians had all been stirred to arms by divine influence.[26])

Written at the time of some of Europe's most savage religious wars,[27] Grotius' work is remarkable for its tolerance: though a pious Protestant, he avoids any statement that might offend Catholic sentiments.[28] Abhorring the 'lack of restraint'[29] that characterized the Wars of Religion, and drawing on the progressive ideas advanced by Franciscus de Victoria[30] (1480–1546) and Gentili[31]—at times without formal acknowledgement—Grotius held that war could not justly be made against those who erred in the interpretation of Christianity[32] or who refused to accept it.[33] These precepts were later reflected in the 1648 Treaty of Westphalia, which provided the foundation for the balance of power policies that remained substantially unchanged until the French Revolution and the Napoleonic wars,[34] and marked the transition of Europe from the medieval period of vertically structured hierarchies under Pope and Emperor to the horizontally organized system of sovereign states.[35] The Treaty affirmed the right of rulers to determine the confessional

---

trans; Washington, DC: Carnegie Institution, 1912) I, ii, §28, states that war may not be declared against infidels merely because they are infidels, but that a just war may be waged on heretics who abandon the Christian faith. He then goes on to state that another just cause of war is where infidels 'are found hindering by their blasphemies and false arguments the Christian faith and also the free preaching of the Gospel rule': ibid I, ii, §30, citing Alfonso of Castile [Alphonsus de Castro], *De justa hæreticorum punitione* [On the Lawful Punishment of Heretics], bk 2.

[26] Gentili, above n 15, I, viii [trans 36].

[27] See Norman Davies, *Europe: A History* (London: Pimlico, 1997) 563–8.

[28] Nussbaum, above n 24, 109.

[29] Grotius, above n 7, Prolegomena, § 28: 'Throughout the Christian world I observed a lack of restraint in relation to war, such as even barbarous races should be ashamed of; I observed that men rush to arms for slight causes, or no cause at all, and that when arms have once been taken up there is no longer any respect for law, divine or human; it is as if, in accordance with a general decree, frenzy had openly been let loose for the committing of all crimes.'

[30] Victoria, above n 10. His name also appears as Vitoria and Vittoria. See Phillipson, above n 15, 34a.

[31] Gentili, above n 15, I, ix. See also Suárez, above n 23, § 5 [trans 823–7].

[32] Grotius, above n 7, II, xx, § 50.

[33] Ibid II, xx, § 48. See also ibid II, xv, § 8 (treaties may be entered into with infidels). Cf Gentili, above n 15, III, xix. See also Covarruvias, *Relectiones on c. peccatum*, ii, § 10, nn 4, 5, cited in Johann Wolfgang Textor, *Synopsis juris gentium* ([1680] Washington, DC: Carnegie Institution, 1916) ch xvii [trans vol 2, 176].

[34] Davies, above n 27, 581–2, 661. The term 'balance of power' was first used in the sixteenth century by Francesco Guicciardini (1483–1540), referring to the regional balance of power between the states of the Italian peninsula: Nussbaum, above n 24, 137. It was formally included in the Peace Treaty of Utrecht (1713) 28 CTS 37, which provided that the 'peace and repose of Christianity' should be achieved by a 'just balance of power [*justum potentiae aequilibrium*]': Nussbaum, above n 24, 137; Rudolf Bernhardt, *Encyclopedia of Public International Law* (Amsterdam: Elsevier, 1995) vol 2, 751. See also Brownlie, above n 5, 14–18.

[35] See, eg, Antonio Cassese, *International Law in a Divided World* (Oxford: Clarendon Press, 1986) 34–8; B V A Röling, 'Are Grotius' Ideas Obsolete in an Expanded World?', in Bull, Kingsbury, and Roberts, above n 16, 289.

allegiance of their states and subject (*cujus regio, ejus religio*)[36] and the corresponding secular supremacy of territorial rulers over their dominions (*Rex in regno suo est Imperator regni sui*).[37] This effectively brought an end to interventions for purely religious differences in Western Europe, though religion remained an important factor in the East.[38]

Nevertheless, Grotius did admit a right to wage war for the purposes of punishment.[39] Such a right had been recognized by his scholastic predecessors as necessary to preserve order in a society lacking any higher tribunal to resolve disputes,[40] but was generally limited to redressing injuries to the person or the state of the sovereign or where some other basis for jurisdiction justified the resort to war.[41] In the manner characteristic of his eclectic work, Grotius cites both scriptural and secular authority for his position;[42] central to his argument is a defence of the right of sovereigns to demand punishment not only for injuries committed against themselves and their subjects, but for those which 'excessively violate the law of nature or of nations in regard to any persons whatsoever':[43]

So we do not doubt that wars are justly waged against those who act with impiety towards their parents, . . . against those who feed on human flesh, . . . and against those who practise piracy.[44]

Grotius states that the 'liberty to serve the interests of human society through punishments' derives not from the position of authority held by sovereigns but from the fact that, in the order of states, they themselves are subject to no one.[45] This in turn depends on his earlier statement that the right of punishment attaches to the wrongdoer, enabling any person free from similar offences to exact punishment.[46]

In substantive terms the doctrinal shift was not great—the scholastics had also recognized the justice of a war to eliminate abnormal practices if it was commanded by God. But the importance of Grotius' work lies in the secular

[36] See Bull, above n 16, 76–7.
[37] See John Gerard Ruggie, 'Territoriality and Beyond: Problematizing Modernity in International Relations' (1993) 47 *International Organization* 139, 157.
[38] Geoffrey Butler and Simon Maccoby, *The Development of International Law* (London: Longmans Green & Co, 1928) 69.
[39] Grotius, above n 7, II, i, § 2; ibid II, xx.          [40] See Eppstein, above n 13, 97–123.
[41] Grotius, above n 7, II, xx, § 40(4), citing Victoria, Vásquez, Azor, and Molina. See also Suárez, above n 23, § 5(5) [trans 825–6].
[42] Grotius, above n 7, II, xx, § 40(3): 'Says Seneca: "If a man does not attack my country, but yet is a heavy burden to his own, and although separated from my people he afflicts his own, such debasement of mind nevertheless cuts him off from us." [*On Benefits*, VII, xix, 9.] Augustine says: "They think that they should decree the commission of crimes of such sort that if any state upon earth should decree them, or had decreed them, it would deserve to be overthrown by a decree of the human race." ' [*City of God*, V, i.]
See also ibid II, xx, § 40(4) (citing Innocent, *On Decr.* III, xxxiv, 8).
[43] Ibid II, xx, § 40(1).          [44] Ibid § 40(3).
[45] Ibid § 40(1).          [46] Ibid § 3(1).

basis for his natural law.[47] Whereas the scholastics characterized a war between equals as punitive by placing one in the position of *minister Dei*,[48] Grotius grounded the state's right to inflict punishment in the natural law right that 'originates in each private person'.[49]

This intellectual shift, together with the political transformations in Europe following the Treaty of Westphalia, established the conditions for the emergence of positivism in international law. The positivists came to reject Grotius' understanding of punitive war—in large part due to fears that such a doctrine might be abused.[50] But his writings in this area are instructive as an example of his more general view that natural law grants each person an executive power to assert not merely his or her own rights, but also the rights of others.[51] This also provided the natural law foundation for his defence of a right to wage war on behalf of the oppressed.

## 1.2. War on behalf of the oppressed

Ellery Stowell cites *Vindicae contra tyrannos*, published in 1579 during the religious wars in France, as the earliest authority asserting the legality of interference 'in behalf of neighboring peoples who are oppressed on account of adherence to the true religion or by any obvious tyranny'.[52] This is somewhat misleading, as the duty to come to the aid of one's religious brethren had been asserted by European leaders for centuries.[53] St Ambrose (*c*339–97), some thousand years earlier, had written that

[47] He reconciled this position with the scholastics by way of an hypothesis: 'What we have been saying would have a degree of validity even if we should concede that which cannot be conceded without the utmost wickedness, that there is no God, or that the affairs of men are of no concern to Him.' Ibid Prolegomena, § 11. See Nussbaum, above n 24, 108. Cf Gentili's rejection of the dogmatic procedure of the theologians: Gentili, above n 15, I, xii [trans 57] ('Let the theologians keep silence about a matter which is outside of their province'). Gentili was writing in Oxford, having fled Italy in 1579 before the Holy Inquisition which sentenced him and his father *in absentia* to penal servitude for life after they converted to Protestantism. In 1603 his works were placed on the Index. Grotius' *De jure belli ac pacis* was also placed on the Index in 1626, with the insignificant qualification '*donec corrigatur* [until amended]'. It remained so until 1899: Nussbaum, above n 24, 94–5, 114.

Grotius' philosophical heritage and his relationship to natural law in particular are now the subject of some debate. See, eg, Benedict Kingsbury, 'A Grotian Tradition of Theory and Practice? Grotius, Law, and Moral Skepticism in the Thought of Hedley Bull' (1997) 3 *Quinnipiac Law Review* 3; Knud Haakonssen (ed), *Grotius, Pufendorf and Modern Natural Law* (Aldershot: Dartmouth, 1999).

[48] See, eg, Suárez, above n 23, § 4(6) [trans 818–19], citing Romans 13: 4.

[49] Hugo Grotius, *De jure praedae commentarius* ([1604] Classics of International Law; Williams trans; Oxford: Clarendon Press, 1950) VIII [trans 92].

[50] See below Sect 2.1.     [51] Grotius, above n 7, II, xxv, § 1(1).

[52] Hubert Languet, *Vindicae contra tyrannos* (1579; Sumpt. Hæred. Lazari Zetzneri, 1622), in Stowell, above n 4, 55.

[53] See Eppstein, above n 13, 59. In lectures first delivered in 1532, Franciscus de Victoria acknowledged a right on the part of the Spanish to wage war against the indigenous Americans

He who does not keep harm off a friend, if he can, is as much in fault as he who causes it. Wherefore holy Moses gave this as a first proof of his fortitude in war. For when he saw an Hebrew receiving hard treatment at the hands of an Egyptian, he defended him, and laid low the Egyptian and hid him in the sand.[54]

Its continued influence can be seen in the work of Gentili, who mixes canonical and natural law justifications for coming to the aid of the oppressed. After quoting St Ambrose's statement that *'plena est justitia quae defendit infirmos'*,[55] he proffers a far more natural law rationale:

But so far as I am concerned, the subjects of others do not seem to me to be outside of that kinship of nature and the society formed by the whole world. And if you abolish that society, you will also destroy the union of the human race, by which life is supported.[56]

Gentili also appears to be one of the first jurists to raise the notion of sovereign accountability, noting that there must be some mechanism to remind the sovereign of his duty and hold him in restraint, 'unless we wish to make sovereigns exempt from the law and bound by no statutes and no precedents'.[57] The circumstances in which this mechanism might be invoked remain vague, however.[58]

In Grotius the justice of war waged on behalf of the oppressed subjects of another sovereign is distinct from Gentili's position in two ways. In the first place, it is more clearly a legal right rather than a moral duty. When considering whether one man is *bound* to defend another from wrong, Grotius limits this to when he can—*with convenience to himself*.[59] (In Hohfeldian terms, this

---

if they prevented the Spaniards from freely preaching the Gospel: Victoria, above n 10, *De Indis*, Sect 3, § 12. Similarly, Suárez asserted a right of war in defence of the innocent but restricted it to Christian princes defending subjects from an unbelieving sovereign: Suárez, above n 23, § 5(7) [trans 826–7].

[54] St Ambrose, *De Officiis*, I, xxxvi, § 179. Cf Gratian, *Decretals*, Pars Secunda, Causa XXIII, Quæstio III, xi, in Eppstein, above n 13, 82.

[55] St Ambrose, *De Officiis*, I, xxvii, § 129 [fulsome is the justice that protects the frail].

[56] Gentili, above n 15, I, xvi, citing Seneca, *On Benefits*, IV, viii, 4.

[57] Gentili, above n 15, I, xvi.

[58] Ibid I, xvi: 'I say that a dispute concerns the commonwealth, when the number of subjects who are aroused to war is so great and of such a character, that since they defend themselves by arms, it is necessary to make war against them. For those who have so much power share as it were in the sovereignty; they are public characters and on an equality with the sovereign . . . And, in fact, if subjects are treated cruelly and unjustly, this principle of defending them is approved by others as well' [trans 75].

[59] Grotius, above n 7, II, xxv, § 7(1): '[I]f danger is evident, it is certain that a man is not so bound, for he may prefer his own life and interests to those of others. In this sense I think we must interpret the words of Cicero: "He who does not prevent or oppose a wrong, if he can [*si potest*], is as much at fault as if he should desert his parents, or country, or associates." [Cicero, *On Duties*, I, vii, 23.] The word "can" [*potest*] we may understand as "with advantage to himself [*cum suo commodo*]".'

Whewell translates the last phrase as 'with convenience to himself'.

would be more accurately described as a *privilege*.[60]) Secondly, it is limited to circumstances where a sovereign has violated the hypothetical rights (in Hohfeld's schema: *claim-rights*) of his subjects. After noting that political associations have always tended to arrogate jurisdiction over internal matters to themselves,[61] he states that

[i]f, however, the wrong is obvious, in case some Busiris, Phalaris, or Thracian Diomede should inflict upon his subject such treatment as no one is warranted in inflicting, the exercise of the right vested in human society is not precluded.[62]

The rights violated are hypothetical because Grotius doubts that subjects themselves may take up arms against the sovereign, even in extreme situations.[63] The bar to action, however, lies not in the unenforceability of the right, but in the incapacity of the subject to act; it is therefore open to another sovereign to assert the rights of the oppressed subjects and intervene on their behalf.[64]

Samuel Pufendorf (1632–94) endorses Grotius' restriction of any right of intervention in the following terms:

In our opinion the safest principle to go on is, that we cannot lawfully undertake the defence of another's subjects, for any other reason than they themselves can rightfully advance, for taking up arms to protect themselves against the barbarous savagery of their superiors.[65]

This is in very limited circumstances indeed as, like Grotius, Pufendorf denied a general right of revolt to citizens oppressed by their sovereign, restricting a

[60] Wesley Newcomb Hohfeld, *Fundamental Legal Conceptions as Applied in Judicial Reasoning and Other Legal Essays* (Walter Wheeler Cook (ed); New Haven: Yale University Press, 1923) 27–64. Briefly, Hohfeld distinguishes two separate uses of the word 'right': (i) a *claim-right*, which has an enforceable *duty* as its correlative, and (ii) a *privilege*, which corresponds not to a duty but to a *no-right* (ie, the lack of a claim-right that something not be done).

[61] Grotius, above n 7, II, xxv, § 8(1): 'This too is a matter of controversy, whether there maybe a just cause for undertaking war on behalf of the subjects of another ruler, in order to protect them from wrong at his hands. Now it is certain that, from the time when political associations were formed, each of their rulers has sought to assert some particular right over his own subjects.'

[62] Ibid § 8(2). Whewell translates the passage as follows: 'But the case is different if the wrong be manifest. If a tyrant like Busiris, Phalaris, Diomede of Thrace, practises atrocities towards his subjects, which no just man can approve, the right of human social connexion is not cut off in such a case.'

Hersch Lauterpacht refers to this as the 'first authoritative statement of the principle of humanitarian intervention': Hersch Lauterpacht, 'The Grotian Tradition in International Law' (1946) 23 *British YBIL* 1, 46.

[63] Grotius, above n 7, II, xxv, § 8(3); ibid I, iv, §§ 1–7. It is this aspect of his work that drew the ire of Rousseau in *The Social Contract* (1762). Note, however, that Grotius qualifies this general rule to the extent that Hersch Lauterpacht argues that the major proposition may be considered all but theoretical. Indeed, these exceptions were cited as justification for the resistance to and deposition of James II: Lauterpacht, above n 62, 45.

[64] Grotius, above n 7, II, xxv, § 8(3)–(4).

[65] Samuel Pufendorf, *De jure naturae et gentium libri octo* ([1688] Classics of International Law; Oxford: Clarendon Press, 1934) VIII, vi, § 14.

citizen's legitimate use of force against the sovereign to extreme circumstances of self-defence.[66] In fact, most commentators of the time either failed
to mention any such right,[67] or rejected it—explicitly, or implicitly in their
adherence to the doctrine of non-intervention.

## 2. NON-INTERVENTION

In counterpoint to the developments outlined above, an opposing intellectual
trend can be observed defending a norm of non-intervention in the affairs of
other states. This can be seen in three areas: the rise of positivism in international law; a more general commitment to sovereignty and to the state as a
morally free entity; and in the changing political climate of the eighteenth and
nineteenth centuries.

### 2.1. Positivism in international law

The idea that states need not account for their actions is most forcefully
expressed in Thomas Hobbes' (1588–1679) observation that a state cannot
injure a citizen, any more than a master could do injury to his slave.[68] In the
*Leviathan*, Hobbes re-emphasized the immunity of the sovereign from temporal accountability in any legal sense:

> Concerning the Offices of one Soveraign to another . . . commonly called the *Law of
> Nations*, I need not say anything in this place; because the Law of Nations, and the
> Law of Nature, is the same thing . . . there being no Court of Naturall Justice, but in
> the Conscience onely where not Man, but God raigneth.[69]

---

[66] Pufendorf, *De jure naturae et gentium libri octo* VII, viii, §§ 1–7.

[67] This was true of the early positivists: Richard Zouche, *Juris et judicii fecialis, sive, juris inter gentes, et quaestionum de eodem explicatio* ([1650] Classics of International Law; Brierly trans; Washington, DC: Carnegie Institute, 1911) (no mention); Samuel Rachel, *De jure naturae et gentium dissertationes* ([1676] Washington, DC: Carnegie Institution, 1916) Second Dissertation, § xl [trans vol 2, 183] (requiring some hurt done wrongfully to one of the acting state's interests); Textor, above n 33, ch xvii [trans vol 2, 167] (requiring a grievance suffered by the party making the war); Cornelius van Bynkershoek, *Quaestionum juris publici libri duo* ([1737] Oxford: Clarendon Press, 1930) vol 1, ch 1 [trans vol 2, 15] (defining war as 'a contest of independent persons carried on by force or fraud for the sake of asserting their rights').

[68] Thomas Hobbes, *De Cive* ([1647] Oxford: Clarendon Press, 1983) ch viii, § 7. Cf Thomas Hobbes, *Leviathan* ([1651] London: Dent, 1914) II, xviii. Cf Jean Bodin, *The Six Books of a Commonweale* ([1577] A facsimile reprint of the English translation of 1606, corrected and supplemented in the light of a new comparison with the French and Latin texts; McRae trans; Cambridge, MA: Harvard University Press, 1962).

[69] Hobbes, *Leviathan*, above n 68, II, xxx. Balthazar Ayala (1548–84) had earlier adopted a similar position that none but God could sit in judgment of the sovereign: Ayala, above n 25, I, ii, §§ 25–6, 33.

As positivism displaced scholasticism in international legal theory, and the balance of power came to dominate international relations in Europe, the excision of theology (and, arguably, ethics[70]) from international law saw sovereignty emerge as its constituent and increasingly inviolable element. The first commentator to advocate an absolute proscription of intervention appears to have been the German philosopher Christian Wolff (1679–1754). Although preceded in his positivist approach to international law by writers such as Richard Zouche (1590–1660), he is credited with being the first to separate the principles of international law from those which constitute the ethics of the individual.[71] Central to his positivism is a rejection of the natural law principles crucial to Grotius' jurisprudence:

Approval is not to be given to the opinion of Grotius, that kings and those who have a right equal to that of kings have the right to exact penalties from any who savagely violate the law of nature or of nations[72] . . . The source of the error is found in the fact that the evil seems to him of such a nature that it can be punished and that it is quite in harmony with reason that it may be punished by him who is not guilty of it.[73]

When he considers the right to wage war, Wolff argues that a punitive war is only legal when waged by a state that has itself received irreparable injury, and where satisfaction cannot otherwise be obtained.[74] A corollary of this is that a punitive war is not legal if it is waged against a nation because it is 'very wicked, or violates dreadfully the law of nature, or offends against God'.[75] Wolff does allow a limited right of intercession on behalf of subjects 'too heavily burdened or too harshly treated' by their sovereign, but draws the line at the use of force.[76]

Borrowing heavily from Wolff, though distinct in his emphasis on the consensual nature of international law, Emmerich de Vattel (1714–67) similarly adopts the basic premise that the domestic jurisdiction is inviolable:

[70] See below Sect 2.2.

[71] Charles Calvo, *Le droit international: théorique et pratique* (Arthur Rousseau (ed); 5th edn; Paris: Librairie nouvelle de Droit et de Jurisprudence, 1896) vol 1, 51; Otfried Nippold, 'Introduction', in Christian Wolff, *Jus gentium methodo scientifica pertractatum* ([1764] Classics of International Law; Drake trans; Oxford: Clarendon Press, 1934) xxxviii.

[72] See Grotius, above n 7, II, xx, § 40.

[73] Wolff, above n 71, § 169. The first writer to raise such objections to Grotius' work appears to be Heineccius, a contemporary of Bynkershoek, who argues that the right to inflict punishment exists only as between a superior and his subjects, and therefore not among nations which are equal: 'punitio nimirum scelerum, eo minus videatur admittenda, quo magis constat, parem a pari, adeoque gentem a gente puniri non posse.' Johann Gottlieb Heineccius, *Elementa juris naturae et gentium* (Turnbull trans; London: J Noon, 1741) § 195, quoted in von Elbe, above n 13, 681 n 126.

[74] Wolff, above n 71, § 636.

[75] Ibid § 637. He adds: 'God himself is capable of punishing a wrong done to himself, nor for that does he need human aid.'

[76] Ibid §§ 256–8.

[The duties of a nation towards itself] are of purely national concern, and no foreign power has any right to interfere [*n'est en droit de s'en mêler ni ne doit y intervenir*] otherwise than by its good offices, unless it be requested to do so or be led to do so by special reasons. To intermeddle [*s'ingère*] in the domestic affairs of another Nation or to undertake to constrain its councils is to do it an injury.[77]

Vattel also criticizes Grotius' assertion that a sovereign may take up arms to chastise a nation guilty of an enormous transgression of the laws of nature:[78] this falsely assumes that the capacity to punish derives from the magnitude of that transgression.[79] Vattel argues that the right of punishment derives solely from the right to provide for one's own safety,[80] and is wary of the dangers attendant to granting a quasi-judicial authority to states:

Did not Grotius perceive that in spite of all the precautions added in the following paragraphs, his view opens the door to all the passions of zealots and fanatics, and gives to ambitious men pretexts without number?[81]

However, after establishing the broad proposition that one sovereign may not sit in judgment of another,[82] Vattel notes that where subjects have a *legal right* to resist their sovereign—'if, by his insupportable tyranny, he brings on a national revolt against him'—any foreign power that is asked to do so may assist the oppressed subjects.[83] This right is distinct from the hypothetical right recognized by Grotius in that it does not depend upon recognition by a foreign sovereign in order to be enforceable.[84] On the contrary, it requires action by the subjects such that the sovereign and his people may be viewed as two distinct powers, the 'political bonds' between them being broken.[85]

Here may be found, perhaps, the origins of the dual meaning of intervention as it came to be understood in the nineteenth century.[86] Vattel himself does not employ the term 'intervention' in any technical sense, using forms of the verb '*intervenir*' to signify both meddling in the internal disputes of another state[87] and mediation by a third power between belligerent states.[88]

---

[77]  Vattel, above n 23, I, iii, § 37.

[78]  See, eg, Grotius, above n 7, II, xx, § 11, referring to nations 'which treat their parents with inhumanity like the Sogdians, which eat human flesh as the ancient Gauls, &c.'.

[79]  Vattel, above n 23, II, i, § 7.

[80]  Ibid I, xiii, § 169.

[81]  Ibid II, i, § 7. Vattel is particularly critical of wars waged in the name of 'true religion', both on the part of 'those ambitious Europeans' who subdued indigenous Americans on the pretext of a civilizing mission, and on that of Islamic states claiming to avenge wrongs done to their god: ibid.

Grotius does appear to have been aware of the danger that the right might be abused, for he observes that 'Perhaps Mithridates was not very wrong when he said of the Romans, that *they did not really attack the vices of kings, but their power and their majesty*': Grotius, above n 7, II, xx, § 43(3).

[82]  Vattel, above n 23, II, iv, § 55.                [83]  Ibid § 56.

[84]  See above nn 63–4 and accompanying text.          [85]  Vattel, above n 23, II, iv, § 56.

[86]  Cf Winfield, above n 1, 137.                     [87]  Vattel, above n 23, I, iii, § 37.

[88]  Ibid III, iii, § 49.

The phrases '*se mêler*' and '*s'ingérer*' occur with far greater frequency.[89] More importantly—and in a distinction that was lost on many subsequent jurists—Vattel establishes two discrete circumstances in which what came to be considered intervention may take place.

In general, where no dispute exists between the sovereign and his subjects, there is an absolute prohibition of intervention. Vattel does not refer to this as intervention, however, but as 'interfer[ing]' [*se mêler*] in the entitlement of each state, subject to the rights of others, to govern itself as it sees fit:[90]

No foreign State may inquire into the manner in which a sovereign rules, nor set itself up as judge of his conduct, nor force him to make any change in his administration . . . The Spaniards acted contrary to all rules when they set themselves up as judges of Inca Atahualpa. If that Prince had violated the Law of Nations in their regard they would have been right in punishing him. But they accused him of having put to death certain of his own subjects, of having had several wives, etc, things for which he was not responsible to them; and, as the crowning point of their injustice, they condemned him by the laws of Spain.[91]

By contrast, when considering a state in which subjects are in revolt against their sovereign, Vattel phrases the legal question as being whether another state may enter into the quarrel [*entrer dans la querelle*]. He concludes that any state may assist or give help [*secourir, assister*] to 'brave people who are defending their liberties', leaving it to the intervening state to determine which of the two parties appears to have justice on its side.[92] Moreover, as a corollary of the voluntary nature of the law of nations he constructs, Vattel argues that the two parties must be allowed to act as if possessed of equal right until the affair is decided. This is clearly an extension of his more general pronouncement on disputes between nations:

When differences arise each Nation in fact claims to have justice on its side, and neither of the interested parties nor other Nations may decide the question. The one who is actually in the wrong sins against its conscience; but as it may possibly be in the right, it can not be accused of violating the laws of the society of Nations.[93]

All this suggests that the confusion over the word 'intervention' arose mainly from the independent meaning that was attributed to its presumed antonym: non-intervention. In fact, the latter concept is better rendered 'non-interference', and restricted to situations where no dispute exists between subjects and sovereign. A similar distinction is found in Kant's *Essay on Perpetual Peace*, in which the fifth of Kant's preliminary articles states that

---

[89] See Winfield, above n 1, 133.
[90] Vattel, above n 23, II, iv, § 54.
[91] Ibid § 55.
[92] Ibid § 56. Vattel cites the example of the assistance granted by the United Provinces to England under the reign of James II.
[93] Ibid Introduction, § 21.

'No state shall forcibly interfere in the constitution and government of another state':[94]

But it would be a different matter if a state, through internal discord, should split into two parts, each putting itself forward as a separate state and laying claim to the whole; in that case a foreign state could not be charged with interfering in the constitution of another state if it gave assistance to one of them (for this is anarchy). But as long as this internal conflict is not yet critical, such interference of foreign powers would be a violation of the right of a people dependent upon no other and only struggling with its internal illness; thus it would itself be a scandal given and would make the autonomy of all states insecure.[95]

For consistency, the term 'non-intervention' will continue to be used here.[96]

## 2.2. Non-intervention and 'the Hegelian myth'

In his book-length defence of a modern right of humanitarian intervention, Fernando Tesón describes the rise of non-intervention as the excision not merely of theology but of ethics from international law.[97] He argues that this was the product of the fetishization of the state as a morally free entity, encouraged by the amorality of positivism and articulated in its most extreme form by G W F Hegel:

257. The state is the actuality of the ethical idea. It is ethical mind . . . knowing and thinking itself . . .

---

[94] Immanuel Kant, 'Toward Perpetual Peace', in Kant, above n 20, 8:346 [trans 319]. Hershey, above n 3, 153 n 18, cites this as the first enunciation of the principle of non-intervention. It must, however, be read in the context of his earlier provision that the constitution of each state was to be republican: Kant, 'Toward Perpetual Peace', 8:350 [trans 352]. In addition, Kant was building on various other plans for world peace developed through the eighteenth century, notably Rousseau's *A Project for Perpetual Peace* (1761), which in turn revived Charles Irénée Castel de Saint-Pierre's *Projet pour rendre la paix perpétuelle en Europe* (1713): see Hemleben, above n 14, 56–95.

[95] Kant, 'Toward Perpetual Peace', 8:346 [trans 319–20]. See also Richard B Lillich, 'Kant and the Current Debate over Humanitarian Intervention' (1997) 6 *Journal of Transnational Law and Policy* 397 (arguing that Kant's republican convictions might have led him to accept unilateral humanitarian intervention in undemocratic states).

[96] The questionable status of intervention as a term of art in English is captured in an exchange in the British Parliament in 1832. During a debate on British relations with Germany, the then Foreign Secretary Palmerston stated that Britain did not follow a policy of non-interference in regard to the internal politics of other states, though this interference would be by words, and not arms. In response to a question about non-intervention, he replied: 'I will not talk of non-intervention, for it is not an English word': Jasper Ridley, *Lord Palmerston* (London: Constable, 1971) 156. The *OED* includes seventeenth-century usages of 'intervention', and a fifteenth-century reference to 'interuencioun'.

[97] Fernando R Tesón, *Humanitarian Intervention: An Inquiry into Law and Morality* (2nd edn; Dobbs Ferry, NY: Transnational Publishers, 1997) 56; see also ibid 6–17.

258. The state is absolutely rational . . . This substantial unity [ie, the state] is an absolute unmoved end in itself, in which freedom comes into its supreme right.[98]

'The Hegelian myth', in Tesón's argot, is the view that foreign intervention is a violation of state autonomy, even when it is undertaken for benign purposes.[99] This view came to predominate, he writes, because the natural law limits to sovereignty recognized by Grotius and Vattel were ignored by theorists such as Wolff and Hegel, who posited an autonomous state independent of domestic political morality.[100] The influence of positivism then came to displace questions of ethics in international law through the nineteenth and twentieth centuries.[101]

Such a schema is neat but deceptive. As indicated above, Grotius and Vattel did recognize a right of intervention on behalf of oppressed subjects, but on very different bases. In particular, it is doubtful that the 'humanitarian component' of international law before the nineteenth century resembled anything comparable to the sort of Kantian ethics being proposed by Tesón. He states that the restriction of humanitarian intervention to 'egregious cases of oppression can be explained by recalling that in the Ancien Régime the right of *revolution* was subject to a similar limitation'.[102] But Grotius admitted no such right of revolution on the part of oppressed subjects, restricting the right of punishment to other sovereigns.[103] Vattel, on the other hand, says little of the right of revolution against the sovereign,[104] but requires such a revolution to take place in fact before a second state has a legal right to intervene.[105]

Tesón's determination to locate the debate over humanitarian intervention squarely in the realms of moral philosophy also leads him to overstate the significance of Hegelianism in international law. He asserts that by the end of the nineteenth century this view had assumed a dominant position in international legal theory,[106] but nevertheless argues that the doctrine of humanitarian intervention had 'considerable acceptance' at the time.[107] While he is correct in pointing to the importance of anthropomorphism as a defining element of modern international legal theory—a phenomenon beginning with the Treaty of Westphalia, in which the state came to be personified as the territorial embodiment of the Prince[108]—his account ignores the practice of

---

[98] G W F Hegel, *Hegel's Philosophy of Right* ([1821] Knox trans; Oxford: Oxford University Press, 1967) §§ 257–8, pp 155–6, cited in Tesón, above n 97, 59. See the critique in Karl Popper, *The Open Society and Its Enemies* (London: Routledge & Kegan Paul, 1966) ch 12.

[99] Tesón, above n 97, 55.    [100] Ibid 58.    [101] Ibid 59.

[102] Ibid 58 (emphasis in original).    [103] See above nn 63–4 and accompanying text.

[104] Vattel does, however, discuss the right of a citizen to *leave* his country, and enumerates at length the cases in which this may be exercised: Vattel, above n 23, I, xix, §§ 220–3.

[105] See above nn 82–5 and accompanying text.    [106] Tesón, above n 97, 59–60.

[107] Ibid 177.

[108] See Lauterpacht, above n 62, 26–30 (discussing Grotius' identification of the individual and the state). Note that Hegel distinguishes the state from private persons due to the depth of

states in the nineteenth century, when the reification of sovereignty came to depend more on the prohibition of the use of force than on a belief as to the moral freedom of states. This is evident most clearly in the doctrine of non-intervention (as distinct from non-interference), which was more concerned with the territorial rather than the moral inviolability of states.

## 2.3. Non-intervention at the start of the nineteenth century

Perhaps the clearest political enunciation of the principle of non-intervention is to be found in the Jacobin Constitution of 1793:

118. Le peuple français est l'ami et l'allié naturel des peuples libres.

119. Il ne s'immisce point dans le gouvernement des autres nations; il ne souffre pas que les autres nations s'immiscent dans le sien.[109]

It is ironic that the Republic that made this declaration in the midst of revolution eventually found internal stability in Napoleon Bonaparte's mission to conquer the world.[110]

In the wake of the French Revolutionary Wars, monarchical Europe formed structures to protect the existing order and attempted to enshrine a right of intervention to keep the peace. Through the Quadruple Alliance of Great Britain, Austria, Prussia, and Russia, the victorious powers affirmed their commitment to a stable and monarchical Europe by agreeing, in the event of similar revolutionary activities,

to concert amongst themselves . . . the measures which they may judge necessary to be pursued for the safety of their respective States, and for the general tranquillity of Europe.[111]

their autonomy: 'so the relation between them differs from a moral relation and a relation involving private rights. . . . Now a relation between states ought also to be right in principle, but in mundane affairs a principle ought also to have power. Now since there is no power in existence which decides in face of the state what is right in principle and actualizes this decision, it follows that so far as international relations are concerned we can never get beyond an "ought". The relation between states is a relation between autonomous entities which make mutual stipulations but which at the same time are superior to these stipulations.' Hegel, above n 98, *Additions*, § 191, p 297. See further Simon Chesterman, 'Law, Subject and Subjectivity in International Relations: International Law and the Postcolony' (1996) 20 *Melbourne University Law Review* 979.

[109] France, Constitution of 1793, arts 118–19, 5 Duvergier 353, 357 (never entered into force) ['118. The French people declares itself the friend and natural ally of free peoples. 119. It does not interfere in the governments of other nations, it does not allow other nations to interfere in its own.']. Cf Convention nationale, résolution du 13 avril 1793: 5 Duvergier 248. See also Robert Redslob, 'La doctrine idéaliste du droit des gens: proclamée par la révolution Française et par le philosophe Emmanuel Kant' (1921) 28 *RGDIP* 441, 443–6.

[110] Davies, above n 27, 701, 715–48. The Constitution was ratified by the primary assemblies on 14 and 21 July 1793, but on 10 Oct 1793 its application was postponed until the conclusion of peace: Jean Brissaud, *A History of French Public Law* (Garner trans; London: John Murray, 1915) 554.

[111] Treaty of Alliance and Friendship, Great Britain–Austria, signed at Paris, 20 Nov 1815, 3 State Papers 273, 277, art 3. (Identical treaties were signed at the same time with other

The Quadruple Alliance became the Quintuple Alliance (or Pentarchy) when France was admitted at the first congress held at Aix-la-Chapelle in 1818.[112] Differences quickly emerged, however. The British held strong reservations about the expeditions to crush revolutions in Naples, Greece, and Spain, and severed relations in 1822.[113] France later withdrew also, leaving Austria, Prussia, and Russia in the Triple Alliance that continued to resist change until the revolutions of 1848.[114] The principle of association lived on in the 'new garb' of the Concert of Europe,[115] but Britain formally dissociated itself from the policy of intervention on the basis of legitimacy in a message of 18 January 1823, when British Foreign Secretary George Canning stated the British Government's view:

We disclaim for ourselves and deny for other powers the right of requiring any changes in the internal institutions of independent States, with the menace of hostile attack in the case of refusal.[116]

When Spain's South American colonies revolted in 1823, Canning joined the United States in opposing any form of European intervention in the Americas.[117] This policy was formalized in the Annual Message of James Monroe in the doctrine that bears his name.[118]

Intervention thus acquired its currency as a term of art only in the nineteenth century,[119] but its usage remained imprecise: in one case it denoted a purely diplomatic intercession or the mere expression of an opinion, in another 'dictatorial interference' in the affairs of another state. When Lord Palmerston asserted Great Britain's readiness to counsel friendship and peace in the 1849 war between Austria and Hungary, Robert Phillimore noted this as an instance of intervention.[120] Subsequent authors suggest that it might

---

powers.) See Henry Wheaton, *Elements of International Law* ([1866] Richard Henry Dana Jr (ed); Classics of International Law; 8th edn; Oxford: Clarendon Press, 1936) 79. At the same time, a more ambitious 'Holy Alliance' was announced by Tsar Alexander I of Russia to provide a spiritual basis for the preservation of peace: Hemleben, above n 14, 97.

[112] Hemleben, above n 14, 102.          [113] Ibid 103.          [114] Ibid.

[115] John Bassett Moore, 'Some Essentials of League for Peace', in Stephen Pierce Duggan (ed), *The League of Nations: The Principle and the Practice* (Boston: Atlantic Monthly Press, 1919) 68.

[116] *Annual Register* (1823) LXV, 114, quoted in J H W Verzijl, *International Law in Historical Perspective* (Leyden: A W Sijthoff, 1968) vol 1, 240.

[117] Moore, above n 11, vol 6, 389–92 (Canning–Rush negotiations), 399–401 (US Cabinet deliberations). See also Davies, above n 27, 762–3.

[118] The Monroe Doctrine amounted to a highly qualified form of non-intervention: it disclaimed any right on the part of the United States to interfere with the existing European colonies and dependencies, but opposed any attempt to extend that system, or 'any interposition for the purposes of oppressing . . ., or controlling in any other manner' the destiny of those states whose independence the United States had recognized: President Monroe, Annual Message, 2 Dec 1823, in Moore, above n 11, vol 6, 401–3.

[119] See Winfield, above n 1, 134–5.

[120] Robert Phillimore, *Commentaries upon International Law* (3rd edn; London: Butterworths, 1879) vol 1, 599.

have been injudicious but hardly constituted intervention.[121] The reasons for the persistence of this dual meaning in the nineteenth century can be understood in light of the emerging norm of non-intervention discussed above,[122] but by the last quarter of the nineteenth century intervention had broadly become synonymous with the use of force which might or might not be justified by international law.[123]

The term 'humanitarian intervention' appears to have been used first by William Edward Hall,[124] although similar terms such as 'intervention on the ground of humanity',[125] 'intervention on behalf of the interests of humanity',[126] and to remove 'abhorrent conditions'[127] appear in the English language literature, and have a longer history still in French.[128] Richard Lillich traces the term back to Wheaton's 1836 treatise, which cites the 'interference' of the Christian Powers of Europe in aid of Greek insurgents against the Ottoman Empire (discussed below[129]) as an illustration that international law authorizes

such an interference . . . where the general interests of humanity are infringed by the excesses of a barbarous and despotic government.[130]

From the preceding discussion, it is clear that the ethical and legal origins of this doctrine stretch back much further to the moral impetus to war over religious differences, and the legal restraints that came to be placed on intervention as sovereignty emerged as the axiom of an international society of equals. Having sketched out its pedigree, it is now possible to consider the content of this 'right' in customary international law through the nineteenth and early twentieth century.


## 3. STATE PRACTICE, 1815–1945

An analysis of pre-Charter state practice illustrates the paucity of evidence of a general right of humanitarian intervention in customary international law.

---

[121] See, eg, Winfield, above n 1, 141.                    [122] See above Sect 2.1.
[123] Brownlie, above n 5, 45.
[124] William Edward Hall, *International Law* (1st edn; Oxford: Clarendon Press, 1880) 247 n 1; William Edward Hall, *Treatise on International Law* (2nd edn; Oxford: Clarendon Press, 1884) 266 n 1.
[125] H W Halleck, *International Law; or, Rules Regulating the Intercourse of States in Peace and War* (1st edn; San Francisco: H Bancroft & Co, 1961) 87; Hall (2nd edn), above n 124, 264.
[126] Edward S Creasy, *First Platform of International Law* (London: John van Voorst, 1876) 300; Robert Phillimore, *Commentaries upon International Law* (London: Benning & Co, 1954) vol 1, 442; Oppenheim, above n 3, vol 1, 186.                    [127] Moore, above n 11, vol 6, 3.
[128] See Antoine Rougier, 'La théorie de l'intervention d'humanité' (1910) 17 *RGDIP* 468. See also the discussion of Vattel in Sect 2.1.
[129] See below Sect 3.3.
[130] Henry Wheaton, *Elements of International Law* (1st edn; Philadelphia: Carey Lea & Blanchard, 1836) II, i, § 10, p 91. See Richard B Lillich (ed), *Humanitarian Intervention and the United Nations* (Charlottesville: University Press of Virginia, 1973) 25 (Lillich).

Of the various examples raised by modern writers seeking to prove the existence of such a right, most either do not involve the threat or use of force, or
retrospectively attribute motives alien to those expressed by the acting states
at the time.

This section reviews these examples before proceeding to a closer analysis
of the three main examples of allegedly humanitarian intervention in the
period: the joint intervention of Great Britain, France, and Russia in aid of
Greek insurgents in 1827; the French occupation of Syria in 1860–1; and the
United States intervention in Cuba during its war with Spain in 1898.

## 3.1. Non-coercive interference

There are numerous instances of purely diplomatic intercessions that various
writers confuse with humanitarian intervention. Efforts by the European
Powers to protect Christian populations within the Ottoman Empire provided the two major examples of allegedly humanitarian intervention in the
pre-Charter era,[131] but also gave rise to lesser disputes sometimes included as
such. Mistreatment of the Christian population in Crete caused a revolt
against Turkish rule in 1866, but the peremptory demands made by the
European Powers were based on Turkey's treaty obligations and the issue was
resolved peacefully.[132] The intercession by Austria-Hungary and Russia on
behalf of Christians in Macedonia in 1903 was similarly restricted to peremptory demands upon the Sultan to provide for future protection and the pay-
ment of compensation to the Christian population.[133] The United States and
others made various protests to Turkey on behalf of its Armenian population
in the years 1904–17,[134] but despite deaths in the order of a million Armenians
it appears that military intervention was never seriously contemplated.[135] In

[131] See below Sects 3.3 and 3.4.
[132] Manouchehr Ganji, *International Protection of Human Rights* (Paris: Minard, 1962) 26–9.
Great Britain acted as an intermediary, prompting Reisman to make the unusual observation
that 'adroit and creative diplomacy may achieve the objectives of forcible humanitarian inter-
vention without necessary resort to armed intervention in the territory in question' while still
including it as an example of such intervention: W Michael Reisman and Myres S McDougal,
'Humanitarian Intervention to Protect the Ibos', in Lillich, above n 130, 167, 181. See further R B
Mowat, *A History of European Diplomacy, 1815–1914* (London: Edward Arnold, 1923) 274 ff;
Jean-Pierre L Fonteyne, 'The Customary International Law Doctrine of Humanitarian
Intervention: Its Current Validity Under the UN Charter' (1974) 4 *California Western ILJ* 203,
210–11.
[133] *Contra* Ganji, above n 132, 33–7; Reisman and McDougal, above n 132, 183; Fonteyne,
above n 132, 212–13.
[134] Myres S McDougal, Harold D Lasswell, and Lung-chu Chen, *Human Rights and World
Public Order: The Basic Policies of an International Law of Human Dignity* (New Haven and
London: Yale University Press, 1980) 240. See, eg, President Theodore Roosevelt, Annual
Message, 6 Dec 1904, in Moore, above n 11, vol 6, 31–2.
[135] See documents collected in Louis B Sohn and Thomas Buergenthal, *International
Protection of Human Rights* (Indianapolis: Bobbs-Merrill, 1973) 181–94; Charles G Fenwick,

1913 Russia's Foreign Minister warned of such intervention if there was an Armenian uprising against the Turkish government,[136] but its motives were far from humanitarian.[137]

Between the Powers themselves, representations were often made on behalf of oppressed groups. In 1857 France and Great Britain interceded on behalf of Neapolitan political agitators striving for Italian national unity and freedom from Austrian rule.[138] In 1863 the treatment of its Polish subjects caused Great Britain, France, and Austria to make concurrent representations to Russia.[139] This coincidence was only in time, however, as each of the three Powers pursued an agenda independent of the others and only tangentially humanitarian.[140]

In the Americas, the United States threatened to intervene militarily during the Cuban insurrection of 1868–78 (as it eventually did in the subsequent insurrection of 1898[141]) but this was largely caused by more proximate non-humanitarian concerns[142] and no action was taken.[143] In Africa, the Congo 'Red Rubber' Crisis of 1898–1908 is cited by one commentator as a 'paradigm' of the term 'humanitarian intervention', but involved popular demonstrations calling for the reform of colonial practices rather than any form of intervention.[144]

## 3.2. Non-humanitarian interventions

Interventions *stricto sensu* were not unusual in the nineteenth century, but of the various occasions on which humanitarian motives were asserted—either at the time or subsequently—many can be dismissed as opportunistic or optimistic interpretations of the doctrine.

---

'Intervention: Individual and Collective' (1945) 39 *AJIL* 645, 650–1; Charles Hyde, *International Law* (2nd edn; Boston: Little Brown, 1947) vol 1, 250; Robert H Ferrell, *American Diplomacy: A History* (3rd edn; New York: Norton, 1975) 735–6.

[136] G P Gooch and Harold William Vazeille Temperly (eds), *British Documents on the Origins of the War 1898–1914* (London: HMSO, 1926) vol 10, part i, nos 429, 494.

[137] Ibid nos 492, 542, no 556; Brownlie, above n 5, 340.       [138] Stowell, above n 4, 88 n 24a.

[139] Ibid 89–120.                                    [140] Ibid 94–5 n 33; Brownlie, above n 5, 340.

[141] See below Sect 3.5.

[142] Mr Fish, Secretary of State, to Mr Cushing, Minister to Spain, No 266, 5 Nov 1875, in Moore, above n 11, vol 6, 85, especially 91. Cf Ann Van Wynen Thomas and A J Thomas, *Non-Intervention: The Law and Its Import in the Americas* (Dallas: Southern Methodist University Press, 1956) 22.

[143] Stowell, above n 4, 480–1; Brownlie, above n 5, 340.

[144] The incident concerned the popular outcry that followed British Consul General Sir Roger Casement's reports of abuses in the Belgian regime administering the Free State of the Congo. This led to a conference being called and the eventual establishment of the Belgian Congo: Lillich, above n 130, 44–6 (Goldie). The incident does not appear to be mentioned by other commentators.

In 1877–8 Russia declared war upon the Ottoman Porte, ostensibly to protect the Christian populations of Bosnia, Herzegovina, and Bulgaria from inhumane treatment and in an action sanctioned by Austria, Prussia, France, and Italy.[145] As Stowell notes, however, Russia was also motivated by its desire to acquire new territory in the Balkans and had signed a secret agreement with Austria to this effect. Though Stowell makes a valiant attempt to salvage it as an example of humanitarian intervention,[146] most authorities agree (as the British Government argued at the time) that the action, though 'based in theory upon religious sympathy and upon humanity . . . was a move, in fact, upon the Straits and Constantinople in pursuance of Russia's century-long program'.[147] Similarly, the 1913 invasion of Macedonia by Bulgaria, Greece, and Serbia had more to do with traditional power politics than a desire to protect the Macedonian Christians.[148] The intervention of the United States and Great Britain during the Boxer Rebellion in China in 1900, cited by Rougier,[149] was justified at the time as an instance of the protection of nationals and property, but also had the aim of ensuring that China remained 'open' to Western trade.[150]

The closest approximation to an intervention justified on humanitarian grounds between 1913 and 1945 was in the Proclamation on the German occupation of Bohemia and Moravia, made by Hitler on 15 March 1939. In that declaration, he referred to 'assaults upon life and liberty' by the 'intolerable terroristic régime of Czecho-Slovakia'. German troops were ordered to 'disarm the terrorist bands and the Czech troops who are shielding them; they will take under their protection the lives of all who are threatened'.[151] This

---

[145] Moore, above n 11, vol 6, 3; Rougier, above n 128, 474–5; Stowell, above n 4, 128–31; Ganji, above n 132, 29–33; Reisman and McDougal, above n 132, 182; Fonteyne, above n 132, 211–12; Tesón, above n 97, 178.

[146] Stowell, above n 4, 131 n 61: 'But even though conquest may have been the motive of the Russian Government, humanitarian intervention to prevent the inhumane treatment of the Christians was the justification of Russia's intervention.'

[147] Theodore Salisbury Woolsey, *America's Foreign Policy* (New York: Century, 1898) 74. See also Fenwick, above n 135, 650; Thomas M Franck and Nigel S Rodley, 'After Bangladesh: The Law of Humanitarian Intervention by Military Force' (1973) 67 *AJIL* 275, 283. Reisman concludes that the case does not undercut the authority of humanitarian intervention, but points to the need for structural and functional checks to avoid abuse by an intervening power: Reisman and McDougal, above n 132, 182.

[148] *Contra* Tesón, above n 97, 178; Fonteyne, above n 132, 213. See Douglas Dakin, *The Greek Struggle in Macedonia, 1897–1913* (Thessaloniki: Institute for Balkan Studies, 1966) 446–71.

[149] Rougier, above n 128, 470; David S Bogen, 'The Law of Humanitarian Intervention: United States Policy in Cuba (1898) and in the Dominican Republic (1965)' (1966) 7 *Harvard International Law Club Journal* 296, 299.

[150] See Moore, above n 11, vol 5, 476–93.

[151] Sir N Henderson to Viscount Halifax, 15 Mar 1939, in E L Woodward and Rohan Butler (eds), *Documents on British Foreign Policy 1919–1939* (London: HMSO, 1949) *Series Three*, iv, no 259, 257; ibid no 257, 256. See also Ian Brownlie, 'Humanitarian Intervention', in John N Moore (ed), *Law and Civil War in the Modern World* (Baltimore, Maryland: Johns Hopkins University Press, 1974) 217, 221; Thomas and Thomas, above n 142, 374.

'embarrassing exception'[152] has, unsurprisingly, not been invoked by writers seeking to establish such a general right.[153] Similarly self-serving claims were made by Japan to justify its invasion of Manchuria.[154]

Tesón concludes his brief survey of pre-Charter practice by stating that the most important precedent for a right of humanitarian intervention is the Second World War itself.[155] Citing Michael Walzer's just war analysis of the conflict,[156] he claims that the Allies fought Fascism not *just* because Hitler and Mussolini engaged in military aggression, but to defend 'dignity, reason, human rights, and decency . . . against degradation, authoritarianism, irrationality, and obscurantism'.[157] Though it may be argued that humanitarian concerns played a part in the Allied involvement in the war, they were nevertheless subsidiary to more traditional motives such as self-defence. In any case, the conflict hardly serves as an example of limited intervention in defence of those concerns.[158]

### 3.3.  Joint intervention of Great Britain, France, and Russia in aid of Greek insurgents, 1827

> The emancipation of Greece was a high act of policy above and beyond the domain of law. As an act of policy it may have been and was justifiable; but it was not the less a hostile act, which, had she dared, Turkey might properly have resented by war.
>
> Historicus, 1863[159]

The joint intervention of Great Britain, France, and Russia in aid of Greek insurgents against Turkish rule in 1827 is frequently cited in the literature as the earliest example of true humanitarian intervention.[160] Stowell notes that some writers class it as a defence of the right to self-determination,[161] but concludes that it has 'usually' been classed as an instance of humanitarian

---

[152] Brownlie, above n 5, 340.

[153] Tesón, above n 97, 31 n 24. Franck and Rodley, above n 147, 284.

[154] Franck and Rodley, above n 147, 284. See Philip Marshall Brown, 'Japanese Interpretation of the Kellogg Pact' (1933) 27 *AJIL* 100.

[155] Tesón, above n 97, 178–9.

[156] Michael Walzer, 'World War II: Why Was This War Different?' (1971) 1 *Philosophy and Public Affairs* 3.

[157] Tesón, above n 97, 178.

[158] Tesón himself does not rely on the example to justify his broader thesis, merely noting it as 'the paradigm of a just war': ibid 178–9.

[159] William Vernon Harcourt, *Letters by Historicus on Some Questions of International Law: Reprinted from 'The Times' with Considerable Additions* (London: Macmillan, 1863) 6.

[160] See, eg, Stowell, above n 4, 126–7, 489; Fenwick, above n 135, 650; Fonteyne, above n 132, 208; Anthony D'Amato, 'The Invasion of Panama was a Lawful Response to Tyranny' (1990) 84 *AJIL* 516, 519.

[161] Harcourt, above n 159, 6.

intervention motivated by the 'uncivilized methods' in which the war was being conducted.[162] This rationale has the support of various authorities,[163] but it is hardly a complete explanation of events.

The treaty between the three Powers, signed at London on 6 July 1827,[164] sets forth in the preamble the specific grounds on which they justified their intervention.[165] Of primary concern appears to have been 'all the disorders of anarchy' caused by the struggle, which both impeded the commerce of the states of Europe and gave opportunity to pirates, 'which not only expose the subjects of the High Contracting Parties to grievous losses, but also render necessary measures which are burthensome for their observation and suppression'.[166] Secondly, mention is made that two of the Powers (Great Britain and France) had 'received from the Greeks an earnest invitation to interpose their Mediation with the Ottoman Porte',[167] and together with the Emperor of Russia, 'animated with the desire of putting a stop to the effusion of blood, and of preventing the evils of every kind',[168] had resolved to combine and regulate their efforts with a view to re-establish peace—efforts demanded 'no less by sentiments of humanity, than by interests for the tranquillity of Europe'.[169]

The treaty was, first and foremost, an offer of mediation in the transition to Greek autonomy,[170] but contained a secret 'Additional Article' outlining

---

[162] Stowell, above n 4, 126.

[163] See, eg, Wheaton, above n 130, II, i, § 10, p 91; James Kent, *Kent's Commentary on International Law* (J T Abdy (ed); 1st edn; Cambridge: Deighton Bell & Co, 1866) 55; Augustus Granville Stapleton, *Intervention and Non-Intervention: The Foreign Policy of Great Britain from 1790 to 1865* (London: J Murray, 1866) 32; Sheldon Amos, *Lectures on International Law* (London: Stevens and Sons, 1874) 40; Theodore D Woolsey, *Introduction to the Study of International Law* (4th edn; London: Sampson, Low, Marston, Low & Searle, 1875) 45; Hermann Strauch, *Zur Interventionslehre* (1879) 277, cited in Stowell, above n 4, 127 n 59; Hersch Lauterpacht, *International Law and Human Rights* (London: Stevens & Sons, 1950) 120; Ganji, above n 132, 22–4. See now Lassa Francis Lawrence Oppenheim, *International Law* (Robert Jennings and Arthur Watts (eds); 9th edn; London: Longman, 1996) vol 1, 442 n 18: 'Thus Great Britain, France and Russia intervened in 1827 in the struggle between revolutionary Greece and Turkey when public opinion reacted with horror to the cruelties committed during the struggle.' On the US attitude towards the war, see Moore, above n 11, vol 6, 33–4.

[164] This was the formalization of a protocol signed at Petersburg, 4 Apr 1826, by the Russian Chancellor (Count Nesselrode), the Russian Ambassador to London (Prince Lieven), and the Duke of Wellington. This was duly communicated to Paris, Vienna, and Berlin but gained no support except in Paris: Mowat, above n 132, 48–9.

[165] Treaty Between Great Britain, France, and Russia, for the Pacification of Greece, signed at London, 6 July 1827, in Edward Hertslet, *The Map of Europe by Treaty* (London: Butterworths, 1875) vol 1, 769–70.

[166] Ibid preamble para 1; John Westlake, *International Law* (2nd edn; Cambridge: Cambridge University Press, 1910) 319 n 3.

[167] As the intervention took place within what was then Turkish territory, it is not an instance of intervention by consent.

[168] Treaty for the Pacification of Greece, above n 165, preamble para 2.

[169] Ibid. See Kent, above n 163, 57.

[170] Treaty for the Pacification of Greece, above n 165, art 1. This was qualified by an obligation on the part of Greece to pay a tribute to the Sultan: ibid art 1, 3.

the consequences that would follow rejection of the offer. (The Additional Article remained secret for all of six days before being published in *The Times*.[171]) Again, the primary concern appears to have been the 'inconveniences and evils' associated with the disorder in the East: these would necessitate the Powers 'forming a connection with the Greeks', by establishing commercial relations and exchange of diplomatic agents.[172] However, if either of the contending parties failed to observe the armistice, the Powers noted that they would enforce it, using 'all the means which circumstances may suggest to their prudence'. They further noted that instructions to this effect would be transmitted to their respective squadrons in the Levant.[173]

The declarations were rejected and a blockade imposed on 31 August 1827, leading ultimately to the Battle of Navarino on 20 October 1827 and a decisive defeat of the Turkish forces.[174] Great Britain's aims in the conflict appear to have been satisfied when the withdrawal of the Egyptian army from Morea was secured,[175] but after the termination of the Russo-Persian war, Tsar Nicholas declared war upon Turkey on 26 April 1828.[176] The Porte declared its acceptance of the terms of the London Treaty by a Declaration signed on 9 September 1829,[177] and in the peace treaty with Russia, signed five days later.[178]

Ian Brownlie dismisses characterization of the action as an instance of humanitarian intervention as 'ex post factoism',[179] stating that the governments of the day did not refer to a legal justification for intervention[180] and that jurists and historians have ascribed numerous motives to the action.[181] He concludes that the substantial motive was the prevention of racial extermination in the Morea, but that this cannot be discussed 'in terms of a legal concept which probably did not exist at the time'.[182] In so far as this refers to the absence of a customary norm prohibiting genocide at the time he is clearly correct. But when considered as an example of the abuse of sovereign power over subjects within its control, this statement seems at odds with his earlier

---

[171]  *The Times*, 12 July 1827. See C W Crawley, *The Question of Greek Independence: A Study of British Policy in the Near East, 1821–1833* (Cambridge: Cambridge University Press, 1930) 79.

[172]  Treaty for the Pacification of Greece, above n 165, Additional Article, § 1.

[173]  Ibid Additional Article, § 2.

[174]  See generally C M Woodhouse, *The Battle of Navarino* (London: Hodder & Stoughton, 1965).

[175]  Mowat, above n 132, 50.

[176]  Ibid 51.

[177]  Declaration of Accession of the Ottoman Porte to the Treaty of 6 July 1827 for the Pacification of Greece, signed at Constantinople, 9 Sept 1829, in Hertslet, above n 165, vol 2, 812.

[178]  Treaty of Peace Between Russia and Turkey, signed at Adrianople, 14 Sept 1829, art 10, in Hertslet, above n 165, vol 2, 813, 820–1.

[179]  Brownlie, above n 151, 220.

[180]  Brownlie, above n 5, 339; Brownlie, above n 151, 220–1.

[181]  Brownlie, above n 5, 339. Cf Halleck, above n 125, 340.

[182]  Brownlie, above n 5, 339, citing H A L Fisher, *A History of Europe* (rev edn; London: Eyre and Spottiswoode, 1943) vol 1, 881.

acknowledgement that a majority of nineteenth-century publicists recognized a right of humanitarian intervention, at least by the end of that century.[183]

Of more weight is his claim that Great Britain and France might have participated in the action due to fears of unilateral intervention by Russia.[184] Although this may explain the diplomacy behind the London Treaty and the protocol that preceded it,[185] the underlying attitudes were more complex. During the middle stages of the revolt, support for Greece was in large part explained by the sentimental interest of Europe:[186] it is likely that, regardless of Russian involvement, public opinion in the two countries would have forced their governments to do something.[187] This was reflected in the orders from Lord Bathurst, Secretary of State for the Colonies, to Sir Harry Neale, then Commander-in-Chief of the Mediterranean Station, dated 8 February 1826:

His Majesty has long had reason to lament the atrocities which have disgraced the contest in which Greece has been for many years unhappily involved . . . His Majesty, however in deploring the continuance of these excesses, has not thought fit hitherto to interpose, except in those cases in which the rights of his subjects . . . have been clearly compromised. But when it is understood, that, whether with the consent of the Porte or not, designs are avowed by Ibrahim Pacha to extirpate systematically a whole community, to seize upon the women and children of the Morea, to transport them to Egypt, and to re-people the Morea from Africa and Asia, to change, in fact, that part of Greece from an European State, into one resembling the States of Barbary; His Majesty cannot, as the Sovereign of an European State, hear of such an attempt without demanding of Ibrahim Pacha, either an explicit disavowal of his ever having entertained such an intention, or a formal renunciation of it, if ever entertained.[188]

There is, however, evidence that Ibrahim's alleged plan was merely a pretext for an alliance between Britain and Russia against Turkey.[189] The urgency of these matters (if true) had waned considerably by the time the London Treaty was signed and intervention actually took place. In response to enquiries by the British Government, both the Porte and Ibrahim expressly denied any such intention and the then Prime Minister Canning apparently accepted their word.[190] The orders to Admiral Sir Edward Codrington, Commander-in-Chief at the time of the 1827 intervention, made no mention of motive beyond reiterating the terms of the London Treaty and stating:

---

[183] Brownlie, above n 5, 338.

[184] Phillips notes that the 1826 protocol (above n 164) put the Russian Czar 'in a somewhat awkward position', as he had sent an ultimatum to the Porte only a few days earlier, demanding the immediate dispatch of plenipotentiaries to discuss Russian grievances: W Alison Phillips, *The War of Greek Independence* (London: Smith Elder & Co, 1897) 246. See also H W Halleck, *Halleck's International Law* (Sherston Baker (ed); 4th edn; London: Kegan Paul Trench Trubner & Co, 1908) 564; Crawley, above n 171, 77.

[185] Crawley, above n 171, 77.
[186] Ibid 13–16; Woodhouse, above n 174, 23–5.
[187] Mowat, above n 132, 47.
[188] Woodhouse, above n 174, 35–6.
[189] Crawley, above n 171, 49, 54.
[190] Woodhouse, above n 174, 37; Crawley, above n 171, 66, 68.

If the Greeks consent to a truce, you are to consider, in concert with your colleagues, of the measures which may be most proper and most expeditious for putting a period to hostilities and to the effusion of blood.[191]

The incident is at best a questionable precedent for the doctrine of humanitarian intervention.[192] Russian involvement had little to do with humanitarian concerns and—despite the public statements of British (and, to a lesser extent, French) officials—it was this that served as the catalyst for intervention.

### 3.4. French occupation of Syria, 1860–1

In June and July 1860 thousands of Maronite Christians were killed by Druzes and Muslims on Mount Lebanon and in Damascus, then part of Greater Syria but within the Ottoman Empire. On 31 July 1860 the ambassadors of Austria, Great Britain, France, Prussia, and Russia met in Paris with a representative of Turkey. A protocol was adopted[193] and incorporated into a convention signed on 5 September.[194] Under the terms of the convention, the Sultan, 'wishing to stop, by prompt and efficacious measures, the effusion of blood in Syria, and to show his firm resolution to establish Order and Peace amongst the Populations placed under his Sovereignty', agreed to up to 12,000 troops being sent to Syria 'to contribute towards the re-establishment of tranquillity'.[195] France was to furnish half this number immediately, with the other Powers agreeing to provide further troops as necessary.[196] The occupation was originally set to last six months,[197] but was extended until 5 June 1861.[198] A French force was duly dispatched, but found that the disturbances had subsided and that order had been restored by the Ottoman authorities. Nevertheless, its troops occupied parts of Greater Syria and its warships policed the coast from August 1860 to June 1861.[199]

---

[191] Woodhouse, above n 174, 44.

[192] See, eg, Charles de Visscher, *Theory and Reality in Public International Law* (Corbett trans; rev edn; Princeton, NJ: Princeton University Press, 1968) 126.

[193] Protocols of Conferences Between Great Britain, France, Prussia, Russia, and Turkey, Relative to the Pacification of Syria, signed at Paris, 3 Aug 1860, in Hertslet, above n 165, vol 2, 1451.

[194] Convention Between Great Britain, Austria, France, Prussia, Russia, and Turkey, respecting measures to be taken for the Pacification of Syria, signed at Paris, 5 Sept 1860, in Hertslet, above n 165, vol 2, 1455, preamble para 1.

[195] Ibid art 1.                    [196] Ibid art 2.                    [197] Ibid art 5.

[198] Convention Between Great Britain, Austria, France, Prussia, Russia, and Turkey, prolonging the European Occupation of Syria, signed at Paris, 19 Mar 1861, in Hertslet, above n 165, vol 2, 1469.

[199] See Istvan Pogany, 'Humanitarian Intervention in International Law: The French Intervention in Syria Re-Examined' (1986) 35 *ICLQ* 182, 186 and sources there cited.

Brownlie includes this as the most likely exception to his general statement that international practice in the nineteenth century discloses no genuine case of humanitarian intervention,[200] an evaluation shared by a number of other publicists.[201] The emphasis that has been placed on the French action as a paradigm example of humanitarian intervention appears misplaced, however. It has been argued that the measures taken by the Ottoman Sultan and local authorities rendered foreign action unnecessary and suspicious in light of European interest in the declining Ottoman Empire,[202] and that ultimate responsibility for the conflict lay with actions of the Christians themselves.[203] More significantly, it has been argued that the consent of the Sultan and the extremely limited mandate of the French forces may take the action outside of traditional definitions of intervention.[204] Stowell notes that the Sultan gave his consent only 'through constraint and a desire to avoid worse',[205] but this makes the action a very dubious precedent for a right of unilateral action.

Perhaps the most important element of the incident as a possible instance of humanitarian intervention is the relative disinterestedness of the acting parties. Despite its occurrence within the context of French colonialism in the region, the occupying force did arrive under the mandate of five European Powers and departed when that mandate concluded. In the second protocol signed at the conference in August 1860, the Powers declared 'in the most formal manner' that they would not seek any territorial advantage, exclusive influence, or concession under the pretext of the occupation.[206] The humanitarian concerns of the Powers—albeit only for the well-being of fellow Christians—appear to have been genuine.

### 3.5. US intervention in Cuba, 1898

There may be an explosion any day in Cuba which would settle a great many things.
Senator Henry Cabot Lodge to Henry White, January 1898[207]

---

[200] Brownlie, above n 5, 340.
[201] See, eg, Rougier, above n 128, 525; Bernhardt, above n 34, vol 2, 927. Cf Stowell, above n 4, 63, and sources there cited.  [202] Pogany, above n 199, 185–8.
[203] See Franck and Rodley, above n 147, 282, citing the Minute of the British Commissioner to Syria, who concluded that 'the original provocation proceeded from the Christians, who had been for months beforehand preparing an onslaught on the Druses, which their leaders confidently expected would terminate, if not in the extermination, at all events in the expulsion, of that race.' Minute of British Commissioner on the Judgments proposed to be passed on the Turkish Officials and Druse Chiefs by the Extraordinary Tribunal of Beyrout, in Sohn and Buergenthal, above n 135, 165.
[204] Thomas and Thomas, above n 142, 22; Pogany, above n 199, 188–90 (though this appears at odds with his argument that the action should be seen as French colonialism); Natalino Ronzitti, *Rescuing Nationals Abroad Through Military Coercion and Intervention on Grounds of Humanity* (Dordrecht: Martinus Nojhoff, 1985) 90. Cf Fonteyne, above n 132, 208–9.
[205] Stowell, above n 4, 66; Ganji, above n 132, 26.
[206] Protocol of 3 Aug 1860, above n 193, § 2.  [207] Quoted in Ferrell, above n 135, 347.

The United States' intervention in Cuba in 1898 is perhaps the closest example to unilateral humanitarian intervention in pre-Charter state practice. Stowell refers to it as 'one of the most important instances of humanitarian intervention',[208] though it is cited in the literature less often than the preceding two examples—presumably because of the numerous other and less altruistic motives behind the action, which was but the flashpoint of the broader war with Spain.[209] In a matter of months, the Spanish navy was defeated, Spain had relinquished the remnants of its empire, the United States had established itself as a world power, and Cuba was an American protectorate.[210]

The initial intervention followed reports of atrocities committed by Spanish military authorities attempting to suppress the insurrection that commenced in 1895. Some of these were clearly exaggerated by the 'yellow journalism' of the day, which is cited as a cause of the war in its own right.[211] Nevertheless, it is not doubted that the Spanish policy of forcing the disaffected population into concentration camps in order to identify revolutionaries caused genuine outrage in the United States. Some 200,000 Cubans were estimated to have died in the camps.[212] Two other factors were the leaking of a particularly undiplomatic personal letter, written by the Spanish Minister to the United States, Enrique Dupuy de Lôme,[213] and the untimely destruction of the US battleship *Maine*, probably by a Spanish submarine mine.[214]

In his special Message to Congress of 11 April 1898, President McKinley outlined four justifications for US intervention in the conflict: 'the cause of humanity', protection of US citizens and their property in Cuba, protection of US commercial interests, and self-defence.[215] A joint resolution was subsequently passed, authorizing intervention on the basis of

---

[208] Stowell, above n 4, 481. One American commentator states that '[o]ne would search in vain the records of the world's history to find a more striking example of a war undertaken by any nation from motives more singularly humane and free from selfish interests and purposes': Oscar S Straus, 'Humanitarian Diplomacy of the United States' (1912) 6 *ASIL Proc* 45, 50. It is also cited by Reisman and McDougal, above n 132, 182–3.

[209] See, eg, Fonteyne, above n 132, 206.

[210] Ferrell, above n 135, 347–8, 367; Michael Walzer, *Just and Unjust Wars: A Moral Argument with Historical Illustrations* (2nd edn; New York: Basic Books, 1992) 103–4.

[211] Ferrell, above n 135, 353. In the search for sensational coverage, William Randolph Hearst dispatched an artist to Cuba for battle sketches. Told that there was no war after all, he is famously alleged to have wired the artist in reply: 'You furnish the pictures; I'll furnish the war': H Wayne Morgan, *William McKinley and His America* (Syracuse, NY: Syracuse University Press, 1963) 330.

[212] Ferrell, above n 135, 350.      [213] Ibid 353.

[214] Moore, above n 11, vol 6, 181–4 (report of US Board of Inquiry); ibid 223–4 (report of Senate Committee on Foreign Relations). But see Richard A Falk, *Legal Order in a Violent World* (Princeton, NJ: Princeton University Press, 1968) 194–5.

[215] President McKinley, Special Message to Congress, 11 Apr 1898, in Moore, above n 11, vol 6, 211, 219–20.

the abhorrent conditions which . . . have shocked the moral sense of the people of the United States, have been a disgrace to Christian civilization, culminating, as they have, in the destruction of a United States battle ship.[216]

The stated goals of intervention were to guarantee Cuban independence and compel Spain to relinquish its authority over the island. For its part, the United States expressly disclaimed any intention to exercise control over the island beyond pacification of the current dispute.[217]

Subsequent writers, as Brownlie notes, have failed to agree on a characterization of the action.[218] Jean-Pierre Fonteyne, who cites six instances of humanitarian intervention in the period, excludes the intervention in Cuba as lacking a clearly humanitarian motive.[219] Theodore Salisbury Woolsey, writing at the time of the Spanish American War, noted that 'it is not on the score of humanity alone . . . that the President justifies intervention', but that American interests were 'deeply involved' to the point where the action might be properly regarded as self-defence.[220] Other jurists have described it as a case of intervention to protect nationals[221] or their property,[222] and as abatement of a nuisance.[223] Walzer less charitably characterizes the action as being perhaps an example of 'benevolent imperialism, given the "piratical times", but it is not an example of humanitarian intervention'.[224]

## 4. HUMANITARIAN INTERVENTION IN THE EARLY TWENTIETH CENTURY

It is unsurprising, then, that the status of humanitarian intervention at the start of the twentieth century was unclear. A century on, the common statement that a 'right of humanitarian intervention' was recognized at this time is at best a partial, at worst a misleading, rendering of the true position. As Brownlie notes, the doctrine was 'inherently vague' and found a variety of forms.[225] But in addition to the different contents attributed to this 'right', more fundamental differences can be seen in its normative status. Evaluation of this status is made particularly difficult by the fact that, as noted earlier, war itself was not prohibited by international law.[226] Nevertheless, a survey of the literature discloses certain lines of demarcation between those who confidently asserted a right of unilateral humanitarian intervention, those who

---

[216] 30 Stat 738 (1898), in Moore, above n 11, vol 6, 226.  [217] Ibid.
[218] Brownlie, above n 5, 46.  [219] Fonteyne, above n 132, 206.
[220] Woolsey, above n 147, 76.  [221] Sohn and Buergenthal, above n 135, 180.
[222] Derek W Bowett, *Self-Defence in International Law* (Manchester: Manchester University Press, 1958) 97.
[223] John Bassett Moore, *The Principles of American Diplomacy* (New York: Harper and Brothers, 1918) 208, citing Alphone Rivier.
[224] Walzer, above n 210, 104.  [225] Brownlie, above n 5, 338.
[226] See above nn 5–11 and accompanying text.

confidently rejected it, and those who held that international law could or should have little to say about the matter. And it is only by combining the first and third groups of publicists that one may conclude that a majority of theorists recognized such a right.[227] Curiously, only a few writers explicitly linked the question of the justification for intervention with that of the manner in which it was exercised. Of these, most held the view that if there was to be an exception to the general rule of non-intervention, collective action was more appropriate than allowing one state unilaterally to take the law into its own hands.

## 4.1. Humanitarian intervention as a legal right

Of those who argued that humanitarian intervention existed as a legal right, a distinction may be drawn between those who justified it as a quasi-judicial police measure against the crimes of a sovereign, and those who characterized it as a defence of the rights of the oppressed.

### 4.1.1. Intervention as a police measure

In the first category are publicists such as Antoine Rougier, who defined the theory of humanitarian intervention as the attempt to give a juridical basis to the right of one state to exercise international control over the internal acts of another state that are contrary '*aux lois de l'humanité*'.[228] Some other notable proponents of this view are Wheaton,[229] Woolsey,[230] Arntz,[231] and Borchard.[232] This view is the most explicitly linked to Grotius' conception of punitive war, and was, on occasion, adopted by representatives of 'civilized' governments intervening in the affairs of other states. Thus Theodore Roosevelt stated in 1904 that

[c]hronic wrongdoing, or an impotence which results in a general loosening of the ties of civilized society, may in America, as elsewhere, ultimately require intervention by some civilized nation, and in the Western Hemisphere the adherence of the United States to the Monroe doctrine may force the United States, however reluctantly, in

---

[227] See, eg, Brownlie, above n 5, 338; Richard B Lillich, 'Humanitarian Intervention: A Reply to Ian Brownlie and a Plea for Constructive Alternatives', in Moore, above n 151, 229, 233.

[228] Rougier, above n 128, 472.

[229] Wheaton, above n 130, II, i, § 10, p 91. See above n 130.

[230] Woolsey, above n 163, § 42, p 32.

[231] E R N Arntz, letter quoted in G Rolin-Jaequemyns, 'Note sur la théorie du droit d'intervention' (1875) 8 *Revue du droit international et de la législation comparée* 673, 675.

[232] Edwin Montefiore Borchard, *The Diplomatic Protection of Citizens Abroad* (New York: Banks Law, 1928). See also W E Lingelbach, 'The Doctrine and Practice of Intervention in Europe' (1900) 16 *Annals of the American Academy of Political and Social Science* 1, 25.

flagrant cases of such wrongdoing or impotence, to the exercise of an international police power.[233]

Some writers also referred to the burdens that power imposed on the bearer,[234] or explicitly limited any right of intervention to civilized states.[235] As indicated above, however, such a right was disclaimed by the early positivists as too open to abuse,[236] and in practice states more commonly relied on less controversial grounds to justify their actions.[237]

### 4.1.2. Intervention on behalf of the oppressed

The second group of writers recognizing the legality of humanitarian intervention did so on the basis that a state is, in certain circumstances, entitled to assert the rights of subjects vis-à-vis their sovereign. This may be further divided into three subcategories.

First, it was sometimes argued in general terms that where a state grossly violated the rights of its citizens, any other state with the means and the will to do so was entitled to intervene. This is the modern equivalent of Grotius' right to wage war on behalf of the oppressed,[238] but it was not a view held in an unqualified form by many writers due to the same fear of abuse that led to its abandonment by the later positivists. Johann Caspar Bluntschli, for example, held that a state is authorized to intervene to ensure respect for individual rights and international law, but only where these have been violated in internal conflict within a state and constituted a general danger.[239] (It is this form of right that writers such as Tesón and Michael Reisman defend in the modern era.[240])

More commonly, and in line with the writings of Vattel, theorists restricted the right of intervention on humanitarian grounds to situations where civil war had broken out[241] or acts of rebellion led to the political bonds between sovereign and citizens being broken.[242] Although this encompassed

---

[233] President Roosevelt, Annual Message, 6 December 1904, in Moore, above n 11, vol 6, 596.

[234] See, eg, A T Mahan, *Some Neglected Aspects of War* (Boston: Little Brown, 1907) 107.

[235] Edwin DeWitt Dickinson, *The Equality of States in International Law* (Cambridge, MA: Harvard University Press, 1920) 262–3; Georgee Fréderic de Martens, *Traite de droit international* (Léo trans, 1883) vol 1, 398, quoted in Fonteyne, above n 132, 219: '*Vis-à-vis* non civilized nations . . . intervention by the civilized powers is in principle legitimate, when the Christian population of those countries is exposed to persecutions or massacres. In those circumstances, it is justified by common religious interests and humanitarian considerations. . . . These motives are not applicable to relations between civilized powers.'
See also Stowell, above n 4, 64–5 n 14.

[237] See above Sect 3.

[236] See above nn 73–85.

[238] See above Sect 1.2.

[239] Johann Caspar Bluntschli, *Le droit international codifié* (Paris: Librairie de Guillaumin, 1870) § 478.

[240] See Ch 2.

[241] A G Heffter, *Le droit international public de l'Europe* ([1844] Bergson trans; Berlin: E H Schroeder, 1857) 105; Halleck, above n 125, 340.

[242] William Oke Manning, *Commentaries on the Law of Nations* (Sheldon Amos (ed); London: Sweet, 1875) 97; Amos, above n 163, 39–41.

humanitarian motives—notably in the desire to 'stay the effusion of blood', a phrase included in the 1827[243] and 1860[244] treaties authorizing the interventions in Greece and Syria—it was also concerned with maintaining order, seen in the references to averting 'a general danger',[245] 'prolonged unrest',[246] and 'public order'.[247]

A third presentation of the doctrine limited it still further to situations where a particular race was 'grievously oppressed' by power of a different race, perhaps akin to the modern war of liberation from colonial domination.[248]


## 4.2. Humanitarian intervention proscribed

Those who opposed a right of humanitarian intervention also fall broadly into two camps. The first recognized an absolute right of non-intervention, either on the Hobbesian basis that subjects hold no rights vis-à-vis their sovereign,[249] or, more commonly, because any intervention on their behalf—no matter how great the moral claim—is incompatible with sovereignty.[250]

It is only this first group that might be accused of succumbing to Tesón's 'Hegelian myth'.[251] A far larger group adopted a more pragmatic position, spurred by the same concerns that led Vattel to reject Grotius' assertion of a quasi-judicial authority held by sovereigns as 'open[ing] the door to all the passions of zealots and fanatics'.[252] A form of utilitarian reasoning was commonly invoked, countering the moral arguments in favour of a right of humanitarian intervention with the practical danger of its abuse:

The occasional benefits of such intervention would be outweighed by its liability to abuse. In theory no doubt it is regrettable that international law should prohibit, even by implication, the suppression of outrage, but in practice the number of national Don Quixotes is not found to be considerable, and thinkers of very different schools are content to distinguish between the moral standards applicable respectively to individuals and communities.[253]

---

[243] See above n 168.                         [244] See above n 195.
[245] Bluntschli, above n 239, § 478 ('un danger général').
[246] Heffter, above n 241, 105 ('inquiétude prolongé').
[247] Manning, above n 242, 97.            [248] Creasy, above n 126, § 316, pp 303–4.
[249] Nassau William Senior, 'Book Review: Wheaton's International Law' (1843) 156 *Edinburgh Review* 334, 365. Cf Hobbes, above n 68.
[250] See, eg, Richard Wildman, *Institutes of International Law* (London: William Benning, 1849) 62–3; James Reddie, *Inquiries in International Law: Public and Private* (2nd edn; Edinburgh: William Blackwood and Sons, 1851) 389–404; Montague Bernard, *On the Principle of Non-Intervention* (Oxford: J H & J Parker, 1860) 16–20; Halleck, above n 125, 340; Brierly, above n 6, 156–7; Thomas Erskine Holland, *Lectures on International Law* (London: Sweet & Maxwell, 1933) 108–10.
[251] See above Sect 2.2.                      [252] See above n 81 and accompanying text.
[253] F E Smith, *International Law* (J Wylie (ed); 4th edn; London: J M Dent, 1911) 63–4. Cf Thomas Alfred Walker, *The Science of International Law* (London: Clay and Sons, 1893) 151–2:

Phillimore notes that the general interests of humanity may be defensible as an accessory motive, but as a 'substantive and solitary justification' of intervention in the affairs or another country it cannot be admitted into international law, 'since it is manifestly open to abuses, tending to the violation and destruction of the vital principles of that system of jurisprudence'.[254] Even writers who allowed a right of humanitarian intervention nevertheless made note of the dangers of its abuse.[255]

### 4.3. Humanitarian intervention as political and unavoidable

The major difficulty in evaluating the legal status of humanitarian intervention in this period is that a large number of writers put the question outside the realm of international law entirely. Historicus (Sir William Harcourt) expressed this in an often-quoted passage published in 1863:

Intervention is a question rather of policy than of law. It is above and beyond the domain of law, and when wisely and equitably handled by those who have the power to give effect to it, may be the highest policy of justice and humanity.[256]

Various writers echoed his view that international law had little to say about such 'high politics'.[257]

Others adopted a more subtle position, noting that there is scope for moral evaluation of state behaviour independent of the legal regime. Herman Rodecker von Rotteck, whom Stowell credits as the first to establish the theory of intervention on the ground of humanity,[258] nevertheless held that it should be considered as a violation of the law, but sometimes excused or even

'Englishmen, who shelter the Nihilist, and cry loud and long on the horrors of Siberian prisons and the anti-Jewish zeal of the Muscovite, require to remember that, however conscious they may be of their philanthropic motives, the world is apt to be suspicious. There are philanthropists beyond the bounds of England.' See also George Grafton Wilson, *Handbook of International Law* (2nd edn; St Paul, Minn: West, 1927) 57; A Pearce Higgins, *Studies in International Law and Relations* (Cambridge: Cambridge University Press, 1928) 27.

[254] Phillimore, above n 126, vol 1, 442. But see his discussion of intervention on religious grounds: ibid 470 ff.

[255] Amos, above n 163, 40; Lingelbach, above n 232, 25; Rougier, above n 128, 478. Cf Senior, above n 249, 366.

[256] Harcourt, above n 159, 14.

[257] See, eg, John Norton Pomeroy, *Lecture on International Law in Time of Peace* (Theodore Salisbury Woolsey (ed); Cambridge, MA: Riverside Press, 1886) 244–5; T J Lawrence, *The Principles of International Law* (London: Macmillan, 1895) 132 ('interventions on the ground of humanity have under very exceptional circumstances a moral, though not a legal, justification'); Amos S Hershey, 'The Calvo and Drago Doctrines' (1907) 1 *AJIL* 26, 42; Frederick Charles Hicks, 'The Equality of States and the Hague Conferences' (1908) 2 *AJIL* 530, 541; Foulke, above n 4, vol 2, 66; T J Lawrence, *A Handbook of Public International Law* (Percy H Winfield (ed); 11th edn; London: Macmillan, 1938) 46.

[258] Stowell, above n 4, 469.

applauded, as one may excuse a crime.[259] Hall explains the apparent political
and juristic acceptance of humanitarian intervention as reflecting 'considerations of sentiment to the exclusion of law'.[260] His own position is that no such
intervention is legal unless 'the whole body of civilized states have concurred
in authorising it'.[261] Where such authorization is not possible, he argues that
such measures should be justified

> as measures which, being confessedly illegal in themselves, could only be excused in
> rare and extreme cases in consideration of the unquestionably extraordinary charac-
> ter of the facts causing them, and of the evident purity of the motives and conduct of
> the intervening state. The record of the last hundred years might not have been much
> cleaner than it is; but evildoing would have been at least sometimes compelled to show
> itself in its true colours; it would have found more difficulty in clothing itself in a gen-
> erous disguise; and international law would in any case have been saved from com-
> plicity with it.[262]

Similarly, T J Lawrence modified his position in later editions to state that in
extreme circumstances of cruelty 'there is nothing in the law of nations which
will brand as a wrongdoer the state that steps forward and undertakes the
necessary intervention':

> There is a great difference between declaring a national act to be legal, and therefore
> part of the order under which states have consented to live, and allowing it to be
> morally blameless as an exception to ordinary rules.[263]

Brierly points out that it is precisely this contradiction between law and
morality that led some writers to regard humanitarian reasons as a legal justification for intervention.[264]


### 4.4. Collective intervention

Lassa Francis Oppenheim, in a passage that remained unchanged through
five editions of his work, doubted whether there was a rule admitting 'interventions in the interests of humanity', but did note that 'public opinion and
the attitude of the Powers are in favour of such interventions'.[265] He con-

---

[259] Herman Rodecker von Rotteck, *Das Recht der Einmischung in die inneren Angelegenheiten
eines fremden Staates vom vernunftrechtlichen, historischen und politischen Standpunkte erörtert*
(1845), in Stowell, above n 4, 525.
[260] Hall (2nd edn), above n 124, 265.      [261] Ibid 266.      [262] Ibid.
[263] T J Lawrence, *The Principles of International Law* (6th edn; Boston: D C Heath, 1915) 129.
[264] Brierly, above n 6, 156. Cf Westlake, above n 166, vol 1, 320: 'Laws are made for men and
not creatures of the imagination, and they must not create or tolerate for them situations which
are beyond the endurance, we will not say of average human nature, since laws may fairly expect
to raise the standard by their operation, but of the best human nature that at the time and place
they can hope to meet with.'
[265] Oppenheim, above n 3, vol 1, 186. This is misrepresented somewhat in Tesón, above n 97,
60.

*can it be allowed to be a collective interest*

cluded that such a right may be recognized at some point in the future, but restricted it to *collective* intervention by the Powers:

Many jurists maintain that intervention is likewise admissible, or even has a basis of right, when exercised in the interest of humanity for the purpose of stopping religious persecution and endless cruelties in time of peace and war. That the Powers have in the past exercised intervention on these grounds, there is no doubt. Thus Great Britain, France, and Russia intervened in 1827 in the struggle between revolutionary Greece and Turkey, because public opinion was horrified at the cruelties committed during this struggle. And many a time interventions have taken place to stop the persecution of Christians in Turkey. But whether there is really a rule of the Law of Nations which admits such interventions may well be doubted. Yet, on the other hand, it cannot be denied that public opinion and the attitude of the Powers are in favour of such interventions, and it may perhaps be said that in time the Law of Nations will recognise the rule that interventions in the interests of humanity are admissible provided they are exercised in the form of a *collective* intervention of the Powers.[266]

This was Hall's position,[267] and it finds support in a few other writers such as Pasquale Fiore[268] and Amos Hershey.[269] It is curious that more writers did not comment on the modality of humanitarian intervention, given the amount of ink spilt on the question of its legitimacy.

The most probable explanation is that its doubtful status meant that little of substance could be said within the positivist paradigm. Those who recognized it as subsisting outside the bounds of international law could not qualify their observation by reference to a norm of conduct; those who sought to evaluate it (if at all) solely in ethical terms apparently saw no significance in whether one or many states intervened. Nevertheless, as Oppenheim stresses, the major instances of alleged humanitarian intervention in the nineteenth century against the Ottoman Empire were collective in character, orchestrated by the Concert of Europe. Moreover, when Russia asserted a right to intervene unilaterally on behalf of Christian subjects persecuted by the Sultan in 1853–4, this provoked the Crimean War in which Great Britain

---

[266] Oppenheim, above n 3, vol 1, 186–7.         [267] See above n 261.

[268] Fiore prohibited unilateral intervention, but held that there was nevertheless an *obligation* for collective intervention when its object is to protect or restore the authority of 'common' law violated by one or more states: Pasquale Fiore, *International Law Codified and Its Legal Sanction* (Borchard trans; 5th edn; New York: Baker Voorhis & Co, 1918) 265, 268–72. It is not clear that this would extend beyond the violation of conventional and customary law obligations, however: ibid 270–1.

[269] Hershey notes that non-intervention is 'a fundamental principle of International Law', but that that body of law must rest upon international practice as well as such principles: Hershey, above n 3, 148. He thus acknowledges that '[f]orcible interference in the internal affairs of another State has been justified on grounds of humanity in extreme cases like those of Greece, Bulgaria, and Cuba, where great evils existed, great crimes were being perpetrated, or where there was a danger of race extermination': ibid 151. To avoid the danger of abuse, he recommends that any such intervention should be collective in character, or if one state intervenes it should do so only as the agent or mandatory of the other: ibid.

and France sided with the Sultan in defence of Turkish sovereignty and independence.[270]

## CONCLUSION

[Intervention] is a high and summary procedure which may sometimes snatch a remedy beyond the reach of law. Nevertheless, it must be admitted that in the case of Intervention, as that of Revolution, its essence is illegality, and its justification is its success. Of all things, at once the most unjustifiable and the most impolitic is an unsuccessful Intervention.

Historicus, 1863[271]

These excursions on the theory and practice of intervention from the sixteenth century to the inter-war period are of more than simply historical interest. Most of the themes in contemporary debates on humanitarian intervention are represented in the writings of this period: the moral impetus to act on behalf of the oppressed and not to let evil go unpunished; the concern about abuse of any unilateral right of intervention on subjectively determined grounds; the emerging public discourse on human rights issues and the countervailing desire to maintain independence despite increasingly permeable international borders. Central to these concerns is the perception that international law can neither sanction nor ignore actions that 'shock the conscience of mankind'.[272]

There is, however, no consensus on what it *can* do. The origins of humanitarian intervention lie largely in the dubious legitimacy of wars against the infidel Other and in defence of missionaries to the East. In 1648 the Treaty of Westphalia signalled a new political commitment to sovereignty, heralding the development of a new norm of non-intervention. It is the tension between these principles that gave rise to the doctrine of humanitarian intervention (complicated further by the related doctrine of protection of nationals abroad), but it remains difficult to establish the customary law status of this 'right'. Analysis of the relevant state practice is confused by the imprecise use of the term 'intervention' and the failure to distinguish humanitarian concerns from other motives, with the result that few (if any) bona fide examples of humanitarian intervention can be discerned.

In the first half of the twentieth century, the status of humanitarian intervention became still more problematic. Although true collective action on the part of the international community was politically difficult, the notion of

[270] Wheaton, above n 111, 99 n 38; Butler and Maccoby, above n 38, 442–51; Davies, above n 27, 870.

[271] Harcourt, above n 159, 41.

[272] Lassa Francis Lawrence Oppenheim, *International Law* (Hersch Lauterpacht (ed); 8th edn; London: Longmans, 1955) 312.

unilateral intervention by a state or group of states sat uncomfortably with the increasing emphasis on the inviolability of the domestic jurisdiction. Again, however, there is little in the way of state practice to support a doctrine of humanitarian intervention.

The Covenant of the League of Nations neither prohibited nor explicitly allowed for humanitarian intervention. The primary aim of the Covenant was peace, to be secured by 'the acceptance of obligations not to resort to war' and 'the maintenance of justice and a scrupulous respect for all treaty obligations in the dealings of organised peoples with one another'.[273] The use of force was not outlawed as such, but war was made a matter of concern to the entire League; members were required at first instance to submit any dispute to arbitration, judicial settlement, or to enquiry by the Council.[274] It is at least arguable that internal human rights violations could have constituted such a dispute,[275] though the Council explicitly disclaimed any capacity to make recommendations on a matter that 'by international law is solely within the domestic jurisdiction of [a] party'.[276]

Similarly, the Kellogg–Briand Pact said nothing of humanitarian intervention, though its tenor is clearly inconsistent with any such right. States parties stated their conviction that 'all changes in their relations' should be sought only by pacific means,[277] condemned recourse to war for the 'solution of international controversies', and renounced it as an instrument of national policy.[278] There was considerable diplomatic activity concerning reservations to this prohibition, but the reservations were limited to the right of legitimate defence or self-defence.[279] (Whether the Pact in fact created a legal prohibition of the use of force, and whether that included forceful measures short of war, were topics of some academic debate.[280])

The suspicion with which later theorists regarded Grotius' claim that one state may enforce the rights of subjects in another state remains a central dilemma in a horizontally organized state system. In the absence of a hegemon to act on behalf of oppressed subjects, some theorists recommended collective police action as a response. Many more held that in extreme circumstances any state could (or would) simply act on its own initiative. More than anything, humanitarian intervention appears to occupy a lacuna

---

[273] Covenant of the League of Nations, preamble.     [274] Ibid art 12.

[275] Sean D Murphy, *Humanitarian Intervention: The United Nations in an Evolving World Order* (Philadelphia: University of Pennsylvania Press, 1996) 59.

[276] Covenant of the League of Nations, art 15.

[277] Treaty Providing for the Renunciation of War as an Instrument of National Policy, 27 Aug 1928, signed at Paris, in force 1929, 94 LNTS 57, preamble.

[278] Ibid art 1.

[279] See generally Brownlie, above n 5, 74–92, 235–47. Thus Japan's alleged vital interests in Manchuria were rejected by the United States and the United Kingdom as excuses for its actions: ibid 243–4.

[280] See, eg, Brownlie, above n 5, 83–9 and sources there cited.

in the primitive international legal regime of the time. As the norm prohibiting the use of force coalesced in the twentieth century, however, that lacuna
became more constrained. This process of coalescence and the prohibition
enshrined in the Charter of the United Nations are the subjects of the next
Chapter.

# 2

# The Scourge of War

## *Humanitarian intervention and the prohibition of the use of force in the UN Charter*

WE THE PEOPLES OF THE UNITED NATIONS DETERMINED to save succeeding generations from the scourge of war, which twice in our lifetime has brought untold sorrow to mankind, and to reaffirm faith in fundamental human rights, in the dignity and worth of the human person . . .

UN Charter, Preamble

The tension between sovereignty and human rights in the international legal order established after the Second World War is manifest in the opening words of the UN Charter. War is to be renounced as an instrument of national policy. Human rights are to be affirmed. But in its substantive provisions, the Charter clearly privileges peace over dignity: the threat or use of force is prohibited in Article 2(4); protection of human rights is limited to the more or less hortatory provisions of Articles 55 and 56.[1] Most contemporary writing on humanitarian intervention recounts this tension, then proceeds to consider a series of alleged instances of intervention on humanitarian grounds in order to conclude whether or not such a right exists in practice. The failure to reconcile the relevant Charter provisions with such customary international law analysis is indicative of how little has changed in the tenor of debate on humanitarian intervention over the last hundred or so years.[2] One

---

[1] UN Charter, arts 55–6:

*Article 55*

With a view to the creation of conditions of stability and well-being which are necessary for peaceful and friendly relations among nations based on respect for the principle of equal rights and self-determination of peoples, the United Nations shall promote:
(a) higher standards of living, full employment, and conditions of economic and social progress and development;
(b) solutions of international economic, social, health, and related problems; and international cultural and educational cooperation; and
(c) universal respect for, and observance of, human rights and fundamental freedoms for all without distinction as to race, sex, language, or religion.

*Article 56*

All Members pledge themselves to take joint and separate action in co-operation with the Organization for the achievement of the purposes set forth in Article 55.
[2] See Ch 1.

reason for this failure is that many proponents of humanitarian intervention justify it as promoting human rights, and are loath to do so at the expense of the closest thing international law has to a constitution. A second reason is that the few instances of alleged state practice that are routinely cited were not accompanied by clear legal justifications on the part of the acting states.

The only occasion on which an alleged instance of humanitarian intervention has been litigated before an international tribunal was in relation to the North Atlantic Treaty Organization's 1999 air campaign against the Federal Republic of Yugoslavia (FRY) concerning its actions in Kosovo (an incident considered in depth in Chapter 5). The FRY instituted proceedings against ten NATO-members before the International Court of Justice, alleging that their joint and several acts were unlawful violations of Article 2(4).[3] The FRY's requests for provisional measures were denied for lack of prima facie jurisdiction,[4] though its actions against eight of the original respondent states remain on foot. In the joint hearings on the ten requests for provisional measures, only Belgium presented a clear argument that its actions were justified on the basis of a right of humanitarian intervention. Counsel stated that NATO 'intervened to protect fundamental values enshrined in the *jus cogens*', such as the right to life and the prohibition of torture, 'and to prevent an impending catastrophe recognized as such by the Security Council'.[5] Other states also used the formula 'humanitarian catastrophe'[6]—alluding directly or indirectly to the language of Security Council resolution 1199 (1998)[7]—but avoided making reference to humanitarian intervention. For the most part, all ten states focused their arguments on questions of jurisdiction and admissibility. Belgium's arguments were necessarily brief, but echoed the trend identified in academic works on this subject indicated above:

[T]he Kingdom of Belgium takes the view that this is an armed humanitarian intervention, compatible with Article 2, paragraph 4, of the Charter, which covers only intervention against the territorial integrity or political independence of a State.

There is no shortage of precedents. India's intervention in Eastern Pakistan; Tanzania's intervention in Uganda; Vietnam in Cambodia; the West African countries' interventions first in Liberia and then in Sierra Leone. While there may have been certain doubts expressed in the doctrine, and among some members of the international community, these interventions have not been expressly condemned by the relevant United Nations bodies. These precedents, combined with Security Council resolutions and the rejection of the draft Russian resolution on 26 March . . . undoubtedly support and substantiate our contention that the NATO intervention is entirely legal.[8]

---

[3] *Legality of Use of Force Case* (*Provisional Measures*) (ICJ, 1999).

[4] Ibid, order of 2 June 1999. See Ch 5, Sect 4.2.3.

[5] Ibid pleadings of Belgium, 10 May 1999, CR 99/15 (uncorrected translation).

[6] See, eg, ibid, pleadings of the United Kingdom, 11 May 1999, CR 99/23, para 17.

[7] SC Res 1199 (1998) preamble: '*alarmed* at the impending humanitarian catastrophe.'

[8] *Legality of Use of Force Case* (*Provisional Measures*) (ICJ, 1999), pleadings of Belgium, 10 May 1999, CR 99/15 (uncorrected translation).

Belgium gave no indication of the way in which such intervention is compatible with Article 2(4), what, exactly, the 'precedents' stand for, or the significance to be attributed to the Security Council resolutions cited (both adopted and rejected).

This Chapter considers the relationship between arguments for a right of humanitarian intervention and the law of the Charter. In order to establish a right of humanitarian intervention in international law, it is necessary to demonstrate either that such a right is not incompatible with the clear provisions of Article 2(4), or that Article 2(4) does not preclude unilateral action as a form of self-help justified in customary international law when the collective security regime envisaged by the Charter fails to address a crisis. These two schools of thought are considered in Sections 1 and 2 of this Chapter. (A third argument that certain regimes by their actions forfeit sovereignty and thereby lose the rights attendant to it will be considered in Chapter 3. Security Council authorized intervention and its limits will be considered in Chapters 4 and 5.)

The most noticeable aspect of the debates recounted in this Chapter is, in the end, the disjunction between the positions of publicists and state practice. No state has ever justified an intervention in terms corresponding to the doctrine as articulated by its most enthusiastic academic proponents. By the same token, it is clear that a small number of interventions have been tolerated (if not expressly approved) by a large number of states, apparently out of recognition of the relatively benign motives and positive consequences of those interventions. This suggests that a flat condemnation of humanitarian intervention *qua* doctrine also overstates the case. Attempts have been made to resolve this tension by reference to the ways in which municipal law deals with controversial issues such as euthanasia and domestic violence. Such analogies merely serve to beg the question, however, of how international law responds to the disjunction between recognized norms and enforceable law. These issues will be pursued in Chapter 6.

## 1. HUMANITARIAN INTERVENTION AS COMPATIBLE WITH ARTICLE 2(4) OF THE UN CHARTER

The Organization and its Members, in pursuit of the Purposes stated in Article 1, shall act in accordance with the following Principles: . . .
   4. All Members shall refrain in their international relations from the threat or use of force against the territorial integrity or political independence of any state, or in any other manner inconsistent with the Purposes of the United Nations.

UN Charter, Article 2(4)

Article 2(4) of the UN Charter prohibits 'the threat or use of force against the territorial integrity or political independence of any state, or in any other manner inconsistent with the Purposes of the United Nations'. The only exceptions to this prohibition in the text of the Charter are the 'inherent right of individual or collective self-defence' in Article 51, and Security Council authorized enforcement actions under Chapter VII. In order to establish that a right of humanitarian intervention is compatible with the terms of the Charter, it is necessary to show that it would not violate Article 2(4). This section considers two sets of arguments that attempt to do just this: that a genuinely humanitarian intervention would not be a use of force 'against the territorial integrity or political independence' of the target state, or that it would not be 'inconsistent with the Purposes of the United Nations'.

The Charter is a multilateral treaty and is thus subject to many of the same customary law rules of interpretation as other treaties.[9] The Vienna Convention on the Law of Treaties, now frequently applied by the ICJ as custom,[10] provides that

A treaty shall be interpreted in good faith in accordance with the ordinary meaning to be given to the terms of the treaty in their context and in the light of its object and purpose.[11]

The 'context' comprises the text, including its preamble and annexes, as well as related agreements.[12] Other matters to be taken into account include subsequent agreements, as well as 'any subsequent practice in the application of the treaty which establishes the agreement of the parties regarding its interpretation'.[13] In circumstances where such an interpretation leaves the meaning ambiguous or obscure, or leads to a result that is manifestly absurd or unreasonable, recourse may be had to the 'preparatory work of the treaty and the circumstances of its conclusion'.[14]

## 1.1. 'Against the territorial integrity or political independence of any State'

On reading Article 2(4), it is not immediately clear whether the phrase 'against the territorial integrity or political independence' is intended to qualify the words 'threat or use of force'. According to the interpretative principle of *inclusio unius est exclusio alterius*[15] it might be argued that this is the only type of force that is to be prohibited. Alternatively, when read as modifying

---

[9] Cf Vienna Convention on the Law of Treaties 1969, art 5: 'The present Convention applies to any treaty which is the constituent instrument of an international organization . . . without prejudice to any relevant rules of the organization.'

[10] See, eg, *Maritime Delimitation and Territorial Questions Case* [1995] ICJ Rep 6, 18 para 33, citing the *Territorial Dispute* (*Libyan Arab Jamahiriya/Chad*) *Case* [1994] ICJ Rep 6, 21–2 para 41. The Vienna Convention does not apply directly to the UN Charter as it specifically applies only to treaties adopted after it came into force. This is, however, without prejudice to rules of customary international law: Vienna Convention on the Law of Treaties 1969, art 4.

[11] Vienna Convention on the Law of Treaties 1969, art 31(1).                    [12] Ibid art 31(2).

[13] Ibid art 31(3).                                                            [14] Ibid art 32.

[15] The inclusion of one is the exclusion of the other.

the prohibition of the *threat* or use of force, the phrase might be seen as denoting an expansive interpretation of 'force'.

Reference to the *travaux préparatoires* makes it clear, however, that there was no intention for the words to restrict the scope of the prohibition of the use of force. The phrase was not part of the Dumbarton Oaks Proposals,[16] but an Australian amendment inserting the phrase[17] was adopted at the San Francisco Conference in response to the desire of several smaller states to emphasize the protection of territorial integrity and political independence.[18] The possibility of the phrase being interpreted differently was raised by the delegates of Brazil and Norway, with the latter suggesting deletion of the words.[19] This was a minority position, however. The UK delegate opined that the wording was adequate,[20] and the US delegate defended the modified Article 2(4) in even stronger terms:

The Delegate of the United States made it clear that the intention of the authors of the original text was to state in the broadest terms an absolute all-inclusive prohibition; the phrase 'or in any other manner' was designed to insure that there should be no loopholes.[21]

The Rapporteur of Committee 1 to Commission I subsequently emphasized that 'the unilateral use of force or any other coercive measure of that kind is neither authorized nor admitted'.[22]

In the first edition of their commentary on the Charter, Leland Goodrich and Edvard Hambro observed that, although the intention behind the inclusion of the phrase was clear, it was possible to construe the language as allowing certain limited uses of force, such as a temporary intervention for

[16] The Dumbarton Oaks Proposals, Ch II, para 4, simply read: 'All members of the Organization shall refrain in their international relations from the threat or use of force in any way inconsistent with the purposes of the Organization': 3 UNCIO 3.

[17] 3 UNCIO 543 (Amendments to the Dumbarton Oaks Proposals submitted on behalf of Australia, 5 May 1945). See also 1 UNCIO 174 (Australian speech at the Second Plenary Session, 27 Apr 1945).

[18] See, eg, 6 UNCIO 304 (Summary Report of Seventh Meeting of Committee I/1, 16 May 1945) ('several delegates'); 6 UNCIO 334–5 (Summary Report of Eleventh Meeting of Committee I/1, 4 June 1945) (Australia, New Zealand, Belgium, UK, US); 3 UNCIO 578–9 (Proposals of the Delegation of the Republic of Bolivia for the Organization of a System of Peace and Security, 5 May 1945) (Bolivia). See also Leland M Goodrich and Edvard Hambro, *Charter of the United Nations: Commentary and Documents* (2nd edn; London: Stevens & Sons, 1949) 103–5; Ian Brownlie, *International Law and the Use of Force by States* (Oxford: Clarendon Press, 1963) 267–8.

[19] 6 UNCIO 334–5 (Summary Report of Eleventh Meeting of Committee I/1, 4 June 1945) (Norway): '[I]t should be made clear in the Report to the Commission that this paragraph 4 did not contemplate any use of force, outside of action by the Organization, going beyond individual or collective self-defense. He was himself in favour of omitting the specific phrase relating to "territorial integrity and political independence" since this was, on the one hand, a permanent obligation under international law and, on the other hand, could be said to be covered by the phrase "sovereign equality" as suggested in the commentary by the Rapporteur.'

[20] 6 UNCIO 335.     [21] Ibid.

[22] 6 UNCIO 400 (Report of Rapporteur of Committee 1 to Commission I, 9 June 1945).

'protective purposes'. Whether the words would serve their original purpose would depend on member states, and particularly the permanent members of the Security Council, 'loyally respect[ing] the spirit and intent of the words in question'.[23] As it turned out, the issue came swiftly before the ICJ. In the *Corfu Channel* case, the United Kingdom argued that a minesweeping operation 'threatened neither the territorial integrity nor the political independence of Albania. Albania suffered thereby neither territorial loss nor [loss to] any part of its political independence.'[24] Though the argument was not specifically addressed in the judgment, the Court's finding that the operation violated Albanian sovereignty impliedly rejects it.[25]

By the third edition of Goodrich and Hambro, the question had all but disappeared.[26] In Hersch Lauterpacht's 1952 edition of *Oppenheim*, the phrase was taken to indicate the breadth of the provision: 'Territorial integrity, especially where coupled with "political independence", is synonymous with territorial inviolability.'[27] Similarly, Ian Brownlie writes that it was included to give more specific guarantees to small states, rather than to have a restrictive effect.[28] This is now the dominant view.[29]

Nevertheless, the restrictive interpretation continues to enjoy occasional currency.[30] Anthony D'Amato is one of the strongest contemporary advo-

---

[23] Leland M Goodrich and Edvard Hambro, *Charter of the United Nations: Commentary and Documents* (1st edn; Boston: World Peace Foundation, 1946) 68–9. The passage was reproduced in the second edition: Goodrich and Hambro, above n 18, 104–5.

[24] [1948] ICJ Pleadings, *Corfu Channel Case*, vol 3, 296.          [25] See below nn 53–9.

[26] See Leland M Goodrich, Edvard Hambro, and Anne Patricia Simons, *Charter of the United Nations: Commentary and Documents* (3rd edn; New York: Columbia University Press, 1969) 51–2.

[27] Lassa Francis Lawrence Oppenheim, *International Law* (Hersch Lauterpacht (ed); 7th edn; London: Longmans, 1952) vol 2, 154.

[28] Brownlie, above n 18, 267–8.

[29] In addition to the writers already cited, see Djura Nincic, *The Problem of Sovereignty in the Charter and in the Practice of the United Nations* (The Hague: Martinus Nijhoff, 1970) 72–3; D W Greig, *International Law* (2nd edn; London: Butterworths, 1976) 871; Eduardo Jiménez de Aréchaga, 'International Law in the Part Third of a Century' (1978) 159 *Recueil des cours de l'académie de droit international* 1, 89–92; Josef Mrazek, 'Prohibition on the Use and Threat of Force: Self-Defence and Self-Help in International Law' (1989) 27 *Canadian Yearbook of International Law* 81, 86–7; Albrecht Randelzhofer, 'Article 2(4)', in Bruno Simma (ed), *The Charter of the United Nations: A Commentary* (Oxford: Oxford University Press, 1994) 106, 117–18; Rudolf Bernhardt, *Encyclopedia of Public International Law* (Amsterdam: Elsevier, 1995) vol 2, 927; Michael Akehurst, *A Modern Introduction to International Law* (Peter Malanczuk (ed); 7th edn; London: Routledge, 1997) 309–11.

[30] See, eg, Derek W Bowett, *Self-Defence in International Law* (Manchester: Manchester University Press, 1958) 152 (discussing self-defence); Julius Stone, *Aggression and World Order* (London: Stevens, 1958) 43 (noting that a restrictive interpretation is 'far from impossible'); G Dahm, 'Das Verbot der Gewaltanwendung nach Art 2(4) der UNO-Charta und die Selbsthilfe gegenüber Völkerrechtsverletzungen, die keinen bewaffneten Angriff enthalten' (1962) 11 *Jahrbuch für Internationales Recht* 48–9 (cited in Randelzhofer, above n 29, 118); Richard B Lillich, 'Forcible Self-Help by States to Protect Human Rights' (1967) 53 *Iowa Law Review* 325, 336; W Michael Reisman and Myres S McDougal, 'Humanitarian Intervention to Protect the Ibos', in Richard B Lillich (ed), *Humanitarian Intervention and the United Nations* (Charlottesville: University Press of Virginia, 1973) 167, 177.

cates of a restrictive reading of Article 2(4) that would permit limited interventions.[31] In a historical review of the of the terms 'territorial integrity' and 'political independence' (notably focusing on periods in which war itself was not prohibited), he concludes that by 1945 there was, at least, some uncertainty as to whether these terms encompassed all transborder acts of armed force.[32] On the strength of this analysis, and after examining the *travaux préparatoires* of Article 2(4), he presents the curious argument that the delegates simply did not understand the words they were using. Despite the clear intention of the states parties—including the US delegate, who emphasized that there were 'no loopholes' in the provision[33]—D'Amato abandons this interpretation of Article 2(4) by asserting that 'history since 1945 has proved to be richer than the imaginations of the delegates to the San Francisco conference'.[34] Fernando Tesón, in a doctoral thesis on humanitarian intervention supervised by D'Amato, draws upon this work to argue that if the drafters had wanted to prohibit all transboundary force, they would have done so.[35] Tesón then argues by tautology that 'genuine humanitarian intervention does not result in territorial conquest or political subjugation'.[36] Two years later D'Amato demonstrated the implications of such a doctrine, when he asserted that the US invasion of Panama in 1989 complied with Article 2(4) because 'the United States did not intend to, and has not, colonialized [sic], annexed or incorporated Panama'.[37] (In the second edition of his work, Tesón notably avoided citing Panama as an instance of humanitarian intervention.[38])

As Oscar Schachter observed in 1984, the idea that a war waged in a good cause would violate neither the territory integrity nor political independence of the target state demands an Orwellian construction of those terms.[39] Such an interpretation runs contrary to numerous statements by the General Assembly and the ICJ concerning the meaning of non-intervention,[40] and is

[31] Anthony D'Amato, *International Law: Process and Prospect* (Dobbs Ferry, NY: Transnational, 1987) 57–73.
[32] Ibid 59–69.      [33] 6 UNCIO 335. See above n 21.      [34] D'Amato, above n 31, 73.
[35] See now Fernando R Tesón, *Humanitarian Intervention: An Inquiry into Law and Morality* (2nd edn; Dobbs Ferry, NY: Transnational Publishers, 1997) 150.
[36] Ibid 151.
[37] Anthony D'Amato, 'The Invasion of Panama was a Lawful Response to Tyranny' (1990) 84 *AJIL* 516, 520.
[38] Indeed, the invasion is mentioned only once (without approval or disapproval), in a footnote: Tesón, above n 35, 173 n 143.
[39] Oscar Schachter, 'The Legality of Pro-Democratic Invasion' (1984) 78 *AJIL* 645, 649. See also Bernhardt, above n 29, vol 2, 927.
[40] See, eg, Declaration on Friendly Relations, GA Res 2625(xxv) (1970) (unanimous): 'No State or group of States has the right to intervene, directly or indirectly, *for any reason whatever*, in the internal or external affairs of any other State'; 'Every State has an inalienable right to choose its political, economic, social and cultural systems, *without interference in any form by another State*' (emphasis added). Cf GA Res 45/150 (1990) (adopted 128-8-9): 'the efforts of the international community to enhance the effectiveness of the principle of periodic and genuine elections should not call into question each State's sovereign right freely to choose and develop

inconsistent with the practice of the Security Council, which has on numerous occasions condemned and declared illegal the unauthorized use of force notwithstanding its temporary nature.[41]

## 1.2. '. . . or in any other manner inconsistent with the Purposes of the United Nations'

A second element of Article 2(4) that has provided the basis for arguments that humanitarian intervention may be lawful under the Charter concerns the phrase 'or in any other manner inconsistent with the Purposes of the United Nations'. In 1983, at the time of the US intervention in Grenada, the US Permanent Representative to the United Nations, Jeane Kirkpatrick, argued that this language provided 'ample justification for the use of force in pursuit of other values also inscribed in the Charter—freedom, democracy, peace'.[42]

As a matter of construction it seems clear that the provision does not limit the prohibition of the use of force to instances where its application is inconsistent with the Organization's purposes. On the contrary, the use of the words 'or in any *other*' suggests an inclusive meaning: that the use of force against the territorial integrity or political independence of a state is inconsistent with the purposes of the United Nations. The better reading, then, is that any threat or use of force that is not directed against the territorial integrity or political independence of a state but is inconsistent with Article 1 of the Charter is *also* illegal.[43]

Tesón uses this phrase as one of his arguments (each presented, implicitly, in the alternative) to justify a right of humanitarian intervention. Asserting that the promotion of human rights is as important a purpose in the Charter as the control of international conflict, he concludes that to argue that humanitarian intervention is prohibited by Article 2(4) is a 'distortion'.[44] It is highly questionable that the drafters regarded human rights as of equal importance to peace,[45] but in any case the text of the Charter simply does not support Tesón's conclusion. The first listed purpose is 'to maintain international peace and security', which is to be attained by prevention and

its political, social, economic and cultural systems, *whether or not they conform to the preferences of other States*' (emphasis added). On the ICJ, see below nn 55–9.

[41] SC Res 332 (1973) (Israeli invasion of Lebanon); SC Res 455 (1979) (declaring temporary Rhodesian incursion into Zambia a violation of Zambia's territorial integrity); SC Res 545 (1983) (South Africa in Angola). See also the statements during debates on the Indian intervention in East Pakistan, discussed in Sect 2.3.4.

[42] (1983) 83(2081) *Dept of State Bull* 74. On the Grenada intervention, see Ch 3, Sect 2.1.

[43] Manfred Lachs, 'The Development and General Trends of International Law in Our Time' (1980) 169 *Recueil des cours de l'académie de droit international* 9, 161–2. See also above n 21.

[44] Tesón, above n 35, 151.

[45] See, eg, Mary Ellen O'Connell, 'Regulating the Use of Force in the 21st Century: The Continuing Importance of State Autonomy' (1997) 36 *Columbia JTL* 473.

removal of threats to the peace, the suppression of breaches of the peace, and peaceful settlement of disputes.[46] The third purpose is:

To achieve *international co-operation* in solving international problems of an economic, social, cultural, or humanitarian character, and in *promoting and encouraging* respect for human rights and for fundamental freedoms for all.[47]

To interpret this as in any way justifying a right of unilateral humanitarian intervention would stretch even the Orwellian school of interpretation.

A related argument is that action taken in support of Security Council resolutions may be an acceptable use of force. Though the argument was not presented in these terms, this is one possible inference from statements made justifying operations in the no-fly zones in Iraq (1991– ) and against the FRY in relation to the situation in Kosovo in 1999. These incidents will be considered in Chapter 5.

## 2. HUMANITARIAN INTERVENTION AS CUSTOMARY INTERNATIONAL LAW

A more common argument in support of a right of humanitarian intervention is that it exists in parallel with the UN Charter. In *Nicaragua*, the ICJ observed that the Charter does not cover the whole area of the regulation of the use of force in international relations.[48] Notably, Article 51 refers to the '*inherent* right of self-defence'.[49] Most arguments in favour of a customary right of humanitarian intervention proceed on the basis that it is a legitimate form of self-help. Writing in 1967, Richard Lillich argued that, in the absence of effective action by the United Nations, unilateral intervention by states was permissible in cases involving gross deprivations of basic human rights.[50] This was followed shortly after by 'Humanitarian Intervention to Protect the Ibos' by Michael Reisman and Myres McDougal, urging UN action in Nigeria, or, in its absence, unilateral action by one or more states.[51]

This section will consider two arguments in favour of an independent customary law right of humanitarian intervention: as a form of self-help that survived the adoption of the Charter, and as an emerging norm of customary international law that has modified existing Charter obligations. This provides the doctrinal background for the examination of state practice that follows.

---

[46] UN Charter, art 1(1).  [47] Ibid art 1(3) (emphasis added).
[48] *Nicaragua (Merits)* [1986] ICJ Rep 14 para 176.
[49] UN Charter, art 51 (emphasis added).
[50] Lillich, 'Forcible Self-Help', above n 30, 344–51. See also Richard B Lillich, 'Intervention to Protect Human Rights' (1969) 15 *McGill LJ* 205, 206–7.
[51] Reisman and McDougal, above n 30.

## 2.1.  Self-help and the UN Charter

The creation of an international legal order in which recourse to force was prohibited soon raised the question of what was to happen if the mechanisms for conflict resolution failed to operate.[52] The ICJ was confronted with such an issue in its very first case. In October 1946 two British warships were damaged by mines in Albanian territorial waters in the North Corfu Channel.[53] Three weeks later, the United Kingdom launched Operation Retail, a minesweeping operation that was carried out against the clearly expressed wishes of the Albanian government.[54] This operation was the subject of a counterclaim against the United Kingdom, alleging that it was an unlawful intervention in Albanian sovereignty.

The United Kingdom argued that it had acted to secure the *corpora delicti* as quickly as possible, in order to support its action for state responsibility. This justification took two forms. First, the United Kingdom claimed that this was a 'new and special application of the theory of intervention', enabling an aggrieved state to secure evidence in the territory of another state in order to submit it to an international tribunal. The Court did not accept this argument:

> The Court can only regard the alleged right of intervention as a policy of force, such as has, in the past, given rise to the most serious abuses and such as cannot, *whatever be the present defects in international organization*, find a place in international law. Intervention is perhaps still less admissible in the particular form it would take here, for, from the nature of things, it would be reserved to the most powerful States, and might easily lead to perverting the administration of international justice itself.[55]

This was regarded as an 'emphatic rejection' of the right of intervention,[56] though Brownlie argued in 1963 that the statement was ambiguous. In particular, it was unclear whether the 'right' referred to was that alleged by the United Kingdom,[57] or a general right of intervention.[58] This ambiguity appears to have been resolved in *Nicaragua*, where the Court cited the case in support of a general principle of non-intervention.[59]

The United Kingdom's second line of argument was to characterize Operation Retail as an instance of self-protection or self-help. The Court did

[52]  See generally Brownlie, above n 18, 281–316.

[53]  Part of this channel was in Albanian territorial waters, but the Court later held that it belonged to the class of international highways through which innocent passage cannot be prohibited by a coastal state in time of peace: *Corfu Channel Case* [1949] ICJ Rep 4, 29.

[54]  Ibid 33.                                        [55]  Ibid 35 (emphasis added).

[56]  See, eg, Hersch Lauterpacht, *The Development of International Law by the International Court* (London: Stevens, 1958) 90, 317.

[57]  That is, to secure evidence in the territory of another state for submission to an international tribunal: *Corfu Channel Case* [1949] ICJ Rep 4, 34.

[58]  Brownlie, above n 18, 288–9.

[59]  *Nicaragua (Merits)* [1986] ICJ Rep 14, 106–7 para 202.

not accept this submission either. Noting that respect for territorial sovereignty is an essential foundation of international relations, the Court held that, although the complete failure of Albania to fulfil its obligations constituted extenuating circumstances, it was bound to declare that the actions of the British Navy violated Albanian sovereignty. Significantly, however, the Court further held that such a declaration was in itself appropriate satisfaction for that violation.[60]

Nevertheless, there have been occasional attempts to justify a right of humanitarian intervention on the uncertain basis of a right to self-help. For present purposes, concern is limited to attempts to bring such an action within the language of the UN Charter. The two most prominent examples of such arguments have been presented by Reisman and Tesón.

### 2.1.1. Self-help as world order: Reisman

Reisman presented an extreme form of this type of argument in a 1984 editorial comment in the *American Journal of International Law*, calling for a radical re-interpretation of Article 2(4) that would allow one state unilaterally to depose a despotic government in another.[61] Noting that the absence of an effective international security system required the preservation of a right to self-defence, he used simple premises and forceful rhetoric to argue that the failure of the United Nations to achieve peace and order not only legitimates but *requires* individual states to resort to self-help.[62] The question, he asserted, is no longer whether but *when* self-help is lawful, which means that the overthrow of despotic governments may be a legitimate goal of states seeking to enhance order and further human rights in an essentially anarchic world.[63] His rhetorical blurring of the line between self-defence and non-defensive uses of force serves only to beg the question of the legitimacy of such action, however, as Schachter pointed out in his response to Reisman's piece.[64]

Reisman proposed to avoid the legal problems attendant to his doctrine of self-help by re-interpreting Article 2(4) as imposing a two-stage test for legitimacy in the use of force: First, will a particular use of force enhance world order? And, if so, will it enhance 'the ongoing right of peoples to determine their own political destinies'?[65] Such a test recalls D'Amato's position on the US invasion of Panama.[66] Reisman argues that the failure to do more than

---

[60] *Corfu Channel Case* [1949] ICJ Rep 4, 35. See further Brownlie, above n 18, 283–9.

[61] W Michael Reisman, 'Coercion and Self-Determination: Construing Charter Art 2(4)' (1984) 78 *AJIL* 642. See also the discussion of the Reagan Doctrine in Ch 3.

[62] Cf Myres S McDougal, 'Authority to Use Force on the High Seas' (1980) 61 *International Law Studies* 551, 559.

[63] Reisman, above n 61, 643.

[64] See Schachter, above n 39, 646. See also Bowett, above n 30, 11.

[65] Reisman, above n 61, 643.                    [66] See above n 37.

condemn violations of Article 2(4) means that they are 'to all intents and purposes validated'.[67] This argument, however, conflates the problem of the enforcement of international law and the utility of a normative system in any form, as became more clear in Reisman's 1990 editorial comment in the same *Journal*:

> Because rights without remedies are not rights at all, prohibiting the unilateral vindication of clear violations of rights when multilateral possibilities do not obtain is virtually to terminate those rights.[68]

It is not clear whether this was intended as a legal argument. Certainly, it bears no relation to the text of Article 2(4) and establishes no limits on which rights may be 'vindicated' or by whom. As for its strength as a political argument, while there may be reasons to support vigilante justice in some lawless situations, this is a far cry from conceding that sheriff's badges should be handed out to any right-minded person with a gun.

### 2.1.2. *Fundamental change of circumstances: Tesón*

Tesón, in a third argument for a positive right of humanitarian intervention,[69] presents an argument similar to that of Reisman: that the provisions of Article 2(4) must be linked to the collective security arrangements in the UN Charter. The failure of those security arrangements, he argues, amounts to a fundamental change of circumstances. Under the Vienna Convention on the Law of Treaties, the modern doctrine of *rebus sic stantibus* provides for a limited right to suspend, terminate, or withdraw from a treaty where the relevant circumstances constituted 'an essential basis of the consent of the parties' and the effect of the change is 'radically to transform the extent of obligations still to be performed under the treaty'.[70]

The International Law Commission's Commentary to the Vienna Convention notes the reluctance of many jurists to admit the existence of such a right, and the strong caveats that are commonly entered as to the need to confine the doctrine within narrow limits: 'The principle of *rebus sic stantibus* has not infrequently been invoked in State practice either *eo nomine* or in the form of a reference to a general principle claimed to justify the termination or modification of treaty obligations by reason of changed circumstances.'[71] Such concerns appear particularly applicable to a state unilaterally asserting an exception to the prohibition of the use of force in Article 2(4). An illustration of this principle may be the approach taken by the ICJ in the *Gabcíkovo-*

---

[67] Reisman, above n 61, 643.
[68] W Michael Reisman, 'Sovereignty and Human Rights in Contemporary International Law' (1990) 84 *AJIL* 866, 875.
[69] See also above nn 35–8 and n 44.
[70] Vienna Convention on the Law of Treaties 1969, art 62(1). See Tesón, above n 35, 157–62.
[71] [1966] 2 *YILC* 257.

*Nagymaros* case, where the Court rejected Hungary's submission that 'profound changes of a political nature' constituted a fundamental change of circumstances for the purposes of Article 62 of the Vienna Convention.[72]

In any case, it is inconceivable that an 'essential basis' of the consent of the member states of the United Nations was an expectation that domestic affairs would be subject to intervention by the United Nations or any other body. This is clear from the domestic jurisdiction provision in Article 2(7), as well as from the limited obligations undertaken by states in 1945 with respect to human rights. It is, moreover, ironic that such an argument should be advanced at precisely the time when it was thought that the United Nations might assume a more significant role in international relations. In the second edition of his work, Tesón observes in a footnote that the argument has become 'somewhat moot', but goes on to state that:

> The new question is: given that the Security Council is sometimes willing to intervene to protect human rights, do individual states still retain the right to intervene unilaterally? I am inclined to answer in the affirmative, at least until the Security Council can fully discharge its responsibilities in the alleviation of human suffering.[73]

This amounts to an abandonment of the *rebus sic stantibus* argument in favour of a more general customary international law right of intervention.

## 2.2. A new norm of customary international law?

None of the preceding arguments that a right of humanitarian intervention survived the passage of the Charter (if, indeed, a coherent doctrine existed before the enactment of the Charter[74]) is persuasive. It remains to be considered whether such a right might have arisen *after* the Charter was adopted. Such a modification of the Charter obligation in Article 2(4) could potentially occur either as a result of subsequent practice of the parties or by the emergence of a new norm of customary international law.[75]

### 2.2.1. Modification of treaties by custom

The modification of treaty rules by custom is a contested area of international law.[76] In its 1966 Draft Articles on the Law of Treaties, the ILC included a

---

[72] See *Gabcikovo-Nagymaros Case* [1997] ICJ Rep 7, 61–2 para 104.
[73] Tesón, above n 35, 158 n 81.      [74] See Ch 1.
[75] See Nancy Kontou, *The Termination and Revision of Treaties in the Light of New Customary International Law* (Oxford: Clarendon Press, 1994) 125.
[76] See generally Gennady Danilenko, *Law-Making in the International Community* (Dordrecht: Martinus Nijhoff, 1993) 162–72; Kontou, above n 75; Michael Byers, *Custom, Power and the Power of Rules: International Relations and Customary International Law* (Cambridge: Cambridge University Press, 1999) 166–80.

provision that '[a] treaty may be modified by subsequent practice in the application of the treaty establishing the agreement of the parties to modify its provisions'.[77] This clause did not receive the necessary support to be included in the Vienna Convention on the Law of Treaties, however.[78] Instead, the Vienna Convention allows for the interpretation of treaties in light of 'any subsequent practice in the application of the treaty which establishes the agreements of the parties regarding its *interpretation*'.[79] In its commentary, the ILC noted that although the line between interpretation and amendment through subsequent practice may be blurred, legally the processes are distinct.[80] This position has not been affected by the 1986 Vienna Convention on the Law of Treaties Between States and International Organizations or Between International Organizations.[81] The issue of treaty modification is therefore itself governed by customary international law.[82]

In the commentary to its 1966 Draft Articles, the ILC refers to two cases in which international tribunals have recognized such a process of modification in customary international law.[83] In the *Temple* case, the ICJ held that the practice of the parties with respect to a boundary line was irreconcilable with the ordinary meaning of the terms of the treaty; the effect of that practice was to amend the treaty.[84] Similarly, in an arbitration between France and the United States regarding the interpretation of an air-transport services agreement, the Arbitration Tribunal held that the relevant treaty had been modified 'by virtue of an agreement that implicitly came into force'.[85]

Numerous examples of multilateral treaties being modified by subsequent practice may be found in the Law of the Sea. The concepts of the 12-mile territorial sea and the 200-mile exclusive economic zone both arose as a form of custom, significantly modifying provisions of the 1958 Geneva Convention on the High Seas,[86] and the 1958 Geneva Convention on the Territorial Sea and the Contiguous Zone.[87] Article 5(5) of the 1958 Geneva Convention on the Continental Shelf required states parties that abandoned an oil platform on the continental shelf to remove it entirely;[88] subsequent practice established that abandoned platforms may be left in place provided that appropri-

---

[77] [1966] 2 *YILC* 236.                          [78] See Danilenko, above n 76, 165–6.

[79] Vienna Convention on the Law of Treaties 1969, art 31(3)(b) (emphasis added).

[80] [1966] 2 *YILC* 236.                          [81] UN Doc A/Conf.129/15 (1986).

[82] The preamble of the Vienna Convention on the Law of Treaties affirms that 'the rules of customary international law will continue to govern questions not regulated by the provisions of the present Convention'.

[83] [1964] 2 *YILC* 198; [1966] 2 *YILC* 236.         [84] *Temple Case* [1962] ICJ Rep 6, 33–4.

[85] *Air Transport Services Agreement Arbitration* (1963), reprinted in 38 ILR 182, 253.

[86] (1958) 450 UNTS 82.

[87] (1958) 516 UNTS 205. See Danilenko, above n 76, 168–9; Kontou, above n 75, 37–71; Byers, above n 76, 173–4.

[88] (1958) 499 UNTS 311, art 5(5).

ate safety measures are taken.[89] (Which practice is now reflected in the 1982 UN Convention on the Law of the Sea.[90])

Turning to the UN Charter, there is at least one instance in which its provisions appear to have been affected by subsequent practice. Article 27(3) provides that decisions of the Security Council on non-procedural matters 'shall be made by an affirmative vote of nine members *including the concurring votes of the permanent members*'.[91] On 29 April 1946 the USSR abstained from a vote on the Spanish question, specifically insisting that this did not constitute a precedent.[92] The resolution was nevertheless considered adopted and such abstentions became an increasingly common feature of Security Council procedure.[93] Cautious doubts as to the legality of this procedure were expressed in the early years of the United Nations,[94] but the issue was only confronted directly in the *Namibia* advisory opinion 25 years later.[95] In that case, South Africa argued that the Security Council resolution requesting the advisory opinion of the Court was invalid due to the abstention of two permanent members from the vote. The Court rejected this submission. It held that there was 'abundant evidence' that members of the Council had consistently and uniformly interpreted the practice of voluntary abstention as not constituting a bar to the adoption of resolutions. Moreover, this procedure had continued unchanged after the 1965 amendment to Article 27 and had been 'generally accepted by Members of the United Nations and evidences a general practice of that Organization'.[96]

It is unclear whether this 'general practice' amounted to an authoritative interpretation of the Charter,[97] or to a modification of its provisions by subsequent practice or by the emergence of a new rule of customary international law.[98] The representative of the UN Secretary-General had submitted that the 'constant practice' of allowing voluntary abstentions was 'customary law',[99] but the judgment itself is ambiguous, referring to both

---

[89] See Danilenko, above n 76, 168; Byers, above n 76, 173–4.

[90] See 1982 UN Convention on the Law of the Sea, UN Doc A/Conf.62/122 (1982), 21 ILM 1261, art 60(3).

[91] UN Charter, art 27(3) (emphasis added).     [92] 1 SCOR (39th mtg) (1946) 243.

[93] See Sydney D Bailey and Sam Daws, *The Procedure of the Security Council* (3rd edn; Oxford: Clarendon Press, 1998) 250–9.

[94] See Leo Gross, 'Voting in the Security Council: Abstention from Voting and Absence from Meetings' (1951) 60 *Yale LJ* 209.

[95] *Namibia* [1971] ICJ Rep 16.     [96] Ibid 22 para 22.

[97] See, eg, Kontou, above n 75, 124; Bruna Simma, 'Article 27', in Simma, above n 29, 430, 447–52; Ian Brownlie, *Principles of Public International Law* (5th edn; Oxford: Clarendon Press, 1998) 695.

[98] See, eg, *Certain Expenses Case* [1962] ICJ Rep 151, 291 (Bustamante J, dissenting) (referring to it as an 'unwritten amendment'); Leo Gross, 'Voting in the Security Council: Abstention in the Post-1965 Amendment Phase and its Impact on Article 25 of the Charter' (1968) 62 *AJIL* 315, especially 327–30; G I Tunkin, *Theory of International Law* (London: George Allen & Unwin, 1974) 339–40.

[99] [1970] ICJ Pleadings, *Namibia*, vol 2, 39–40.

'interpret[ation]' and 'practice'.[100] It is not necessary to resolve this debate here. It is sufficient to note, for present purposes, that it *may* be possible to amend the Charter in such a way, though the threshold of requisite practice would be high.[101]

### 2.2.2. *Norms of* jus cogens *and treaty modification*

The Vienna Convention as adopted does preserve one method by which a treaty may be voided by the development of customary international law. Article 64 provides that if a new peremptory norm of general international law emerges, any existing treaty that is in conflict with that norm becomes void and terminates.[102] This must be read in conjunction with Article 53, which provides that a treaty is void if, at the time of its conclusion, it conflicts with a peremptory norm.[103] Article 53 also explains that, for the purposes of the Vienna Convention, a peremptory norm is

a norm accepted and recognized by the international community of States as a whole as a norm from which no derogation is permitted and which can be modified only by a subsequent norm of general international law having the same character.[104]

These provisions are of interest for two reasons. First, the emergence of a norm of *jus cogens* does not modify but *voids* a treaty. Such a provision could not sensibly apply to the UN Charter. Secondly, and more importantly, the Vienna Convention makes it clear that one norm of *jus cogens* can only be modified by another such norm. As there is now considerable support for the view that the prohibition of the use of force is such a norm,[105] this would raise the threshold for evidence of a countervailing norm still higher.

### 2.2.3. *The* Nicaragua *case*

In fact, the possible emergence of a customary law right of intervention was canvassed by the ICJ in *Nicaragua*. The Court was not considering Article 2(4)

---

[100]  *Namibia* [1971] ICJ Rep 16, 22 para 22.
[101]  See the discussion in Simma, above n 97, 449–52 and sources there cited.
[102]  Vienna Convention on the Law of Treaties 1969, art 64.       [103]  Ibid art 53.
[104]  Ibid.
[105]  The ICJ has noted that the prohibition of the use of force 'is frequently referred to in statements by State representatives as being not only a principle of customary international law but also a fundamental or cardinal principle of such law. The International Law Commission, in the course of its work on the codification of the law of treaties, expressed the view that "the law of the Charter concerning the prohibition of the use of force in itself constitutes a conspicuous example of a rule in international law having the character of *jus cogens*".' *Nicaragua (Merits)* [1986] ICJ Rep 14, 100 para 190, citing Report of the International Law Commission, 18th Session [1966] 2 *YILC* 172, 247. See also *Nicaragua (Merits)* [1986] ICJ Rep 14, 153 (Separate Opinion of President Singh), 199 (Separate Opinion of Sette-Camara J); American Law Institute, *Restatement (Third) of the Foreign Relations Law of the United States* (1987) § 102, Comment *k*, vol 1, 28. *Contra* G A Christenson, 'The World Court and *Jus Cogens*' (1987) 81 *AJIL* 93, 101.

of the Charter but the comparable obligations in customary international law.[106] When evaluating the acts of intervention that formed the basis of Nicaragua's claim against the United States, the Court found that it first had to consider whether there was evidence of a general right for states to intervene in support of an internal opposition in another state, where that opposition 'appeared particularly worthy by reason of the political and moral values with which it was identified'.[107] After referring to the *North Sea Continental Shelf* cases on the formation of customary international law,[108] the Court noted that it had no jurisdiction to rule on the legality of the conduct of states not parties to the dispute. It went on to discuss the evidence that it could consider:

*nor has it authority to ascribe to States legal views which they do not themselves advance.* The significance for the Court of cases of State conduct prima facie inconsistent with the principle of non-intervention lies in the nature of the ground offered as justification. Reliance by a State on a novel right or an unprecedented exception to the principle might, if shared in principle by other States, tend towards modification of customary international law.[109]

There was no evidence of such reliance. On the contrary, where the United States had elaborated its grounds for intervening, these were for reasons connected with the domestic politics of the target state, its ideology, its level of armaments, or its foreign policy. These were not assertions of rules of existing international law, but statements of policy.[110] In the case at bench, the United States had offered some legal justifications, but these were solely by reference to the 'classic' rules involved: collective self-defence against an armed attack.[111]

In a passage considering the alleged humanitarian justifications for the US intervention, the Court observed that there could be

no doubt that the provision of strictly humanitarian aid to persons or forces in another country, whatever their political affiliations or objectives, cannot be regarded as unlawful intervention, or in any other way contrary to international law.[112]

Nevertheless, the Court could not contemplate the creation of 'a new rule opening up a right of intervention by one State against another on the ground that the latter has opted for some particular ideology or political system'.[113]

In terms of the specific allegation that Nicaragua had violated human rights (made in a finding of the US Congress), the Court stated that where human rights are protected by international conventions, that protection

---

[106] *Nicaragua (Merits)* [1986] ICJ Rep 14, 98–101 paras 185–90.
[107] Ibid 108 para 206.
[108] *North Sea Continental Shelf Cases* [1969] ICJ Rep 3, 44 para 77.
[109] *Nicaragua (Merits)* [1986] ICJ Rep 14, 109 para 207 (emphasis added).
[110] Ibid 109 para 207.     [111] Ibid 109 para 208.
[112] Ibid 114 para 242.     [113] Ibid 133 para 263. See also Ch 3, Sect 2.3.

takes the form provided for in those conventions.[114] And, while the United States was entitled to form its own opinion of Nicaragua's respect for human rights,

the use of force could not be the appropriate method to monitor or ensure such respect. With regard to the steps actually taken, the protection of human rights, a strictly humanitarian objective, cannot be compatible with the mining of ports, the destruction of oil installations, or . . . the training, arming and equipping of the *contras*. The Court concludes that the argument derived from the preservation of human rights in Nicaragua cannot afford a legal justification for the conduct of the United States, and cannot in any event be reconciled with the legal strategy of the respondent State, which is based on the right of collective self-defence.[115]

The ICJ's position is clearly inconsistent with a customary international law right of humanitarian intervention.[116] Nevertheless, some commentators have attempted to interpret it narrowly.[117] According to one such view, the judgment can be confined to its statements on the *disproportionate* use of force. Read in conjunction with the Court's earlier statements concerning the provision of humanitarian *aid*,[118] the judgment can (at best) be said to be not incompatible with a narrow right of humanitarian intervention. Such an analysis is merely directed at importing common-law principles to narrow the *ratio* of the case, however, and in no way provides support for the contrary position.[119]

### 2.2.4. *Criteria for the formation of new rules of customary international law*

In *Nicaragua*, the ICJ reaffirmed the criteria for the formation of new rules of customary international law outlined in the *North Sea Continental Shelf* cases. Thus the acts concerned must 'amount to a settled practice' and be accompanied by the *opinio juris sive necessitatis*:

Either the States taking such action or other States in a position to react to it, must have behaved so that their conduct is 'evidence of a belief that this practice is rendered obligatory by the existence of a rule of law requiring it.'[120]

Although a detailed consideration of the formation of rules of customary international law is not within the scope of the present work, one issue must be considered before turning to look at the practice of states. Some writers

---

[114] *Nicaragua (Merits)* [1986] ICJ Rep 14, 134 para 267.    [115] Ibid 134–5 para 268.

[116] See, eg, Nigel S Rodley, 'Human Rights and Humanitarian Intervention: The Case Law of the World Court' (1989) 38 *ICLQ* 321, 332.

[117] See Sean D Murphy, *Humanitarian Intervention: The United Nations in an Evolving World Order* (Philadelphia: University of Pennsylvania Press, 1996) 129–30; Tesón, above n 35, 270.

[118] See above n 112.

[119] Tesón, above n 35, 305 ('distinguish[ing]' the Grenada case from the situation in *Nicaragua*).

[120] *Nicaragua (Merits)* [1986] ICJ Rep 14, 109 para 207.

such as D'Amato and Wolfke have taken the position that only acts and not statements constitute state practice for the purposes of customary international law.[121] In so far as it concerns the change of customary rules, this position would seem to require violations of customary international law. With respect to the law governing the use of force, it accords great weight to acts of intervention and no weight at all to protests, resolutions and declarations condemning them.[122] Brownlie has aptly referred to this theory as '"Rambo" superpositivism';[123] as Michael Akehurst observes, it is hardly a jurisprudence to be recommended to anyone who wishes to strengthen the rule of law in international relations.[124] It leaves little room for diplomacy and peaceful persuasion and, perhaps most importantly, marginalizes less-powerful states within the international legal system. It is a view that has repeatedly been contradicted by the ICJ[125] and by a majority of scholars.[126]

### 2.3. State practice and *opinio juris*

It is necessary, then, to review the various incidents commonly marshalled as examples of humanitarian intervention. Such a historical survey has been undertaken by many authors, with results that depend upon the choice of incidents, the credibility attributed to official reasons for a given action, and the weight attached to the response of the international community. The end of the Cold War and the increased activity of the UN Security Council radically changed the nature of such interventions. For these reasons, interventions after 1990 will be considered in Chapters 4 and 5. That being said, divers examples in the period 1945–89 appear in the literature. The factual circumstances of most have been discussed at length elsewhere;[127] the focus here will be on the value each has as evidence of state practice and *opinio juris* in the emergence of a norm of customary international law. As virtually all the

[121] See, eg, Anthony D'Amato, *The Concept of Custom in International Law* (Ithaca: Cornell University Press, 1971) 88; D'Amato, above n 31; Karol Wolfke, *Custom in Present International Law* (2nd edn; Dordrecht: Martinus Nijhoff, 1993) 42.

[122] See, eg, Anthony D'Amato, *International Law: Process and Prospect* (rev edn; Irvington, NY: Transnational, 1995) 123–4, arguing that the Security Council resolution condemning the US intervention in Grenada, blocked only by a US veto, was 'purely verbal': 'There could be boycotts. There are many things that you can do to harass US citizens abroad, I suppose. There are many ways you can hurt the United States. But nobody did that. The only thing any state did was engage in verbal condemnation.'

[123] Panel Discussion, 'Comparative Approaches to the Theory of International Law' (1986) 80 *ASIL Proc* 152, 156 (Brownlie).

[124] Michael Akehurst, 'Custom as a Source of International Law' (1974) 47 *British YBIL* 1, 8.

[125] See, eg, *Asylum Case* [1950] ICJ Rep 265, 277; *Rights of Nationals of the USA in Morocco Case* [1952] ICJ Rep 176, 200.

[126] See Byers, above n 76, 134–6 and citations therein.

[127] See, eg, Murphy, above n 117, 83–281.

*Just War or Just Peace?*

situations discussed were resolved in a non-judicial manner, the methodology adopted here is consistent with Reisman's 'incidents' technique.[128]

As a preliminary matter, it is possible to dispense quickly with six incidents in which humanitarian concerns were marginal, if they operated at all. This applies to the intervention by Egypt and other states into Palestine/Israel (1948),[129] the Soviet invasions of Hungary (1956)[130] and Czechoslovakia (1968),[131] the early stages of the United States' involvement in Vietnam (1964–75),[132] South

---

[128] W Michael Reisman, 'International Incidents: Introduction to a New Genre in the Study of International Law' (1984) 10 *Yale JIL* 1. An 'incident' is (1) an overt conflict between two or more actors in the international system; (2) perceived as such by other key actors; (3) resolved in some non-judicial fashion; (4) such that the attitudes of 'functional elites' as to whether the resolution was acceptable behaviour may be assessed: ibid 12.

[129] The day after Israel proclaimed its independence on 14 May 1948, five states—Egypt, Syria, the Lebanon, Transjordan, and Iraq—commenced military action against the new Jewish state, which responded in kind. At the time, Egypt declared that it had decided to intervene 'to put an end to massacres and establish respect for the laws of universal morality and the principles recognized by the United Nations', adding: 'This intervention is not directed against the Jews of Palestine but against Zionist terrorist bands, and has no other object than the re-establishment of order, peace, and security in that country': *Keesing's* (1948) 9275–6. These sentiments were repeated by Egypt in the Security Council, but were not given much credence: 3 SCOR (292nd mtg) (1948) 3. A US proposal that the Council should determine that a breach of the peace existed failed to muster sufficient votes, but on 1 Apr 1948 the Council adopted a resolution calling on both groups to cease fire immediately: SC Res 43 (1948) para 3.

[130] On 4 Nov 1956, the USSR invaded Hungary, deposing the popular socialist regime of Imre Nagy. The Soviet delegate to the UN Security Council stated that the action was 'helping to put an end to the counter-revolutionary intervention and riots', thus saving the Hungarian people from 'anti-popular elements' and their efforts 'to stab the Hungarian people in the back': S/PV.754 (1956) para 53 (USSR); S/PV.746 (1956) para 165 (USSR). These statements were rejected and the invasion was condemned by most of the international community. A Security Council resolution calling on the USSR to desist from its intervention was vetoed by the USSR, but a similar resolution was adopted by the General Assembly: GA Res 1004(ES-II) (1956). In addition to the dubious humanitarian justifications for the invasion, the primary justification asserted by the USSR was that of invitation. Given the Nagy government's explicit repudiation of this claim, this argument was also tenuous: see Quincy Wright, 'Intervention, 1956' (1957) 51 *AJIL* 257, 274–6.

[131] As in the case of Hungary, Warsaw Pact forces allegedly came to the aid of the people of Czechoslovakia in 1968 because 'enemies [had] . . . shaken the foundations of law and order . . . [f]louting socialist laws . . . in preparation for seizing power': S/PV.1445 (1968) para 201 (USSR). The humanitarian (and other) motives asserted in the Security Council were rejected and a draft resolution condemning the intervention failed only by reason of a Soviet veto. Initially, the USSR claimed that Czech party and government leaders had requested its assistance in repulsing reactionary forces: [1965] *UN YB* 298, 300–2. It later articulated a broader justification that the socialist community had a *duty* to intervene whenever socialism came under attack in a fraternal socialist state. This became known as the Brezhnev Doctrine: see 'Text of Pravda Article Justifying Invasion of Czechoslovakia', *NYT*, 27 Sept 1968, reprinted in 7 ILM 1323.

[132] One of the early justifications offered by the United States for its intervention in Vietnam was that it acted to 'protect [South Vietnam's] people from the acts of terror perpetrated by Communist insurgents from the north' and help them create the conditions in which they could exercise their right of self-determination: President Johnson, New Year's Message to the Chairman of the Military Revolutionary Council in South Viet-Nam, 1 Jan 1964, in [1963–4] 1 *Johnson Papers* 106; President Johnson, Address at Johns Hopkins University, 7 Apr 1965, in [1965] 1 *Johnson Papers* 395. This was never formulated as a legal argument, however, and the United States came to justify its intervention on the basis of collective self-defence against the alleged aggression by the North against an independent South Vietnam: see, eg, Letter from US Representative to the UN, Adlai E Stevenson, to the President of the Security Council, Roger

Africa's intervention in the Angolan civil war (1975–6),[133] and Indonesia's invasion and annexation of East Timor (1975).[134] A further eleven incidents warrant some consideration.

### 2.3.1. *Belgian intervention in the Congo (Léopoldville), 1960*

Shortly after achieving independence from Belgium in 1960, the Republic of the Congo (Léopoldville) was the object of the UN's largest military assistance operation directed by the Organization itself.[135] This operation overlapped with a Belgian intervention, perhaps explaining why this incident is often overlooked in analyses of state practice. An alternative explanation is that it is not a very convincing instance of humanitarian intervention.[136]

Belgian Congo became independent on 1 July 1960 under the name of the Republic of the Congo.[137] On the night of 5/6 July, mutinies broke out in what came to be seen as a general movement against Belgian and other European residents.[138] On 7 July Europeans began fleeing into neighbouring French Congo; the following day Belgium announced that troop reinforcements were being sent to the Congo. Belgian troops went into action against Congolese soldiers on 10 July, notably in the Katanga province, the independence of which was soon proclaimed by Prime Minister Moise Tshombe. With the situation becoming more confused by the hour, on 11 July the Congolese Government appealed for assistance from the United Nations. The Security Council passed a resolution on 13 July authorizing the

Seydouz, dated 27 Feb 1965, in (1965) 59 *AJIL* 632; US Dept of State, Office of the Legal Adviser, 'The Legality of United States Participation in the Defense of Viet-Nam', 4 Mar 1966, in (1966) 60 *AJIL* 565.

[133] In Aug 1975, several thousand South African troops intervened from Namibia in the ongoing civil war in Angola. When the matter finally came before the Security Council in Mar 1976, South Africa retreated from its initial assertion that Portugal had invited South African troops into Angola and claimed instead that it had been motivated essentially by protective and humanitarian considerations: it had initially sought to protect a hydroelectric project in the Calueque area and had later been forced to undertake the purely humanitarian task of caring for the thousands of displaced persons fleeing the violence of the Soviet- and Cuban-backed MPLA: [1976] *UNYB* 175. These reasons were also rejected, and the Security Council adopted a resolution condemning South Africa's 'aggression': SC Res 387 (1976) para 1, adopted 9-0-5 (France, Italy, Japan, UK, US abstaining; China not participating). See generally Fred Bridgland, *The War for Africa: Twelve Months That Transformed a Continent* (Rivonia: Ashanti, 1990).

[134] When it invaded East Timor on 7 Dec 1975, Indonesia claimed that it was acting, *inter alia*, to protect Timorese people who favoured integration with Indonesia: [1975] *UNYB* 858. These statements were not taken seriously, and the invasion was deplored by the General Assembly and the Security Council: GA Res 3485(xxx) (1975); SC Res 384 (1975).

[135] See Ch 4, Sect 1.1.1. See generally G Abi-Saab, *The United Nations Operation in the Congo 1960–1964* (Oxford: Oxford University Press, 1978); Rosalyn Higgins, *United Nations Peacekeeping 1946–1967: Documents and Commentary: Vol 3, Africa* (London: Oxford University Press, 1980).

[136] The incident is not mentioned in the extensive discussions of state practice in Murphy, above n 117, or Tesón, above n 35.

[137] See *Keesing's* (1960) 17594.     [138] Ibid 17639.

Secretary-General to provide Congo with military assistance and calling upon Belgium to withdraw its troops.[139]

In the Security Council debate and elsewhere, Belgium asserted that it had 'decided to intervene, with the sole purpose of ensuring the safety of European and other members of the population and of protecting human lives in general'.[140] This received some support,[141] but the 13 July resolution linked the provision of UN military assistance to Belgium's withdrawal.[142] A Soviet amendment that would have 'condemned' Belgium for 'armed aggression' against the Congo was supported only by the USSR and Poland.[143] During the debate, France made a reference to 'intervention on humanitarian grounds' that has been remarked upon occasionally in the literature.[144] This was in response to accusations that the Belgian action constituted aggression, however, and the statement in full makes it clear that the primary justifications given credence are a request from the Congolese Government and protection of *Belgian* nationals.[145]

Over the course of the following months it became clear that Belgium's assistance was being channelled into support for the Katangese rebels. It is often argued that this was more out of concern for future access to the copper-rich province than any genuinely 'humanitarian' concern.[146] The Belgian troops withdrew by September 1960.[147]

### 2.3.2. *Belgian and US intervention in the Congo, 1964 (the Stanleyville Operation)*

Congo was again the target of intervening foreign forces in 1964. When the UN troops of ONUC withdrew on 30 June 1964, the post-independence war

---

[139] *Keesing's* (1960) 17639; [1960] *UNYB* 52–3; SC Res 143 (1960) adopted 8-0-3 (China, France, UK).

[140] S/PV.873 (1960) para 183 (Belgium).

[141] See, eg, S/PV.873 (1960) para 130 (UK), para 144 (France).

[142] SC Res 143 (1960).                [143] [1960] *UNYB* 53.

[144] See, eg, Natalino Ronzitti, *Rescuing Nationals Abroad Through Military Coercion and Intervention on Grounds of Humanity* (Dordrecht: Martinus Nijhoff, 1985) 31; Francis Kofi Abiew, *The Evolution of the Doctrine and Practice of Humanitarian Intervention* (The Hague: Kluwer Law International, 1999) 106.

[145] S/PV.873 (1960) para 144 (France) (emphasis added): 'In this connexion, I wish to repeat that the accusation of aggression . . . appears to us unfounded. The presence of Belgian troops in the Congo is in fact in conformity with the Belgian–Congolese treaty of friendship of 29 June 1960. Their mission of protecting lives and property is the direct result of the failure of the Congolese authorities and is in accord with a recognized principle of international law, namely, intervention on humanitarian grounds [*l'intervention d'humanité*]. It has been established that in several places *such intervention has been expressly requested by Congolese authorities . . .*'

[146] See, eg, Wil D Verwey, 'Humanitarian Intervention', in Cassese, above n 123, 57, 61; Anthony C Arend and Robert J Beck, *International Law and the Use of Force: Beyond the UN Charter Paradigm* (London: Routledge, 1993) 116.

[147] See Donald W McNemar, 'The Postindependence War in the Congo', in Richard A Falk (ed), *The International Law of Civil War* (Baltimore: Johns Hopkins Press, 1971) 244, 253.

had concluded and the country was united. Tshombe, previously leader of the secessionist regime in Katanga, became Prime Minister of the Republic on 9 July 1964.[148] Nevertheless, one-third of the Congo remained under the control of a new rebel group, the Conseil National de Liberation (CNL) based in Stanleyville, in the north-eastern province of Orientale.[149] In September 1964 the rebel forces took over a thousand foreign residents hostage at Stanleyville and Paulis, threatening to kill them unless the central government agreed to certain concessions. After peaceful attempts to free the hostages failed, Belgian forces entered the Congo once again on 24 November 1964, this time with the aid of US aeroplanes and using British military facilities.[150] The troops were withdrawn three days later after a successful rescue mission in which all but about sixty to eighty of the European hostages were released. The main objective of the intervening states was the protection of their own nationals, but many other hostages—primarily foreign and white—were also freed.[151]

Described in 1970 as 'one of the clearest modern instances of true humanitarian intervention and [one that] should be viewed as lawful in character',[152] the Stanleyville Operation's star has faded somewhat with time.[153] From the outset, it was not clear that this was an instance of humanitarian intervention *stricto sensu*—arguably, it was more properly characterized as intervention with the consent of the legitimate government. In addition, the colonial context of the operation renders it a problematic example of the more general doctrine.

In a note to the President of the Security Council sent on the same day as the operation commenced, Belgium stated that

In exercising its responsibility for the protection of its nationals abroad, [the Belgian Government] found itself forced to take this action in accordance with the rules of international law codified by the Geneva Conventions. What is involved is a legal, moral and humanitarian operation which conforms to the highest aims of the United Nations: the defence and protection of fundamental human rights in respect for national sovereignty.[154]

In its own letter, the United States stated that the 'sole purpose of this humanitarian mission was to liberate hostages whose lives were in danger'.[155]

The issue came onto the agenda of the Security Council in December 1964, in response to both a twenty-two-power complaint against the Belgian–US intervention and a complaint by the Congo itself against various other states

---

[148] *Keesing's* (1964) 20217.  [149] McNemar, above n 147, 256.
[150] [1964] *UN YB* 95.  [151] *Keesing's* (1965) 20561.
[152] Gerhard von Glahn, *Law Among Nations* (2nd edn; London: Macmillan, 1970) 168. See also Lillich, 'Forcible Self-Help', above n 30, 340; Howard L Weisberg, 'The Congo Crisis 1964: A Case Study in Humanitarian Intervention' (1972) 12 *Virginia JIL* 261. Cf Gerhard von Glahn, *Law Among Nations* (6th edn; London: Macmillan, 1992) 166.
[153] Tesón does not even include it as an example.
[154] S/6063 (1964).  [155] S/6062 (1964).

said to be assisting the rebel movement. After debate occupying seventeen meetings, in which most states supporting the intervention emphasized both the humanitarian motives and the authorization of the legitimate government, the Council adopted resolution 199 (1964). The first operative paragraph requested 'all States to refrain or desist from intervening in the domestic affairs of the Congo'.[156] After the vote, the US delegate declared that this paragraph obligated those states providing assistance to the rebels to end such intervention. The delegates for the USSR and Czechoslovakia countered that the paragraph was directed at those who had been condemned by the Council in their armed intervention—Belgium and the United States.[157]

As indicated earlier, the Stanleyville Operation is no longer regarded as a paradigm of humanitarian intervention. First, the intervention may be more properly characterized as intervention with consent of the legitimate government.[158] In a letter to the American Ambassador, the Congolese Prime Minister stated that in view of 'the deteriorating situation in Stanleyville and the failure of all humanitarian efforts', his government had

accordingly decided to authorize the Belgian Government to send an adequate rescue force to carry out the humanitarian task of evacuating the civilians held as hostages by the rebels, and to authorize the American Government to furnish necessary transport for this humanitarian mission.[159]

In letters of the same date, Belgium and the United States informed the Security Council of the operation, noting that it took place with the consent of the Congolese Government.[160] This was reiterated by the US State Department in its announcement of the landing on 24 November 1964.[161]

It has, however, been argued that even if the first phase of the operation was undertaken with the consent of the government, this does not apply to the second phase. After completion of the rescue mission in Stanleyville on 26 November, the paratroop force became aware that a further several hundred hostages, including US citizens, were being held near the town of Paulis. The force flew to the area and completed its evacuation mission on the same day.[162] It is at least arguable that this second mission is distinct from the first, there being no explicit consent on the part of the Government to this further action. Moreover, when the US Ambassador to the Security Council reported the second operation, he did not refer to the Congolese Government's consent, emphasizing instead that

---

[156] SC Res 199 (1964) para 1, adopted 10-0-1 (France).
[157] [1964] *UNYB* 100.                          [158] Brownlie, above n 123, 500.
[159] Letter of Prime Minister Tshombe of the Democratic Republic of the Congo to the American Ambassador in Léopoldville dated 21 Nov 1964, in Marjorie M Whiteman, *Digest of International Law* (Washington, DC: US Govt Printing Office, 1963–73) vol 12, 213.
[160] S/6055 (1964); S/6056 (1964).               [161] Whiteman, above n 159, vol 12, 211–13.
[162] Ibid 213.

the sole aim of my Government has been and is to assist in the rescue of innocent civilians endangered by rebel activity in violation of international law. It is clear from the statements of the rescued persons themselves that further delay would have meant an even greater number of wanton and tragic killings. Time, for the lives of those people, was calculable only in minutes.[163]

Nevertheless, when charged with military intervention in a communiqué issued in Nairobi by the Ad Hoc Commission on the Congo of the Organization of African Unity (OAU), the United States defended its action as being 'for purely humanitarian reasons *and with the authorization of the Government of the Congo*'.[164]

A second reason for the diminished fortunes of the Stanleyville Operation as an instance of humanitarian intervention is that it was tarred with the brush of colonialism.[165] One of the consequences of the intervention was the shoring up of the Tshombe regime's position vis-à-vis the rebels and it was suggested by many African and Eastern bloc states that the humanitarian issues were, once again, a pretext for intervention to protect political and economic interests.[166] In addition, some representatives in the Security Council pointed to the apparent racial prejudice underlying the motives of the rescuers.[167]

As Thomas Franck and Nigel Rodley observe, there are many parallels between the Stanleyville Operation and the Great Power interventions inside the Ottoman Empire of the nineteenth century.[168] Like the Ottoman Empire, the Congo was too weak to assert control over the whole of its territory, let alone protect white hostages in a dissident province; like the Ottoman Sultans, Prime Minister Tshombe was prepared to accept foreign forces in his country to help him re-establish his authority.[169] As an example of humanitarian intervention it is, at best, questionable.

### 2.3.3. US intervention in the Dominican Republic, 1965

On 24 April 1965 military officers and members of the Dominican Revolutionary Party staged a *coup d'état* against the Cabral Government of the Dominican Republic. The situation deteriorated to the point where the newly installed military junta informed the US Embassy that it was not able to guarantee the safety of US nationals.[170] On 28 April 1965 US Marines

---

[163] S/6068 (1964).     [164] (1964) 51(1329) *Dept of State Bull* 848 (emphasis added).

[165] See Thomas M Franck and Nigel S Rodley, 'After Bangladesh: The Law of Humanitarian Intervention by Military Force' (1973) 67 *AJIL* 275, 288; Verwey, above n 146, 62.

[166] [1964] *UNYB* 96–8. The action significantly assisted the Léopoldville Government's white mercenary-led troops in their efforts to suppress the dissident regime of Christophe Gbenye: Franck and Rodley, above n 165, 288.

[167] See, eg, S/PV.1170 (1964) paras 84–99 (Congo (Brazzaville)).

[168] See Ch 1, Sect 3.3.     [169] Franck and Rodley, above n 165, 289.

[170] [1965] *UNYB* 140.

landed in Santo Domingo with the objective of protecting US and other nationals.[171] The intervention is commonly considered in two parts: the first comprising the evacuation of foreign nationals (primarily, though not exclusively, US citizens); the second extending to the control exercised over the Republic by the occupying troops. Few argue that the second phase was legal.[172] The first phase is often considered to be an intervention in protection of nationals abroad.[173] The incident is further complicated by the fact that by mid-May the initial US intervention had been absorbed into an operation under the authority of the Organization of American States (OAS).[174]

In statements made a few days after the first five hundred marines had landed, US President Johnson declared that the intervention was intended to 'preserve law and order'[175] and help 'the people of that country . . . freely choose the path of political democracy, social justice, and economic progress'.[176] The credibility of these humanitarian objectives diminished when it did not withdraw its troops after the foreigners were evacuated, but reinforced them, giving the United States de facto control of the Republic. Moreover, President Johnson soon suggested a different motive for the intervention: 'The American nations cannot, must not, and will not permit the establishment of another Communist government in the Western Hemisphere.' He went on to suggest that the political context of the situation was not merely an important consideration but was determinative of the US intervention:

[R]evolution in any country is a matter for that country to deal with. It becomes a matter calling for hemispheric action only—repeat—*only* when the object is the establishment of a Communistic dictatorship.[177]

There was some small support for the action in Security Council debate, which rejected a Soviet-sponsored resolution condemning the intervention (supported only by the USSR itself) and calling upon the United States to withdraw (supported by the USSR and Jordan).[178] Statements in support of the US action focused on its claim to be acting in protection of its nationals abroad.[179] The Council eventually adopted a compromise resolution calling

---

[171] *Keesing's* (1965) 20813.
[172] See, eg, Lillich, *Humanitarian Intervention*, above n 30, 81 (Friedmann); Abiew, above n 144, 112. Indeed, Ved Nanda quotes one of the marines as complaining to the last American to depart: 'You can't go, you can't leave, because if you leave, then our very presence here is going to be illegal!' Lillich, *Humanitarian Intervention*, above n 30, 77 (Nanda).
[173] See, eg, Charles G Fenwick, 'The Dominican Republic: Intervention or Collective Self-Defense' (1966) 60 *AJIL* 64; Bernhardt, above n 29, vol 2, 928.
[174] See below nn 181–4.
[175] President Johnson, Statement of 30 Apr 1965, in [1965] 1 *Johnson Papers* 465.
[176] President Johnson, Statement of 1 May 1965, in ibid 467.
[177] President Johnson, Statement of 2 May 1965, in ibid 472–3 (emphasis in original).
[178] *Keesing's* (1965) 20856.                    [179] [1965] *UNYB* 142–3 (UK, France).

for a ceasefire and inviting the Secretary-General to send a representative to the Dominican Republic to report back to the Council.[180]

Parallel manoeuvres were underway at the OAS. At the time of the initial intervention, the United States called for an emergency meeting of the OAS Council and announced the military action the day after it commenced. The OAS then became involved in diplomatic moves to broker a ceasefire.[181] On 3 May 1965 the US representative to the OAS proposed the creation of an Inter-American Peace Force, which was approved in principle by an OAS resolution adopted on 6 May.[182] Following the resolution, the United States withdrew some of its forces (then numbering 22,000) and the remainder were incorporated within the multinational force under unified Brazilian command. Forces were also offered by six Latin American states; with the exception of 1,115 Brazilian troops, however, the numbers were small.[183] The OAS involvement in this incident is of interest as an embryonic peacekeeping operation by a regional organization, but in no way served to authorize the initial US intervention.[184]

### 2.3.4. Indian intervention in East Pakistan/Bangladesh, 1971

The Indian intervention in East Pakistan in 1971 is commonly held up as one of the more promising examples of alleged humanitarian intervention. Tesón calls it 'an almost perfect example';[185] Fonteyne observes that it 'probably constitutes the clearest case of forceful individual humanitarian intervention in this century';[186] Bowett includes it as the only possible illustration of the practice in the period 1945–86.[187] It therefore merits consideration in some detail.

[180] SC Res 203 (1965). SC Res 205 (1965) requested that the suspension of hostilities be transformed into a permanent ceasefire. See [1965] *UNYB* 146–7.

[181] (1965) 1(1) *OAS Chronicle* 1–4.

[182] Under the 6 May 1965 resolution, the OAS Tenth Meeting of Consultation of Ministers of Foreign Affairs requested that willing and capable governments make forces available to the OAS to form an Inter-American Peace Force that would operate under the authority of the Tenth Meeting of Consultation: (1965) 1(1) *OAS Chronicle* 23–4.

[183] By 3 July 1965, the IAPF had the following composition: Brazil—1,115; Costa Rica—20; El Salvador—3; Honduras—250; Nicaragua—164; Paraguay—183; United States—10,900: (1965) 1(1) *OAS Chronicle* 5.

[184] See generally Inter-American Institute of International Legal Studies, *The Inter-American System: Its Development and Strengthening* (Dobbs Ferry, NY: Oceana, 1966) 205; A J Thomas and Ann Van Wynen Thomas, *The Dominican Republic Crisis 1965* (Background Paper and Proceedings of the Ninth Hammarskjöld Forum; Dobbs Ferry: Oceana, 1967) 107–10; Abraham F Lowenthal, *The Dominican Intervention* (Cambridge, MA: Harvard University Press, 1972).

[185] Tesón, above n 35, 207.

[186] Jean-Pierre L Fonteyne, 'The Customary International Law Doctrine of Humanitarian Intervention: Its Current Validity Under the UN Charter' (1974) 4 *California Western ILJ* 203, 204.

[187] Derek W Bowett, 'The Use of Force for the Protection of Nationals Abroad', in Cassese, above n 123, 39, 50.

By the late 1960s the political and economic domination of East Pakistan by its Western counterpart had given much support to campaigns for autonomy.[188] In the November–December 1970 general election, the pro-autonomy Awami League won 167 of the 169 seats in East Pakistan. President Yahya Khan interpreted this as a threat to the territorial integrity of Pakistan and postponed the National Assembly indefinitely.[189] Calls for autonomy in East Pakistan soon became calls for independence; on 23 March 1971 the leader of the Awami League, Sheik Mujibur Rahman, issued a 'Declaration of Emancipation'.[190] Two days later, on 25 March 1971, the Pakistan Army moved into Dacca.

The brutality of the military operation that followed is well-documented.[191] The International Commission of Jurists summarized events as follows:

The principle [*sic*] features of this ruthless oppression were the indiscriminate killing of civilians, including women and children and the poorest and weakest members of the community; the attempt to exterminate or drive out of the country a large part of the Hindu population; the arrest, torture and killing of Awami League activists, students, professional and business men and other potential leaders among the Bengalis; the raping of women; the destruction of villages and towns; and the looting of property. All this was done on a scale which is difficult to comprehend.[192]

It is estimated that in the following nine months, at least one million people were killed and up to ten million fled to India.[193]

Relations between Pakistan and India deteriorated as a result of the crisis. By late November both India and Pakistan had called up reservists and were poised for all-out conflict; border skirmishes became more frequent and widespread. On 3 December, for reasons that are unclear,[194] the Pakistani airforce launched a 'pre-emptive air strike' against Indian airfields. Indian Prime Minister Indira Gandhi declared that Pakistan had 'launched a full-scale war against us' and the Indian Army invaded Pakistan on both the eastern and western fronts. Three days later India recognized Bangladesh as an independent state. The war lasted 12 days, formally ending with Pakistan's surrender on 16 December.[195]

---

[188] The partition of India in 1947 left Pakistan composed of two entities, divided by ethnicity, culture, language, and a distance of over 1,000 miles: see International Commission of Jurists, *The Events in East Pakistan 1971* (1972) 7–10; Ved P Nanda, 'Self-Determination in International Law: The Tragic Tale of Two Cities—Islamabad (West Pakistan) and Dacca (East Pakistan)' (1972) 66 *AJIL* 321.

[189] See International Commission of Jurists, above n 188, 12–14.          [190] Ibid 15–21.

[191] See also Nanda, above n 188, 322–3; Subrata Roy Chowdhury, *The Genesis of Bangladesh: A Study in International Legal Norms and Permissive Conscience* (London: Asia Publishing House, 1972) 76–148 and sources there cited.

[192] International Commission of Jurists, above n 188, 26–7.          [193] Ibid 24–6, 97.

[194] See, eg, D K Palit, *The Lightning Campaign: The Indo-Pakistan War, 1971* (New Delhi: Lancer, 1998) 77.

[195] International Commission of Jurists, above n 188, 43–4.

Even in this supposedly clearest of examples, there were mixed motives on the part of the intervening state. In the Security Council, speaking on 4 December 1971, India's representative stated that

we have on this particular occasion absolutely nothing but the purest of motives and the purest of intentions: to rescue the people of East Bengal from what they are suffering.[196]

India's Prime Minister had previously appealed to foreign governments and the United Nations to do something about the situation in which 'the general and systematic nature of inhuman treatment inflicted on the Bangladesh population was evidence of a crime against humanity'.[197] In the absence of any alternatives, India had been forced to act.

Such apparently genuine humanitarian concerns were commingled, however, with others.[198] In particular, India raised the issue of Pakistani aggression to justify an argument of self-defence.[199] It also made reference to giving support to the new government of Bangladesh (problematic due to the fact that it was recognized only after the invasion).[200] This mix of motives is apparent in the following passage from the statement of the representative of India to the Security Council:

So long as we have any light of civilized behaviour left in us, we shall protect [the people of East Pakistan]. We shall not fight their battle. Nobody can fight other people's battles. There are great Powers seated around this table that have found out to their own cost that people cannot fight other people's battles, that they have to fight them themselves. But whatever help we can give, whether in the form of aid to the refugees, in the form of medicines, or in any other form, we shall continue to give it. Secondly, we shall continue to save our own national security and sovereignty . . .[201]

In discussions within the United Nations, such humanitarian concerns appear to have tempered criticism of India but were not accepted as a justification for its intervention.[202]

---

[196] S/PV.1606 (1971) para 186.

[197] Quoted in Wil D Verwey, 'Humanitarian Intervention Under International Law' (1985) 32 *Netherlands ILR* 357, 401.

[198] See, eg, Michael Walzer, *Just and Unjust Wars: A Moral Argument with Historical Illustrations* (2nd edn; New York: Basic Books, 1992) 105 (concluding that 'circumstances sometimes make saints of us all').

[199] See, eg, S/PV.1606 (1971) para 155 (Pakistan's break up is 'creating aggression against us'); ibid para 163 ('They have been accustomed to killing their own people. I do not believe that is their privilege. I think this is a barbaric act. But after having killed their own people they now turn their guns on us. . . . We decided to silence their guns, to save our civilians').

[200] The question of self-determination will not be considered here: see Nanda, above n 188; Chowdhury, above n 191; James Crawford, 'The Criteria for Statehood in International Law' (1976) 48 *British YBIL* 93, 170–2.     [201] S/PV.1606 (1971) para 175 (India).

[202] See, eg, S/PV.1611 (1971) para 19 (US): 'The fact that the use of force in East Pakistan in March can be characterized as a tragic mistake does not, however, justify the actions of India in intervening militarily and placing in jeopardy the territorial integrity and political independence of its neighbour Pakistan.'

The Security Council only became seized of the situation on 4 December 1971, in a meeting called by nine members on 'the deteriorating situation which has led to armed clashes between India and Pakistan'.[203] A Soviet veto prevented adoption of a US-sponsored resolution calling for a ceasefire and the immediate withdrawal of armed forces.[204] Subsequent discussion proved circular, with most states calling for India's withdrawal. Unable to reach a conclusion, the Council referred the question to the General Assembly.[205]

The General Assembly considered the question at two plenary meetings held on 7 December 1971 and eventually adopted resolution 2793(xxvi) (1971). In its operative paragraphs, the General Assembly called upon India and Pakistan to conclude a ceasefire and withdraw their troops.[206] At the same time, it urged that 'every effort be made to safeguard the lives and well-being of the civilian population in the area of conflict'.[207] Although the resolution was directed at both India and Pakistan, Schachter states that 'it was clearly directed against the Indian forces in East Pakistan'.[208] Tesón disagrees with this reading,[209] emphasizing the importance of achieving a satisfactory solution *within* Pakistan in the speeches of representatives concerning the resolution.[210] Certainly, concern was expressed about the fate of the civilian population. However, the fact remains that the issue only came onto the agenda when Indian troops crossed the border and the main step taken was to call upon the two states to respect each other's territory. In fact, a second draft resolution had been proposed by the USSR, calling for a ceasefire and simultaneously calling upon Pakistan to take effective action towards a political settlement in East Pakistan, reflecting the results of the December 1970 election. The draft resolution was never put to a vote.[211]

Although India's intervention in East Pakistan is generally referred to as one of the better instances of humanitarian intervention, there are relatively few writers who actually claim that it was legal for this reason. The International Commission of Jurists did not accept India's claims of self-defence and assistance to a new government, but concluded its legal study on the events in East Pakistan by stating that India's armed intervention 'would have been justified if she had acted under the doctrine of humanitarian intervention'.[212] This highlights the essential problem with the East Pakistan incident: although India initially asserted humanitarian motives, it ultimately relied on the more traditional ground of self-defence.[213] Similarly, although the debates within the United Nations expressed concern about the humani-

---

[203] [1971] *UNYB* 146.                    [204] Ibid 147–8.                [205] SC Res 303 (1971).
[206] GA Res 2793(xxvi) (1971) para 4.      [207] Ibid para 4.
[208] Oscar Schachter, 'The Right of States to Use Armed Force' (1984) 82 *Michigan Law Review* 1620, 1629 n 19.
[209] Tesón, above n 35, 210 n 199.          [210] Ibid 209 n 194.            [211] [1971] *UNYB* 151.
[212] International Commission of Jurists, above n 188, 96.
[213] See Ronzitti, above n 144, 96, 108–9; Verwey, above n 197, 401–2; Bowett, above n 187, 50.

tarian situation, there was no suggestion that this did anything more than mitigate India's position. Even if one accepts that India's action constitutes state practice for the purposes of establishing customary international law, there is little evidence of *opinio juris*.[214]

At the same time, however, few writers (and relatively few states) were prepared simply to condemn the intervention as illegal; caveats were typically entered to the effect that the intervention may nevertheless have been *morally* justified.[215] A number of commentators stressed the distinction between legal and moral condemnation. This led to a polarization of views in the academic community: some writers asserted that it was possible to regard an act as illegal and yet moral; others rejected this as inherently contradictory—if such an act is *moral*, the law should recognize it as *legal*.[216] Quite apart from the legality of the incident itself, then, East Pakistan highlighted a cleavage in the attitudes of international lawyers to the 'right' of humanitarian intervention. The different positions reflected distinct views on the status of the prohibition of the use of force, the manner in which international law develops, and the treatment of acts inconsistent with established legal norms. As Chapter 1 has shown, this cleavage is new neither to international law in general nor to humanitarian intervention in particular.

### 2.3.5. Israeli intervention in Uganda, 1976 (the Entebbe Operation)

The Israeli commando operation at Entebbe, Uganda, is normally classed as a case of protection of nationals abroad and distinguished from humanitarian intervention.[217] The 3 July 1976 operation was launched to free the remaining 104 of over 250 passengers and crew taken hostage by Palestinian terrorists while on a flight to Paris. Uganda's permission for the operation was not sought, apparently due to Israel's belief that Uganda was complicit in the terrorists' acts.[218] The commandos successfully freed almost all of the hostages, killing their captors, three hostages, and some Ugandan soldiers in the process.[219]

When the matter came before the Security Council, Israel specifically relied on the ground of protection of nationals abroad as a species of self-

---

[214] See, eg, Bernhardt, above n 29, vol 2, 928.

[215] See, eg, Lillich, *Humanitarian Intervention*, above n 30, 114 (Friedman).

[216] See, eg, the discussion between numerous participants in Lillich, *Humanitarian Intervention*, above n 30, 114–22.

[217] See, eg, John F Murphy, 'State Self-Help and Problems of Public International Law', in Alona E Evans and John F Murphy (eds), *Legal Aspects of International Terrorism* (Lexington, MA: Lexington, 1978) 553, 554–61; Arend, above n 146, 99; Murphy, above n 117, 15–16. But see Louis Henkin, 'The Invasion of Panama Under International Law: A Gross Violation' (1991) 29 *Columbia JTL* 293, 296–7.

[218] Letter from the Representative of Israel to the Secretary-General, S/12123–A/31/122 (1976); [1976] *UNYB* 315.

[219] *Keesing's* (1976) 27888.

defence.[220] The United States agreed that Israel's action was consistent with the 'well-established right to use limited force for the protection of one's own nationals from an imminent threat of injury or death in a situation where the State in whose territory they are located either is unwilling or unable to protect them'. This right was said to flow from the right of self-defence and was limited to 'such use of force as is necessary and appropriate to protect the threatened nationals from injury'.[221]

Other states were more ambivalent about the action and a number were sharply critical, labelling it 'aggression' and an 'excessive use of force'. A draft resolution proposed by Benin, Libya, and Tanzania condemning Israel's action was not put to a vote.[222] A draft resolution sponsored by the United Kingdom and the United States condemning hijacking failed to obtain a majority of votes.[223] Though most commentators consider the Entebbe operation to have been a justifiable (if not legal) intervention, it is at most authority for the right to protect nationals abroad.[224]

### 2.3.6. Belgian and French intervention in Zaïre, 1978

The names had changed, but in 1978 Belgium once again sent troops to evacuate foreign nationals from a rebellion in the copper-rich southern province of Shaba (formerly Katanga) in Zaïre (formerly Congo). The Congolese National Liberation Front (FLNC) entered the town of Kolwezi on 11–12 May 1978 and in ten days killed some 700 civilians, including 200 white foreigners (mainly Belgian and French nationals). On 19 May a paratroop regiment of about 800 from the French Foreign Legion entered Zaïre, shortly joined by 1,750 Belgian paratroopers, infantry, and medical staff.[225] A statement from the French President's office announced that troops had been sent 'at the request of the Zaïre Government' and with the aim of 'protecting the French and foreign residents of Kolwezi and re-establishing security there'.[226] The Belgian Prime Minister, Léo Tindemans, said that 'the French operation is quite different in character from the Belgian operation', whose purpose was to 'bring help to the European and local population'.[227]

The French troops soon gained control of Kolwezi while Belgian forces began to organize evacuations. By 21 May all those Europeans who wished to leave had been evacuated (including 1,700 Belgians, 400 French, 150 Italians, 150 British, 150 Greeks, and some other nationals). Belgium began a phased withdrawal of its paratroops the following day, but French troops

[220] S/PV.1939 (1976) paras 106–15 (Israel).
[221] S/PV.1941 (1976) para 77 (US). See also the US State Dept Internal Memorandum reprinted in (1979) 73 *AJIL* 122.
[222] S/12139 (1976); [1976] *UNYB* 319.          [223] S/12138 (1976); [1976] *UNYB* 320.
[224] See further Francis A Boyle, 'The Entebbe Hostages Crisis' (1982) 29 *Netherlands ILR* 32.
[225] *Keesing's* (1978) 29125–6.          [226] Ibid 29126.
[227] Ibid.

continued search-and-destroy operations in the surrounding bush. The foreign troops departed by mid-June.[228]

As in the previous interventions in the Congo, the 1978 intervention combined various motives of protecting (white, foreign) nationals and maintaining control over the mineral resources of this troubled region. The incident never appeared on the Security Council's agenda.

### 2.3.7. Tanzanian intervention in Uganda, 1978–9

The outcome of Tanzania's intervention in Uganda—the ouster of dictator Idi Amin—is widely supported as a desirable result. This is, of course, different from determining that the intervention was legal (and on what basis). Though it is often regarded as a victory for human rights, analyses of Tanzania's actions typically equivocate between its humanitarian motives and the more base motive of self-defence.

Years of animosity between Amin and Tanzanian President Julius Nyerere came to a head in October 1978, when Ugandan forces occupied a part of bordering Tanzania. Amin asserted that the occupation was an act of self-defence in response to Tanzania's support for Ugandan dissidents, but on 1 November he announced that all territory north of the Kagera River was 'now part of Uganda'. Nyerere denounced this as an act of war. With reference to Amin, he stated: 'We have the capacity to hit him; we have the reason to hit him; and we have the determination to hit him.' International support fell clearly behind Tanzania, and on 8 November Amin offered to withdraw his troops, provided that the OAU guaranteed that Tanzania would no longer invade Uganda or support Ugandan exiles in Tanzania. Nyerere rejected this conditional offer, and on 12 November announced that Tanzania had launched its own offensive. In the following days, Amin began to withdraw his troops unilaterally, but a broadcast from Dar es Salaam stated that Amin could not be 'let off' as the two weeks of Ugandan occupation had seen its army indulge in 'pillage, massacre, destruction and rape' and created 'a state of war' between the two countries. The Tanzanian army penetrated into Uganda, joined by organizations of Ugandans who had lived in exile and opposed Amin. Amin's regime was effectively overthrown when Uganda's capital, Kampala, fell on 10–11 April 1979. Amin fled Uganda and a new government was formed.[229]

Tanzania's military action was clearly precipitated by Uganda's armed attack on Tanzania, though it was variously characterized as defensive and punitive in character. When he announced Tanzania's recognition of the new government under President Lule, Nyerere stated:

---

[228] Ibid 29126–7; Verwey, above n 146, 65.    [229] *Keesing's* (1979) 29669–72.

Those who say [that] Tanzania created a bad precedent [by acting against Uganda] are liars. What we did was exemplary at a time when the OAU found itself unable to condemn Amin. I think we have set a good precedent inasmuch as when African nations find themselves collectively incapable of punishing a single country, then each country has to look after itself.[230]

With reference to its actions in deposing Amin, Nyerere said that the exiled Ugandans had decided to go into Uganda, which coincided with Tanzania's desire to punish Amin.[231]

The intervention appears to have been tolerated by the majority of the international community. The clearest evidence of this is the swift recognition of the new regime in Kampala.[232] A few states spoke out in favour of Tanzania, though this was largely restricted to its actions taken in self-defence.[233] Other states spoke out against the second phase of the action. The Nigerian Government warned on 9 April that interfering in another country's affairs in this way presented the danger of a chain reaction in Africa, where 'a few militarily powerful countries would be able to determine the leadership of other states'.[234] The matter was not debated in either the Security Council[235] or the General Assembly; the Secretary-General became involved only late in the day as part of efforts to mediate a ceasefire.[236]

Tesón concludes from this that 'on the whole the Tanzanian action was legitimized by the international community',[237] which 'virtually approved the Tanzanian intervention'.[238] This is an exaggeration. Most states acknowledged Tanzania's right to defend itself and were subsequently content to see Amin's regime replaced, but this is not the same as saying that they regarded the intervention as a lawful use of force.

Natalino Ronzitti notes that Nyerere argued that there were two wars being fought: one being fought in self-defence by Tanzania; one fought by Ugandan dissidents seeking to topple Amin.[239] Academic opinion on the action reflects these mixed motives. A few writers conclude that it was a legitimate instance of humanitarian intervention.[240] Others are more reticent. In addition to the problem of conflating the 'two wars' into one, some note that

---

[230] *Keesing's* (1979) 29673.              [231] Ibid.                         [232] Ibid 29838.
[233] See, eg, the statement of US Secretary of State Cyrus Vance: 'Our position is very clear; there is a clear violation of Tanzania's frontier by Uganda. We support President Nyerere's position according to which Ugandan troops must withdraw immediately': ibid 29669.
[234] Ibid 29673.
[235] By a letter dated 28 Mar 1979, Uganda requested that an urgent meeting of the Security Council be convened. On 5 Apr Uganda informed the Council President that its request had been withdrawn as a result of an appeal by the African group of states at the UN: [1979] *UNYB* 262–3.
[236] Murphy, above n 117, 106.        [237] Tesón, above n 35, 187.        [238] Ibid 191.
[239] Ronzitti, above n 144, 103–4. See also Murphy, above n 117, 107. Cf S K Chatterjee, 'Some Legal Problems of Support Role in International Law: Tanzania and Uganda' (1981) 30 *ICLQ* 755.
[240] In addition to Tesón, see U O Umozurike, 'Tanzania's Intervention in Uganda' (1982) 20 *Archiv des Völkerrecht* 301, 312–13; Reisman, above n 61, 644.

the installation of the new regime served the policy goals of Tanzania—humanitarian motives may have been operative, but were far from paramount.[241] As an example of state practice, one can say with confidence only that the action was not condemned. Once again, there is little evidence of *opinio juris* beyond an affirmation of the right of self-defence. With regard to the second aspect of the conflict, Nyerere himself emphasized that the war within Uganda was, ultimately, one that had to be fought by the Ugandans themselves.[242]

### 2.3.8. Vietnamese intervention in Kampuchea (Cambodia), 1978–9

Both the Tanzanian overthrow of Idi Amin and the Vietnamese ousting of Pol Pot were cited by Belgium in support of its participation in NATO's action in Kosovo in 1999.[243] The Vietnamese intervention is also one that is commonly regarded as having had a positive impact on the region. At the time of the intervention, however, Vietnam came under stern criticism for its actions—actions which, in any case, it justified primarily as taken in self-defence.

Following sporadic fighting along the Vietnamese–Kampuchean border throughout 1978, Vietnamese troops invaded Kampuchea on 25 December 1978. The Vietnamese forces included members of the United Front for National Salvation of Kampuchea, an insurgent group formed earlier in the month by exiled Kampucheans. The United Front had adopted an eleven-point programme, the first of which was to overthrow the 'reactionary Pol Pot–Ieng Sary clique', hold general elections, and adopt a new constitution. The Vietnamese Army captured Phnom Penh on 7 January 1979 and in the following months established control over most of the territory. Pol Pot fled into the mountains, where the Khmer Rouge continued to maintain a guerrilla resistance.[244]

In a telegram to the President of the Security Council on 31 December 1978, Democratic Kampuchea's Foreign Minister, Ieng Sary, accused Vietnam of invading Kampuchea and requested a meeting of the Security Council. A spokesperson for the US State Department said on 3 January that, although the US 'takes great exception to the human rights record' of the Kampuchean Government, 'as a matter of principle, we do not feel that a

---

[241] See, eg, Jack Donnelly, 'Human Rights, Humanitarian Intervention and American Foreign Policy: Law, Morality and Politics' (1984) 37 *Journal of International Affairs* 311, 316; Bernhardt, above n 29, vol 2, 928.

[242] See *Keesing's* (1979) 29671 (quoted in Ch 3, Sect 3). See further Tony Avirgan and Martha Honey, *War in Uganda: The Legacy of Idi Amin* (Westport, CT: Lawrence Hill, 1982).

[243] See above n 8.

[244] *Keesing's* (1979) 29613. See generally Gary Klintworth, *Vietnam's Intervention in Cambodia in International Law* (Canberra: AGPS, 1989).

unilateral intervention against that regime by a third power is justified'. The
United States therefore supported the request for a Council meeting.[245]

In the Security Council meetings of 11–15 January 1979, Vietnam's representative argued that a distinction had to be drawn between the
Kampuchean–Vietnamese border war and the revolutionary war of the
Kampuchean people. With respect to the first conflict, Vietnam asserted its
right to defend its independence, sovereignty, and territorial integrity. With
respect to the second, Vietnam recognized the new regime as the sole representatives of Kampuchea.[246] Vietnam thus refrained from asserting any right
of intervention, a position that was reflected in the statements of other representatives. Nearly all states making speeches referred to the principle of non-
interference in the internal affairs of states. France, for example, stated:

The notion that because a régime is detestable foreign intervention is justified and
forcible overthrow is legitimate is extremely dangerous. That could ultimately jeopar-
dize the very maintenance of international law and order and make the continued existence of various régimes dependent on the judgement of their neighbours.[247]

Norway admitted that it had

strong objections to the serious violations of human rights committed by the Pol Pot
Government. However, the domestic policies of that government cannot—we repeat,
cannot—justify the actions of Viet Nam over the last days and weeks.[248]

Similar statements were made by the United Kingdom[249] and Portugal,[250]
among others.[251]

China introduced a draft resolution that would have strongly condemned
Vietnam's 'aggression',[252] but withdrew it in view of a resolution introduced
by Kuwait. The second resolution would have reaffirmed that the preservation of the sovereignty, territorial integrity and political independence of
every state was a fundamental principle of the Charter and called upon all foreign forces to withdraw.[253] It received thirteen votes in favour but failed by
reason of a Soviet veto.[254] In the end, no resolution was adopted by the
Council in relation to Kampuchea (Cambodia) until 1990. This was also the

[245] *Keesing's* (1979) 29614–15.
[246] [1979] *UN YB* 274. Cf Bernhardt, above n 29, vol 2, 928.
[247] S/PV.2109 (1979) para 36 (France).                    [248] Ibid para 18 (Norway).
[249] 'Whatever is said about human rights in Kampuchea, it cannot excuse Viet Nam, whose
own human rights record is deplorable, for violating the territorial integrity of Democratic
Kampuchea': S/PV.2110 (1979) para 65 (UK).
[250] 'There are no nor can there be any socio-political reasons that would justify the invasion
of the territory of a sovereign State by the forces of another State': S/PV.2110 (1979) para 26
(Portugal).
[251] See S/PV.2109 (1979) para 10 (Kuwait), para 20 (Czechoslovakia), para 50 (Bangladesh),
para 59 (Bolivia), para 91 (Sudan); S/PV.2110 (1979) para 39 (Malaysia), paras 48–9 (Singapore,
stating that 'No other country has a right to topple the Government of Democratic Kampuchea,
however badly that Government may have treated its people'), para 58 (New Zealand).
[252] S/13022 (1979); [1979] *UN YB* 273–5.                 [253] S/13027 (1979).
[254] [1979] *UN YB* 275.

year in which the United States first recognized the legitimacy of the Vietnamese-backed regime that had been in power since 1979.[255]

In the General Assembly, the new Kampuchean regime challenged the right of the ousted regime to be represented in the Assembly. In September 1979, however, the Assembly voted to accept the credentials of Pol Pot's delegate.[256] A number of states emphasized that, despite what they considered to be the deplorable record of Democratic Kampuchea, there was no justification for accepting the credentials of a regime installed through external intervention.[257] Other states explained their position on the issue as being based on respect for the Charter and emphasized that this did not imply any support for the Pol Pot regime.[258] Later in the year, the Assembly considered the ongoing conflict within Kampuchea and the related refugee crisis. The Assembly voted not to make a decision on a draft resolution that would have supported the Kampuchean people's right to receive support in the exercise of their right of self-determination,[259] and instead adopted a resolution calling for the immediate withdrawal of all foreign forces and an end to foreign interference in the internal affairs of states in south-east Asia.[260]

As in the case of Tanzania's intervention, Vietnam's concern with Kampuchea was, at best, only partly humanitarian in origin. In terms of state practice this is not conclusive of the issue, but when one looks for *opinio juris* there is an immediate problem that neither the acting state nor any of the (few) states that supported the action articulated anything resembling a right of humanitarian intervention. Indeed, it appears clear that any assertion of such a right would have been rejected.

### 2.3.9. *French intervention in the Central African Empire/Republic, 1979*

In his extensive analysis of state practice during the Cold War, Sean Murphy concludes that France's role in deposing Jean-Bedel Bokassa in the Central African Empire is 'probably the best example of humanitarian intervention . . . that was accepted as lawful by the international community'.[261] Tesón also included the Central African case as an instance of humanitarian intervention '*par excellence*'.[262] It is mentioned by few other writers, however.[263]

---

[255] See Thomas L Friedman, 'US Shifts Cambodia Policy: Ends Recognition of Rebels; Agrees to Talk to Hanoi', *NYT*, 19 July 1990. Cf Thomas M Franck, 'Of Gnats and Camels: Is There a Double Standard at the United Nations?' (1984) 78 *AJIL* 811, 812–13.

[256] GA Res 32/2A (1979) adopted 71-35-34.

[257] [1979] *UNYB* 292 (Malaysia, New Zealand, Pakistan, Singapore, Somalia, US).

[258] Ibid 293 (Colombia, Denmark, FRG, Greece, Italy, Sri Lanka).

[259] A/34/L.7/Rev/1 and Rev.1/Add.1 (1979); motion not to take a decision adopted 62-36-38: [1979] *UNYB* 294.

[260] GA Res 34/22 (1979) adopted 91-21-29.      [261] Murphy, above n 117, 108.

[262] Tesón, above n 35, 199.

[263] Exceptions to this include Michael Akehurst, 'Humanitarian Intervention', in Hedley Bull (ed), *Intervention in World Politics* (Oxford: Clarendon Press, 1984) 95, 99; Oscar Schachter, 'Is

Certainly, Bokassa's departure from Central African politics was little mourned.[264] His fourteen years as self-styled 'emperor' were marked by atrocities, and—unique in the incidents under consideration—the French action was preceded by a judicial inquiry into his conduct. In response to Amnesty International reports that schoolchildren had been tortured and murdered following unrest in January 1979, the Sixth Franco-African conference despatched an African judicial commission to investigate.[265] Its report was made public on 16 August, confirming that the atrocities had taken place and stating that Bokassa had 'almost certainly' participated in them himself. On the night of 20/21 September 1979, while Bokassa was in Libya, his predecessor and personal adviser (and cousin), David Dacko, flew into Central Africa on a French military aircraft with 1,800 French paratroopers and concluded a bloodless *coup*.[266]

France initially suggested that its involvement had followed the *coup* and been in response to the request of the new regime,[267] though this was clearly inconsistent with Dacko's statements. Tesón (on whom Murphy relies exclusively) argues that the French Government therefore reversed its position and indicated that the intervention was based on humanitarian concerns.[268] To be sure, there is evidence that France was genuinely concerned by Bokassa's human rights record—it had cut off financial aid after publication of the report of the judicial commission[269]—but is the installation of a new and more favourable government in such a manner to be regarded as a 'humanitarian intervention'? As in the case of Tanzania's statements concerning its ouster of Amin, it appears that the action against Bokassa was more in the nature of punishment than prevention. This was particularly acute in the case of Bokassa whose retention of power had long been dependent upon French assistance.[270] Charles Rousseau also notes that Opération Barracuda had been planned from the end of July—before the judicial commission's report was released—and was the fifth French military intervention in Africa in just over two years.[271] Seen in its full colonial context, he concludes that this was hardly an action from which France should draw pride.[272]

---

There a Right to Overthrow an Illegitimate Regime?', in *Le droit international au service de la paix, de la justice du dévelopement: mélanges Michel Virally* (Paris: A Pedone, 1991) 423, 429–30; Arend, above n 146, 125–6.

[264] Only Libya, Chad, and Benin appear to have protested the action: Charles Rousseau, 'Chronique des faits internationaux' (1980) 83 *RGDIP* 351, 365.

[265] *Keesing's* (1979) 29751.

[266] Ibid 29933–4; Rousseau, above n 264, 364–5; Samuel Decalo, *Psychoses of Power: African Personal Dictatorships* (2nd edn; Gainesville, FL: Florida Academic Press, 1997) 233–5.

[267] See *Keesing's* (1979) 29934.

[268] Murphy, above n 117, 108; Tesón, above n 35, 198.

[269] *Keesing's* (1979) 29933.                          [270] Rousseau, above n 264, 365.

[271] Ibid 364–5, citing Zaïre (Apr 1977 and May 1978), Chad (May 1978), Mauritania (Autumn 1978).

[272] Ibid 365.

## 2.3.10. *US intervention in Grenada, 1983*

Though commonly included in the recitation of alleged humanitarian interventions, the United States never articulated a justification for its 1983 intervention in Grenada in these terms. In fact, in one of the more sophisticated legal explanations of the invasion, it went some way to specify the grounds on which it did *not* rely: an expanded view of self-defence, 'new interpretations' of Article 2(4), or 'a broad doctrine of "humanitarian intervention"'.[273] Most attempts to bring it under this rubric concern the allegedly pro-democratic elements of the action and it will be considered under that heading in Chapter 3.[274] For present purposes, it is sufficient to note that the Security Council failed to protest the intervention only by reason of a US veto,[275] and that the General Assembly adopted a resolution 'deeply deplor[ing]' the intervention as 'a flagrant violation of international law' by the margin of 108 to 9.[276]

## 2.3.11. *US intervention in Panama, 1989–90*

The US Operation 'Just Cause' against the Noriega regime in Panama is similar to the Grenada episode: humanitarian issues beyond the installation of a 'democratic regime' do not appear to have been at issue; a Security Council resolution was blocked by vetoes;[277] and a General Assembly resolution condemning the unilateral action was adopted by a substantial majority.[278] It will also be considered further in Chapter 3.[279]

## 2.3.12. *'Collective' humanitarian interventions, 1990–9*

There are other examples that might be considered. In particular, the 1990s saw a number of collective interventions that are sometimes viewed as being justified on the basis of the norm under consideration here. Unlike the examples above, however, the primary legal justification in those incidents was typically linked to the Security Council (however tenuously). For this reason, the following incidents will be considered in Chapters 4 and 5:

* Economic Community of West African States (ECOWAS) intervention in Liberia, 1990;[280]

---

[273] Davis R Robinson, 'Letter dated 10 February 1984, addressed to Professor Edward Gordon, Chairman of the Committee on Grenada of the American Bar Association's Section on International Law and Practice' (1984) 78 *AJIL* 661, 664. This is cheerfully dismissed by Tesón, who marshals it as evidence of precisely such a right: Tesón, above n 35, 216–17.

[274] See Ch 3, Sect 2.1.      [275] [1983] *UNYB* 211.

[276] GA Res 38/7 (1983) para 1, adopted 108-9-27.

[277] [1989] *UNYB* 175. The draft resolution was voted down 10-4-1 (Canada, France, UK, and US against; Finland abstaining).

[278] GA Res 44/240 (1989) adopted 75-20-40.      [279] See Ch 3, Sect 2.2.

[280] See Ch 4, Sect 3.1.3.

- US, UK, and French no-fly zones in Iraq, 1991– ;[281]
- ECOWAS intervention in Sierra Leone, 1997–8;[282] and
- NATO intervention in the FRY, 1999.[283]

## 2.4. Evaluation of state practice and *opinio juris*

It seems clear that writers who claim that state practice provides evidence of a customary international law right of humanitarian intervention grossly overstate their case. In addition to the six spurious incidents listed earlier,[284] the humanitarian elements of the three US interventions in the Western hemisphere—Dominican Republic (1965), Grenada (1983), and Panama (1989–90)—must be considered highly dubious. As indicated above, the United States specifically *disclaimed* any right of humanitarian intervention in relation to its action in Grenada. All three interventions in the Congo/Zaïre (1960, 1964, 1978) were, at best, interventions to protect nationals abroad; at worst they were post-colonial adventures to secure access to mineral resources in the newly independent state. Similarly, France's intervention in the Central African Republic (1979) cannot be understood without reference to its colonial history in the region.

Of the four remaining examples, the Entebbe operation (1976) can be set aside as being an example of protection of nationals abroad, explicitly relied upon as a species of self-defence. This leaves three examples of interventions that are, at least, regarded favourably in retrospect by the international community: East Pakistan (1971), Uganda (1978–9). and Kampuchea (1978–9). As indicated above, however, in none of these cases was humanitarian concerns invoked as a justification for the use of military force.

Tesón, drawing on the work of D'Amato, argues that such an analysis is flawed because it privileges what states *say* rather than what they *do*.[285] The difficulties associated with a theory of custom that values only actions have been indicated earlier.[286] Of more concern here is Tesón's willingness to disregard the statements of leaders completely:

Finding customary law is trying to provide an interpretation of a largely amorphous diplomatic material. Indeed, we read historical events in the light of a complex set of empirical and normative assumptions. That complexity is poorly conveyed by the theory that customary law is determined by the speeches of politicians. A theory of law devoid of any moral underpinnings, one whose only currency is the sanctimonious language of government officials, is hardly deserving of the name. It matters little that

[281] See Ch 5, Sect 4.1.                    [282] See Ch 4, Sect 3.3.2.
[283] See Ch 5, Sect 4.2.                     [284] See above nn 129–34.
[285] Tesón, above n 35, 192–3, citing Anthony D'Amato, 'Reply to letter of Michael Akehurst' (1986) 80 *AJIL* 148, 149.
[286] See above nn 121–6.

the Tanzanians (wrongly) thought that they were acting in self-defense or said that they were so acting. The *logic of the situation*, revealed by world reaction, tells a different story: that the observance of a minimum of human rights is a precondition of the protection afforded governments by article 2(4) of the United Nations Charter.[287]

There are a number of problems with such a conception of customary law. First, it suggests that analyses of state practice such as that undertaken here rely exclusively on the 'sanctimonious language' of government leaders. Relatedly, and more importantly, it appears to do away with the notion of *opinio juris*, leaving in its place the 'logic of the situation'. This 'logic' is to be assessed by commentators, who are assumed to be in a position to assess what the Tanzanians were *really* doing.[288] Such a position might be appropriate in the case of a widespread practice, whose character as law is uncertain. Where there is evidence of a general practice or a consensus in the literature, for example, the ICJ has shown itself willing to assume the existence of *opinio juris*.[289] This could not apply to such a controversial doctrine as humanitarian intervention, however. Tesón also conveniently dispenses with the wealth of treaty law and resolutions of international organizations that affirm a right of *non*-intervention as yet more rhetoric. Aside from the fact that such a conception of customary law is incompatible with the vast majority of writing on the subject, it would be completely unworkable as a legal system.

This view of the formation of custom is, moreover, inconsistent with D'Amato's own position, relied upon in the passage by Tesón just quoted. In response to a letter from Akehurst,[290] D'Amato's piece is a brief defence of his position that what states do is more important in the formation of custom than what they say.[291] The justifications he gives for this position are, however, unhelpful to Tesón's argument—in particular, D'Amato warns that reliance on the statements of government officials opens the door to 'self-serving formulations' that may assert that even the most blatantly illegal acts are consistent with a rule of international law.[292] To be sure, D'Amato has elsewhere warned that states may give the 'wrong' reasons for their actions that might otherwise be lawful.[293] But his theory of customary international law (at least, as originally formulated) incorporates a qualitative element of *opinio juris* that requires the articulation of an objective claim of international legality.[294]

---

[287] Tesón, above n 35, 193.

[288] 'We try to impose order on diplomatic history. Humanitarian intervention is the best explanation of the Tanzanian action; it is the one that *interprets* that piece of history in its best light': Tesón, above n 35, 191, citing Ronald Dworkin, *Law's Empire* (London: Fontana, 1986) 87–113.

[289] Brownlie, above n 97, 7. See, eg, *Gulf of Maine Case* [1984] ICJ Rep 246, 293–4 paras 91–3.

[290] Michael Akehurst, 'Letter' (1986) 80 *AJIL* 147.          [291] D'Amato, above n 285.

[292] D'Amato, above n 285, 149.

[293] See, eg, Anthony D'Amato, 'Nicaragua and International Law: The "Academic" and the "Real"' (1985) 79 *AJIL* 657, 662–4.

[294] See D'Amato, above n 121, 74–87.

There is no explanation from D'Amato or Tesón as to why this requirement is dropped in favour of a rule previously considered only in respect of the possibility of its abuse.

At the same time, Tesón makes much of what states do *not* say. The failure to criticize some of the incidents cited as humanitarian interventions may in some circumstances amount to tacit approval, but this is not evidence of *opinio juris*. Consistent waiver of illegality may indicate a change or the beginnings of a change in the law; sporadic waiver is just that. The fact that certain actions appear to have been tolerated by the international community is an insufficient basis on which to ground a right of humanitarian intervention. It does, however, challenge the bland claim that such actions are illegal.

This position is broadly consonant with that adopted by the UK Foreign and Commonwealth Office (FCO) in an internal document on intervention produced in 1984.[295] The FCO noted that the state practice to which advocates of a right of humanitarian intervention have appealed provides an uncertain basis for their claims: in particular, humanitarian ends are almost always mixed with 'other less laudable motives', and the humanitarian benefits of an intervention are commonly either not claimed or only put forward *ex post facto*.[296] The best case that could be made in support of humanitarian intervention, the FCO concluded in tortured (if accurate) prose, 'is that it cannot be said to be unambiguously illegal'.[297]

## CONCLUSION

> I would prefer to advise politicians contemplating such intervention to look to political rather than legal justifications and mitigation. Political leaders who are contemplating unilateral military intervention should not be encouraged to believe that international law is firmly on their side. It is not. At best, it is unclear. They could still take their chances on a cogent political justification being accepted as genuine by the international community.
>
> Thomas M Franck, 1972[298]

This Chapter has considered two classes of argument that a right of humanitarian intervention might have survived or emerged after the enactment of the UN Charter: that such interventions may somehow fit within the provisions of Article 2(4), or that such action may be a legitimate form of self-help. In doing so, it has sought to challenge the superficial manner in which the legality of a right of humanitarian intervention is usually examined—by commen-

---

[295] Planning Staff of the Foreign and Commonwealth Office, 'Is Intervention Ever Justified?' (internal document 1984), released as Foreign Policy Document No 148, excerpted in (1986) 57 *British YBIL* 614.
[296] Ibid 618–19.    [297] Ibid 619.
[298] Lillich, *Humanitarian Intervention*, above n 30, 64 (Franck).

tators and in the sole example of a state arguing the validity of such a right in an international tribunal.[299] Such examinations typically proceed with an assertion that Article 2(4) should not preclude all action to promote human rights, followed by an account of alleged examples supporting a customary international law right of intervention. Closer analysis shows that the doctrinal and historical basis for such a right is shaky indeed. None of the arguments that humanitarian intervention is compatible with Article 2(4) is persuasive, and the scope for modification of its provisions through custom is narrow. State practice discloses at most three 'best cases' of humanitarian intervention, but even these lack the necessary *opinio juris* that might transform the exception into the rule.

The various attempts to justify a right of intervention considered here are, for the foreseeable future, unlikely to receive the support of more than a handful of states. As such, humanitarian intervention will remain at most in a legal penumbra—sometimes given legitimacy by the Security Council, sometimes merely tolerated by states.

[299] See above n 8.

# 3

## 'You, the People'

### Unilateral intervention to promote democracy

> What difference does it make to the dead, the orphans and the homeless,
> whether the mad destruction is wrought under the name of totalitarianism
> or the holy name of liberty or democracy? I assert in all humility, but with all
> the strength at my command, that liberty and democracy become unholy
> when their hands are dyed red with innocent blood.
>
> M K Gandhi[1]

There is now a considerable literature on 'the emerging right to democratic
governance',[2] arguing in essence that the democratic entitlements spelt out in
human rights treaties are at last achieving more than hortatory status.[3] For
the greater part of the twentieth century, the relatively small number of actual
democracies and uncertainty as to the precise content of such a right precluded general endorsement of a principle of democracy.[4] Moreover, as
James Crawford argues, the manner in which classical international law con-
ceptualized sovereignty and the state was deeply *un*democratic, or at least
capable of operating in deeply undemocratic ways.[5]

In the course of the 1980s, however, democracy came to assume far greater
importance: the number of states legally committed to open, multiparty,
secret-ballot elections with universal franchise grew from about one-third in
the mid-1980s to as many as two-thirds in 1991;[6] new discourses in inter-

---

[1] M K Gandhi, *Non-Violence in Peace and War* (2 vols; Ahmedabad: Navajivan Publishing
House, 1942) vol 1, 357.

[2] The seminal articles on this concept are Thomas M Franck, 'The Emerging Right to
Democratic Governance' (1992) 86 *AJIL* 46; Gregory H Fox, 'The Right to Political
Participation in International Law' (1992) 17 *Yale JIL* 539. See now Gregory H Fox and Brad R
Roth (eds), *Democratic Governance and International Law* (Cambridge: Cambridge University
Press, 2000).

[3] See especially Universal Declaration on Human Rights, GA Res 217A(III) (1948) art 21;
International Covenant on Civil and Political Rights 1966, art 25; European Convention for the
Protection of Human Rights and Fundamental Freedoms 1950, Protocol 1, art 3; American
Convention on Human Rights 1969, art 23.

[4] James Crawford, 'Democracy and International Law' (1993) 44 *British YBIL* 113–16.

[5] Ibid 117–19.

[6] Franck, above n 2, 47, puts the number at 110 states, citing the US Department of State's
*Country Reports on Human Rights Practices* for 1990 and reports in the *New York Times*. The
annual 'Comparative Survey of Freedom' conducted by Freedom House states that of the 165
states monitored in 1991 there were 76 formal liberal democracies and 36 states 'in varying stages
of transition to a democratic system': 'The Comparative Survey of Freedom: 1991' (1991) 22(1)

national law and international relations stressing democracy as a value emerged[7] (notably the 'democratic peace' thesis[8]); and the international community showed a greater willingness to encourage or apply pressure upon a state to hold or recognize the results of elections, or take part in election-monitoring.[9] Although the 'right' to democratic governance remains, at best, inchoate, the crucial questions that will be addressed in this Chapter are *whether* and *how* any such right may be enforced.

A preliminary distinction must be made between a unilateral right of pro-democratic intervention, and situations where the Security Council makes a determination that disruption to democracy constitutes a threat to international peace and security within the meaning of Chapter VII of the UN Charter. The fact of Security Council authorized action in such circumstances provides support for the view that the right to democratic governance may be acquiring some substance, but a finding that its absence may constitute a threat to the peace does not establish a unilateral right of intervention. Such interventions will be considered in Chapter 4.[10] It is also necessary to distinguish the more general questions of intervention by invitation,[11] or in a time of civil war[12] or anarchy (sometimes referred to as 'failed states'),[13] and

---

*Freedom Review* 5, 6. In 1996 the same survey classed 117 of 191 states as democracies: 'The Comparative Survey of Freedom' (1996) 27(1) ibid 5. Democracy is defined as, at a minimum, 'a political system in which the people choose their authoritative leaders freely from among competing groups and individuals who were not chosen by the government': ibid 11.

Another study suggests that in 1995 half of states could be classed as 'liberal democracies', with one quarter being 'authoritarian' and the remainder being 'partially democratic'. This contrasts with the position in 1975, where less than a quarter of states were liberal democracies and over two-thirds authoritarian: David Potter *et al*, *Democratization* (Malden, MA: Polity Press/Open University, 1997) 9.

[7] See Crawford, above n 4, 122 n 39 and sources there cited.      [8] See Ch 4, Sect 3.3.3.

[9] See Agenda for Democratization, UN Doc A/51/761 (1996); Support by the United Nations System of the Efforts of Governments to Promote and Consolidate New or Restored Democracies, UN Doc A/50/332 and Corr.1 (1995). See also Fox, above n 2; Crawford, above n 4, 123–6; Karl J Irving, 'The United Nations and Democratic Intervention: Is "Swords Into Ballot Boxes" Enough?' (1996) 25 *Denver JILP* 41.

[10] See Ch 4, Sect 3.3.

[11] See Ian Brownlie, *International Law and the Use of Force by States* (Oxford: Clarendon Press, 1963) 317–27; Georg Nolte, *Eingreifen auf Einladung—Zur völkerrechtlichen Zulässigkeit des Einsatzes fremder Truppen im internen Konflikt auf Einladung der Regierung (Intervention upon Invitation: Use of Force by Foreign Troops in Internal Conflicts at the Invitation of a Government under International Law (English Summary))* (Berlin: Springer Verlag, 1999); David Wippman, 'Pro-Democratic Intervention by Invitation', in Fox and Roth, above n 2, 293; Brad R Roth, 'The Illegality of "Pro-Democratic" Invasion Pacts', in Fox and Roth, above n 2, 328.

[12] See generally Tom J Farer, 'Intervention in Civil Wars: A Modest Proposal; (1967) 67 *Columbia Law Review* 266; Richard A Falk (ed), *The International Law of Civil War* (Baltimore: Johns Hopkins Press, 1971); John N Moore (ed), *Law and Civil War in the Modern World* (Baltimore: Johns Hopkins, 1974); Gregory H Fox, 'International Law and Civil Wars' (1994) 26 *NYUJILP* 633.

[13] The clearest recent example of this is Somalia after the ouster of the Siad Barre regime in Jan 1991. The civil war that ensued was accompanied by the complete collapse of the governments, legislature, courts, police, and prisons: Yemi Osinbajo, 'Legality in a Collapsed State: The Somali Experience' (1996) 45 *ICLQ* 910. See further Ch 4, Sect 3.2.1.

whether recognition of governments continues to have legal significance despite recent protestations that recognition is now accorded only to states.[14] These issues will be considered only in so far as they touch upon the subject at hand.

This Chapter will first consider the theories of international law that have been said to support a doctrine of unilateral pro-democratic intervention. A number of modern writers have adopted positions that recall Grotius' right to wage war on behalf of the oppressed. As indicated in Chapter 1, this view fell from favour with the emergence of a principle of non-intervention.[15] Such a right of intervention is premised upon the entitlement of A to assert and enforce B's rights as against C—a doctrine of self-help that violates cardinal principles of the international legal order as argued in Chapter 2. A more extreme position asserts that an undemocratic regime loses the protection of international law by effectively voiding its sovereignty. If taken literally, such a rule would render up to a third of the world's states susceptible to intervention on this basis. More realistically, it opens the way to selective application of a principle that is prone to abuse. The argument presented here is that such a norm is neither legally accurate nor politically desirable—both conclusions being borne out by the two major examples of unilateral intervention sometimes characterized as 'pro-democratic': the US interventions in Grenada in 1983 and in Panama in 1989–90. (The US intervention in the Dominican Republic in 1965 and US actions in Nicaragua in the early 1980s are occasionally referred to as additional examples of 'pro-democratic' intervention, but have been considered and rejected elsewhere.[16] Similarly, the ECOWAS intervention in Sierra Leone is occasionally invoked in support of such a right. As it was at least partially justified by Security Council authorization, it is considered in Chapter 4.[17])

Discussion of the 'democratic entitlement' in terms of external enforcement is fundamentally to misconceive its nature. 'Popular sovereignty' may well represent the converging aspirations of many peoples around the globe, but the only vehicle in which this particular human right may find meaningful expression remains—in all but the most exceptional situations—sovereignty of a more traditional kind.

---

[14]  This issue is considered briefly in Sect 1.4.

[15]  See Ch 1, Sect 2.

[16]  On the Dominican Republic, see Ch 2, Sect 2.3.3. On Nicaragua, see Ch 2, Sect 2.2.3, and see below n 28. See also Brad R Roth, *Governmental Illegitimacy in International Law* (Oxford: Clarendon Press, 1999) 297–303.

[17]  See Ch 4, Sect 3.3.2.

## 1. UNILATERAL PRO-DEMOCRATIC INTERVENTION IN THEORY

### 1.1. Popular sovereignty

In an editorial comment published in 1990, Michael Reisman argued that the term 'sovereignty' constituted an anachronism when applied to undemocratic governments or leaders, and that traditional concepts of sovereignty were being replaced by a 'popular sovereignty' vested in the individual citizens of a state.[18] This meant that unilateral intervention to support or restore democracy did not violate sovereignty—and therefore international law—but instead upheld and vindicated it.

Such a justification of unilateral intervention to promote democracy (or other noble ends) depends on a radical reconceptualization of sovereignty. Much has been written on the decline of sovereignty as the defining concept of international law and international relations;[19] indeed, the very idea of a 'right to democracy' itself is testimony to this change. At its most extreme, 'popular sovereignty' is said to have displaced the traditional notion of sovereignty as the 'critical new constitutive policy' of international law.[20] On this view, the Austinian conception of the sovereign as (by definition) the repository of legal authority has been supplanted by the state authorized to represent and protect the individuals from whom it derives its *raison d'être*.[21] Reisman, writing in 1990, used this rationale to argue that

[t]he Chinese Government's massacre in Tiananmen Square to maintain an oligarchy against the wishes of the people was a violation of Chinese sovereignty. The Ceausescu dictatorship was a violation of Romanian sovereignty. President Marcos violated Philippine sovereignty, General Noriega violated Panamanian sovereignty. . . .[22]

Pursuing the argument yet further, Reisman concluded that it was 'anachronistic' to say that the United States violated Panama's sovereignty in 1989 by launching an invasion to capture its (allegedly) illegitimate head of state.[23]

This is not so much a logical conclusion as an *auto-da-fé*. No matter what role the concept of popular sovereignty plays in modern international law, it simply does not follow that the illegitimacy of one regime entitles a foreign

[18] W Michael Reisman, 'Sovereignty and Human Rights in Contemporary International Law' (1990) 84 *AJIL* 866.

[19] See, eg, Simon Chesterman, 'Law, Subject and Subjectivity in International Relations: International Law and the Postcolony' (1996) 20 *Melbourne University Law Review* 979 and sources there cited.

[20] Reisman, above n 18, 874. See also J G Starke, 'Human Rights and International Law', in Eugene Kamenka and Alice Erh-Soon Tay (eds), *Human Rights* (London: Edward Arnold, 1978) 113–31.

[21] See, eg, L J Macfarlane, *The Theory and Practice of Human Rights* (London: Temple Smith, 1985) 7.

[22] Reisman, above n 18, 872.        [23] Ibid 874.

state—*any* foreign state (though one can guess *which* foreign state)—to use force to install a new and more 'legitimate' regime.[24] Although similar positions are adopted by Anthony D'Amato and Fernando Tesón, who dismiss any defence of the principle of non-intervention as examples of 'the rhetoric of statism'[25] and 'the Hegelian myth'[26] respectively, what they and Reisman do not appear to consider is the possibility that *both* Noriega's voiding of the 1989 election *and* the US invasion violated Panamanian sovereignty, albeit in different ways.

Within any normative system, rights will inevitably conflict. It is not enough to assert that the rights of Panamanians are being violated and that this must trump a conflicting right that prohibits the unilateral use of force in international relations. Despite the fact that sovereignty has to some degree been transformed since the adoption of the UN Charter, democracy has not displaced peace as the principal concern of that instrument, and of the international legal system more generally. A comparison may be made with the right to self-determination: enshrined in the major human rights instruments and numerous resolutions of the General Assembly, it is nevertheless commonly accepted that any right of secession to which it might give rise is limited—as a result, in part, of Articles 2(4) and 2(7) of the Charter—to the colonial context and by the principle of *uti possidetis*.[27]

This view finds support in the International Court of Justice's judgment in *Nicaragua*. The Court held that, regardless of what the United States thought of Nicaragua's Sandinista regime,

adherence by a State to any particular doctrine does not constitute a violation of customary international law; to hold otherwise would make nonsense of the fundamental principle of State sovereignty, on which the whole of international law rests, and the freedom of choice of the political, social, economic and cultural system of a State. Consequently, Nicaragua's domestic policy options, even assuming that they corre-

---

[24] To be fair, Reisman sometimes emphasizes that popular sovereignty should not be the 'single variable determinative of lawfulness in all future cases': Reisman, above n 18, 874. Nevertheless, his support for the US intervention in Panama suggests the limited nature of this restriction on the position he advocates.

[25] Anthony D'Amato, 'The Invasion of Panama was a Lawful Response to Tyranny' (1990) 84 *AJIL* 516, 518; see also Reisman, above n 18, 874.

[26] Fernando R Tesón, *Humanitarian Intervention: An Inquiry into Law and Morality* (2nd edn; Dobbs Ferry, NY: Transnational Publishers, 1997) 55–61. See Ch 1, Sect 2.2. Interestingly, in the second edition of his book-length defence of a right of humanitarian intervention, Tesón does not include the example of the US invasion of Panama.

[27] See generally Clyde Eagleton, 'Self-Determination in the United Nations' (1953) 47 *AJIL* 88; U O Umozurike, *Self-Determination in International Law* (Hamden, CT: Shoe String Press, 1972); Eyassu Gayim, *The Principle of Self-Determination* (Oslo: Norwegian Institute of Human Rights, 1990). See also below n 64. On *uti possidetis* see Steven Ratner, 'Drawing a Better Line: Uti Possidetis Juris Today' (1996) 90 *AJIL* 590; Malcolm N Shaw, 'The Heritage of States: The Principle of *Uti Possidetis Juris* Today' (1996) 67 *British YBIL* 75; *Frontier Dispute Case (Burkina Faso/Republic of Mali)* [1986] ICJ Rep 554, 565–7 paras 20–6.

spond to the description given of them by the Congress finding, cannot justify on the legal plane the various actions of the Respondent complained of.[28]

And, as indicated in Chapter 2, the *fact* of occasional incidents of self-help by states in contravention of these norms does not—and should not—justify a change in the law.

## 1.2. The Reagan Doctrine

The closest that a state administration has come to articulating a foreign policy consistent with a right of pro-democratic intervention is the Reagan Doctrine:

Mirroring basic American constitutional principles, the Reagan Doctrine rests on the claim that *legitimate* government depends on the consent of the governed and on its respect for the rights of citizens. A government is not legitimate merely because it exists, nor merely because it has independent rulers. Nazi Germany had a de facto government headed by Germans; that did not make it legitimate.[29]

Leaving aside the obvious question of whether Nazi Germany's illegitimacy in 1945 derived from the treatment of its civilian population or its campaign of aggressive war, the implication appears to be that legitimacy under President Ronald Reagan was linked to the consent and the rights of the governed. In fact, however, the Reagan Doctrine's application was much more limited. Writing in 1989, Jeane Kirkpatrick and Allan Gerson (US permanent representative to the United Nations and counsel to the US mission respectively from 1981 to 1985), went on to emphasize that the Reagan Doctrine had been developed primarily as a response to the Brezhnev Doctrine, countering the perceived Soviet objective of global empire.[30] As such, the legal basis for the 'support—including military support—for insurgencies'[31] was justified (if at all) on the grounds of self-defence.[32] This was made clear by Reagan himself in the 1985 State of the Union address that came to be seen as a significant articulation of the doctrine:

[W]e must not break faith with those who are risking their lives—on every continent, from Afghanistan to Nicaragua—to defy Soviet-supported aggression and secure rights which have been ours from birth. . . . Support for freedom fighters is self-defense.[33]

---

[28] *Nicaragua (Merits)* [1986] ICJ Rep 14, 133 para 263.
[29] Jeane J Kirkpatrick and Allan Gerson, 'The Reagan Doctrine, Human Rights, and International Law', in Louis Henkin (ed), *Right v Might: International Law and the Use of Force* (New York: Council on Foreign Relations, 1989) 19, 23 (emphasis in original).
[30] Ibid 23.          [31] Ibid 20.          [32] Ibid 31–3.
[33] President Reagan, State of the Union Address, 6 Feb 1985, in [1985] 1 *Reagan Papers* 135.

The doctrine was criticized in its day and its applications in Grenada and Nicaragua were condemned by the General Assembly and the ICJ respectively.[34] As the basis for a right of democratic intervention or even democratic legitimacy, it is severely limited: it did not prevent the United States maintaining normal relations with states that made no pretence to be democratic, such as Saudi Arabia, South Africa, and Indonesia. For present purposes, it is sufficient to note that the circumstances that were alleged to justify such actions in self-defence no longer exist.[35]

## 1.3. The Copenhagen Document

It has been argued that some support for the democratic intervention thesis may be found in the document adopted by the CSCE in its 29 June 1990 meeting in Copenhagen.[36] One of a series of instruments elaborating the non-binding Final Act of Helsinki,[37] the Copenhagen Document contains broad provisions concerning respect for human and minority rights. Of particular interest here are its provisions on the link between human rights, representative government, and the responsibility of states to defend and protect these institutions.

The participating states declare that 'the will of the people, freely and fairly expressed through periodic and genuine elections, is the basis of the authority and legitimacy of all government'.[38] And, as quoted by Malvina Halberstam, they

> recognize their responsibility to defend and protect . . . the democratic order freely established through the will of the people against the activities of persons, groups or organizations that engage in or refuse to renounce terrorism or violence aimed at the overthrow of that order *or of that of another participating state.*[39]

Halberstam thus asserts that a 'strong argument' can be made that the Copenhagen Document 'authorizes' one state to intervene (including the use

---

[34] See Sect 2.1.

[35] Rein Mullerson, 'Self-Defense in the Contemporary World', in Lori Fisler Damrosch and David J Scheffer (eds), *Law and Force in the New International Order* (Boulder: Westview, 1991) 13, 15–16. See further Nicholas O Berry, 'The Conflict Between United States Intervention and Promoting Democracy in the Third World' (1987) 60 *Temple Law Quarterly* 1015, 1017; Christopher C DeMuth, *The Reagan Doctrine and Beyond* (Washington, DC: American Enterprise Institute for Public Policy Research, 1988).

[36] Conference on Security and Co-operation in Europe, Document of the Copenhagen Meeting of the Conference on the Human Dimension, 29 June 1990, reprinted in 29 ILM 1305 (Copenhagen Document). See Malvina Halberstam, 'The Copenhagen Document: Intervention in Support of Democracy' (1993) 34 *Harvard ILJ* 163.

[37] Conference on Security and Co-operation in Europe, Final Act of Helsinki, 1 Aug 1975, reprinted in 14 ILM 1292.

[38] Copenhagen Document, above n 36, para 6.

[39] Ibid as quoted in Halberstam, above n 36, 165 (Halberstam's emphasis).

of force) to protect a freely elected government in another state: 'While paragraph 6 does not specifically authorize the use of force,' she states, 'neither
does it prohibit the use of force.'[40] Such pedantry is correct but misleading. In
particular, it is instructive to quote in full the words omitted by the ellipsis in
Halberstam's extract: the participating states 'recognize their responsibility to
defend and protect, *in accordance with their laws, their international human
rights obligations and their international commitments*, the democratic order
freely established . . .'.[41] By implication, this would make such defence and
protection subject to Article 2(4) of the UN Charter.

In some circumstances, a request from the legitimate regime in time of crisis may justify intervention—an issue that will not be considered here.[42]
Halberstam extends this, however, to cover a freely elected government that
does *not* request assistance. Citing the justifications presented by D'Amato
and Abraham Sofaer for the US invasion of Panama,[43] she argues that such
an intervention would not contravene Article 2(4) of the UN Charter.[44] At
the same time, however, Halberstam suggests that the document in fact provides evidence of a new or emerging right of intervention independent of
Article 2(4). Referring to Franck's analysis of another international instrument, she argues by analogy that the provisions of the Copenhagen
Document are also 'weighted with the terminology of *opinio juris*' and are
'deliberately norm creating'.[45] Franck was, however, discussing the UN
Charter. There is some dispute as to the extent to which CSCE (and now OSCE)
documents are to be considered evidence of customary international law.
Though not enforceable in themselves, it is arguable that they provide evidence of (or will influence the development of) customary international law.[46]
Nevertheless, her case for this influence is certainly overstated.

Though she notes that the 'right' she interprets as being created or recognized in the Copenhagen Document is more limited than that proposed by

---

[40] Halberstam, above n 36, 166–7. Cf Louis E Fielding, 'Taking the Next Step in the
Development of New Human Rights: The Emerging Right of Humanitarian Assistance to
Restore Democracy' (1995) 5 *Duke JCIL* 329, 347 (considering this a 'reasonable interpretation',
but supporting Security Council authorized intervention).

[41] Copenhagen Document, above n 36, para 6 (emphasis added).

[42] See above n 11.                              [43] See below Sect 2.2, especially nn 94–104.

[44] Halberstam, above n 36, 167.                [45] Ibid 175, citing Franck, above n 2, 67.

[46] See, eg, Thomas Buergenthal, 'The Copenhagen CSCE Meeting: A New Public Order for
Europe' (1990) 11 *Human Rights Law Journal* 217, 231; Arie Bloed, 'A New CSCE Human
Rights "Catalogue": The Copenhagen Meeting of the Conference on the Human Dimension of
the CSCE', in Arie Bloed and Pieter van Dijk (eds), *The Human Dimension of the Helsinki
Process: The Vienna Follow-up Meeting and Its Aftermath* (Dordrecht: Martinus Nijhoff, 1991)
54, 72–3; Lori Fisler Damrosch, 'International Human Rights Law in Soviet and American
Courts' (1991) 100 *Yale LJ* 2315; Thomas M Franck, 'The Democratic Entitlement' (1995) 29
*University of Richmond Law Review* 1, 26. The non-binding diplomatic nature of the Helsinki
process was criticized in its early stages, but is now recognized as having yielded more detailed
and extensive results than its counterparts: Henry J Steiner and Philip Alston, *International
Human Rights in Context: Law, Politics, Morals* (Oxford: Clarendon Press, 1996) 577–9.

Reisman or the Reagan Doctrine, the fact that she implies that it would have provided a legal basis for the US invasion of Panama suggests its probable scope of operation.[47] Such an interpretation is, moreover, inconsistent with the Moscow Document adopted by the CSCE in 1991. Once again, the participating states condemned forces that seek to take power from a representative government of a participating state, and committed themselves to

> support vigorously, *in accordance with the Charter of the United Nations*, in case of overthrow or attempted overthrow of a legitimately elected government of a participating State by undemocratic means, the legitimate organs of that State.[48]

Although Halberstam's analysis of the Copenhagen Document is footnoted by a number of writers in support of a right of pro-democratic intervention,[49] her conclusions do not stand up to much scrutiny.[50] With the dubious exception of the Reagan Doctrine, discussed earlier, there is no state practice to support her interpretation, and the status of the document itself would undermine any pretensions to *opinio juris*.

## 1.4. Legitimacy, recognition, and intervention

Underlying the various approaches to the external consequences of the installation of particular regimes is the more basic question of the international legal status of governments. This is not the place for an excursion into the various theories of recognition.[51] It is interesting, however, to note that in the years immediately preceding the period currently under discussion, both the United States and the United Kingdom abandoned the practice of granting formal recognition to regimes that came into power by unconstitutional

---

[47] See Halberstam, above n 36, 171.

[48] Conference on Security and Co-operation in Europe: Document of the Moscow Meeting of the Conference on the Human Dimension, Emphasizing Respect for Human Rights, Pluralistic Democracy, the Rule of Law, and Procedures for Fact-Finding, 3 Oct 1991, reprinted in 30 ILM 1670, para 17 (emphasis added).

[49] See, eg, W Michael Reisman, 'Humanitarian Intervention and Fledgling Democracies' (1995) 18 *Fordham ILJ* 794, 802 n 26; Francis Kofi Abiew, *The Evolution of the Doctrine and Practice of Humanitarian Intervention* (The Hague: Kluwer Law International, 1999) 257 n 88; W Michael Reisman, 'Sovereignty and Human Rights in Contemporary International Law', in Fox and Roth, above n. 2, 239, 256 n 54.

[50] See, eg, David Wippman, 'Defending Democracy Through Foreign Intervention' (1997) 19 *Houston JIL* 659, 679.

[51] See generally Ian Brownlie, *Principles of Public International Law* (5th edn; Oxford: Clarendon Press, 1998) 85–104; Stefan Talmon, *Recognition of Government in International Law: With Particular Reference to Governments in Exile* (Oxford: Clarendon Press, 1998); Roth, above n 16. On the relationship between democratic legitimacy and recognition, see Sean D Murphy, 'Democratic Legitimacy and the Recognition of States and Governments', in Fox and Roth, above n. 2, 123.

means. This position is consistent with the practice of the majority of states, which formally recognize states rather than governments.[52]

For the United Kingdom, Lord Carrington explained that this change in policy occurred because the previous practice of recognition had been mis-understood as implying approval of a new regime, particularly where there might be public concern about human rights violations or the manner in which the regime came to power. This was not seen as affecting the capacity of that state to act on the international plane, however:

> We have therefore concluded that there are practical advantages in following the pol-
> icy of many other countries in not according recognition to Governments. Like them,
> we shall continue to decide the nature of our dealings with régimes which come to
> power unconstitutionally in the light of our assessment of whether they are able of
> themselves to exercise effective control of the territory of the State concerned, and
> seem likely to continue to do so.[53]

In fact, the United States under President Rutherford Hayes (1877–81) had required a demonstration of popular support as a criterion for *political* recog-nition of a government. This was part of an elaborate set of criteria for recog-nition that developed over the nineteenth century. In 1977, however, the State Department explicitly de-emphasized the use of recognition in favour of focusing on whether the United States wished to have diplomatic relations with new governments. The establishment of such relations, according to the State Department, 'does not involve approval or disapproval but merely demonstrates a willingness on our part to conduct our affairs with other gov-ernments directly'.[54]

As Stefan Talmon argues, however, reports of the death of recognition of governments as a meaningful practice in international law are somewhat exaggerated.[55] Despite modification of the *practice* of recognition—specif-ically, the abandonment of formal public statements of recognition—legal consequences continue to flow from 'dealing with' or 'not dealing with' par-ticular regimes.[56] In addition, where two or more rival authorities claim to be the government of the same state (such as Beijing/Taipei, Cambodia after the ouster of Pol Pot, occupied Kuwait, Haiti under Cédras), state practice con-tinues to demonstrate the importance of formal recognition even by states

---

[52] This has led some writers to conclude that the doctrine of recognition of governments has been abolished: see Talmon, above n 51, 3 and sources there cited. Cf Tesón, above n 26, 81 n 1, arguing that there is no need to distinguish between recognition of states and recognition of gov-ernments for the purposes of his analysis.

[53] UK Parliamentary Debates, Lords, 28 Apr 1980, cols 1121–2, reprinted in (1980) 51 *British YBIL* 367. See Colin Warbrick, 'The New British Policy on Recognition of Governments' (1981) 30 *ICLQ* 568; Stefan Talmon, 'Recognition of Governments: An Analysis of the New British Policy and Practice' (1992) 53 *British YBIL* 231.

[54] 'Diplomatic Recognition: A Foreign Relations Outline' (1977) 77 (1998) *Dept of State Bull* 462, 463.

[55] Talmon, above n 51. Cf Brownlie, above n 51, 91–3.     [56] Talmon, above n 51, 5–7.

that claim to have eschewed such procedures.[57] Indeed, the Security Council has, on occasion, called upon states not to recognize any regime set up by an illegitimate occupying power,[58] and even decided, acting under Chapter VII, that member states 'shall refrain from recognizing [the] illegal régime' of Ian Smith in Southern Rhodesia.[59]

The recognition or non-recognition of regimes depending on their commitment to democracy may well prove the most effective means of fostering a right to this form of polity. There is some evidence from the break-up of the USSR and the former Yugoslavia that a regime's respect for democratic and other human rights may be required as a precondition for the recognition of a *state*.[60] There is, however, no evidence that states generally withhold recognition from non-democratic regimes: such regimes are commonly allowed to participate in intergovernmental organizations and to enjoy the benefits and protections of international law[61]—notably, a large proportion of the international community supported military action in defence of Kuwaiti sovereignty in 1990–1, though it had no pretensions to democracy. An exception to this is the Organization of American States (OAS), which in 1997 amended its Charter to permit suspension of a member whose democratic government is overthrown by force.[62] Nevertheless, it is not seriously argued that the failure to recognize a particular regime deprives that state of the protection of Article 2(4) of the UN Charter.

There is also a certain question of consistency here. If one accepts that non-democratic states are international legal persons capable of acting as such (for example, in their capacity to conclude binding treaties), it seems odd to argue that their international legal rights do not extend to the basic principle pro-

---

[57] Talmon, above n 51, 8–10.

[58] SC Res 661 (1990) para 9(b) (Iraq–Kuwait) adopted 13-0-2 (Cuba, Yemen). Cf GA Res 3411D(xxx) (1975) para 3 (calling upon governments and organizations not to deal with any institutions or authorities of the South African bantustans 'or to accord any form of recognition to them') adopted 99-0-8 (Belgium, France, FRG, Italy, Luxembourg, Netherlands, UK, US abstaining).

[59] SC Res 277 (1970) para 2 (Rhodesia) adopted 14-0-1 (Spain).

[60] See EC Guidelines on the Recognition of New States in Eastern Europe and in the Soviet Union, reprinted in (1991) 62 *British YBIL* 559. The Community and its member states affirmed their readiness to recognize those new states that 'have constituted themselves on a democratic basis'. To this end, they adopted a common position on the process of recognition, requiring, *inter alia*, 'respect for the provisions of the Charter of the United Nations and the commitments subscribed to in the Final Act of Helsinki and in the Charter of Paris, especially with regard to the rule of law, democracy and human rights'. A similar approach was adopted with respect to the break-up of the former Yugoslavia: EC Declaration on Yugoslavia, reprinted in (1991) 62 *British YBIL* 560. For criticism of this practice, see, eg, Danilo Türk, 'The Dangers of Failed States and a Failed Peace in the Post Cold War Era' (1995) 27 *NYUJILP* 625, 626.

[61] See Murphy, above n 51, 128–9.

[62] OAS Charter (1948) art 9, as amended by the Protocol of Washington, adopted on 14 Dec 1992 by the Sixteenth Special Session of the General Assembly of the OAS, amendment entered into force 1997. Suspension is not automatic, however, and must be approved by a two-thirds majority of the OAS member states. For US ratification, see (1994) 88 *AJIL* 719.

hibiting the use of force. This inconsistency is exacerbated by the fact that the prohibition of force is widely regarded as having achieved the status of a peremptory, *jus cogens* rule. (A treaty condoning an otherwise illegal use of force would thus be void under Article 53 of the 1969 Vienna Convention on the Law of Treaties.[63]) By contrast, even the most ardent supporters of the 'right to democratic governance' do not claim that this specific right has achieved *jus cogens* status. In this context it is important to note that the 'right to democratic governance' is not coterminous with the right to self-determination, which is regarded by some as a *jus cogens* rule[64] and does not necessarily require the operation of democratic processes. How a non-peremptory rule could trump a peremptory rule remains unexplained.

## 2. UNILATERAL PRO-DEMOCRATIC INTERVENTION IN PRACTICE

Having considered the arguments advanced in favour of a unilateral right of pro-democratic intervention *in abstracto*, this section considers the two major examples of unilateral intervention sometimes characterized as 'pro-democratic': the US interventions in Grenada (1983) and Panama (1989).

### 2.1. US intervention in Grenada, 1983

On 25 October 1983 a force of about 400 US Marines and 1,500 paratroops, together with 300 soldiers from neighbouring Caribbean states, landed in Grenada, where a violent *coup d'état* had been staged by radical Marxist opponents of the leftist Maurice Bishop regime. The newly self-appointed Revolutionary Military Council was deposed after three days of fighting. US troops withdrew by 15 December, leaving only a small number of US and Caribbean support personnel on the island. Precise casualty figures were disputed, but appear to have numbered in the low hundreds (including up to forty-seven in the accidental bombing of a hospital).[65]

---

[63] See Ch 2, Sect 2.2.2.

[64] See, eg, Antonio Cassese, *Self-Determination of Peoples: A Legal Reappraisal* (Hersch Lauterpacht Memorial Lectures; Cambridge: Cambridge University Press, 1995) 140; Brownlie, above n 51, 515. Cf *East Timor Case* [1995] ICJ Rep 90, 102 para 29 (self-determination has an *erga omnes* character and is 'one of the essential principles of contemporary international law').

[65] An initial figure of approximately one hundred casualties was quickly revised up. On 9 Nov 1983, the US Defence Department stated that 42 US soldiers had died, along with 59 'enemy soldiers'. Major General Schwarzkopf, deputy commander of 'Urgent Fury' gave the latter figure as 160 Grenadian and 71 Cuban soldiers killed. An indeterminate number of Grenadian civilians were also killed, including those in the hospital: see generally *Keesing's* (1984) 32614–18; Edward Gordon *et al*, 'International Law and the United States Action in Grenada: A Report' (1984) 18 *International Lawyer* 331, 334.

The Reagan Administration provided three justifications for Operation Urgent Fury.[66] First, it cited an invitation from the Governor-General of Grenada, received on 24 October 1983. According to Deputy Secretary of State Kenneth Dam, the 'legal authorities of the Governor-General remained the sole source of governmental legitimacy on the island in the wake of the tragic events'.[67] As a point of constitutional law, this is open to question.[68] Moreover, the invasion was already in an advanced stage of implementation by the time the request was supposedly received—just one day before the troops landed. Although the proximity of the request to the invasion is not determinative of its legality, it does indicate clearly that even the United States did not regard it as decisive.[69] *The Economist* (which strongly supported the action) concluded that the 'request was almost certainly a fabrication concocted between the OECS [Organization of Eastern Caribbean States] and Washington to calm the post-invasion diplomatic storm'.[70]

Secondly, the United States cited a request to intervene from the OECS. On 2 November 1983, Dam referred to Articles 3, 4, and 8 of the OECS Treaty, which, he stated, 'deal with local as well as external threats to peace and security'.[71] This reference was misleading—the treaty does refer to such threats, but not in terms that could possibly justify the use of force against a member state. Three months later, State Department Legal Adviser Davis Robinson presented a modified position, relying instead on Article 6, which grants plenary authority to the heads of government of the OECS states.[72] He then referred to Article 3(2) which, he stated, 'expressly empowers the heads of government to pursue joint policies in the field of mutual defense and security, and "such other activities calculated to further the purposes of the Organization as the member States may from time to time decide"'.[73] He

[66] See Kenneth W Dam, 'Statement Before the House Committee on Foreign Affairs, 2 November 1983' (1984) 78 *AJIL* 200, 203; Davis R Robinson, 'Letter dated 10 February 1984, addressed to Professor Edward Gordon, Chairman of the Committee on Grenada of the American Bar Association's Section on International Law and Practice' (1984) 78 *AJIL* 661.

[67] Dam, above n 66, 203.

[68] Under the 1973 Constitution, the Governor-General apparently had such power as part of his unenumerated reserve powers. It is unlikely that these were in effect in 1983, however, after the promulgation of the People's Laws in 1979 following the revolution: see Michael J Levitin, 'The Law of Force and the Force of Law: Grenada, the Falklands, and Humanitarian Intervention' (1986) 27 *Harvard ILJ* 621, 646–7.

[69] Robert J Beck, 'International Law and the Decision to Invade Grenada: A Ten-Year Retrospective' (1993) 33 *Virginia JIL* 765, 789–90.

[70] 'Britain's Grenada Shut-Out', *The Economist*, 10 Mar 1984, 31, 34. It further stated that the decision to invade 'had been 75% made on Saturday', the day before the alleged request: ibid 32. Cf Nolte, above n 11, 286 ff; Roth, above n 16, 303–10.

[71] Dam, above n 66, 203 (statement before the House Committee on Foreign Relations).

[72] Robinson, above n 66, 663 (letter addressed to Professor Edward Gordon, Chairman of the Committee on Grenada of the American Bar Association's Section on International Law and Practice).

[73] Robinson, above n 66, 663, citing Treaty Establishing the Organization of Eastern Caribbean States, 18 June 1981, signed at Basseterre, St Kitts/Nevis, 20 ILM 1166, art 3(2)(r) [OECS Treaty].

omitted to mention that Article 3(2) merely states the fields in which member states will endeavour to co-ordinate, harmonize, and pursue joint policies. The 'Major Purposes' listed in Article 3(1) include the defence of member states' 'sovereignty, territorial integrity and independence'.[74] In both statements, the United States relied upon Chapter VIII of the UN Charter in a manner that conflated 'pacific means of dispute settlement' under Article 52 with enforcement actions under Article 53—measures that require Security Council authorization. Only the former article was cited by the United States to justify an action that was clearly *not* 'pacific' (and therefore could only have fallen within the scope of the latter).[75]

Thirdly, the United States invoked the protection of nationals abroad as a legal justification. The facts supporting this thesis have been contested—in particular, the United States asserted that Grenadian officials refused to let US citizens leave the island, although Canada claimed to have flown a chartered plane to and from the island on the very day of the intervention.[76] In any case, it was acknowledged even by US officials that the scale of the operation went beyond the limits of this 'narrowly drawn ground for the use of force'.[77]

A Security Council resolution deploring the intervention as a violation of international law was vetoed by the United States.[78] The General Assembly did, however, pass a resolution that 'deeply deplore[d]' the US-led intervention as a flagrant violation of international law.[79] Subsequent events also undermined the US legal position. None of the Eastern Caribbean states involved referred to the humanitarian motives initially stressed by the United States. Instead, they claimed that the action was 'to help stabilize the country', 'to restore law and order', but above all 'to block the Russians and the Cubans', 'to prevent another Angola' and 'to prevent Marxist revolution from spreading to all the islands'. They described the landing as 'a pre-emptive defensive action'.[80]

In the attempt to find support for a unilateral right of pro-democratic intervention, even a regional one, Grenada is a strained example. The United States itself did not seek to raise this justification, or any justification that could be seen to imply a right of pro-democratic intervention. In a letter to

---

[74] OECS Treaty, above n 73, art 3(1)(b).

[75] See Dam, above n 66, 203; Robinson, above n 66, 663. It therefore seems disingenuous of the Legal Adviser to have stated that '[w]e are not aware of any serious contention that actions falling within the scope of Article 52 could violate Article 2(4) of the Charter': Robinson, above n 66, 663.

[76] Levitin, above n 68, 649.                     [77] Robinson, above n 66, 664.

[78] [1983] *UN YB* 211. The draft resolution was voted down 11-1-3 (US against; Togo, UK, and Zaïre abstaining).

[79] GA Res 38/7 (1983) adopted 108-9-27.

[80] See Wil D Verwey, 'Humanitarian Intervention', in Antonio Cassese (ed), *The Current Legal Regulation of the Use of Force* (Dordrecht: Martinus Nijhoff, 1986) 57, 65 and sources cited therein.

the American Bar Association, a State Department Legal Adviser stressed that the United States specifically did *not* rely on an expanded view of self-defence, 'new interpretations' of Article 2(4), or 'a broad doctrine of "humanitarian intervention"'.[81] Even if it had invoked the restoration of democracy as a justification, the preponderance of *opinio juris* in this instance is to be found in the negative reaction of other states, and thus supports the contrary rule.

## 2.2. US intervention in Panama, 1989[82]

Supporters of a unilateral right of pro-democratic intervention rely most heavily on the US invasion of Panama in 1989 as a paradigmatic example of their theory at work. Close examination, however, confirms that the case of Panama supports precisely the opposite conclusion.

On 20 December 1989, 24,000 US troops began an operation to overthrow the government of Panama and capture its head of state, General Manuel Noriega. President George Bush explained and justified the action on four grounds: 'to safeguard the lives of Americans, to defend democracy in Panama, to combat drug trafficking and to protect the integrity of the Panama Canal Treaty.'[83] Having rendered Noriega fugitive, the United States now recognized the 'rightful leadership' of the likely victors of elections held earlier that year; diplomatic relations would resume immediately and steps would be taken to lift economic sanctions imposed against the Noriega regime.[84] The US forces would be withdrawn 'as quickly as possible'. With no apparent irony, Bush added that he would 'continue to seek solutions to the problems of this region through dialogue and multilateral diplomacy'.[85]

Analysis of the legal basis for the action—somewhat hopefully code-named Operation 'Just Case'—is made difficult by the conflation of policy and legal reasoning in statements such as these. Of the four grounds outlined above, the exercise of an 'inherent right of self defence' protected under Article 51 of the UN Charter and extending to the protection of nationals abroad most closely resembled a legal argument.[86] But if self-defence was the primary legal justi-

---

[81] Robinson, above n 66, 664.

[82] See generally Association of the Bar of the City of New York, *The Use of Armed Force in International Affairs: The Case of Panama* (*Report of The Committee on International Arms Control and Security Affairs and The Committee on International Law*) (1992); Simon Chesterman, 'Rethinking Panama: International Law and the US Invasion of Panama, 1989', in Guy S Goodwin-Gill and Stefan A Talmon (eds), *The Reality of International Law: Essays in Honour of Ian Brownlie* (Oxford: Oxford University Press, 1999) 57.

[83] President Bush, 'Address to the Nation Announcing United States Military Action in Panama', 20 Dec 1989, in [1989] 2 *Bush Papers* 1722, para 2 (Bush Address).

[84] See Memorandum Terminating Economic Sanctions Against Panama, 20 Dec 1989, in [1990] 2 *Bush Papers* 1726 (lifting economic sanctions imposed by Executive Order No 12635).

[85] Bush Address, above n 83, para 10.      [86] See generally Chesterman, above n 82, 62–80.

fication put forward by the Bush Administration, it was the claim that intervention may be justified in support of democracy that won the most vocal
support from legal academics.[87] D'Amato described US actions in Panama
and, previously, Grenada as 'milestones along the path to a new non-statist
conception of international law'.[88] Reisman similarly heralded a new era in
which 'the people, not governments, are sovereign'.[89] In an endearingly iso-
lationist conception of customary international law, each regarded the invasion as a significant and positive development,[90] apparently oblivious to the
broad condemnation of the intervention by the international community.
Once again a Security Council resolution was blocked by the US veto;[91] once
again the General Assembly condemned the unilateral action.[92] On the other
side of the Atlantic, Sir Elihu Lauterpacht was a rare non-US voice in support
of the invasion, stating that the only justification offered by the United States
with any merit was that it had 'acted in support of the democratic process—
a concept of internationally recognized relevance'.[93]

The Bush Administration invoked democracy in support of the invasion in
two ways: as the exercise of a right to act unilaterally to promote democracy
in another state, and as legitimate assistance to a democratically elected head
of state, Guillermo Endara, who, it was claimed, had consented to that
action. According to Abraham Sofaer, Legal Adviser to the State
Department at the time of the invasion, when Endara was informed of the
impending arrival of US troops on 19 December 1989, he

decided to be sworn in as president. He welcomed the US action, presented his views
as to the proper objectives of US efforts and immediately began to cooperate fully in
their implementation. He appealed to the Panamanian forces 'not to resist' the US
action, which he said was unavoidable and 'seeks to end the Noriega dictatorship and
reestablish democracy, justice and freedom.' He also began exercising the functions of
his office, appointing officials to assume direction over components of the
Panamanian government and progressively asserting control over all Panamanian territory.[94]

---

[87] See, eg, D'Amato, above n 25; Reisman, above n 18; Panel Discussion, 'The Panamanian
Revolution: Diplomacy, War and Self-Determination in Panama: I Self-Determination and
Intervention in Panama' (1990) 84 *ASIL Proc* 182, 192 (Tesón).

[88] D'Amato, above n 25, 517.

[89] Reisman, above n 18, 874, quoting S/PV.2899 (1989) (Statement of Mr Pickering). In his
1990 article, Reisman distances himself somewhat from Pickering's statement. His position in
2000 is less qualified: see Reisman, 'Sovereignty', above n 49, 252.

[90] See D'Amato, above n 25, 523; Reisman, above n 18, 874–6; Reisman, 'Fledgling
Democracies', above n 49, 803.

[91] [1989] *UNYB* 175. The draft resolution was voted down 10-4-1 (Canada, France, UK, and
US against; Finland abstaining).

[92] GA Res 44/240 (1989) adopted 75-20-40.

[93] Elihu Lauterpacht, 'Letter to the Editor: Legal Aspects of Panama Invasion', *The Times*, 23
Dec 1989.

[94] Abraham D Sofaer, 'The Legality of the United States Action in Panama' (1991) 29
*Columbia JTL* 281, 289. In a press briefing, Gen Colin Powell stated that Endara was sworn in

Even if one accepts the legitimacy of Endara and his colleagues, the United States never claimed that he actually requested the invasion. Although Bush stated that Endara 'welcomed the assistance' of the United States[95] and there was some reference to his being 'consulted',[96] he was informed of the plans for a military intervention only when troops were already in the air.[97] Bob Woodward reports that Bush had decided that this was the point of no return—if Endara refused to 'play ball', Secretary of Defense Dick Cheney and General Colin Powell, who were overseeing the operation, were to check with Bush personally.[98] Endara was sworn in at Fort Clayton, a US military base in the Canal Zone, less than an hour before the invasion began.[99]

There is, in fact, some evidence that Endara was not entirely happy about the invasion, which he later described as a 'kick in the head', stating that he 'would have been happier without it'.[100] In a profile on him written in January 1990, he explained his reaction to the news from US officials that an invasion was imminent and that they wanted him to take the oath as President:

It would have been very easy for me to say, 'I'm not going to take this job under occupation by American forces' . . . But I knew that I couldn't do that. I had to assume the responsibility of Government—the people chose me to be President. I couldn't simply tell the US: 'You pick the Government. You are the occupying power and you do what you want.'[101]

This squarely raises the question of what might have happened had he refused to 'play ball'. Sofaer argues that one reason Endara's consent was not secured prior to the invasion is that it would have exposed him to unjustifiable political and physical risk.[102] But as the New York Bar Association observes, the claim that unilateral intervention is justified in support of democratic choice is weakened when elected leaders are unable to ask openly for such interven-

'shortly before the operation. He was sworn in by a Panamanian justice of some kind . . .': 'Fighting in Panama: The Pentagon; Excerpts From Briefings on US Military Action in Panama', *NYT*, 21 Dec 1989.

[95] Letter from President Bush to Speaker of the House Thomas Foley, 21 Dec 1989, in [1989] 2 *Bush Papers* 1734, para 5.

[96] See Letter from Mr Pickering, Permanent Representative of the United States to the United Nations, to the President of the Security Council, 20 Dec 1989, S/21035 (1989) para 2: 'The United States undertook this action after consultation with the democratically-elected leaders of Panama'. See also 'Fighting in Panama: The State Dept; Excerpts From Statement by Baker on US Policy', *NYT*, 21 Dec 1989.

[97] Association of the Bar of the City of New York, above n 82, 66 n 282.

[98] Bob Woodward, *The Commanders* (London: Simon & Schuster, 1991) 182.

[99] The swearing appears to have taken place at 12:39 am on the morning of the invasion: ibid 182. In a press statement that was later discredited, Endara said that he had been sworn in at 2 am: 'Panamanians in Secret Pact on Oath-Taking', *LA Times*, 27 Dec 1989.

[100] Philip Geyelin, 'Noriega Was Only Part of the Problem', *Washington Post*, 1 Jan 1990; Michael L Conniff, *Panama and the United States: The Forced Alliance* (Athens, GA: University of Georgia Press, 1991) 167.

[101] David E Pitt, 'To Many in Panama, the New President is an Enigma Wrapped in a Smile', *NYT*, 28 Jan 1990.

[102] Sofaer, above n 94, 290.

tion for fear of popular disapproval.[103] It might have been such concerns that led Endara to claim initially that he was sworn in on Panamanian territory—an assertion contradicted by witnesses and uniformly disregarded by the press.[104]

After noting that Endara's consent would have been sufficient to justify the invasion had he controlled the territory of Panama and been able to exercise governmental powers prior to 19 December 1989,[105] Sofaer asserts that the fact that he lacked such control 'does not deprive his consent of legal significance'.[106] It is not clear what Sofaer intends by this, but it may indicate an argument that a new government may retrospectively validate the action that brought it to power. This appears to be the import of Lauterpacht's comment that

[w]hat matters in law is not the technical propriety of the United States action at its inception but whether the Government of Panama itself now regards that action as lawful.[107]

The implication is that a newly installed regime may pardon violations of international law committed against its predecessor. With regard to their *inter se* obligations under the rules of state responsibility, this may be the case, although if the norm breached was one of *jus cogens*, then it is extremely doubtful that any *ex post facto* waiver would be effective.[108] There is now considerable support for the view that the prohibition of the use of force is such a peremptory norm;[109] as indicated earlier, a treaty condoning a violation of this norm would thus be void under Article 53 of the Vienna Convention.[110] Although the Convention applies only to written agreements,[111] this does not affect the independent application of the rules it sets forth to other agreements.[112]

Even if it were effective, third states and international tribunals are not bound to accept such a waiver.[113] In the *Barcelona Traction* case, the ICJ held that certain rules of international law entail obligations *erga omnes*, with all states having a legal interest in the protection of the rights involved—as an illustration, the Court referred to those obligations outlawing acts of aggression.[114] If an intervention were considered to violate such an obligation, all

---

[103] Association of the Bar of the City of New York, above n 82, 67.
[104] 'Panamanians in Secret Pact on Oath-Taking', *LA Times*, 27 Dec 1989.
[105] Sofaer, above n 94, 290 (citing Lassa Francis Lawrence Oppenheim, *International Law* (Hersch Lauterpacht (ed); 8th edn; London: Longmans, 1955) 305).
[106] Sofaer, above n 94, 290.      [107] Lauterpacht, above n 93.
[108] See Natalino Ronzitti, 'Use of Force, *Jus Cogens* and State Consent', in Cassese, above n 80, 147, 160–1.
[109] See Ch 2, Sect 2.2.2.      [110] See above Sect 1.4.
[111] Vienna Convention on the Law of Treaties 1969, art 2(1)(a).
[112] Ibid art 3(b).
[113] See Brownlie, above n 11, 317–18 and citations therein; Ronzitti, above n 108, 161–3.
[114] *Barcelona Traction Case* [1970] ICJ Rep 3, 32.

other states may be considered individually as 'injured' parties.[115] Allowing the target state to consent to such an invasion retrospectively would do little to allay concerns that this doctrine is open to abuse precisely in order to impose regimes sympathetic to the acting state.

In the event, most Latin American states withdrew their ambassadors from Panama after the invasion and refused to recognize the Endara Administration, stating that diplomatic relations would be normalized only when US troop numbers returned to pre-invasion levels and some form of plebiscite demonstrated popular support for the new regime.[116] The Permanent Council of the OAS initially refused to accept the credentials of the ambassador dispatched by Endara to represent Panama. Noriega's ambassador remained and participated in the vote criticizing the invasion.[117] Over the course of the following months, however, most governments extended recognition to the Endara regime.[118]

In May 1994 Panama held its first effective democratic elections in over twenty-five years. Ironically, the victor was Ernesto Perez Balladares of the Revolutionary Democratic Party, the party formerly controlled by Noriega.[119]

### 2.3. Evaluation of state practice

The immediate obstacle to adopting the arguments advanced in favour of a unilateral right of pro-democratic intervention is that they are simply not accepted by even a significant minority of states.[120] Although there is some

[115] Report of the ILC, 37th Session [1985] 2(2) *ILC YB* 25–7. See further M Mohr, 'The ILC's Distinction Between "International Crimes" and "International Delicts" and Its Implications', in Marina Spinedi and Bruno Simma (eds), *United Nations Codification of State Responsibility* (New York: Oceana, 1987) 115; Yoram Dinstein, *War, Aggression and Self-Defence* (2nd edn; Cambridge: Cambridge University Press, 1994) 112.

[116] Robert Pear, 'US Says Latin American Nations are Resuming Ties with Panama', *NYT*, 9 Mar 1990. Developed Western states were among the first to recognize the new regime: Don Shannon, 'Panama's New Government Slowly Gains in World Acceptance Envoys: President Endara's Diplomatic Corps Has Re-Established Ties with 17 Nations', *LA Times*, 6 Jan 1990.

[117] Tom J Farer, 'Panama: Beyond the Charter Paradigm' (1990) 84 *AJIL* 503, 510.

[118] In Latin America, El Salvador, Guatemala, Costa Rica, and Honduras were among the first to recognize the Endara Administration. Colombia, Argentina, Ecuador, Venezuela, and Peru joined them in March 1990: Pear, above n 116.

[119] See Erich Schmitt, 'Washington Talk: A Panama Enemy Becomes an Ally', *NYT*, 21 July 1994. Five years earlier, Perez Belladares had managed the campaign of Carlos Duque, Noriega's hand-picked presidential candidate.

[120] See generally Oscar Schachter, 'The Legality of Pro-Democratic Invasion' (1984) 78 *AJIL* 645, 649; Louis Henkin, 'The Use of Force: Law and US Policy', in Henkin, above n 29, 37; Ved P Nanda, 'The Validity of United States Intervention in Panama Under International Law' (1990) 84 *AJIL* 494, 498; Franck, above n 2, 85; Dinstein, above n 115, 89; Karsten Nowrot and Emily W Schabacker, 'The Use of Force to Restore Democracy: International Legal Implications of the ECOWAS Intervention in Sierra Leone' (1998) 14 *American University International Law Review* 321, 378–87.

evidence of support on the part of the United States and perhaps the United Kingdom,[121] upholding or restoring democracy has not previously been asserted as an independent basis for intervention. It was not raised by Tanzania when it deposed Idi Amin in Uganda in 1979,[122] by Vietnam when it overthrew the genocidal regime of Pol Pot in 1978–9,[123] nor by France when it helped overthrow 'Emperor' Bokassa in the Central African Republic in 1979.[124] On those occasions when it has been invoked by the United States to justify its actions in Grenada, Nicaragua, and Panama (explicitly, or by the implication of commentators), the action has been condemned by the international community and—when the issue came before it—by the ICJ.[125]

There is also a wealth of evidence supporting precisely the opposite conclusion. The Declaration on Friendly Relations, adopted without a vote by the General Assembly in 1970, affirms that '[e]very State has an *inalienable* right to choose its political, economic, social and cultural systems, without interference in any form by another State'.[126] General Assembly resolution 45/150 (1990), adopted by a large majority, recognizes that

the efforts of the international community to enhance the effectiveness of the principle of periodic and genuine elections should not call into question each State's sovereign right freely to choose and develop its political, social, economic and cultural systems, whether or not they conform to the preferences of other States.[127]

Resolution 45/151 (1990), adopted by a smaller but still substantial majority, went further, affirming that any 'extraneous activities that attempt, directly or indirectly, to interfere in the free development of national electoral processes' violate the spirit and letter of the Charter and the Declaration on Friendly Relations.[128]

Aside from the normative problems such an argument faces, it is also highly questionable that such a doctrine would be desirable. In the *Nicaragua* case, the Court refused 'to contemplate the creation of a new rule opening up a right of intervention by one state against another on the ground that the latter has opted for some particular ideology or political system'.[129] Such a rule

---

[121] In a statement on the subject of the US intervention in Panama, the Secretary of State for Foreign and Commonwealth Affairs, Mr Douglas Hurd, observed in part: 'We fully support the American action to remove General Noriega, which was undertaken with the agreement of the leaders who clearly won the elections held last May. Noriega's arbitrary rule was maintained by force. We and many others have repeatedly condemned Noriega and called for the election result to be respected. Every peaceful means of trying to see the results of the democratic elections respected has failed.' UK Parliamentary Debates, Commons, 20 Dec 1989, col 357, reprinted in (1989) 40 *British YBIL* 692.

[122] See Ch 2, Sect 2.3.7.  [123] See Ch 2, Sect 2.3.8.

[124] See Ch 2, Sect 2.3.9.  [125] See above n 28.

[126] Declaration on Friendly Relations, GA Res 2625(xxv) (1970) (emphasis added).

[127] GA Res 45/150 (1990) para 4, adopted 128-8-9.

[128] GA Res 45/151 (1990) para 3, adopted 111-29-11. See also GA Res 49/180 (1994) adopted 97-57-14.

[129] *Nicaragua (Merits)* [1986] ICJ Rep 14, 133. See Ch 2, Sect 2.2.3.

would, *ex hypothesi*, be exercised arbitrarily. In his landmark paper on the right to democratic governance, moreover, Thomas Franck argued that for such a right to be meaningful, precisely the opposite approach is necessary:

[S]teps should be taken to meet the fear of some smaller states that election monitoring will lead to more Panama-style unilateral military interventions by the powerful, perhaps even for reasons less convincing than those which provoked the 1989 US military strike against the Noriega dictatorship. That a new rule might authorize actions to enforce democracy still conjures up just such chilling images to weaker states, which see themselves as the potential objects of enforcement of dubious democratic norms under circumstances of doubtful probity.[130]

Reisman disputes this. He argues that a commitment to democracy coupled with an unwillingness to allow for its unilateral enforcement (if that is the only 'feasible option') produces anomalous results such as sanctions regimes that 'severely [punish] the victims while enriching the villains'.[131] Such an assertion not only conflates ongoing debates about the utility of sanctions with the right of unilateral intervention, it assumes its own answer by positing the use of force as the only 'feasible option'.

There are other ways for one state to manifest its concern at the undemocratic behaviour of another. The most common manner of doing so is simply to refuse to recognize a regime's representative authority, or at least refuse to deal with it in certain—particularly economic—ways. As Reisman rightly notes, isolation is a blunt instrument and may in fact cause harm to those whom the acting state desires to protect.[132] Another possibility may be to require third parties dealing with a grossly unrepresentative regime to assume the risks that may be involved—for example, the risk that a subsequent government will refuse to honour the commitments of its predecessor—by modifying the applicable rules of state responsibility.[133] And, in exceptional circumstances where there is broad consensus that some form of enforcement action to support or restore democracy is required, collective action through the Security Council provides the only appropriate—and legal—alternative.[134]

[130] Franck, above n 2, 84. Cf Thomas M Franck, 'Legitimacy and the Democratic Entitlement', in Fox and Roth, above n 2, 25, 47.

[131] Reisman, 'Sovereignty', above n 49, 256.

[132] Ibid 256–7. Cf Crawford, above n 4, 128–9.

[133] Crawford, above n 4, 129–30. *Contra* the *Tinoco Concessions Arbitration* (1923) 1 RIAA 369. An obvious problem would be that the spectre of sovereign risk would dissuade investment and much useful intercourse with many developing states.

[134] See Ch 4, Sect 3.3.

## CONCLUDING THOUGHTS ON 'KIND-HEARTED GUNMEN'[135]

It is not my responsibility to overthrow Amin. That is the responsibility of the Ugandans. It was my task to chase him from Tanzanian soil. I have done so. The Amin Government is a government of thugs, and the Ugandans have the right to overthrow it.

Julius Nyerere, 1979[136]

Twenty years ago, Michael Walzer proposed a thought experiment concerning what might be considered an ideal case of pro-democratic intervention. He posited a country named Algeria in which a nominally democratic revolution has evolved into a theocratic military dictatorship that suppresses civil liberties and brutally represses its citizens. The new elite allows no challenge to its authority; women are returned to their traditional religious subordination to patriarchal authority. Nevertheless, the regime has deep roots in Algeria's history, as well as its political and religious culture (a questionable claim for the regime the revolutionaries had in mind). Walzer further posited that the Swedish Government has in its possession a 'wondrous chemical' which, if introduced into the water supply, would turn all Algerians into Swedish-style social democrats. They would have no memory of their former views and experience no loss; they would be empowered to create a new regime in which civil liberties would be respected and women treated as equals. Should Sweden use the chemical?[137]

Although this thought experiment includes issues that go far beyond the scope of the present Chapter, it is raised here because it makes an important point: that how one answers the question depends on whether one accepts that the 'right to democratic governance' is more complex than a simple assertion that sovereignty must be popular. This Chapter has argued that it is, and that this is reflected in tensions between different principles of international law commonly invoked in support of such a right: hence the contradiction between rights to self-determination and limits on intervention to give expression to it; hence the paradox that the United Nations exists to promote human rights but not to interfere in the domestic jurisdiction of states. To assert that these tensions mean something at the beginning of the twenty-first century is neither anachronistic nor evidence of a simplistic 'statist' approach to international law. Rather, it reflects the fact that there will usually be

---

[135] See Ian Brownlie, 'Thoughts on Kind-Hearted Gunmen', in Richard B Lillich (ed), *Humanitarian Intervention and the United Nations* (Charlottesville: University Press of Virginia, 1973) 139.

[136] *Keesing's* (1979) 29671.

[137] Michael Walzer, 'The Moral Standing of States' (1978) 9 *Philosophy and Public Affairs* 209, 226–7.

differences between what a political community is, what it can be, and what it should be.[138]

Indeed, the position adopted here is that pro-democratic intervention may—in all but the most exceptional of circumstances—actually be inimical to human rights. As Walzer notes, it seems paradoxical to assert a people's right to a state within which their rights are violated, but such a state is the only one that they, as a political community, are likely to call their own.[139] It could be said that the argument is a straw one: altering a people's culture through despotic control is more intrusive than 'surgical' military strikes aimed at removing an undemocratic government. But the important point is that the right of self-determination that is at the heart of the democratic entitlement vests in none other than 'the people', and that it is they—and not some foreign power that they have similarly *not* elected—who must determine their own destiny.

Clearly there are limits to such a principle. These, it is submitted, are those presently recognized by international law. Governments are no longer completely shielded by principles of sovereignty and domestic jurisdiction when they engage in egregious violations of human rights or otherwise expose their populations to widespread or systematic abuse. However, those who seek to intervene are also subject to constraints of a legal character. States may not use force other than in self-defence (within the strict limits of the law governing that principle), or pursuant to a legitimate request from the authorities (or, in some circumstances, from a separatist movement fighting a war of liberation from colonial domination) in advance of the intervention, or where the Security Council has authorized the use of force pursuant to a finding (which is credible and not contrary to the purposes of the Charter) that a situation is a threat to international peace and security. The constraints on forcible means do not demand that a concerned international community sit on its hands in the face of great human suffering, only that its response must be limited to peaceful means unless one of these situations applies.

The attempt by Reisman and others to justify US actions in the Western hemisphere as evidence of a new right of unilateral pro-democratic intervention poses a threat to the prohibition of the use of force and, therefore, to the embattled organization that is charged with principal responsibility for issues of peace and security in an increasingly interdependent world. It is also disingenuous: Grenada could equally be explained as one of the last Cold War battlefields; Panama as an embarrassed President Bush dealing clumsily with

---

[138] See further Anne Orford, 'Locating the International: Military and Monetary Interventions After the Cold War' (1997) 38 *Harvard ILJ* 443, 460–4; Simon Chesterman, 'Human Rights as Subjectivity: The Age of Rights and the Politics of Culture' (1998) 27(1) *Millennium: Journal of International Studies* 97.

[139] Walzer, above n 137, 226. Cf Claude Ake, 'The Unique Case of African Democracy' (1993) 69 *International Affairs* 239; Martti Koskenniemi, 'The Police in the Temple: Order, Justice and the UN: A Dialectical View' (1995) 6 *European JIL* 325, 343.

a former US protégé. (Similarly, the Security Council authorized action in Haiti might be characterized as a refugee crisis remarkable only for the fact that the United States sought UN approval to intervene in the Western hemisphere.[140]) To hold these incidents up as models of a new era of pro-democratic intervention is to ignore the history of invasions that has characterized the relationship between the United States and its southern neighbours. To use them as the foundation of a new international legal order is to drape the arbitrary use of force by the sole remaining superpower in the robes of dubious legality.

With history stubbornly refusing to end, there will always be a conflict between what is possible and what is right. But if the right to democratic governance means anything, it is that its content *and the manner of its expression* must be determined by the people in whom it vests.

[140] See Ch 4, Sect 3.3.1.

# 4

# The New Interventionism

*Threats to international peace and security*
*and Security Council actions under*
*Chapter VII of the UN Charter*

> The lesson of the Cold War, finally, was not that the evolution of the UN
> into a global policeman was thwarted, but that the difficulties and dangers
> of intervention were masked by the Security Council's paralysis.
>
> *Independent*, 1993[1]

A great deal has been written on the transformations that have affected the
United Nations in general and the Security Council in particular since the
thawing of Cold War tensions in the late 1980s. The rise and fall of hopes for
a more effective Council has littered the pages of law reviews and international relations journals, tempered by only occasional murmuring as to the
dangers attendant to such inconstancy. In this Chapter and the one that follows, it is argued that the trends established in the period 1990–9 herald a
more basic challenge to the international legal order: by blurring the bound-
aries of the exception to the prohibition of the use of force established by
Chapter VII they threaten to undermine this cardinal principle of the international legal order. Paralleling the argument advanced in Chapters 2 and
3—that nominally humanitarian motives may be used to justify intervention
that is at best arbitrary and at worst maleficent—at issue here is the normative significance to be attributed to explicitly political compromises reached
in the informal (and unrecorded) consultations that dominate the work of the
Security Council,[2] and the consequences for an international rule of law.

Here two factors may be identified: the *plasticity* of the circumstances in
which the Security Council may act, and the *contingency* of these actions on
the willingness of states to follow them through on its behalf. It is beyond the
scope of the present work to examine the whole of Security Council practice
in this area, or even to cover completely the range of actions taken under
Chapter VII. Nor will the present work attempt comprehensively to discuss the

---

[1] Editorial, 'The Possible and the Defensible', *Independent*, 16 July 1993.
[2] Sydney D Bailey and Sam Daws, *The Procedure of the Security Council* (3rd edn; Oxford:
Clarendon Press, 1998) 44.

susceptibility of Security Council decisions to judicial review.[3] The focus will be on the invocation of humanitarian justifications for enforcement actions by the Security Council, and the process of delegation through which such mandated actions have been carried out. This Chapter considers the changing nature of 'threats to international peace and security' as understood in Security Council practice. Chapter 5 then turns to the shibboleth of enforcement actions in the 1990s—'all necessary means'—and analyses the nature and extent of the mandate this confers upon acting states.

## 1. THE EXPANDING ROLE OF THE SECURITY COUNCIL

It is curious that in the voluminous literature on the Security Council's recent activism the logic of Article 39 is often overlooked. Many writers critical of the measures taken pursuant to Security Council resolutions authorizing enforcement actions base their concern on the failure of the Security Council to respect the limits of Article 39, without acknowledging the burgeoning number of other resolutions adopted under Chapter VII.[4]

As Vera Gowlland-Debbas has pointed out, an attempt to analyse recent practice solely in terms of the strict legal basis for its actions in particular Charter provisions is unlikely to bear fruit. Whereas she shifted the focus from the Security Council's role in the progressive development of international law onto its function in the *enforcement* of international obligations,[5] however, the present work is primarily concerned with the normative consequences of a watering down of the procedural limits on enforcement actions. The analysis begins with an account of the Security Council's rise to activism and the broadening scope of 'threats to international peace and security' as this term has been used in the past decade.

---

[3] See generally Tom J Farer, 'Human Rights in Law's Empire: The Jurisprudence War' (1991) 85 *AJIL* 117; Mohammed Bedjaoui, *The New World Order and the Security Council: Testing the Legality of its Acts* (Dordrecht: Martinus Nijhoff, 1994); Ian Brownlie, 'The Decisions of Political Organs of the United Nations and the Rule of Law', in Ronald St John Macdonald (ed), *Essays in Honour of Wang Tieya* (Dordrecht: Martinus Nijhoff, 1994) 91; Martti Koskenniemi, 'The Police in the Temple: Order, Justice and the UN: A Dialectical View' (1995) 6 *European JIL* 325; Krzysztof Skubiszewski, 'The International Court of Justice and the Security Council', in Vaughan Lowe and Malgosia Fitzmaurice (eds), *Fifty Years of the International Court of Justice: Essays in Honour of Sir Robert Jennings* (Cambridge: Grotius, 1996) 606. See also *Certain Expenses Case* [1962] ICJ Rep 151, 230 (Winiarski J, dissenting); *Namibia* [1971] ICJ Rep 16, 293 (Fitzmaurice J, dissenting), 340 (Gros J, dissenting); *Lockerbie Case (Preliminary Objections)* [1998] ICJ Rep 9, 24–5 paras 40–5.

[4] See, eg, Mary Ellen O'Connell, 'Regulating the Use of Force in the 21st Century: The Continuing Importance of State Autonomy' (1997) 36 *Columbia JTL* 473.

[5] Vera Gowlland-Debbas, 'Security Council Enforcement Action and Issues of State Responsibility' (1994) 43 *ICLQ* 55, 56–7.

## 1.1. Chapter VII actions prior to 1990

The central role assigned to the Security Council by the UN Charter is made manifest in the prohibition of the use of force in Article 2(4) and the conferral of 'primary responsibility for the maintenance of international peace and security' on the Council in Article 24(1). This is given substance in Article 25, which provides that its decisions are binding on all member states, and Article 103, which provides that obligations under the Charter override conflicting international legal obligations.[6] The legal pre-eminence accorded to the Council by the San Francisco Conference in 1945 was, nevertheless, tempered by political realism: permanent membership was granted to the major powers of the day, along with a veto over non-procedural matters.[7] In the event, the collective security system envisaged by the Charter was never fully implemented, in large part due to the political climate of the Cold War.[8]

Article 39 provided that the coercive powers conferred on the Council in Chapter VII were to be triggered by a determination of 'any threat to the peace, breach of the peace, or act of aggression'.[9] In the first forty-four years of the UN—a period not noted for the abandonment of the use of force in international relations—the Council made only three determinations of a 'breach of the peace' under Article 39: Korea (1950);[10] the Falkland Islands/Islas Malvinas (1982);[11] and Iran–Iraq (1987—the eighth year of that conflict).[12] Prior to the General Assembly's adoption of the 1974 definition of 'aggression'[13] no state acts had been condemned as such; between then and 1989, the acts of only three attracted the label: Israel,[14] South Africa,[15] and the illegal regime of Southern Rhodesia.[16] In the same period (1946–89), the

---

[6] Cf *Lockerbie Case* (*Provisional Measures*) [1992] ICJ Rep 3, 47 para 29 (Bedjaoui J, dissenting) (distinguishing between obligations and rights as protected by provisional measures); *Genocide Convention Case* (*Provisional Measures*) [1993] ICJ Rep 325, 440 para 100 (Lauterpacht J, separate opinion) (suggesting that art 103 might not apply to norms of *jus cogens*).

[7] UN Charter, art 27(3).

[8] Until 1966, the veto was regarded as merely an extension of Soviet foreign policy. Following the expansion of the Security Council to fifteen members, however, Western states ceased to dominate the Council. Between 1966 and 1997, Western states were responsible for 86% of the vetoes cast: Bailey and Daws, above n 2, 228. Cf Martti Koskenniemi, 'The Place of Law in Collective Security' (1996) 17 *Michigan JIL* 455, 457.

[9] UN Charter, art 39(1).

[10] SC Res 82 (1950) (Korea) adopted 9-0-1 (Yugoslavia abstaining) (USSR not present).

[11] SC Res 502 (1982) (Falklands/Malvinas) adopted 10-1-4 (Panama against; China, Poland, Spain, USSR abstaining).

[12] SC Res 598 (1987) (Iran–Iraq) adopted unanimously.

[13] General Assembly Resolution on the Definition of Aggression: GA Res 3314(XXIX) (1974).

[14] SC Res 573 (1985) (Israel–Tunisia); SC Res 611 (1988) (Israel–Tunisia).

[15] See, eg, SC Res 387 (1976) (South Africa–Angola) adopted 9-0-5 (China did not participate in the voting); SC Res 567 (1985) (South Africa–Angola); SC Res 568 (1985) (South Africa–Botswana); SC Res 571 (1985) (South Africa–Angola); SC Res 577 (1985) (South Africa–Angola) adopted unanimously; SC Res 574 (1985) (South Africa–Angola).

[16] SC Res 455 (1979) (Southern Rhodesia–Zambia) adopted by consensus.

Council also explicitly determined the existence of threats to the peace in relation to three situations:[17] Palestine (1948);[18] Southern Rhodesia (1965);[19] and South Africa's nuclear weapons programme (1977).[20] Finally, the Council expressed *concern* that events in the Congo (1961)[21] and Cyprus (1974)[22] threatened international peace and security, and implied the same of East Pakistan in 1971.[23]

Chapter VII provides for three types of response to such situations. Article 40 provides that, before making recommendations or deciding upon measures provided for in Article 39, the Council may '*call upon* the parties concerned to comply with such provisional measures as it deems necessary or desirable'.[24] Article 41 empowers it to '*decide* what measures not involving the use of armed force are to be employed to give effect to its decisions'.[25] Finally, Article 42 allows it to '*take such action* . . . as may be necessary to maintain or restore international peace and security'.[26] This neat schema assumed the existence of standing agreements under Article 43 and a level of co-operation in the Security Council that now appears almost Panglossian. In fact, prior to 1990, action under Chapter VII was as inconsistent as it was infrequent.

### 1.1.1. Enforcement actions prior to 1990

Before the action against Iraq in 1990–1, the Council had authorized what might be considered enforcement actions only twice: in 1950 the Council '*recommended*' action in Korea under the unified command of the United States; in 1966 it '*called upon*' the United Kingdom to use force to prevent the violation of sanctions against Southern Rhodesia. In addition, the Council authorized the use of force by the United Nations and the Secretary-General in the course of the peacekeeping operation in the Congo. The Council also imposed mandatory sanctions on two occasions in this period: the economic blockade of Southern Rhodesia (1966–79)[27] and the arms embargo on South Africa (1977–94).[28]

---

[17] Situations where a breach of the peace or act of aggression was also determined are excluded. Where a situation continued to constitute a threat to the peace, it is only listed once.

[18] SC Res 54 (1948) para 1.          [19] SC Res 217 (1965) para 1.

[20] SC Res 418 (1977) para 1.

[21] SC Res 161 (1961) preamble B: '*Gravely concerned* at the continuing deterioration of the situation in the Congo and the prevalence of conditions which seriously imperil peace and order and the unity and territorial integrity of the Congo, and threaten international peace and security'.

[22] SC Res 353 (1974) preamble: '*Gravely concerned* about the situation which has led to a serious threat to international peace and security'.

[23] SC Res 307 (1971) preamble: '*Having discussed* the grave situation . . . which remains a threat to international peace and security'.

[24] UN Charter, art 40 (emphasis added).          [25] Ibid art 41 (emphasis added).

[26] Ibid art 42 (emphasis added).

[27] SC Res 232 (1966); SC Res 253 (1968); SC Res 277 (1970).          [28] SC Res 418 (1977).

The Council's involvement in the Korean question began in June 1950, when the United States obtained a Security Council resolution to respond to North Korea's invasion of South Korea[29]—a move made possible only by the non-attendance of the representative of the USSR.[30] In the absence of agreements under Article 43,[31] command and control of the operation was delegated to Washington.[32] Resolution 84 (1950) was conspicuously vague as to the authority it conferred on the United States: having recommended that member states provide such assistance as may be necessary to repel North Korea's armed attack and to restore international peace and security in the area, the Council directed that this assistance be co-ordinated by the United States and authorized it to use the UN flag. In the final paragraph of the resolution, the Council requested the United States to provide it with reports 'as appropriate'.[33] On 1 August 1950 the representative of the USSR resumed his seat on the Security Council, which then ceased to play an active part in the war.[34] The legal basis of the Korean operation remains the subject of some dispute. The fact that the Council merely 'recommended' that states provide assistance to South Korea in repelling the attack of North Korea militates against grounding the action in Article 42. On this basis, some writers have argued that the true foundation lay in the collective self-defence provisions of Article 51.[35] In light of statements at the time and subsequent practice, however, it seems more plausible that the recommendation should be seen as an enforcement action, either under Article 39 or a residual power grounded in Chapter VII.[36]

Resolution 221 (1966) gave ambiguous authorization to the United Kingdom to use force to prevent ships carrying oil to Southern Rhodesia in

[29]  SC Res 82 (1950); SC Res 83 (1950).

[30]  The Soviet representative had withdrawn from the Council on 13 Jan 1950, stating that he would not participate in the Council's work until 'the representative of the Kuomintang group had been removed', and that the USSR would not recognize as legal any decision of the Council adopted with the participation of that representative. He returned to the Council on 1 Aug 1950: [1950] *UN YB* 220–30.

[31]  See 5 UN SCOR (476th mtg) No 18, p 3 (1950) (UK): 'Had the Charter come fully into force and had the agreement provided for in Article 43 of the Charter been concluded, we should, of course, have proceeded differently, and the action to be taken by the Security Council to repel the armed attack would no doubt have been founded on Article 42. As it is, however, the Council can naturally act only under Article 39, which enables the Security Council to recommend what measures should be taken to restore international peace and security.'

[32]  SC Res 84 (1950) adopted 7-0-3 (Egypt, India, Yugoslavia) (USSR not present).

[33]  SC Res 84 (1950).                                        [34]  See below, n 47.

[35]  See, eg, Julius Stone, *Legal Controls of International Conflict* (rev edn; Sydney: Maitland, 1959) 234–7; Jochen Abr Frowein, 'Articles 39–43', in Bruno Simma (ed), *The Charter of the United Natons: A Commentary* (Oxford: Oxford University Press, 1994) 614, 630.

[36]  See, eg, Derek W Bowett, *United Nations Forces: A Legal Study of United Nations Practice* (London: Stevens, 1964) 47; Oscar Schachter, 'The Place of Law in the United Nations' [1950] *Annual Review of UN Affairs* 203, 219–21; Leland M Goodrich, Edvard Hambro, and Anne Patricia Simons, *Charter of the United Nations: Commentary and Documents* (3rd edn; New York: Columbia University Press, 1969) 315; Malcolm N Shaw, *International Law* (4th edn; Cambridge: Cambridge University Press, 1997) 866.

contravention of resolution 217 (1965).[37] Reference to Articles 41 and 42 was specifically rejected in the debates on the resolution, and it has been argued that the preference for the hortatory expression 'calls upon' in its text suggests that although it may have been adopted under Chapter VII of the Charter, it cannot be considered an enforcement action.[38] The difficulty with this view is that this use of force was to be directed against the vessel of a third state. Opinion remains divided.[39]

The UN peacekeeping force in the Congo was authorized to use force to end the civil war between 1961 and 1964, but remained under the command and control of the Secretary-General, first Dag Hammarskjöld and later U Thant. UN troops were initially provided at the request of the Congo in July 1960[40] and their original standing orders were to use force only in self-defence. As the situation deteriorated, however, the Security Council authorized the use of force 'as a last resort' to prevent civil war,[41] and later to remove mercenaries.[42] It has been argued that this constituted an enforcement action under Chapter VII,[43] but this is a minority position. The Secretary-General stated that the operation was essentially an internal security measure taken by the Security Council at the invitation of the Congolese government, perhaps implicitly under Article 40.[44] In the *Certain Expenses* case that arose from disputes as to the financing of the operation, the International Court of Justice similarly rejected the view that the action was an enforcement action.[45]

---

[37] SC Res 221 (1966) authorized the United Kingdom to patrol Beira harbour in Mozambique, to prevent oil from reaching Rhodesia.

[38] Vera Gowlland-Debbas, *Collective Responses to Illegal Acts in International Law: United Nations Actions in the Question of Southern Rhodesia* (Dordrecht: Martinus Nijhoff, 1990) 416–19.

[39] See, eg, Frowein, above n 35, 634; John F Murphy, 'Force and Arms', in Oscar Schachter and Christopher C Joyner (eds), *United Nations Legal Order* (Cambridge: Cambridge University Press, 1995) 247, 280–2.

[40] SC Res 143 (1960) adopted 8-0-3 (China, France, UK).

[41] SC Res 161A (1961) adopted 9-0-2 (France, USSR) para 1: 'The Security Council . . . *Urges* that the United Nations take immediately all appropriate measures to prevent the occurrence of civil war in the Congo, including arrangements for cease-fires, the halting of all military operations, the prevention of clashes, and the use of force, if necessary, in the last resort.'

[42] SC Res 169 (1961) adopted 9-0-2 (France, USSR) para 4.

[43] See, eg, Finn Seyersted, 'United Nations Forces: Some Legal Problems' (1961) 37 *British YBIL* 351, 446.

[44] 15 UN GAOR, 5th Committee (839th mtg) (1961) para 6 (Secretary-General).

[45] *Certain Expenses Case* [1962] ICJ Rep 151, 177: 'It is not necessary for the Court to express an opinion as to which article or articles of the Charter were the basis for the resolutions of the Security Council, but it can be said that the operations of ONUC did not include a use of armed force against a State which the Security Council, under Article 39, determined to have committed an act of aggression or to have breached the peace.' See also Rosalyn Higgins, *The Development of International Law Through the Political Organs of the United Nations* (London: Oxford University Press, 1963) 107.

### 1.1.2. *Alternatives to Security Council action*

As Rosalyn Higgins has observed, 'the Charter is an extraordinary instrument, and . . . a huge variety of possibilities are possible under it'.[46] The two most prominent such adaptations to the problem of Security Council inaction during the Cold War were the *Uniting for Peace* resolution passed by the General Assembly in 1950, and the emergence of peacekeeping forces, whose legal basis Dag Hammarskjöld famously located in Chapter 'VI½' of the Charter.

In August 1950 the return of the Soviet representative to the Security Council precluded any further action in response to the situation in Korea.[47] This led to moves to avoid the problem of the veto by asserting a new role for the General Assembly. At the initiative of Western states, the General Assembly adopted the *Uniting for Peace* resolution. This provided that the Assembly would meet to recommend collective measures in situations where the veto prevented the Council from fulfilling its primary responsibility for the maintenance of international peace and security. In the case of a breach of the peace or act of aggression, the measures available were said to include the use of armed force.[48] On 1 February 1951, in accordance with the *Uniting for Peace* procedures, the Assembly passed a resolution condemning China's armed intervention in Korea as an act of aggression, and recommended that all states lend every assistance to the UN action in Korea.[49]

The legal status of the *Uniting for Peace* procedure is questionable, as noted in *obiter dicta* by the ICJ in the *Certain Expenses* case. The Court stated that Article 11(2) of the Charter allows the General Assembly to *recommend* peacekeeping operations at the request, or with the consent, of the state(s) concerned, but that this is limited by the requirement that any question on which 'action' (here understood to mean enforcement action within the meaning of Chapter VII) is required be referred to the Security Council.[50] Further restrictions are imposed by Article 12, which prevents the Assembly making recommendations on situations in respect of which the Security Council is 'exercising . . . the functions assigned to it in the . . . Charter',[51] and Article

---

[46] Rosalyn Higgins, *Problems and Process: International Law and How We Use It* (Oxford: Clarendon Press, 1994) 184.

[47] See Anjali V Patil, *The UN Veto in World Affairs 1946–1990: A Complete Record and Case Histories of the Security Council's Veto* (London: Mansell, 1992) 189–96.

[48] GA Res 377A(v) (1950).                           [49] GA Res 498(v) (1951).

[50] *Certain Expenses Case* [1962] ICJ Rep 151, 164–5. The Court decided the case by adopting a principle of 'institutional effectiveness', and held that 'when the Organization takes action which warrants the assertion that it was appropriate for the fulfilment of one of the stated purposes of the United Nations, the presumption is that such action is not *ultra vires* the Organization': ibid 168. See Ian Brownlie, *Principles of Public International Law* (5th edn; Oxford: Clarendon Press, 1998) 700–1.

[51] UN Charter, art 12(1). See N D White, *The United Nations and the Maintenance of International Peace and Security* (Manchester: Manchester University Press, 1990) 103–5.

2(7).[52] Nevertheless, the procedure was subsequently employed on a number of occasions and the question of its legality is now probably moot.[53] It was followed (at least in part) in relation to:[54] the Suez Crisis (1956)—against France and the United Kingdom, two of its original sponsors;[55] Hungary (1956);[56] Lebanon and Jordan (1958);[57] the Congo (1960);[58] the Middle East (1967);[59] East Pakistan/Bangladesh (1971);[60] Afghanistan (1980);[61] the Palestine Situation (1980, 1982);[62] and Namibia (1981).[63]

The procedure that came to characterize UN involvement in peace and security during the Cold War, however, was peacekeeping. A product of its time, peacekeeping operations were traditionally non-threatening and impartial, governed by the principles of consent and minimum force.[64] The first such operation to have a mandate going beyond mere observer status[65] was the first UN Emergency Force (UNEF I), established by the General Assembly in 1956 to supervise the ceasefire in the Middle East after the Suez invasion. As Israel did not consent to the operation, it operated only on Egyptian soil; when Egypt withdrew its consent just prior to the Six Day War in 1967, UNEF I was withdrawn from the Middle East.[66]

It is possible to challenge the legality of peacekeeping operations on the basis that Chapter VII must be read as providing the only legitimate basis for the decision to use a military force (though this would not preclude observer missions). Such an argument is difficult to accept. On the same basis, the use of force under Article 42 would be precluded by the absence of agreements under Article 43. This was rejected by the ICJ in *Certain Expenses*[67] and has been refuted by long-standing practice. By the end of 1989, a total of eighteen operations had been established, ten of which were ongoing (this had increased by five in the previous two years); all but two of these operations were authorized by the Security Council.[68] With regard to traditional

---

[52] See White, above n 51, 105–8.

[53] See Ian Brownlie, *International Law and the Use of Force by States* (Oxford: Clarendon Press, 1963) 334; White, above n 51, 110.

[54] D J Harris, *Cases and Materials on International Law* (4th edn; London: Sweet & Maxwell, 1991) 894; Shaw, above n 36, 881.

[55] GA Res 997(ES-I) (1956); GA Res 1000(ES-I) (1956).

[56] SC Res 120 (1956); GA Res 1004(ES-II) (1956).     [57] GA Res 1237(ES-III) (1958).

[58] SC Res 157 (1960); GA Res 1474(ES-IV) (1960).     [59] See [1967] *UN YB* 191–2.

[60] SC Res 303 (1971); GA Res 2793(XXVI) (1971).

[61] SC Res 462 (1980); GA Res ES-6/2 (1980).

[62] SC Res 500 (1982); GA Res ES-9/1 (1982).     [63] GA Res ES-8/2 (1981).

[64] Mats R Berdal, *Whither UN Peacekeeping?* (Adelphi Paper 281; London: IISS, 1993) 3.

[65] The first peacekeeping force *stricto sensu* was the UN Truce Supervision Organization (UNTSO), established in 1948 to observe the truce in Palestine. It remains in existence.

[66] See generally Gabriella Rosner, *The United Nations Emergency Force* (Columbia University Studies in International Organization; New York: Columbia University Press, 1963).

[67] See Ch 5, Sect 1.

[68] UNEF I (1956–67) and the UN Security Force in West New Guinea (West Irian) (UNSF: 1962–3) were established by General Assembly resolutions. The UN Good Offices Mission in Afghanistan and Pakistan (UNGOMAP: 1988–90) was established by a letter from the President of

peacekeeping—that is, where the consent of relevant authorities has been obtained in advance of any operation—such a legal challenge would in any case be limited to the constitutional validity of such an action within the UN Organization. Moves towards more 'muscular' peacekeeping operations in which peacekeepers are authorized to use force in excess of personal self-defence raise more complex issues, discussed in the next Chapter.[69]

### 1.1.3. The Security Council and the Cold War

In *An Agenda for Peace*, Secretary-General Boutros Boutros-Ghali estimated that over 100 conflicts had left some 20 million dead in the time-span considered in this brief overview of UN operations 1946–89.[70] It is clear that Cold War tensions and the exercise of the veto were major factors in the United Nation's apparent paralysis: the veto was exercised on 279 occasions, with the result that when the Council did pronounce on matters that might have attracted its coercive powers, hortatory resolutions were preferred.[71] On the rare occasions that coercive measures were invoked, these were limited by the requirement of UN oversight or to specific circumstances provided for in the resolution.

The clear exception to this was the Korean operation, but most writers regarded it as an aberration.[72] It was, ironically, a Russian who first heralded the potential of the Security Council to play a more active role in international peace and security after the Cold War. After the reappointment of Javier Pérez de Cuéllar in 1986, the Secretary-General challenged the Council to reach a 'meeting of minds' on the conflict between Iran and Iraq;[73] the cooperation between the permanent five members of the Council (P5) on this matter led to a system of regular informal meetings.[74] Most remarkable, however, was President Gorbachev's September 1987 article in *Pravda* and

---

the Security Council to the Secretary-General and subsequently endorsed by Security Council resolutions. The other operations were: UNTSO (1948– ); UNMOGIP (1949– ); UNOGIL (1958); ONUC (1960–4); UNYOM (1963–4); UNFICYP (1964– ); DOMREP (1965–6); UNIPOM (1965–6); UNEF II (1973–9); UNDOF (1974– ); UNIFIL (1978– ); UNIIMOG (1988–91); UNTAG (1989–90); UNAVEM I (1989–91); ONUCA (1989–92).

[69] See Ch 5, Sect 3.1.

[70] An Agenda for Peace: Preventive Diplomacy, Peacemaking and Peace-keeping (Report of the Secretary-General pursuant to the statement adopted by the Summit Meeting of the Security Council on 31 Jan 1992), UN Doc A/47/277-S/24111 (1992) para 14.

[71] See, eg, SC Res 180 (1963) and SC Res 312 (1972) (voluntary measures against Portugal for its colonial possessions); SC Res 283 (1970), SC Res 558 (1984), and SC Res 569 (1985) (voluntary diplomatic, trade, and cultural embargo against South Africa).

[72] See, eg, Higgins, above n 45, 226–7; Erik Suy, 'Peace-Keeping Operations', in René-Jean Dupuy (ed), *Handbook on International Organizations* (Dordrecht: Martinus Nijhoff, 1988) 379, 381; White, above n 51, 86; Harris, above n 54, 882; Shaw, above n 36, 867.

[73] UN Press Release SG/SM/3956 (13 Jan 1986).

[74] See David Malone, *Decision-Making in the UN Security Council: The Case of Haiti, 1990–1997* (Oxford: Clarendon Press, 1998) 8.

*Izvestia* seeking wider use of peacekeeping forces and calling on the P5 to become 'guarantors' of international security.[75] In the following two years, five peacekeeping and observer forces were deployed across three continents.[76] The relative success of these operations established the conditions for an explosion of Council activity at the start of the next decade.

## 1.2. A 'new world order'? Chapter VII actions, 1990–9

> Out of these troubled times . . . a new world order can emerge: a new era, freer from the threat of terror, stronger in the pursuit of justice, and more secure in the quest for peace. . . . A world where the rule of law supplants the rule of the jungle. A world in which nations recognize the shared responsibility for freedom and justice. A world where the strong respect the rights of the weak.
>
> George Bush, 1990[77]

On every conceivable measure, the Security Council has played a far more active role since 1990. At the most basic level, it simply did more. Between 1946 and 1989 it met 2,903 times and adopted 646 resolutions, averaging fewer than 15 a year; between 1990 to 1999 it met 1,183 times and adopted 638 resolutions, an average of about 64 per year. In its first 44 years, 24 Security Council resolutions cited or used the terms of Chapter VII;[78] by 1993 it was adopting that many such resolutions every year.[79]

The Council also came to demonstrate an extraordinarily broad interpretation of its responsibility to maintain international peace and security. Acting under Chapter VII, it has set up international criminal tribunals for the former Yugoslavia and Rwanda,[80] and authorized the use of force to apprehend alleged criminals;[81] it has imposed a war reparations procedure

[75] Mikhail S Gorbachev, 'Reality and the Guarantees of a Secure World', in FBIS *Daily Report: Soviet Union*, 17 Sept 1987, 23–8, cited in Malone, above n 74, 8. See also Anthony Parsons, *From Cold War to Hot Peace: UN Interventions 1947–1994* (London: Michael Joseph, 1995) 15–16.

[76] UNIIMOG (Iran–Iraq, 1988–91); UNGOMAP (Afghanistan–Pakistan, 1988–90); UNTAG (Namibia, 1989–90); UNAVEM I (Angola, 1989–91); ONUCA (Central America, 1989–92).

[77] 'Address Before a Joint Session of the Congress on the Persian Gulf Crisis and the Federal Budget Deficit', 11 Sept 1990, in [1990] 1 *Bush Papers* 1219.

[78] See Appendix 1.

[79] Ch VII resolutions passed in the years 1990 onwards were as follows: 1990—11; 1991—13; 1992—10; 1993—27; 1994—24; 1995—21; 1996—9; 1997—15; 1998—22; 1999—14. See Appendix 2.

[80] SC Res 808 (1993); SC Res 827 (1993); SC Res 955 (1994). The Appeals Chamber in the *Tadic* case found that 'the establishment of the International Tribunal falls squarely within the powers of the Security Council under Article 41': *Prosecutor v Tadic*, IT-94-1-AR72 (Oct 1995) para 36. See further Danesh Sarooshi, *The United Nations and the Development of Collective Security: The Delegation by the UN Security Council of its Chapter VII Powers* (Oxford: Clarendon Press, 1999) 95–8.  [81] SC Res 837 (1993) (Somalia).

for Iraq[82] and demarcated and guaranteed the Iraq–Kuwait boundary;[83] and it has attempted to force Libya and the Sudan to extradite alleged terrorists.[84]

Compared with the two sanctions regimes prior to 1990,[85] mandatory sanctions have been imposed on the following states: Iraq and occupied Kuwait (1990– );[86] successor states of the former Yugoslavia (1991–6);[87] Somalia (1992– );[88] Libya (1992–9);[89] Liberia (1992– );[90] Haiti (1993–4);[91] Rwanda (1994–6);[92] Sudan (1996– );[93] Sierra Leone (1997–8);[94] the Federal Republic of Yugoslavia (FRY) (1998– );[95] and Afghanistan (1999– ).[96] It has also imposed sanctions against a non-state entity: UNITA forces in Angola (1993– ).[97]

Peacekeeping operations have expanded in number and scope. By the end of 1999, a further thirty-five operations had been established, with a total of seventeen ongoing.[98] All received their mandates from the Security Council, increasingly acting under Chapter VII. With peacekeepers now being deployed with more complex tasks and in more dangerous areas, the nature of these mandates has changed somewhat from the original model of an impartial, consent-based operation where force is used only in self-defence.[99] As a result of attacks on peacekeepers in Bosnia, Somalia, and Rwanda, it has become common for the Council to authorize peacekeepers to use 'all necessary means' to achieve specific objectives.[100] Such 'mission creep' has blurred the line between peacekeeping and peace-enforcement, a dichotomy that

---

[82] SC Res 674 (1990); SC Res 687 (1991); SC Res 692 (1991).

[83] SC Res 833 (1993).                    [84] SC Res 748 (1992) (Libya); SC Res 1054 (1996) (Sudan).

[85] See above nn 27–8.

[86] SC Res 661 (1990) (general economic sanctions, following its invasion of Kuwait).

[87] SC Res 713 (1991) (arms embargo, following the outbreak of fighting). General economic sanctions were imposed on the FRY concerning its military involvement in Bosnia and Herzegovina: SC Res 757 (1992).

[88] SC Res 733 (1992) (arms embargo, following the outbreak of internal conflict).

[89] SC Res 748 (1992); SC Res 883 (1993) (arms and air traffic embargo, following demands on Libya to renounce support for terrorism, expanded in Nov 1993).

[90] SC Res 788 (1992) (arms embargo, following ceasefire violations).

[91] SC Res 841 (1993) (arms embargo and petroleum sanctions, in response to refugee flows from Haiti and the failure of the regime to restore the legitimate government).

[92] SC Res 918 (1994) (arms embargo, following continuing and systematic internal violence).

[93] SC Res 1054 (1996); SC Res 1070 (1996) (restrictions on Sudanese officials abroad and on aircraft movements, following an assassination attempt against President Hosni Mubarak of Egypt).

[94] SC Res 1132 (1997) (arms embargo and petroleum sanctions); SC Res 1171 (1998) (terminating sanctions).

[95] SC Res 1160 (1998) (arms embargo, following activities in Kosovo).

[96] SC Res 1267 (1999) (restrictions on flights by or on behalf of the Taliban and freeze of Taliban financial resources, following failure to extradite alleged terrorist Usama bin Laden).

[97] SC Res 864 (1993) (arms embargo and petroleum sanctions, following UNITA's failure to accept the results of elections and observe a ceasefire).

[98] Source: UN Web <http://www.un.org/Depts/dpko>.

[99] ONUC was the only Cold War exception to this principle: see above Sect 1.1.1.

[100] See Ch 5, Sect 3.1.

Secretary-General Boutros-Ghali stressed should be maintained in his *Supplement to An Agenda for Peace*.[101] The primary distinction between these two classes of operation appears now to relate more to the command and control of military forces, with the former remaining (at least nominally) under the operational control of the Security Council and the Secretary-General, whereas the latter allows states to take action on the Council's behalf.

Enforcement actions have also grown in number. Compared with the isolated examples of the Korean and, perhaps, the Rhodesian operations discussed above,[102] since 1990 the Council has explicitly authorized one or more nominated states, regional organizations, or 'coalitions of the willing', to use 'all necessary means' (or 'all measures necessary' or 'all necessary measures') in the following situations:

* Operations Desert Shield and Desert Storm in Kuwait and Iraq (1990–91);
* Operation Restore Hope (or UNITAF) in Somalia (1992–3);
* Opération Turquoise in south-west Rwanda (1994);
* Operation Uphold Democracy in Haiti (1994–5);
* IFOR and SFOR in Bosnia and Herzegovina (1995– );
* a Canadian-led force in eastern Zaïre (1996) (never implemented);
* NATO-led KFOR operations in Kosovo (1999– ); and
* INTERFET in East Timor (1999).

The Council has also authorized more limited uses of force under Chapter VII in the following situations:

* UNPROFOR and member states providing air support in respect of safe areas in Bosnia and Herzegovina (1993–5); and
* Operation Alba in Albania (1997).

In many cases, the two classes of operations have been closely related to one another and even overlapped. Peacekeeping operations in Somalia, Haiti, Rwanda, and Bosnia were followed by enforcement operations when they proved incapable of discharging their mandates. Similarly, enforcement operations were followed by peacekeepers in Somalia and Haiti;[103] resolution 1264 (1999) on East Timor specifically provided that the multinational force INTERFET was to be replaced 'as soon as possible' by a peacekeeping operation.[104]

In addition, the Council has also given implicit retroactive approval to ECOMOG operations in Liberia (1990–2) and Sierra Leone (1997–8), and MISAB and French operations in the Central African Republic (1997–8), as well as

---

[101] Supplement to An Agenda for Peace: Position Paper of the Secretary-General on the Occasion of the Fiftieth Anniversary of the United Nations, UN Doc A/50/60-S/1995/1 (1995) para 36.

[102] See above Sect 1.1.1.                    [103] Cf Malone, above n 74, 25–6.

[104] SC Res 1264 (1999) para 10.

questionable authorization for the air exclusion zone in Iraq (1991– ) and NATO threats and air strikes in relation to FRY operations in Kosovo (1998–9).

Of primary concern in this Chapter is the initial determination by the Security Council that it is empowered to act under Chapter VII. The next section considers the nature of this requirement before moving onto the question of whether recent practice has violated that procedural hurdle or changed it fundamentally.

## 2. THE REQUIREMENT OF A 'THREAT TO THE PEACE'

### 2.1. Chapter VII of the UN Charter

A cursory survey of the relevant Security Council resolutions makes it clear that the terms of Chapter VII have not been used in a studied manner. In the operative paragraphs of resolution 567 (1985), South Africa was condemned for acts of aggression against Angola—acts which were then said to '*endanger* international peace and security',[105] recalling the language of Chapter VI.[106] During the India–Pakistan conflict of 1971, draft resolutions were proposed that referred to hostilities along the India–Pakistan border as constituting a *threat* to international peace and security.[107]

Chapter VII is entitled 'Action with Respect to Threats to the Peace, Breaches of the Peace, and Acts of Aggression'. Article 39 introduces the coercive powers of the Council and provides for a two-step process:

The Security Council shall *determine* the existence of any threat to the peace, breach of the peace or act of aggression *and* shall make recommendations, or decide what measures shall be taken in accordance with Articles 41 and 42, to maintain or restore international peace and security.[108]

This suggests that a determination of a threat to the peace, breach of the peace, or act of aggression must be made before the Security Council can decide what measures should be taken.[109] It is, of course, uncontroversial that the Council can make *recommendations* outside the ambit of Chapter VII, though there are differences of opinion as to whether *decisions* so made are mandatory or binding. This is not a debate that need be pursued here.[110] The significance of reference to Chapter VII for present purposes is that it enables

---

[105] SC Res 567 (1985) para 1 (emphasis added).                    [106] See UN Charter, art 33(1).
[107] S/10416 (1971); S/10423 (1971); S/10461 Rev.1 (1971). All three were vetoed by the USSR: see Patil, above n 47, 207–11.
[108] UN Charter, art 39 (emphasis added).
[109] Gowlland-Debbas, above n 5, 61; Simma, above n 35, 612–13.
[110] See Bailey and Daws, above n 2, 263–73. The ICJ noted in *Namibia* that art 25 'is not confined to decisions in regard to enforcement action but applies to "the decisions of the Security Council" adopted in accordance with the Charter': *Namibia* [1971] ICJ Rep 16, 53.

the Council to authorize enforcement actions and constitutes the only exception to the domestic jurisdiction clause, Article 2(7).

A preliminary question that arises is whether reference to Articles 41 and 42 in Article 39 implies that such a determination must precede action under Article 40. Article 40 provides that

[i]n order to *prevent* an aggravation of the situation, the Security Council may, *before making the recommendations or deciding upon the measures provided for in Article 39*, *call upon* the parties concerned to comply with such provisional measures as it deems necessary or desirable.[111]

On this basis, it has been suggested that Article 40 may not be subject to the same procedural requirements as Articles 41 and 42—that is, it need not follow a determination that a threat to the peace, breach of the peace, or act of aggression exists.[112] Hans Kelsen observed that its position and relation to the other articles of Chapter VII suggest that Article 40 should be subject to the same procedural requirements, but that this had been contradicted by Council practice even in the first years of the United Nations.[113] In later years, the ambiguous status of Article 40 appears to have been closely connected with the political difficulties posed by the crisis in the Congo—notably, the Secretary-General stated that the ONUC operation had been authorized under Article 40, but was at pains to justify its conduct in light of Article 2(7).[114] The significance of Article 40's status is thus closely linked to the binding nature of action taken by the Council under its aegis.[115]

Now, like so many other questions of Council procedure, this issue appears moot. The practice of the 1990s showed a shift away from *any* reference to the specific articles of Chapter VII and a reliance on the Chapter as a whole.

---

[111] UN Charter, art 40 (emphasis added).     [112] Higgins, above n 45, 235–6.

[113] Hans Kelsen, 'Collective Security and Collective Self-Defense Under the Charter of the United Nations' (1948) 42 *AJIL* 783. In SC Res 27 (1947) on Indonesia, the Council *called upon* parties to cease hostilities without making any determination under art 39. In SC Res 54 (1948) on Palestine, by contrast, the Council determined that a threat to the peace existed before making orders pursuant to art 40.

[114] Higgins, above n 45, 236; Thomas M Franck, 'The Security Council and "Threats to the Peace": Some Remarks on Remarkable Recent Developments', in René-Jean Dupuy (ed), *The Development of the Role of the Security Council: Peace-Keeping and Peace-Building* (Dordrecht: Martinus Nijhoff, 1993) 83, 91–5.

[115] Goodrich, Hambro, and Simons, above n 36, 305–8. There is little serious doubt now that the Security Council may make binding decisions as well as recommendations under art 40: see, eg, Frowein, above n 35, 620–1. SC Res 598 (1987) identified a breach of the peace in the Iran–Iraq war and specifically referred to arts 39 and 40; Secretary-General Boutros-Ghali has stated that peace-enforcement units for restoring and maintaining a ceasefire may find their basis in art 40: Agenda for Peace, above n 70, para 44.

## 2.2. Multiple resolutions under Chapter VII

A second preliminary question concerns whether an explicit determination
must be made on each occasion that the Council purports to act under
Chapter VII. This has arisen when the Council has passed multiple resolutions
and, rather than stating that a situation 'continues to constitute a threat to
international peace and security',[116] merely refers to a previous resolution (or
'its previous relevant resolutions') in which such a decision was made and
asserts that it is '*acting* under Chapter VII'. This was initially seen to be con-
stitutionally problematic[117] but in light of the persistence of this practice it
may be more properly viewed as a response to the increased activity of the
Council. Of the thirty Chapter VII resolutions passed in relation to Iraq after
resolution 687 (1991) until the end of 1998, only *one* stated that the situation
continued to constitute a threat to international peace and security.[118]

It could be argued that the requirement to reaffirm such a determination
would force a vote on the continuing appropriateness of Chapter VII actions
in the course of an ongoing dispute. In relation to the actions against Iraq, for
example, it is at least questionable whether the situation in 1998 did in fact
constitute a threat to international peace and security in the absence of any
belligerent activity not directed against the air exclusion zone that had been
imposed upon it (on questionable legal grounds). At the very least, it is doubtful that any such threat warranted the air strikes that took place in December
of that year. Whether the United States and the United Kingdom acted *ultra
vires* the mandate of the Security Council will be considered in the next
Chapter.[119] Nevertheless, although the policy arguments in favour of trans-
parency may be persuasive, it would be extremely difficult to argue now that
all such resolutions are *ultra vires*.

## 2.3. Security Council practice

With the exception of Iraq's invasion of Kuwait, which was determined to be
a breach of the peace,[120] it is the determination of a 'threat to international
peace and security' that has served as the trigger for Chapter VII action in the
recent period of Security Council activism. For the most part, this has been in
the form of a preambular reference *determining* that either 'the situation' or a

[116] See, eg, SC Res 933 (1994) and SC Res 940 (1994) (Haiti).

[117] See, eg, Helmut Freudenschuss, 'Article 39 of the UN Charter Revisited: Threats to the
Peace and the Recent Practice of the UN Security Council' (1993) 46 *Austrian JPIL* 1, 31.

[118] SC Res 1137 (1997). Cf SC Res 949 (1994): '*Recognizing* that any hostile or provocative
action directed against its neighbours by the Government of Iraq constitutes a threat to peace
and security in the region.'

[119] See Ch 5, Sect 4.1.                     [120] SC Res 660 (1990).

particular circumstance constitutes such a threat. These determinations are collected in Appendix 3. Examples of general statements include the initial resolutions on Liberia, Rwanda, and Angola; an example of an extraordinarily detailed determination may be seen in that concerning Libya's failure to extradite suspected terrorists.[121]

In addition, however, the Council has occasionally avoided making a determination by noting that it is '[c]oncerned that the continuation of this situation constitutes a threat to international peace and security'. Such was the terminology used in the first Chapter VII resolutions on Yugoslavia[122] and Somalia.[123] Confusingly, similar words were used in resolution 688 (1991) on Iraq's repression of its Kurdish population, though the Council did not state that it was acting under Chapter VII.[124] In resolution 770 (1992) on Bosnia and Herzegovina, the Council acted under Chapter VII after '[r]ecognizing that the situation . . . constitutes a threat to international peace and security'. Further illustrating the uncertainty of these terms, resolution 743 (1992) on Yugoslavia also stated that the Council was '[c]oncerned that the situation continues to constitute a threat to international peace and security, *as determined in resolution 713 (1991)*'.[125] Though imprecise, these resolutions were all adopted in the early years of the recent period of interventionism—it may not be an exaggeration to suggest that the Council was still experimenting with its new-found powers.

### 3. THE CHANGING DEFINITION OF A 'THREAT TO THE PEACE'

[U]ne menace pour la paix au sens de l'art 39 est une situation dont l'organe compétent pour déclencher une action de sanctions déclare qu'elle menace effectivement la paix.

Jean Combacau, 1974[126]

In a remarkable meeting on 31 January 1992, the Security Council convened for the first time at the level of heads of state and government. The members of the Council affirmed their commitment to the UN Charter system, and

---

[121] SC Res 748 (1992): '*Determining* . . . that the failure by the Libyan Government to demonstrate by concrete actions its renunciation of terrorism and in particular its continued failure to respond fully and effectively to the requests in resolution 731 (1992) constitute a threat to international peace and security.'

[122] SC Res 713 (1991).  [123] SC Res 733 (1992).

[124] Logically, there is of course no problem if the Council makes a determination under art 39 but takes no Chapter VII action: see, eg, SC Res 1078 (1996) on the Great Lakes region.

[125] SC Res 743 (1992) preamble (emphasis added).

[126] Jean Combacau, *Le pouvoir de sanction de l'ONU: Étude théorique de la coercition non militaire* (Paris: Editions A Pedone, 1974) 100 (emphasis in original) ['A threat to the peace in the sense of art 39 is a situation that the organ, competent to impose sanctions, declares to be an actual threat to the peace'].

noted the 'new favourable international circumstances' that had enabled the Council to fulfil more effectively its primary responsibility for the maintenance of international peace and security. At the same time, however, they suggested that the nature of this role was changing:

The absence of war and military conflicts amongst States does not in itself ensure international peace and security. The non-military sources of instability in the economic, social, humanitarian and ecological fields have become threats to peace and security.[127]

It is unclear whether this statement was intended to be taken literally as an indication of the Council's preparedness to use its collective security powers under Chapter VII to address those 'non-military sources of instability' that, in its collective opinion, constitute threats to peace and security justifying action under that head. Certainly, Chapter VII has been invoked in an extraordinarily wide range of circumstances since 1992. Indeed, the difficulty of establishing what substantive meaning (if any) should be attributed to a 'threat to international peace and security' has led to suggestions that such a determination is, increasingly, being treated as a formal rather than substantive hurdle.[128] This may be so, but a more fundamental difficulty in establishing the limits to this concept is the apparent link between such determinations and the political willingness to take measures in response to particular situations.

This section considers three classes of situation that have been recognized by the Security Council as constituting (at least in part) threats to international peace and security: internal armed conflicts, humanitarian crises, and disruption to democracy. Such a reconceptualization of international peace and security, it has been argued, heralds an era of greater international concern for humanitarian issues. But when one looks more closely at these and other 'new' threats to international peace and security, the plasticity of Chapter VII is suggestive of more traditional motives.

## 3.1. Internal armed conflicts

Despite the provision in the Charter that the Organization should not intervene in domestic matters, Member States find it more and more difficult to regard any conflict as domestic or internal.

Boutros Boutros-Ghali, 1992[129]

[127] Security Council Summit Statement Concerning the Council's Responsibility in the Maintenance of International Peace and Security, 47 UN SCOR (3046th mtg) UN Doc S/23500 (1992), [1992] *UNYB* 33.
[128] Cf Christopher Greenwood, 'Legal Constraints on UN Military Operations', *IISS Strategic Comments*, 22 Mar 1995.
[129] Boutros Boutros-Ghali, quoted in Franck, above n 114, 83.

The most basic transformation in the use of Security Council powers is that it now appears to be broadly accepted that a civil war or internal strife may constitute a threat to international peace and security within the meaning of Article 39. The greater preparedness of the United Nations to involve itself in internal armed conflicts is clearest in the evolution of peacekeeping operations, most of which are now deployed with mandates under Chapter VII.[130] In his *Supplement to An Agenda for Peace*, the Secretary-General noted that only one of the five ongoing peacekeeping operations in 1988 related to an intra-state conflict. Of the twenty-one operations established between then and January 1995, thirteen concerned intra-state conflicts (though some, especially those in the former Yugoslavia, also had an inter-state dimension). Of the eleven operations established between 1992 and 1995 all but two related to intra-state conflicts.[131] Although these operations are traditionally conducted only with the consent of the relevant parties, moves towards more 'muscular' peacekeeping have undermined this requirement.[132] In any case, such consent does not bear on the determination that a situation constitutes a threat to the peace.[133]

In the *Tadic* case of 1995, the Appeals Chamber of the International Criminal Tribunal for the Former Yugoslavia (ICTY) stated, in *obiter dicta*, that 'settled practice of the Security Council and the common understanding of the United Nations membership in general' established that a purely internal armed conflict could constitute a 'threat to the peace':

Indeed, the practice of the Security Council is rich with cases of civil war or internal strife which it classified as a 'threat to the peace' and dealt with under Chapter VII, with the encouragement or even at the behest of the General Assembly, such as the Congo crisis at the beginning of the 1960s and, more recently, Liberia and Somalia. It can thus be said that there is a common understanding, manifested by the 'subsequent practice' of the membership of the United Nations at large, that the 'threat to the peace' of Article 39 may include, as one of its species, internal armed conflicts.[134]

For most of the life of the United Nations, this would have been regarded as a controversial proposition indeed.[135] As indicated above, Security

---

[130] See, eg, SC Res 836 (1993):
*Acting* under Chapter VII of the Charter
*Authorizes* UNPROFOR . . . acting in self-defence, to take the necessary measures, including the use of force, in reply to bombardments against the safe areas by any of the parties or to armed incursion into them or in the event of any deliberate obstruction in or around those areas to the freedom of movement of the Force or of protected humanitarian convoys.
[131] Supplement to An Agenda for Peace, above n 101, para 11.
[132] See, eg, Mats R Berdal, 'The Security Council, Peacekeeping and Internal Conflict After the Cold War' (1996) 7 *Duke JCIL* 71, 76. See further Ch 5, Sect 3.1.
[133] *Contra* O'Connell, above n 4, 487 (discussing consent in Somalia).
[134] *Prosecutor v Tadic*, IT-94-1-AR72 (Oct 1995) para 30.
[135] See, eg, Oscar Schachter, 'The United Nations and Internal Conflict', in John Norton Moore (ed), *Law and Civil War in the Modern World* (Baltimore: Johns Hopkins University Press, 1974) 401.

Council practice in this area before 1990 was far from rich.[136] In April 1946 the Council rejected the suggestion that the Franco regime in Spain constituted a threat to the peace, noting that 'a very sharp instrument' had been entrusted to the Council, and that care should be taken that 'this instrument is not blunted or used in any way which would strain the intentions of the Charter or which would not be applicable in all similar cases'.[137] During the debate on the situation in Palestine in 1948, the United Kingdom stressed that any threat to the peace must be a threat to *international* peace,[138] though the United States took a broader approach that internal disorder could constitute a threat to the peace.[139] Relevant Security Council resolutions on the Congo crisis referred repeatedly to the presence of Belgian and other foreign military personnel and mercenaries as contributing to the threat to peace and security[140]—the General Assembly cited them as a central factor in the crisis.[141] And Western powers resisted pressure to condemn the racial policies of South Africa and Rhodesia as threats to the peace for many years—the first Chapter VII resolutions on Rhodesia in 1965 were pre-empted by its 'act of rebellion' against the United Kingdom;[142] the 1977 resolution against South Africa was primarily a response to its nuclear weapons programme.[143]

It is true, nevertheless, that the Council became more prepared to determine the existence of threats to the peace on the basis of internal conflicts in the heady new world order rhetoric that followed the successful operation against Iraq in 1991. This trend has a decidedly uncertain beginning, however, as the first resolution concerned with matters solely within the domestic jurisdiction of Iraq was the first not to be adopted specifically under Chapter VII.

### 3.1.1. *Iraqi treatment of the Kurds, 1991*

It is common to trace the recent preparedness to view internal armed conflicts as threats to the peace back to resolution 688 (1991), which addressed the repression of northern Iraq's Kurds.[144] During the military campaign against

---

[136] See Sec 1.1.

[137] UN Doc S/75, p 12, in Leland M Goodrich and Edvard Hambro, *Charter of the United Nations: Commentary and Documents* (2nd edn; London: Stevens & Sons, 1949) 266. Cf Franck, above n 114, 90–1.

[138] 3 UN SCOR (296th mtg) No 69, p 2 (UK).                    [139] Ibid 7, 10 (US).

[140] SC Res 146 (1960) para 2; SC Res 161 (1961) para 2; SC Res 169 (1961) para 4.

[141] GA Res 1599(xv) (1960) preamble. Nevertheless, as Rosalyn Higgins observed, the degree of fault on the part of Belgium was never assessed: Higgins, above n 45, 225.

[142] SC Res 217 (1965) preamble, para 1. Cf Franck, above n 114, 96.

[143] SC Res 418 (1977).

[144] See, eg, Nigel S Rodley, 'Collective Intervention to Protect Human Rights and Civilian Populations: The Legal Framework', in Nigel S Rodley (ed), *To Loose the Bands of Wickedness: International Intervention in Defence of Human Rights* (London: Brassey's, 1992) 14; Kelly K Pease and David P Forsythe, 'Human Rights, Humanitarian Intervention, and World Politics' (1993) 15 *Human Rights Quarterly* 290, 303; Cedric E Evans, 'The Concept of "Threat to Peace"

Iraq in 1991, US President George Bush publicly expressed his hope that Iraqi citizens would 'take matters into their own hands' and remove Saddam Hussein from power.[145] The apparently crushing defeat of the Iraqi army and the support of foreign leaders reignited the desire for independence among Kurds living in northern Iraq. Previous revolts by the Kurds had been brutally suppressed by Saddam Hussein's Ba'ath regime, including the use of chemical weapons against the Kurdish population.[146] On this occasion, Iraqi troops attacked Kurdish villages, forcing up to two million civilians to flee; by 5 April 1991, Turkey estimated that almost a million Kurds were attempting to reach safety by crossing its borders.[147]

Concern had been expressed about the treatment of the Kurds in northern Iraq and the Shiites and Marsh Arabs in the south at the Council meeting on 3 April 1991. This was the meeting that had adopted resolution 687 (1991), providing for the terms of the ceasefire with Iraq but conspicuously failing to mention the plight of Iraq's civilian population.[148] Two days later, the Council passed resolution 688 (1991). On the basis of this resolution, the United States issued a warning to Iraq on 10 April that any military activity north of the 36th parallel would be met with force. Reversing his previous policy, President Bush committed US troops to set up encampments in northern Iraq to ensure the safety of Kurdish refugees and co-ordinate relief supplies.[149] Allied troops remained in Iraq until 15 July as part of Operation Provide Comfort; the military exclusion zone later became the northern no-fly zone, extended in August 1992 to apply also to Iraqi territory south of the 32nd parallel.

The legality of the measures taken under resolution 688 will be discussed further in Chapter 5.[150] With regard to its significance as an instance in which the Council was prepared to view internal strife as a threat to international peace and security, however, resolution 688 is a dubious precedent for two reasons. First, this was the fourteenth Security Council resolution following

---

and Humanitarian Concerns: Probing the Limits of Chapter VII of the UN Charter' (1995) 5 *Transnational Law and Contemporary Problems* 213, 224; Richard B Lillich, 'The Role of the UN Security Council in Protecting Human Rights in Crisis Situations: UN Humanitarian Intervention in the Post-Cold War World' (1995) 3 *Tulane JICL* 1, 7; O'Connell, above n 4, 484.

[145] See Ch 5, Sect 4.1.

[146] See Editorial, 'Poison Gas: Iraq's Crime', *NYT*, 26 Mar 1988. Howard Adelman, 'Humanitarian Intervention: The Case of the Kurds' (1992) 4 *International Journal of Refugee Law* 4.

[147] S/PV.2982 (1991) 6 (Turkey).

[148] France proposed to include a paragraph demanding an end to the repressive measures, but this was opposed by the US and the UK (who feared a delay in adopting resolution 687) as well as by the USSR and China: Freudenschuss, above n 117, 6. See also S/PV.2981 (1991) 94 (France). For the political consequences in the US, see Thomas L Friedman, 'Decision Not to Help Iraqi Rebels Puts US in an Awkward Position', *NYT*, 4 Apr 1991.

[149] *Keesing's* (1991) 38127. Bush's statement came on 16 Apr 1991.

[150] See Ch 5, Sect 4.1.

the Iraqi invasion of Kuwait, but the first that failed to state explicitly or implicitly[151] that the Council was acting under Chapter VII of the Charter. It was also the first resolution expressly to recall Article 2(7) of the UN Charter. This was inserted by France after it became clear that an earlier draft resolution (which also made no reference to Chapter VII) did not have the support of nine Council members.[152] British officials readily admitted that it was not a Chapter VII resolution, but asserted nonetheless that the establishment of an air exclusion zone was justified in pursuance of the *objects* expressed in resolution 688 (1991) or perhaps under an independent customary international law right of humanitarian intervention.[153]

Secondly, where the Council did refer to the threat to international peace and security, this was very clearly restricted to the transboundary effects of the situation.[154] The preamble referred to the Council's grave concern at

the repression of the Iraqi civilian population in many parts of Iraq, including most recently in Kurdish populated areas, which led to a massive flow of refugees towards and across international frontiers and to cross-border incursions, *which threaten* international peace and security in the region.[155]

The use of the plural verb form 'threaten' makes it clear that it was the two consequences (flow of refugees, cross-border incursions) that were the threat to international security. This was repeated in the operative paragraphs: the Council condemned 'the repression of the Iraqi civilian population . . . *the consequences of which threaten* international peace and security in the region'.[156] These changes appear to have been necessary to secure the support of the USSR, Romania, and Ecuador, as well as the abstention of China.[157] With the exception of France, which sponsored the resolution, every other state that voted in favour of the resolution made statements stressing the international repercussions of Iraq's repression of its civilian population in the flows of refugees to neighbouring states.[158] France alone asserted that '[v]iolations of human rights such as those now being observed become a mat-

---

[151] SC Res 665 (1990) provided for implementation of SC Res 661 (1990), in which the Council decided 'to impose economic sanctions under Chapter VII'; SC Res 669 (1990) referred specifically to art 50 of the Charter. By contrast, SC Res 688 (1991) did not even refer to previous resolutions.

[152] S/22442 (1991). See Freudenschuss, above n 117, 7.

[153] This is discussed further in Ch 5, Sect 4.1.2.

[154] This was accurately predicted in Oscar Schachter, 'United Nations Law in the Gulf Conflict' (1991) 85 *AJIL* 452, 469. See also Peter Malanczuck, *Humanitarian Intervention and the Legitimacy of the Use of Force* (Dordrecht: Martinus Nijhoff, 1993) 17–18; Lois E Fielding, 'Taking a Closer Look at Threats to Peace: The Power of the Security Council to Address Humanitarian Crises' (1996) 73 *University of Detroit Mercy Law Review* 551, 566.

[155] SC Res 688 (1991) preamble (emphasis added).        [156] Ibid para 1 (emphasis added).

[157] Freudenschuss, above n 117, 7.

[158] S/PV.2982 (1991) 22-3 (Romania), 36 (Ecuador), 38 (Zaïre), 41 (Côte d'Ivoire), 56 (Austria), 58 (US), 61 (USSR), 64-5 (UK), 67 (Belgium).

ter of international interest when they take on such proportions that they assume the dimension of a crime against humanity'.[159]

Even so, it was the most controversial and least-supported resolution on Iraq, adopted by ten votes to three (Cuba, Yemen, Zimbabwe) with two abstentions (China, India). Yemen and Zimbabwe argued that the Council was using the flow of refugees across Iraq's borders as a cover to justify a threat to peace determination that in fact rested upon matters solely within Iraq's domestic jurisdiction.[160] They did not deny that Iraq was repressing its Kurdish population, or that refugees were in fact flowing across Iraq's borders into Turkey and Iran, but argued that some UN organ other than the Security Council should provide the refugees with assistance.[161] Cuba stated that the resolution was an unjustified intervention in the internal affairs of Iraq; while it did not deny the humanitarian crisis, it pointed to newspaper reports only the previous day that President Bush had authorized the CIA to aid rebel factions in Iraq.[162]

### 3.1.2. *Yugoslavia, 1991*

A more promising example of internal armed conflict constituting a threat to international peace and security may be found in Yugoslavia prior to its dissolution in 1991–2. The fact that the threat related precisely to this impending dissolution, however, renders suspect claims that it stands for a general principle of Security Council involvement in such conflicts.

Between June and October 1991, four of the six republics comprising Yugoslavia declared their independence. Croatia and Slovenia first made unilateral declarations on 25 June 1991 after internal referenda—war broke out almost immediately.[163] In the early months of the fighting, the European Community (EC) played a leading role; when it was unable to secure a ceasefire by mid-September, Austria, Canada, and Hungary requested that the Security Council convene to consider the situation.[164] The Council adopted resolution 713 (1991), in which it expressed its concern that the 'continuation of this situation constitutes a threat to international peace and security'[165] and imposed an arms embargo under Chapter VII.[166] Only Yugoslavia's consent to the resolution avoided a Chinese veto,[167] though this did not affect the need for a determination under Article 39. A month later, Bosnia and Herzegovina proclaimed its sovereignty by assembly vote on 15 October.[168] Ceasefires were brokered and broken, and on 15 December the Council adopted resolution 724 (1991), in which it strengthened the Chapter VII arms

159 S/PV.2982 (1991) 53 (France).
160 Ibid 27-31 (Yemen), 31-32 (Zimbabwe).
161 Ibid 27 (Yemen), 31-32 (Zimbabwe).
162 Ibid 43 (Cuba), citing *NYT*, 4 Apr 1991.
163 *Keesing's* (1991) 38373.
164 [1991] *UNYB* 214.
165 SC Res 713 (1991) preamble.
166 Ibid para 6.
167 S/PV.3009 (1991) 49-51 (China).
168 *Keesing's* (1991) 38513.

embargo and sought to lay the ground for a peacekeeping operation.[169] December also saw the EC agree in principle to recognizing the independence of the Yugoslav republics,[170] with Germany formally recognizing Croatia and Slovenia on 23 December and the EC following suit on 15 January 1992.[171] Bosnia and Herzegovina conducted a referendum and proclaimed its formal independence on 3 March 1992.[172] On 22 May 1992 Croatia, Slovenia, and Bosnia and Herzegovina were admitted as member states of the United Nations.[173]

From this point there is little question that the conflict was international.[174] Before May 1992—and certainly in September 1991—however, it was questionable whether any threat to peace and security extended beyond the borders of Yugoslavia. In resolution 713 (1991) the Council referred to two elements that supported its initial statement that the situation constituted a threat to international peace and security:[175] the 'heavy loss of human life and material damage, and . . . the consequences for the countries of the region, in particular the border areas of neighbouring countries'.[176] Given that the border-area issue was, at best, a minor one, it is arguable that the Security Council was asserting its ability to intervene in a purely internal conflict. Nevertheless, it is clear that the Council was wary of making such a far-reaching reinterpretation of its Charter role, at least for the moment.[177] In this regard, it is also noteworthy that the Council's reference to Chapter VII was confined to the operative paragraph in which it imposed the arms embargo.[178] This was to become a theme in other controversial resolutions of the early 1990s.

### 3.1.3. Liberia, 1990–2[179]

An often-overlooked example of the Security Council invoking Chapter VII powers in what was arguably an internal armed conflict is Liberia in 1990.[180]

---

[169] SC Res 724 (1991) paras 5, 2–4.               [170] *Keesing's* (1991) 38684.
[171] Ibid (1992) 38703.                              [172] Ibid (1992) 38832.
[173] GA Res 46/236 (1992) (Slovenia); GA Res 46/237 (1992) (Bosnia and Herzegovina); GA Res 46/238 (1992) (Croatia).
[174] See *Prosecutor v Tadic*, IT-94-1-AR72 (October 1995) paras 72–8 (concluding that the conflict comprised both internal and international elements).
[175] Interestingly, the Council stated in the preamble to SC Res 743 (1992) that Resolution 713 (1991) had 'determined' that the situation constituted a threat to international peace and security.
[176] SC Res 713 (1991) preamble.                    [177] Cf O'Connell, above n 4, 486.
[178] SC Res 713 (1991) para 6.
[179] See generally Anthony Chukwuka Ofodile, 'The Legality of ECOWAS Intervention in Liberia' (1994) 32 *Columbia JTL* 381; Abiodun Alao, *The Burden of Collective Goodwill: The International Involvement in the Liberian Civil War* (Aldershot: Ashgate, 1998); Mark Huband, *The Liberian Civil War* (London: Frank Cass, 1998).
[180] See, eg, Helmut Freudenschuss, 'Between Unilateralism and Collective Security: Authorizations of the Use of Force by the UN Security Council' (1994) 5 *European JIL* 492; Evans, above n 144; O'Connell, above n 4.

This was an unusual incident in that the relevant resolutions were largely retrospective—and, arguably, retroactive—with the first Chapter VII resolution not being passed until November 1992.

The conflict began in late 1989, when former minister Charles Taylor organized a rebel force in Côte d'Ivoire and invaded Liberia in an attempt to oust the unpopular President Samuel Doe, who had come to power after a *coup* ten years earlier. Civil war quickly broke out between Taylor's National Patriotic Front of Liberia (NPFL) and Doe's Armed Forces of Liberia (AFL),[181] and was increasingly fought along ethnic lines.[182] By July 1990 Taylor's NPFL appeared close to ousting Doe when a splinter group of the NPFL, the Independent National Patriotic Front of Liberia (INPFL), led by Prince Yormie Johnson joined the fray.[183] By August the conflict was thought to have claimed 5,000 lives and caused 500,000 refugees to flee Liberia, with a further million displaced persons within Liberia—this amounted to 60 per cent of Liberia's population of 2.5 million.[184] The United States launched an operation to evacuate US and other foreign nationals, but took no action with respect to the larger crisis.[185]

In the absence of UN or OAU action, the Economic Community of West African States (ECOWAS)[186] called on the warring parties to observe an immediate ceasefire and established the ECOWAS Cease-fire Monitoring Group (ECOMOG), with the purpose of 'keeping the peace, restoring law and order and ensuring that the cease-fire is respected'.[187] The 4,000-strong force comprised 3,000 Nigerians and smaller contingents from Ghana, the Gambia, Guinea, and Sierra Leone.[188] ECOMOG arrived in Monrovia after just two weeks' preparation and clashed with Taylor's forces within two days. Although nominally a 'peacekeeping' force, ECOMOG was responsible for the first use of aerial bombing in the war; its aggressive interpretation of its role appears to have been instrumental in bringing the warring factions to the negotiating table in November 1990.[189] A ceasefire was agreed, though sporadic fighting continued and support from Taylor to rebels in neighbouring Sierra Leone

---

[181] See Sean D Murphy, *Humanitarian Intervention: The United Nations in an Evolving World Order* (Philadelphia: University of Pennsylvania Press, 1996) 146–7; *Keesing's* (1990) 37174.

[182] Kenneth B Noble, 'From Liberian War, Tales of Brutality', *NYT*, 9 July 1990.

[183] *Keesing's* (1990) 37601.      [184] Ibid 37644.

[185] For a discussion of this as an incident of protection of nationals abroad, see Richard B Lillich, 'Forcible Protection of Nationals Abroad: The Liberian "Incident" of 1990' (1992) 35 *German Yearbook of International Law* 205.

[186] ECOWAS was established in 1975 and comprises sixteen states: Benin, Burkina Faso, Cape Verde, Côte d'Ivoire, The Gambia, Ghana, Guinea, Guinea-Bissau, Liberia, Mali, Mauritania, Niger, Nigeria, Senegal, Sierra Leone, and Togo.

[187] ECOWAS Standing Mediation Committee, Final Communiqué of the First Session, 7 Aug 1990, para 11, in Marc Weller (ed), *Regional Peace-Keeping and International Enforcement: The Liberian Crisis* (Cambridge International Document Series; Cambridge: Cambridge University Press, 1994) 73.

[188] Murphy, above n 181, 151.

[189] Kenneth B Noble, 'Liberian Factions Agree to a Cease-fire', *NYT*, 29 Nov 1990.

sparked its own civil war.[190] After a series of four meetings in Côte d'Ivoire, the Yamoussoukro IV Accord was adopted in October 1991.[191] This provided for the disarmament of the warring factions and the organization of elections under the supervision of foreign observers by April 1992.[192] Due in large part to the non-compliance of Taylor's NPFL, the agreement failed and fighting resumed in earnest in August 1992—including the emergence of the United Liberation Movement of Liberia for Democracy (ULIMO), loyal to the memory of President Doe who had died after being captured by the INPFL.[193]

ECOWAS had previously sought the United Nation's understanding, if not support, for its operations.[194] The Security Council's first involvement was a statement made in January 1991, 5 months after ECOMOG entered the conflict. That intervention had led to a ceasefire and the President of the Council had 'commend[ed]' the ECOWAS efforts to promote peace in Liberia and called upon all parties to the conflict to respect the ceasefire agreement.[195] It was not until November 1992, however, that the Council itself determined that the 'deterioration of the situation in Liberia constitutes a threat to international peace and security, particularly in West Africa as a whole'.[196] In the discussion that accompanied the passage of resolution 788 (1992), however, there was little reference to the transboundary effects of the conflict.[197] Representatives focused on the protracted civil war, the number of displaced persons (as well as refugees), and the humanitarian crisis attendant to these problems. Once again, reference to Chapter VII was confined to the operative paragraph imposing the arms embargo.[198]

The Council thus became involved after the fact. An attempt to bring the matter before the Security Council in May 1990 had been frustrated by Zaïre, reportedly due to fears that intervention in Liberia might serve as precedent for other interventions in Africa.[199] When the conflict became more pronounced in August 1990, the Council was occupied with the Iraq–Kuwait issue.

The legal basis for ECOMOG's intervention (if any) is therefore unclear. Certainly more than a 'peacekeeping' mission, it in any case did not enjoy the consent of the Liberian factions. Samuel Doe, then recognized as head of government, would have welcomed assistance in suppressing the insurgency but ECOMOG sought to replace him as President. The interim President, Amos Sawyer, did support the intervention, but his was a government created by

---

[190] Kenneth B Noble, 'Liberian Conflict Engulfs Neighbor', *NYT*, 16 Apr 1991.

[191] Yamoussoukro IV Accord, 30 Oct 1991, S/24815.     [192] [1992] *UNYB* 191.

[193] *Keesing's* (1992) 39041; Kenneth B Noble, 'Liberian Insurgents Kill President, Diplomats and Broadcasts Report', *NYT* 11 Sept 1990.

[194] S/21485 (1990); Alao, above n 179, 103–4.

[195] S/22133 (1991); Murphy, above n 181, 153.     [196] SC Res 788 (1992) preamble.

[197] S/PV.3138 (1992) 61 (Zimbabwe), 87 (India).

[198] SC Res 788 (1992) para 8.     [199] Alao, above n 179, 101.

and dependent on the ECOMOG forces themselves. Nor was there any basis in ECOWAS law for such an operation.[200]

It is interesting to speculate as to whether it was ECOMOG's involvement itself that transformed the situation into a truly 'international' threat. Resolution 788 (1992), which imposed a mandatory arms embargo,[201] elaborated the Council's determination that 'deterioration of the situation in Liberia constitutes a threat to international peace and security, *particularly in West Africa as a whole*'.[202] This, combined with its implicit endorsement of the peacekeeping efforts of ECOMOG[203]—and the ambiguous preambular recollection of 'the provisions of Chapter VIII'—further confuses the legal status of the ECOMOG action.

It seems likely that such regional intervention, supported by ambiguous Council authorization, will become more common in the future. The Council's response to the situation in Liberia finds parallels in its response to ECOMOG's further adventures in Sierra Leone[204] and France's involvement in the Central African Republic.[205] NATO's operations against the FRY in 1999 may be seen as the natural extension of this trend.[206]

### 3.1.4. Angola, 1992–

Fighting broke out in Angola in late 1992 after the National Union for the Total Independence of Angola (UNITA) refused to accept the validity of the 1992 multi-party elections. (The conflict was, of course, much older.) Peace negotiations resulted in a Memorandum of Understanding and the adoption of a ceasefire. The Security Council extended the mission of the second UN Angola Verification Mission (UNAVEM II), established in 1991, six times.[207] Resolutions passed early in 1993 mentioned the Council's concern at reports of foreign support for and involvement in military actions within Angola,[208] but were primarily directed at the humanitarian crisis that was unfolding.[209] On 25 May 1993 the Secretary-General reported that fighting throughout the country had intensified, causing a humanitarian disaster further aggravated by the recent drought in southern Africa. According to World Food Program estimates, nearly two million Angolans were suffering from hunger and disease, with at least 1,000 dying daily.[210]

The Security Council unanimously adopted resolutions in June and July expressing grave concern at the deteriorating situation and condemning

---

[200] See Murphy, above n 181, 160–1.
[202] Ibid preamble (emphasis added).
[203] Ibid para 1, in which the Council '[c]ommends ECOWAS for its efforts to restore peace, security and stability in Liberia'.
[204] See Sect 3.3.2.
[206] See Ch 5, Sect 4.2.
[208] SC Res 804 (1993) preamble, para 9.
[210] S/25840 & Add 1; [1993] *UNYB* 251.

[201] SC Res 788 (1992) para 8.

[205] See Sect 3.1.5.
[207] [1993] *UNYB* 246.
[209] SC Res 811 (1993) preamble, para 11.

UNITA for its continued military actions.[211] The war intensified through September and the three observer states (Portugal, Russian Federation, United States) recommended that the Council propose measures to undercut UNITA's ability to pursue war and make it resume negotiations.[212] On 15 September the Council unanimously adopted resolution 864 (1993), which determined, for the first time, 'that, as a result of UNITA's military actions, the situation in Angola constitutes a threat to international peace and security',[213] and imposing a mandatory oil and arms embargo against UNITA.[214]

This was an unusually clear instance of the Council intervening under Chapter VII in a civil war. Most remarkable, however, is the Council's treatment of a non-state entity as the object of a Chapter VII resolution. Though it is common now for the Council to call upon various parties to an internal dispute to resolve a dispute peacefully, this was the first occasion on which it used its mandatory powers in this way. For present purposes, however, the Council's Chapter VII involvement was limited to the imposition of sanctions against UNITA. The adoption of the Lusaka Protocol in 1994 raised hopes of a peaceful resolution to the civil war, but UNITA's failure to comply fully with the Lusaka Protocol led to further sanctions in October 1997.[215]

### 3.1.5. *Central African Republic, 1996–8*

In a fashion comparable to its response to the Liberian civil war, the Security Council in 1997 gave its blessing to foreign intervention in the suppression of a rebellion in the Central African Republic (CAR). After a series of army mutinies, French soldiers were deployed in the CAR between April and November 1996—in theory to protect foreign nationals, though widely understood to be providing military support to troops loyal to President Ange-Felix Patasse.[216]

In accordance with the Bangui Agreements, concluded in the CAR capital on 25 January 1997, French troops were replaced by troops from Burkina Faso, Chad, Gabon, Mali, Senegal, and Togo taking part in the Inter-African Mission to Monitor the Implementation of the Bangui Agreements (MISAB).[217] France continued to provide the main logistical and financial support for its operations. Sporadic fighting continued until a ceasefire was agreed on 2 July.[218]

It was not until August that the Security Council adopted its first resolution on the matter. Resolution 1125 (1997) determined that the situation

---

[211] SC Res 834 (1993); SC Res 851 (1993).                    [212] S/26448; [1993] *UN YB* 255.
[213] SC Res 864 (1993) B, preamble.
[214] SC Res 864 (1993) para 19; *Keesing's* (1993) 39623.           [215] Ibid (1997) 41850.
[216] Ibid (1996) 41353. For a discussion of France's involvement in a previous CAR *coup*, see Ch 2, Sect 2.3.9.
[217] UN Press Release SC/6407 (6 Aug 1997); *Keesing's* (1997) 41481.           [218] Ibid 41760.

constituted a threat to international peace and security in the region. Unlike the more ambiguous resolution on Liberia, however, the Council specifically approved 'the continued conduct by member states participating in MISAB of the operation in a neutral and impartial way to achieve its objective to facilitate the return to peace and security'.[219] Acting under Chapter VII, it then authorized 'the Member States participating in MISAB and those States providing logistical support [*sc* France] to ensure the security and freedom of movement of their personnel' for a period of three months.[220] This was interpreted at the time as an authorization for MISAB troops to use force if necessary.[221]

A series of resolutions extended MISAB's mandate until 15 April 1998, when it was replaced by the UN Mission in the Central African Republic (MINURCA) with a view to assisting national forces in maintaining order and preparing for elections.[222]

### 3.1.6. Internal armed conflict as a threat to peace and security

It now seems uncontroversial that internal strife may constitute a threat to international peace and security sufficient to justify action under Chapter VII. Despite the uncertain beginnings with the ambiguous resolutions on Iraq and Yugoslavia, which ostensibly relied heavily on the transboundary effects of internal strife, by the time the Security Council considered the civil war in Angola it was prepared to locate such a threat specifically in the actions of a rebel movement. As in the case of Council action in Liberia and the CAR, however, the consent of the recognized government was significant in establishing the political will to support Chapter VII action.

It would, of course, be idealistic in the extreme to assume that the Council's determination of a threat to peace and security would be entirely objective. Nevertheless, the political process of gauging the preparedness of states to act now commonly precedes any authorization on the part of the Security Council. This is particularly true in the Council's response to humanitarian crises.

---

[219] SC Res 1125 (1997) para 2. This was to be done 'by monitoring the implementation of the Bangui Agreements . . . including through the supervision of the surrendering of arms of former mutineers, militias and all other persons unlawfully bearing arms'.

[220] SC Res 1125 (1997) paras 3–4.

[221] *Keesing's* (1997) 41760. See, eg, 'UN authorizes force "if necessary" by troops in Central African Republic', Agence France Presse English Wire, 6 Aug 1997.

[222] SC Res 1136 (1997); SC Res 1152 (1998); SC Res 1155 (1998); SC Res 1159 (1998). MINURCA's mandate was periodically extended until 15 Feb 2000: see SC Res 1271 (1999).

### 3.2. Humanitarian crises

The nature of the Security Council's power under Chapter VII is such that it is unlikely to be invoked in response to a humanitarian crisis unless it occurs in a time of conflict. There is, therefore, a necessary overlap between these two categories (as seen, for example, in the tension between resolutions 687 and 688 on Iraq[223]). Though the Council appeared to have resolved this dilemma when it came to address the situation in Somalia—asserting that the 'magnitude of the human tragedy' warranted Chapter VII action—the difficulties in backing up this rhetoric with action subsequently made it more cautious. Rwanda was probably a casualty of such caution. By 1996 the Council was more circumspect. In relation to the crisis in eastern Zaïre, two resolutions were passed within six days. In the first, the Council determined that the 'magnitude of the present humanitarian crisis' constituted a threat to international peace and security, but did not act under Chapter VII.[224] In the second, the Council made a more general reference to 'the present situation', and did.[225]

### 3.2.1. Somalia, 1992–3

In the power vacuum that followed the January 1991 ousting of President Mohammed Siad Barre—Somalia's leader for 21 years—Somalia imploded into clan-based civil war.[226] Talks held in Djibouti in June and July 1991 led to the Djibouti Accords and the appointment of Ali Mahdi Mohamed as Interim President, but the leader of a rival faction, General Mohamed Farah Aideed [Aydid, Aidid], rejected the Accords and heavy fighting persisted in the capital Mogadishu [Mogadiscio] from November 1991.[227] On 16 January 1992 the International Committee of the Red Cross (ICRC) reported that hundreds of thousands of refugees from the conflict were on the brink of starvation in camps south of the capital. The office of the UN High Commissioner for Refugees (UNHCR) reported on 31 January that 140,000 Somali refugees had reached Kenya, with another 700 arriving each day.[228]

As in the case of the Council's first Chapter VII resolution on Yugoslavia,[229] resolution 733 (1992), also adopted unanimously, based its *concern* that the situation in Somalia constituted a threat to international peace and security on the 'heavy loss of human life and widespread material damage resulting from the conflict ... and ... its consequences on the stability and peace in [*sic*] the region'.[230] It is possible that the flow of refugees was a relevant 'conse-

[223] See Sect 3.1.1.          [224] SC Res 1078 (1996).          [225] SC Res 1080 (1996).
[226] See John Drysdale, *Whatever Happened to Somalia* (London: Haan Associates, 1994) 27–38.
[227] [1992] *UNYB* 198–9.          [228] *Keesing's* (1992) 38711.
[229] SC Res 713 (1991).          [230] SC Res 733 (1992) preamble.

quence', but this term was not elucidated in the resolution, which was itself adopted without formal discussion.[231] It also confined reference to Chapter VII to the operative paragraph imposing the arms embargo.[232]

By March, an effective ceasefire was yet to be implemented. In light of the immediate threat posed by severe food shortages to a large proportion of Somalia's population, the Secretary-General reported that implementation of the planned relief programme should go ahead, with the consequences of obstructing it made unmistakably clear to the leaders of the two factions.[233] On 17 March 1992 the Security Council unanimously adopted resolution 746 (1992), which—though not acting under Chapter VII—stated that the Council was '[d]*eeply disturbed* by the magnitude of the human suffering caused by the conflict and concerned that the continuation of the situation in Somalia constitutes a threat to international peace and security'.[234] In the discussion on resolution 746 (1992), the Council's primary concern appears to have been the effect of the war on the provision of humanitarian assistance to the starving population, with only passing reference to the massive flow of refugees[235] and non-intervention.[236]

The situation continued to deteriorate through 1992. UNOSOM, deployed with the consent of the two leading factions in Mogadishu in April,[237] was unable to implement its mandate due to the absence of a governing authority capable of maintaining law and order, and the failure of the various factions to co-operate.[238] The provision of 3,500 UNOSOM security personnel for the protection of humanitarian relief efforts was approved in August,[239] but deployment was slow and the situation deteriorated by the day.[240] By October 1992 the Secretary-General reported that almost 4.5 million of Somalia's 6 million population were threatened by severe malnutrition and related diseases. Of those, at least 1.5 million were at immediate mortal risk. An estimated 300,000 had died in the 11 months from November 1991.[241]

On 29 November the Secretary-General advised the Council that the only way in which relief operations could continue was through resort to enforcement provisions under Chapter VII of the Charter, combined with parallel action to promote national reconciliation to remove the main factors that created the human emergency.[242] This recommendation came four days after an offer from the United States to provide 20,000 troops as part of a multinational force authorized by the United Nations,[243] due in large part to the

---

[231] S/PV.3039 (1992).  [232] SC Res 733 (1992) para 5.
[233] S/23693 & Corr.1; [1992] *UNYB* 200–1.
[234] SC Res 746 (1992) preamble. This was repeated in SC Res 751 (1992) preamble, and with minor changes in SC Res 767 (1992) preamble.
[235] S/PV.3060 (1992) 41 (Austria).  [236] S/PV.3060 (1992) 43-44 (China), 52 (Ecuador).
[237] SC Res 751 (1992).  [238] [1992] *UNYB* 208.
[239] S/24480 & Add 1; SC Res 775 (1992); [1992] *UNYB* 206–7.
[240] *Keesing's* (1992) 39181–2. By November 1992, only 500 troops had arrived.
[241] [1992] *UNYB* 593; A/47/553.  [242] S/24868 (1992); [1992] *UNYB* 208.
[243] *Keesing's* (1992) 39218.

unprecedented exposure given to the humanitarian disaster in Somalia by the US media.[244]

On 3 December 1992 the Council unanimously adopted resolution 794 (1992). Though recognizing the 'unique character' of the situation, it stated that the Council,

*Determining* that the magnitude of the human tragedy caused by the conflict in Somalia, further exacerbated by the obstacles being created to the distribution of humanitarian assistance, constitutes a threat to international peace and security, . . .

10. *Acting* under Chapter VII . . . *authorizes* the Secretary-General and Member States cooperating to implement the offer [by the United States to organize and lead an operation] to use all necessary means to establish as soon as possible a secure environment for humanitarian relief operations in Somalia.[245]

Twenty-four hours later, US President George Bush ordered 28,000 troops into Somalia in Operation Restore Hope (also known as UNITAF) to ensure the safe delivery of international aid.[246] US Marines landed on 9 December 1992, with live television links back to the United States.[247]

The primary concern of the Security Council as expressed in statements before and after the vote was the delivery of humanitarian aid. In explanation of its vote on the resolution, the United States stressed the essentially peaceful and limited character of the operation, but stated that the action represented an important step towards a 'post-Cold War world order'.[248] China—which had cast its first affirmative vote for an enforcement resolution—and other non-aligned states emphasized the unique character of the crisis and the role given to the Secretary-General and the Security Council.[249] The Secretary-General later stated that the Security Council had 'established a precedent in the history of the United Nations: it decided for the first time to intervene militarily for strictly humanitarian purposes'.[250]

---

[244] See, eg, Walter Goodman, 'Re Somalia: How Much Did TV Shape Policy?', *NYT*, 8 Dec 1992; Linda Melvern, *The Ultimate Crime: Who Betrayed the UN and Why* (London: Allison & Busby, 1995) 320–1; Walter Clarke, 'Failed Visions and Uncertain Mandates in Somalia', in Walter Clarke and Jeffrey Herbst (eds), *Learning from Somalia: The Lessons of Armed Humanitarian Intervention* (Boulder: Westview, 1997) 3, 8–9; Harry Johnston and Ted Dagne, 'Congress and the Somalia Crisis', in Clarke and Herbst, above, 191, 195–6. On the role of the media in humanitarian crises more generally, see Larry Minear, Colin Scott, and Thomas G Weiss, *The News Media, Civil War, and Humanitarian Action* (Boulder: Lynne Rienner, 1996); Robert I Rotberg and Thomas G Weiss (eds), *From Massacres to Genocide: The Media, Public Policy, and Humanitarian Crises* (Washington, DC: Brookings Institution, 1996).

[245] SC Res 794 (1992).

[246] *Keesing's* (1992) 39225.

[247] George F Kennan, 'Somalia, Through a Glass Darkly', *NYT*, 30 Sept 1993.

[248] S/PV.3145 (1992) 36 (US).

[249] S/PV.3145 (1992) 7 (Zimbabwe), 12-13 (Ecuador), 16-18 (China), 46 (Morocco), 49-50 (India). See also Freudenschuss, above n 180, 514, noting the insertion of the relevant phrases in the draft resolution.

[250] [1993] *UNYB* 51.

Subsequent evaluations of the UNITAF mission suggest that the Council's primary concern was indeed humanitarian,[251] if not necessarily wise.[252] On 4 May 1993, the United States formally turned over the operation to an expanded UNOSOM (UNOSOM II), but it was unable to fulfil the expanded mandate that included 'nation-building' projects such as disarming the factions and arresting faction leaders such as General Aideed.[253] Twenty-four Pakistani soldiers were killed on 5 June while inspecting weapons dumps in accordance with the expanded mandate under resolution 814 (1993).[254] The next day the Security Council passed resolution 837 (1993), 'reaffirming' that the Secretary-General was authorized to 'take all necessary measures against those responsible for the armed attacks . . . to establish the effective authority of UNOSOM II throughout Somalia, including to secure the investigation of their actions and their arrest and detention for prosecution, trial and punishment'.[255]

This was tantamount to a declaration of war against Aideed's militia.[256] A series of confrontations between a heavily reinforced UNOSOM II and Aideed's militia continued through the summer, culminating in the 'Olympic Hotel battle' on 3 October when US Rangers and Delta commandos made an unsuccessful attempt to capture Aideed. Three US Black Hawk helicopters were downed and eighteen Americans died, as did one of the Malaysians who came to extract them. At least 500 and as many as 1,000 Somalis—many of them civilians—were killed in the firefight.[257] The image of a dead US pilot being dragged through the streets before jeering crowds of onlookers became an enduring image of the conflict, and a key symptom of what became known as the 'Somalia syndrome'.[258]

The United States withdrew its peacekeeping forces in March 1994, at which time the UN mission contracted to focus on food relief and distribution. The Security Council voted gradually to withdraw UNOSOM. The last Pakistani UN peacekeepers left on 4 March 1995, escorted by 1,800 US marines.[259]

[251] See, eg, Peter H Kooijmans, 'The Enlargement of the Concept "Threat to the Peace" ', in Dupuy, above n 114, 111, 115; Evans, above n 144, 229; Andrew S Natsios, 'Humanitarian Relief Intervention in Somalia: The Economics of Chaos', in Clarke and Herbst, above n 244, 77, 78.
[252] For various perspectives on the merits of Operation Restore Hope, see the essays collected in Clarke and Herbst, above n 244.
[253] See SC Res 814 (1993).
[254] See John Drysdale, 'Foreign Military Intervention in Somalia: The Root Cause of the Shift from UN Peacekeeping to Peacemaking and Its Consequences', in Clarke and Herbst, above n 244, 118, 132.
[255] SC Res 837 (1993) para 5.          [256] Drysdale, above n 254, 132.
[257] See generally Mark Bowden, *Black Hawk Down: A Story of Modern War* (New York: Atlantic Monthly Press, 1999).
[258] Melvern, above n 244, 328–30; Drysdale, above n 254, 132–3.
[259] Fernando R Tesón, *Humanitarian Intervention: An Inquiry into Law and Morality* (2nd edn; Dobbs Ferry, NY: Transnational Publishers, 1997) 244.

### 3.2.2. Rwanda, 1994[260]

The failure of the international community to respond to the genocide that unfolded in Rwanda in April 1994 gave the lie to the increased activism of the Security Council. Though its roots lay in Rwanda's colonial past and a civil war that first flared in October 1990,[261] the crisis was ignited by a surface-to-air missile that shot down the plane carrying Rwandan President Juvénal Habyarimana and his Burundian counterpart, Cyprien Ntaryamira.[262] Portrayed in Western media as a 'tribal conflict' between the majority Hutu and minority Tutsi,[263] the violence was more properly understood as a brutal attempt by the Hutu-dominated Rwandan military to eradicate its opposition. Fighting broke out within hours; by the end of the next day militant Hutus had killed Prime Minister Agathe Uwilingiyimana and seized control of the government, claiming that Habyarimana had been assassinated by Tutsi rebels. This provoked rampages against Tutsis and moderate Hutus by security forces and armed gangs loyal to the government. Most notorious of the killers were the *Interahamwe* [Those Who Stand Together] and *Impuzamugambi* [The Single-Minded Ones]—predominantly Hutu militias trained by the national army and organized as the youth wings of the major Hutu parties.[264] The Rwandan Patriotic Front (RPF), led by Paul Kagame, recommenced its civil war with the Rwandan Government, but claims that the Tutsi-led RPF committed systematic reprisals against Hutus were unsubstantiated.[265]

The brutality of the conflict was only heightened by the simplicity of the weapons with which it was fought—*pangas* [machete-like agricultural tools] and sharpened sticks. Early UN reports played down the scale of the carnage,[266] but by the end of May, the Secretary-General reported that between 250,000 and 500,000 Rwandans, mostly Tutsi, had been killed. He concluded that

the magnitude of the human calamity that has engulfed Rwanda might be unimaginable but for its having transpired. On the basis of the evidence that has emerged, there can be little doubt that it constitutes genocide.[267]

---

[260] See generally Gérard Prunier, *The Rwanda Crisis: History of a Genocide* (New York: Columbia University Press, 1997); Philip Gourevitch, *We Wish to Inform You that Tomorrow We Will Be Killed with Our Families* (London: Picador, 1999). See also the Report of the Independent Inquiry into the Actions of the United Nations during the 1994 Genocide in Rwanda, UN Doc S/1999/1257 (1999), Annex.

[261] This was fought between Hutu government forces and the Tutsi-led Rwandan Patriotic Front (RPF), which launched an invasion from Uganda. In August 1993 a truce was negotiated in Arusha, Tanzania, calling for an interim administration and new elections: Murphy, above n 181, 243.

[262] The exact circumstances of the crash remain unclear. For a survey of various theories, see Prunier, above n 260, 212–29.

[263] See, eg, Evans, above n 144, 229.           [264] *Keesing's* (1994) 39992.

[265] See Prunier, above n 260, 310.              [266] See Melvern, above n 244, 11.

[267] S/1994/640, 10; [1994] *UNYB* 297.

A further 1.5 million of Rwanda's 7 million people were estimated to be displaced.[268]

The response of the Security Council was, to say the least, ineffectual. At the time of Habyarimana's death there were 2,500 UN peacekeepers stationed in Rwanda as part of the UN Assistance Mission in Rwanda (UNAMIR) to monitor the Arusha Accords. On 21 April, in the middle of the crisis, the Security Council voted to *reduce* that number to 270.[269] After ten Belgian troops assigned to guard the Prime Minister were killed on 7 April, Belgium had stated its intention to withdraw its 440 troops from UNAMIR.[270] The Secretary-General then made a report to the Council in which he said UNAMIR's position had become impossible. He outlined three alternatives for the Council's consideration: a massive reinforcement of UNAMIR to coerce the sides into ceasefire; reduction of the UN's commitment to a small group headed by the Force Commander and supported by a staff of about 270, which would attempt to bring about agreement on a ceasefire; or complete withdrawal.[271] Resolution 912 (1994) merely stated that the Council decided to 'adjust the mandate of UNAMIR . . . as set out in paragraphs 15 to 18 of the Secretary-General's report'.[272]

The decision was condemned by the OAU and aid agencies, who accused the Council of applying different standards to Africa from those applied in Europe.[273] Massacres continued and on 29 April, the Secretary-General urged the Council to reconsider its position and take 'forceful action to restore law and order'.[274] Two weeks later he submitted a plan calling for 5,500 troops to be sent to Kigali under an expanded UNAMIR mandate to provide security assistance to humanitarian organizations for the distribution of relief supplies, and to establish access to sites where displaced persons and refugees were concentrated and ensure their protection.[275] This was initially resisted by the United States, which argued for more detailed planning before going into Kigali lest UN forces and prestige be put at risk, which could in turn threaten US funding for UN peacekeeping operations.[276]

On 17 May the Council adopted resolution 918 (1994), which authorized an expansion of UNAMIR forces up to 5,500.[277] Intense lobbying by the United States ensured that this would take place in two phases, however, with the first comprising only 150 unarmed observers and an 800-strong Ghanaian battalion to secure Kigali airport.[278] Although the preamble to resolution 918 (1994) stated that the Council was '[d]eeply disturbed* by the magnitude of the human suffering caused by the conflict and concerned that the continuation

---

[268] *Keesing's* (1994) 39992.
[269] SC Res 912 (1994) para 7(c).
[270] S/1994/446.
[271] S/1994/470.
[272] SC Res 912 (1994) para 7(c).
[273] *Keesing's* (1994) 39944.
[274] S/1994/518; *Keesing's* (1994) 39944.
[275] S/1994/728 (Report of 13 May 1994).
[276] See Murphy, above n 181, 245.
[277] SC Res 918 (1994) para 5.
[278] *Keesing's* (1994) 39992.

of the situation in Rwanda constitutes a threat to peace and security in the region', Part B of the resolution (which imposed a mandatory arms embargo under Chapter VII) merely *determined* that 'the situation in Rwanda constitutes a threat to peace and security in the region'.[279]

In fact there had been a studied effort *not* to acknowledge the magnitude of the humanitarian crisis. Despite the Secretary-General's report of May 1994, the United States and other governments resisted using the term 'genocide' as it would have made their policies of inaction untenable.[280] In resolution 918 (1994), the Council had avoided the term even in the abstract, referring instead to 'the killing of members of an ethnic group with the intention of destroying such a group in whole or in part'.[281] It was not until 8 June that the Council, in a resolution intended to accelerate the deployment of the expanded UNAMIR, noted '*with the gravest concern* the reports indicating that acts of genocide have occurred in Rwanda'.[282] Ten days later, the UNAMIR force still consisted of only 503 troops under the command of Major-General Romeo A Dallaire, who had remained in Rwanda throughout the crisis. The Secretary-General estimated that UNAMIR would be unable to undertake its full mandate for another three months.[283]

At this point, France's Foreign Minister Alain Juppé announced that France was prepared to intervene in Rwanda, 'with its main European and African partners', to put an end to the massacres and protect groups threatened with 'extinction'.[284] In a letter to the Secretary-General dated 20 June 1994, France requested Chapter VII authorization '[i]n the spirit of resolution 794' (which had authorized the US-led UNITAF operation in Somalia) for itself and Senegal 'to send a force in without delay, so as to maintain a presence pending the arrival of the expanded UNAMIR'.[285] This offer was met with some suspicion due to France's role in arming and training the predominantly Hutu government forces,[286] and was rejected outright by the RPF.[287]

Despite these misgivings, the Security Council adopted resolution 929 (1994) on 22 June 1994. Recognizing that the situation 'constitutes a unique case which demands an urgent response by the international community' and determining 'that the magnitude of the humanitarian crisis in Rwanda constitutes a threat to peace and security in the region', the Council authorized France, under Chapter VII, to conduct an operation under national command

---

[279] SC Res 918 (1994) Part B, preamble.

[280] Tesón, above n 259, 260; Gourevitch, above n 260, 152–4.

[281] SC Res 918 (1994) preamble. This is, of course, a partial definition of genocide. See also the Presidential Statement of 30 Apr 1994: S/PRST/1994/21.

[282] SC Res 925 (1994) preamble.

[283] S/1994/728.

[284] Alain Juppé, 'Intervenir au Rwanda', *Libération*, 16 June 1994, in Prunier, above n 260, 280.

[285] S/1994/734.    [286] Murphy, above n 39, 248; Gourevitch, above n 260, 88–90, 154–5.

[287] *Keesing's* (1994) 40038.

and control aimed at contributing, in an impartial way, to the security and protection of displaced persons, refugees and civilians at risk, using 'all necessary means' to achieve these humanitarian objectives.[288] Helmut Freudenschuss has written that the references to impartiality and humanitarian goals, as well as a two-month time-limit, were added to the resolution during brief but intensive consultations.[289] Even so, a distinct lack of enthusiasm was evidenced by the five abstentions to the resolution.[290]

Regardless of their motivation and their actions prior to June 1994, it is now accepted that the safe areas created in south-western Rwanda by Opération Turquoise saved many lives. When French troops prepared to depart at the conclusion of their two-month mandate, they were asked to stay by aid groups, the UNHCR, the Clinton Administration, and the Ethiopian troops who took their place.[291] Nevertheless, it appears that their main contribution was to save the *génocidaires* from Tutsi-led retribution.[292]

### 3.2.3. Eastern Zaïre, 1996

The situation in the Great Lakes Region in 1996 was without question an international crisis, if not necessarily an international armed conflict. Over a million refugees from Rwanda had gathered in eastern Zaïre, exacerbating ongoing problems of political and ethnic friction in the area. Rwanda and Zaïre (and, to a lesser extent, Burundi and Uganda) accused other countries of provoking armed attacks or supporting rebel movements to destabilize existing governments. Intense fighting in Zaïre in November forced all international humanitarian workers to evacuate and led 600,000 displaced Zaïrians to flee into Rwanda.[293] On 7 November 1996 the Secretary-General proposed to the Council that a multinational force be dispatched to eastern Zaïre.[294] Zaïre agreed to the deployment of such a force the next day[295] and on 9 November the Council passed resolution 1078 (1996), requesting states concerned to make arrangements through the Secretary-General prior to a mission being authorized. Canada offered to lead a temporary and strictly humanitarian operation,[296] which was duly authorized to use 'all necessary means' by resolution 1080 (1996). By 5 December, however, the situation in eastern Zaïre appeared to have improved significantly. The voluntary repatriation of many Rwandan refugees and the increased access of humanitarian

---

[288] SC Res 929 (1994) preamble, paras 2, 3.     [289] Freudenschuss, above n 180, 521.

[290] SC Res 929 (1994) adopted 10-0-5 (Brazil, China, New Zealand, Nigeria, Pakistan abstaining).

[291] Raymond Bonner, 'As French Leave Rwanda, Critics Reverse Position', *NYT*, 23 Aug 1994.

[292] See, eg, Gourevitch, above n 260, 155–61, 188–9. Cf Prunier, above n 260, 284–90 (discussing the decision to intervene).

[293] [1996] *UNYB* 46; *Keesing's* (1996) 41350.     [294] S/1996/916.

[295] S/1996/920.     [296] S/1996/941.

organizations had partially achieved the force's objectives—combined with
the dispersal of the remaining number of refugees over large areas of eastern
Zaïre, this meant that the multinational force was of little utility at its present
level. In a letter dated 13 December, Canada decided to withdraw its command and forces by 31 December.[297]

Of some passing interest is the different terminology used in the two resolutions. Resolution 1078 (1996) was not adopted under Chapter VII, but the
Council did determine 'that the magnitude of the present humanitarian crisis
in eastern Zaïre constitutes a threat to peace and security in the region'.
Resolution 1080 (1996), by contrast, explicitly acted under Chapter VII but
determined merely that 'the present situation in eastern Zaïre constitutes a
threat to international peace and security'.

### 3.2.4. Albania, 1997

Following the collapse of a number of officially sanctioned pyramid investment schemes in March 1997, Albania was thrown into chaos as hundreds of
thousands of people lost their life savings.[298] On 28 March the Council determined in resolution 1101 (1997) that the situation constituted a threat to
international peace and security and, acting under Chapter VII, authorized
Italy to lead a multinational protection force 'to facilitate the safe and prompt
delivery of humanitarian assistance, and to help create a secure environment
for the missions of international organizations in Albania, including those
providing humanitarian assistance'.[299] Comparable to the resolutions on the
CAR, explicit Chapter VII authorization was restricted to ensuring the security
and freedom of movement of the multinational protection force.[300] The resolution was adopted without public debate in the Council, reportedly because
representatives wished to return to their Easter vacations.[301] The exception
was China, whose representative noted that it normally opposed intervening
in a state's internal affairs, but abstained rather than blocked the resolution
because of the seriousness of the situation.[302]

The resolution followed Italy's offer to lead a multinational force,[303] made
in response to the thousands of Albanian refugees crossing into Italy across
the Adriatic Sea.[304] Italy's impartiality in the operation was brought into
question when its navy sank a boat full of refugees as part of its interdiction

---

[297] See *Keesing's* (1997) 41431.
[298] Jane Perlez, 'Albania Calls an Emergency as Chaos Rises', *NYT*, 3 Mar 1997.
[299] SC Res 1101 (1997) paras 4, 2.                    [300] Ibid para 4.
[301] John M Goshko, 'UN Approves Italy-Led Force for Albania: Europeans Commit to
Guard Aid Efforts', *Washington Post*, 29 Mar 1997.
[302] S/PV.3758 (1997) (China).                    [303] S/1997/258.
[304] Goshko, above n 301.

programme;[305] when a second wave of refugees threatened, Italian opposition parties pressed for an extension of the UN mandate to include stopping criminal groups from organizing crossings.[306]

By mid-May it had become clear to international observers (notably Italy) that Albania's long-term objectives were best achieved by organizing elections—and thus ousting President Sali Berisha.[307] In resolution 1114 (1997), the Council extended the mandate of the Italian-led force to include protection of the OSCE mission that was to supervise the coming elections. This was limited to a period of 45 days.[308] Elections were held and a new government elected, with the majority of the multinational force departing within the period specified.[309]

### 3.2.5. East Timor, 1999

The situation in East Timor in 1999 was to some extent *sui generis*, as the origins of the conflict lay in Indonesia's 1975 invasion of the former Portuguese colony. Since the purported annexation of East Timor by Indonesia was never recognized by the vast majority of the international community (with the notable exception of Australia), it is questionable what role Indonesia was entitled to play in the territory's transition to independence.[310] In practice, however, East Timor's independence only became possible following the replacement of Indonesian President Suharto [Soeharto] by B J Habibie, who offered to hold a plebiscite on the territory's future. An agreement dated 5 May 1999, between Indonesia and Portugal (as the administering power of a non-self-governing territory), provided for a 'popular consultation' to be held on East Timor's future on 8 August.[311] The date of the consultation fell squarely in the middle of Indonesia's first Presidential elections in 44 years, apparently in the hope of boosting Habibie's chances of re-election by garnering international support. And, crucially, the agreement left security arrangements in the hands of Indonesia's military, which had actively suppressed the East Timorese population for 24 years. On 11 June the Security Council established the UN Mission in East Timor (UNAMET) to organize and conduct the consultation.[312] A month later, with the consultation postponed until the end of August, the Secretary-General made a report to the Council, noting that 'the situation in East Timor will be rather delicate as the Territory

---

[305] 'Albania Assails Italy, Awaits Security Force', ibid, 30 Mar 1997.
[306] Vera Haller, 'More Albanians Flee to Italy, Despite Peacekeepers' Presence', ibid, 6 May 1997.
[307] Editorial, 'The Albanian Mess', ibid, 21 May 1997.      [308] SC Res 1114 (1997) para 6.
[309] S/PRST/1997/44, 14 Aug 1997. See also Editorial, 'In and out of Albania', *Washington Post*, 16 Aug 1997.
[310] See Antonio Cassese, *Self-Determination of Peoples: A Legal Reappraisal* (Hersch Lauterpacht Memorial Lectures; Cambridge: Cambridge University Press, 1995) 223–30.
[311] S/1999/513, Annexes I–III.      [312] SC Res 1246 (1999).

prepares for the implementation of the result of the popular consultation, whichever it may be'.[313] Despite threats of violence, 98 per cent of East Timorese voted in the referendum, with 78.5 per cent choosing independence.

The violence that ensued took place under the direction of the Indonesian military, if not the government itself.[314] At the time there was great reluctance to intervene, despite the apparent hypocrisy given the international response to the situation in Kosovo. Finally, at the instigation of Australia—driven by domestic political pressure, concern about a refugee crisis, and some measure of contrition for its previous policies on East Timor—the Security Council on 15 September authorized an Australian-led multinational force to restore peace and security to East Timor.[315]

As indicated above, there seems to have been no legal basis for requiring Indonesia's consent to such an operation. Nevertheless, as a practical matter, it was clear that no form of enforcement action was possible unless Indonesia consented to it. Resolution 1264 (1999) therefore welcomed a 12 September statement by the Indonesian President that expressed the readiness of Indonesia to accept an international peacekeeping force through the United Nations in East Timor.[316]

In terms of locating a threat to international peace to security for the purposes of justifying Chapter VII action a number of bases might have been found. These include: the actions of Indonesian troops in a nominally Portuguese territory (from September 1999 or over the preceding 24 years); cross-border violence between Indonesia and the emerging state of East Timor; the transborder effects of a humanitarian catastrophe in East Timor; or violations of international humanitarian and human rights law. In fact it was the last of these that provided the justification for a determination that the situation threatened peace and security,[317] apparently due to the need to secure Indonesian consent for the operation that followed.

The resolution authorizing the Australian-led force (INTERFET) noted that the multinational force should be replaced 'as soon as possible' by a peacekeeping force.[318] On 25 October the Council voted to establish a transitional authority for East Timor (UNTAET), the military component of which was to replace INTERFET 'as soon as possible'.[319]

---

[313] S/1999/862 para 5.

[314] The Security Council mission to Dili and Jakarta included analysis by UNAMET that the violence was 'nothing less than a systematic implementation of a "scorched earth" policy in East Timor, under the direction of the Indonesian military': S/1999/976, Annex, para 1.

[315] SC Res 1264 (1999).                          [316] Ibid preamble.

[317] Ibid: '*Expressing* its concern at reports indicating that systematic, widespread and flagrant violations of international humanitarian and human rights law have been committed in East Timor.'

[318] Ibid para 10.                               [319] SC Res 1272 (1999) para 9.

### 3.2.6. Humanitarian crises as threats to peace and security

A credible argument can be made that refugee flows may, in some circumstances, constitute a threat to international peace and security.[320] Such were the grounds emphasized in the early resolutions on internal armed conflicts, and the Council has justified Chapter VII actions to create safe havens in the Balkans[321] and Rwanda[322] at least in part due to the external effects of refugee flows.[323] In later years the Council also determined that 'serious' or 'systematic, widespread and flagrant' violations of international humanitarian law may contribute to a threat to international peace and security in its resolutions establishing the International Criminal Tribunals for the Former Yugoslavia and Rwanda[324] and on East Timor.[325] This position is supported by the ICRC.[326] Other resolutions have noted the importance of humanitarian assistance in restoring peace and security.[327]

There has been, therefore, a gradual shift away from reliance on the transboundary implications of a situation, paralleling the greater preparedness to view an internal armed conflict as a threat to peace and security. It is difficult to draw normative conclusions from the exercise of this power in the cases discussed in this section, but it appears that such a determination is more likely when the internal armed conflict has transborder consequences, and where serious violations of international humanitarian law are taking place. These are not fixed conditions, however, as the Council's treatment of disruption to democracy shows.

### 3.3. Disruption to democracy

Operation Restore Democracy in Haiti has been seen as the high-water mark of Council activism in the 1990s.[328] Certainly, it was a watershed for at least two reasons. First, resolution 940 (1994) was unprecedented in authorizing the use of force to remove one regime and install another. Seen in the context of the progression of Council resolutions in this period it was unremarkable in recognizing internal strife as warranting a Chapter VII response, but this

---

[320] See Alan Dowty and Gil Loescher, 'Refugee Flows as Grounds for International Action', in Michael Brown, Owen R Coté, Jr, Sean M Lynn Jones, and Steven E Miller (eds), *Nationalism and Ethnic Conflict: An International Security Reader* (Cambridge, MA: MIT Press, 1997) 305.
[321] SC Res 819 (1993); SC Res 824 (1993); SC Res 836 (1993).
[322] SC Res 918 (1994); SC Res 929 (1994).
[323] This trend was also predicted in Schachter, above n 154, 469.
[324] SC Res 808 (1993); SC Res 827 (1993); SC Res 955 (1994).     [325] SC Res 1264 (1999).
[326] International Committee of the Red Cross, 'Report on the Protection of War Victims' (1993) 296 *International Review of the Red Cross* 391, 427.
[327] SC Res 770 (1992) (Bosnia and Herzegovina). See also SC Res 787 (1992).
[328] O'Connell, above n 4, 474.

was the first occasion on which it could be claimed that the Council authorized the use of force in support of democracy. (This link between democracy and peace may be contrasted with the claim, discussed in Chapter 3, that the absence of democracy diminishes sovereignty.) Secondly, this was the first time that the United States sought the imprimatur of the United Nations to use force within its own hemisphere. This may be contrasted with the fig-leaf of OECS support for its intervention in Grenada in 1983,[329] and its blunt unilateralism in Panama in 1989.[330]

For both of these reasons, it is worth considering in some detail. This will be followed by a consideration of the Security Council's response to ECOWAS' intervention in Sierra Leone, sometimes said to be a second instance of collective intervention to restore democracy.

### 3.3.1. Haiti, 1991–4[331]

In 1990, after some years of international pressure to resume democratic elections, Jean-Bertrand Aristide was elected President of Haiti with 67 per cent of the popular vote in an internationally monitored ballot. Aristide was removed from office by a *coup d'état* on 30 September 1991.[332] The Organization of American States (OAS) swiftly condemned the *coup* and recommended the imposition of diplomatic and later economic sanctions by its members.[333] The Security Council failed to adopt a resolution on the issue, reportedly because China and certain non-aligned states were concerned about increased Security Council involvement in areas traditionally considered to be within the sphere of domestic jurisdiction.[334] The General Assembly, by contrast, strongly condemned the 'illegal replacement of the constitutional President of Haiti', affirming that 'any entity resulting from that illegal situation' was unacceptable.[335]

The refusal of Haiti's military dictators to reinstate the Aristide government, combined with the continued persecution of Aristide supporters, eventually led the Security Council to impose a mandatory economic embargo in June 1993. The resolution was adopted explicitly under Chapter VII and listed a variety of factors that had led the Council to determine 'that, in these unique and exceptional circumstances, the continuation of this situation threatens international peace and security in the region'.[336] These included 'the incidence of humanitarian crises, including mass displacements of population', and the 'climate of fear of persecution and economic dislocation which could increase the number of Haitians seeking refuge in neighbouring Member States'.[337]

---

[329] See Ch 3, Sect 2.1.                                    [330] See Ch 3, Sect 2.2.
[331] See generally Malone, above n 74.                      [332] See ibid 48–61.
[333] OAS MRE/RES 1/91, MRE/RES 2/91, MRE/RES 3/91 (1991).
[334] Tesón, above n 259, 250; Malone, above n 74, 63–4.     [335] GA Res 46/7 (1991).
[336] SC Res 841 (1993) preamble.                            [337] Ibid.

This is clearly an atypical conception of a threat to international peace and security. (Interestingly, subsequent resolutions referred to 'a threat to peace and security in the *region*'.[338]) Various commentators have questioned whether the situation actually constituted a threat to the peace,[339] and there is evidence that some Council members placed more reliance on the request for assistance from the Aristide Government-in-exile.[340] Confirmation of this may be found in the preamble to the resolution, which explicitly linked the request from Haiti's representative and actions taken by the OAS and the General Assembly, amounting to a 'unique and exceptional situation warranting extraordinary measures'.[341] In any event, this line of reasoning does not help justify enforcement actions under Chapter VII.

As indicated above, it is at least arguable that the flow of refugees can justify a determination that a situation threatens international peace and security,[342] though this argument is not persuasive in the case of Haiti as the number of refugees was small compared to the millions displaced by the conflicts in Iraq, Somalia, and Rwanda.[343] In any case, the United States was already acting to reduce the number of refugees to pre-*coup* levels by pursuing an interdiction programme that was as aggressive as it was, arguably, illegal.[344] The *political* threat posed by refugees landing on American soil did encourage the Clinton Administration to push for a resolution to the crisis, however. During the 1992 US Presidential election campaign, candidate Clinton had condemned the Bush policy of forced repatriation of Haitian boat people.[345] Two months later, following his inauguration as President and in the absence of viable alternatives, Clinton signalled that he would retain the Bush repatriation policy.[346] Having been forced to adopt precisely those measures for which he had excoriated his predecessor, a solution to the Haitian crisis became urgent.[347]

---

[338] See, eg, SC Res 917 (1994); SC Res 933 (1994); SC Res 940 (1994).

[339] See Douglas Lee Donoho, 'Evolution or Expediency: The United Nations Response to the Disruption of Democracy' (1996) 29 *Cornell LJ* 329, 359 n 160 and sources there cited.

[340] See ibid 347, 372 n 233 and sources there cited.

[341] SC Res 841 (1993) preamble. China specifically noted that the resolution should not be regarded as constituting any precedent for the future: S/PV.3238 (1993) 21.

[342] See above Sect 3.2.6.                    [343] See Donoho, above n 339, 362–3.

[344] The US Supreme Court upheld the validity of the programme as a matter of US law in *Sale v Haitian Centers Inc* 509 US 155 (1993), but the decision was sharply criticized by, *inter alia*, the UNHCR on the basis that the obligation of *non-refoulement* in art 33 of the 1951 Geneva Convention relating to the Status of Refugees applies everywhere, including on the high seas: see Statement of the High Commissioner, 22 June 1993 (1993) 32 ILM 1215. See further Guy Goodwin-Gill, 'Case and Comment: The Haitian Refoulement Case' (1994) 6 *International Journal of Refugee Law* 69.

[345] Malone, above n 74, 71.

[346] Ibid 79. Malone suggests in a footnote that Clinton had learnt the potential impact and cost of refugee flows domestically, when Cuban refugees had rioted in Arkansas following the 'Mariel boatlift'. Citing an interview with Taylor Branch, a historian close to Clinton, Malone writes that the President believed that this riot cost him his first re-election bid as Governor: ibid 215 n 1.

[347] Ibid 95.

The Security Council embargo led the Haitian military junta to accept the Governors Island Agreement (GIA), which provided, *inter alia*, for President Aristide to be returned to power.[348] Sanctions were lifted on 27 August 1993, but the agreement collapsed when violence against Aristide supporters resumed in September and October of that year. This corresponded with severe reservations in the United States about the merits of sending US troops to a volatile country after the death of eighteen soldiers in Mogadishu, Somalia. In an embarrassing volte-face, the USS *Harlan County* arrived in Port-au-Prince harbour on 11 October, only to be withdrawn the next day.[349]

The Security Council responded by reimposing sanctions[350] and authorizing a naval blockade under Chapters VII and VIII of the Charter,[351] but the date set in the GIA for Aristide's return, 30 October 1993, passed with only a Presidential Statement warning that sanctions might be strengthened in the future.[352] At this point, the Clinton Administration began to signal through media leaks that Aristide should be prepared to compromise further in order to broaden his political support.[353] A *New York Times* editorial highlighted the hypocrisy of this position:

The Clinton Administration explains its opposition to broadened sanctions as humanitarian, saying that it doesn't want to impose additional burdens on Haiti's impoverished millions. This is a bit hard to take from an Administration that is willing to use US warships to turn back boatloads of desperate Haitians. Then as now, the real motivation for the . . . policy seems to be a fear of domestic reaction to a massive influx of poor, black Haitian refugees.[354]

In February 1994 Aristide reversed his previous position and publicly signalled support for a surgical intervention to overthrow the *de facto* government and restore him to power.[355] In the face of initial reluctance on the part of the Clinton Administration, Aristide skilfully used the refugee crisis to garner public support, criticizing the US practice of *refoulement* as comparable to a 'floating Berlin Wall'.[356] As public opinion shifted, driven also by the Congressional Black Caucus and a hunger strike by Randall Robinson, Chairman of TransAfrica, the Clinton Administration was pushed to modify and later reverse its policy. By May, it announced that Haitian boat people would be interviewed to determine whether they were political refugees, rather than automatically sending them back to Haiti. The UNHCR, earlier critical of the US repatriation policy, now persuaded other states in the region to assist by providing temporary processing centres for asylum-seekers.[357]

---

[348]  See Malone, above n 74, 86–7.          [349]  Ibid 91–2, 95–6.
[350]  SC Res 873 (1993).                        [351]  SC Res 875 (1993).
[352]  S/26668 (1993). The sanctions were strengthened in May: SC Res 917 (1994).
[353]  Malone, above n 74, 94.
[354]  Editorial, 'No Time to Hesitate on Haiti', *NYT*, 7 Nov 1993.
[355]  A/48/867-S/1994/150 (1994).              [356]  Malone, above n 74, 103.
[357]  Ibid 104–5.

On 29 July 1994, nearly three years after the *coup*, the Aristide Government-in-exile formally requested 'prompt and decisive action' by the international community.[358] Two days later, the Security Council, acting under Chapter VII, passed resolution 940 (1994), which authorized a multinational force to use

all necessary means to facilitate the departure from Haiti of the military leadership, . . . the prompt return of the legitimately elected President and the restoration of the legitimate authorities of the Government of Haiti, and to establish and maintain a secure and stable environment that will permit implementation of the Governors Island Agreement.[359]

Six weeks later, Clinton delivered a televised speech advising the *de factos* that their time was up and indicating that military action was imminent. This was despite serious domestic concerns about the merits of an invasion. In what David Malone has described as a political *coup de théâtre*, a violent invasion was avoided when former US President Jimmy Carter secured an agreement with the Haitian military to return Aristide to power.[360] By the end of September over 17,000 US troops were peacefully deployed in Haiti, with Aristide himself returning to Port-au-Prince on 15 October 1994.[361] There were no US casualties, though a number of Haitians died during violent demonstrations.[362] International reaction to the events was generally positive, with only a few states expressing serious reservations.[363]

### 3.3.2. Sierra Leone, 1997–8

In May 1997 the recently elected government of Sierra Leone was overthrown by the Armed Forces Revolutionary Committee (AFRC). Sierra Leone had been in a state of civil war since unrest in Liberia spilled across the border in 1991.[364] The *coup* met with a hostile reaction throughout the region and internationally. ECOWAS, which already had troops in a peacekeeping role in Sierra Leone, made clear its determination to reverse the *coup*. A week later, the OAU unanimously condemned the *coup* and implicitly authorized ECOWAS to take military action to restore the elected government, urging Sierra Leone's

---

[358] S/1994/905, Annex. This was regarded as insufficient, however, and so a letter was sent stating the 'agreement' of the Aristide Government with the draft resolution: S/1994/910 (1994).
[359] SC Res 940 (1994) adopted 12-0-2 (Brazil and China abstaining; Rwanda not participating) para 4.
[360] Malone, above n 74, 110–12. See also Elaine Sciolino, 'On the Brink of War, a Tense Battle of Wills', *NYT*, 20 Sept 1994.
[361] Donoho, above n 339, 348.
[362] These included a firefight between American troops and a Haitian military contingent in which ten Haitians died: Malone, above n 74, 113.
[363] Tesón, above n 259, 252.      [364] See above Sect 3.1.3.

neighbours 'to take all necessary measures' to return President Kabbah to office.[365]

On 8 October 1997 the Security Council unanimously adopted resolution 1132 (1997). Determining that 'the situation' constituted a threat to international peace and security, the Council demanded that the military junta relinquish power to make way for the restoration of the democratically elected government.[366] To enforce this objective, it expressly authorized ECOWAS under Chapter VIII to cut the AFRC off from foreign supplies of war *matériel*.[367] South Korea's representative on the Council gave the remarkable explanation that the '*coup* had had a destabilizing effect on the whole region by reversing a new wave of democracy which was spreading across the African continent'.[368]

As with the intervention in Liberia, this was in reality a case of the Council purporting to give retrospective validation to acts that had already taken place. The embargo had been in force since August 1997,[369] and ECOWAS forces had engaged in sporadic attacks over the following months. Despite the reference to Chapter VIII, ECOWAS continued to operate in advance of its Council mandate—Nigerian ECOMOG forces launched a major military assault in February 1998, action subsequently welcomed in a Presidential Statement[370] and later a resolution.[371]

Following the return of the democratically elected president on 10 March 1998, the Council terminated the petroleum and later the arms embargoes.[372] Fighting between government and rebel forces continued, however, and the Council established UNOMSIL to monitor the security situation, disarmament, and observance of international humanitarian law.[373] An ill-fated peace agreement was subsequently signed in Lomé on 7 July 1999; in October 1999 UNOMSIL's mandate was taken over by UNAMSIL, with a more robust mandate to 'afford protection to civilians under imminent threat of physical violence'.[374] This mandate was sorely tested when the peace agreement broke down the following year.

[365] Decision of the 33rd Summit of the OAU (2–4 June 1997). See Brad R Roth, *Governmental Illegitimacy in International Law* (Oxford: Clarendon Press, 1999) 405–6; David Wippman, 'Pro-Democratic Intervention by Invitation', in Gregory H Fox and Brad R Roth (eds), *Democratic Governance and International Law* (Cambridge: Cambridge University Press, 2000) 293, 303–5.

[366] SC Res 1132 (1997) para 1. It had earlier strongly deplored the *coup* in a Presidential Statement: S/PRST/1997/36 (11 July 1997).

[367] SC Res 1132 (1997) para 8.　　[368] UN Press Release SC/6425 (8 Oct 1997) 10.

[369] ECOWAS Twentieth Session of the Authority of Heads of State and Government, Decision on Sanctions Against the Junta in Sierra Leone, in Wippman, above n 365, 304.

[370] S/PRST/1998/5.

[371] SC Res 1162 (1998) (commending ECOMOG on its role in restoring peace and security).

[372] SC Res 1156 (1998); SC Res 1171 (1998). The resolution provided that arms were allowed to be sold only to the government, however.

[373] SC Res 1181 (1998).

[374] SC Res 1270 (1999) para 14: '*Acting* under Chapter VII of the Charter of the United Nations, *decides* that in the discharge of its mandate UNAMSIL may take the necessary action to

### 3.3.3. *Disruption to democracy as a threat to peace and security*

Tesón cites the US action in Haiti as 'the most important precedent support-ing the legitimacy both of an international principle of democratic rule and of collective humanitarian intervention'.[375] Dismissing the argument that this might more properly be characterized as an enforcement action under Chapter VII (read broadly), he argues that '[n]o one can seriously argue that the Haitian situation posed a threat to international peace and security in the region' and that in resolution 940, the Security Council 'sensibly abandoned the reference to the language of article 39'.[376] Tesón, however, ignores the preambular determination that 'the situation in Haiti continues to constitute a threat to peace and security in the region',[377] and his analysis is not sup-ported even by Reisman.[378]

It is, however, difficult to reconcile the Council action with any principled interpretation of the provisions of Article 39. Three possible types of inter-pretation suggest themselves. First, and most obviously, the act of disruption *itself* may threaten international peace and security. This was arguably the case in two incidents that are sometimes identified as early precedents for Security Council intervention in support of democracy.[379] The Security Council responded to the 1966 declaration of independence by the white minority government in Southern Rhodesia by imposing mandatory eco-nomic sanctions and authorizing a limited use of force (by the United Kingdom) to stop oil tankers from violating the embargo.[380] The Southern Rhodesian question is perhaps unique in that the Council explicitly recog-nized the legitimacy of the Zimbabwean people's struggle against a colonial regime, specifically invoking the Declaration on the Granting of Independence to Colonial Territories and Peoples.[381] Subsequent resolutions referred to allegations of armed aggression on the part of the Ian Smith regime against neighbouring states.[382] Similarly, the Chapter VII resolution imposing an arms embargo on South Africa strongly condemned the racist regime, but ultimately located a threat to international peace and security in

---

ensure the security and freedom of movement of its personnel and, within its capabilities and areas of deployment, to afford protection to civilians under imminent threat of physical violence, taking into account the responsibilities of the Government of Sierra Leone and ECOMOG.'

[375] Tesón, above n 259, 249. Cf Lillich, above n 144, 9 (referring to it as 'the purest form of humanitarian intervention to date').

[376] Tesón, above n 259, 254.          [377] SC Res 940 (1994).

[378] See, eg, W Michael Reisman, 'Haiti and the Validity of International Action' (1995) 89 *AJIL* 82, 83.

[379] See, eg, ibid.          [380] See Sect 1.1.1.

[381] SC Res 232 (1966) para 4, referring to GA Res 1514(xv) (1960). See also SC Res 253 (1968) preamble; SC Res 277 (1970) preamble.

[382] See SC Res 386 (1976); SC Res 403 (1977); SC Res 411 (1977); SC Res 423 (1978); SC Res 445 (1979).

the prospect of South Africa acquiring nuclear weapons.[383] Whether any given situation lends itself to being characterized as a threat to international peace and security will depend on the specific circumstances, including the consequences for neighbouring states, such as (arguably) refugee flows. It is possible, though difficult, to fit the Security Council resolutions on Haiti within such a framework.

Secondly, at a different level of analysis, some scholars argue that the absence of democracy may itself constitute a threat to international peace and security. This is an extreme form of the 'democratic peace' thesis that authentic democracies do not fight each other, or—depending on the definition of 'democracy' or 'fighting'—that such conflicts are exceptional.[384] (The gunboat diplomacy between Spain and Canada over fishing rights in 1995 may be such an exception,[385] as might the involvement of the United States in the 1973 overthrow of the democratically elected government in Chile.) As a general principle this clearly cannot stand, as it would deprive at least one-third of the world's states of the protection of Article 2(7).[386]

Thirdly, what might be called the Humpty Dumpty school of interpretation[387] grants the Security Council an absolute licence to determine what constitutes a 'threat to international peace and security'. This approach has the attraction of fitting all such determinations, but at the cost of any normative framework within which to situate them. Although decisions of the Security Council are in practice not subject to review (judicial or otherwise), the ICJ's 1998 decision on preliminary objections in the *Lockerbie* case at least affirms that they are subject to the Charter, Article 24 of which provides that, in fulfilling its 'primary responsibility' for the maintenance of international peace and security, 'the Security Council shall act in accordance with the Purposes and Principles of the United Nations'.[388]

[383] SC Res 418 (1977).

[384] See generally Michael E Brown, Sean M Lynn Jones, and Steven E Miller, *Debating the Democratic Peace* (Cambridge, MA: MIT Press, 1996). See also Tom J Farer, 'Collectively Defending Democracy in a World of Sovereign States: The Western Hemisphere's Prospect' (1993) 15 *Human Rights Quarterly* 716, 724–6; Fernando R Tesón, 'Collective Humanitarian Intervention' (1996) 17 *Michigan JIL* 323, 332–3. For a discussion of the somewhat embarrassing finding that autocracies in the process of democratization actually become *more* likely to go to war, see Edward D Mansfield and Jack Snyder, 'Democratization and the Danger of War', in Brown, Jones, and Miller, above 301–4.

[385] See Peter Davies, 'The EC/Canadian Dispute in the Northwest Atlantic' (1995) 44 *ICLQ* 927; Peter Davies and Catherine Redgwell, 'The International Legal Regulation of Straddling Fishing Stocks' (1996) 67 *British YBIL* 199; Michael Byers, *Custom, Power and the Power of Rules: International Relations and Customary International Law* (Cambridge: Cambridge University Press, 1999) 97–101.

[386] See Ch 3.

[387] '"When *I* use a word," Humpty Dumpty said in a rather scornful tone, "it means just what I choose it to mean—neither more nor less"': Lewis Carroll, *Through the Looking-Glass* (London: Macmillan, 1872) ch 6.

[388] UN Charter, art 24. See above n 3.

It is, moreover, arguable whether the disruption to democracy actually constituted the basis for resolution 940 (1994). The preamble to the resolution states that the Security Council was '[g]*ravely concerned* by the significant further deterioration of the humanitarian situation in Haiti, in particular the continuing escalation by the illegal de facto regime of systematic violations of civil liberties, the desperate plight of Haitian refugees and the recent expulsion of the staff of the International Civilian Mission'. Democracy is not mentioned until later in the preamble, in a passage that states: '*Reaffirming* that the goal of the international community remains the restoration of democracy in Haiti and the prompt return of the legitimately elected President, Jean-Bertrand Aristide, within the framework of the Governors Island Agreement.' The disruption of democracy is thus only one of several factors identified by the Security Council as contributing to a threat to international peace and security. Moreover, given the order and language of the two passages—and despite the fact that the *coup* was preceded by internationally monitored elections—the democracy factor appears to have been considered less important than the humanitarian situation giving rise to 'grave concern'.

But the aspect of resolution 940 (1994) that most diminishes its value as a precedent in respect of any more general preparedness to view disruption to democracy as a legitimate ground for Security Council action is the emphasis placed therein on the request for UN action made by the Aristide Government-in-exile in July 1994. Although the Council does not require an invitation from the government of a state in order to authorize an intervention within that state's territory, an invitation of this kind is widely acknowledged to legitimate unilateral or collective intervention in the absence of Security Council authorization.[389] It is therefore arguable that the United States did not require a Security Council resolution to intervene in Haiti as it did. And if the resolution was indeed unnecessary, its precedential effect in terms of radically redefining the international law on the use of force must then be called into question.

More recently, Brad Roth has suggested that the action in Sierra Leone is

the best evidence yet of a fundamental change in international legal norms pertaining to 'pro-democratic' intervention. The Security Council in this case took authorization of action against the 'illegitimate' regime beyond the context of United Nations peacemaking *cum* electoral 'arbitration', not even bothering to take refuge in assertions of 'extraordinary', 'exceptional', or 'unique' circumstances in invoking Chapter VII. Moreover, its *post hoc* ratification of the regional organization's forcible acts neither comported with a literal interpretation of Chapter VIII nor could be rationalized by a threat of imminent humanitarian disaster. The argument can be made, with at least a modicum of plausibility, that *coups* against elected governments are now, *per se*, violations of international law, and that regional organizations are now licensed to use force to reverse such *coups* in member states.[390]

Cautious as this statement is, the two conclusions (from which Roth ultimately retreats) simply do not follow. If the argument is that customary international law has evolved to the point where the nature of regime-change attracts international legal consequences (though implicitly restricted to violent overthrows of elected regimes), more evidence than a Security Council determination that such a *coup* constitutes a threat to peace and security must be established. Similarly, the retrospective validation of acts by the Council can hardly be equated with the granting of a licence to perform such acts in future.

## CONCLUSION

We have been told that one of the pillars of the new world order is respect for law and the rule of law. That statement has given us cause for hope. What we are witnessing, however, is in point of fact a gradual retreat from law and the rule of law and, in some cases, an attempt to circumvent the international rule of law for political ends.

We find this new world order ominous. We see a lack of balance. Indeed, there is an imbalance here. We see no firm application of law, and unless we are extremely careful this may lead to a change of the rules that have contributed to stability over the past four decades. It is indeed a strange world, and we may be in for many surprises.

Representative of Yemen, 1991[391]

Michael Reisman has referred to the intended role of the Security Council in conflict resolution as comparable to that of a *deus ex machina* in theatre: the providential intervenor 'is assumed to be untainted by the political objectives of the belligerents'; it harbours no long-term objectives of its own 'other than the selfless, altruistic one of securing a peace agreement. These traits do indeed approach the divine.'[392] As the preceding review of the new interventionism of the Security Council has shown, it is extremely difficult to reconcile the practice of the Council in the 1990s with any principled interpretation of its legal mandate.

A process of evolution is inevitable in an institution like the Council. Notably, the practice of regarding an abstention (or an absence) as a 'concurring' vote for the purposes of Article 27(3) was an initially problematic

[390] Roth, above n 365, 407.    [391] S/PV.2982 (1991) 30–1 (discussing SC Res 688 (1991)).
[392] W Michael Reisman, 'Stopping Wars and Making Peace: Reflections on the Ideology and Practice of Conflict Termination in Contemporary World Politics' (1998) 6 *Tulane JICL* 5, 29. Cf Richard K Betts, 'The Delusion of Impartial Intervention' (1994) 73(6) *Foreign Affairs* 20.

position that is now regarded as uncontroversial.[393] But in the past decade it appears that a great many procedural questions have been rendered moot. Notably, the plasticity of the Council's mandate to take enforcement actions appears reducible primarily to the political will of those states prepared to act. The danger, here, is that subjecting such an ostensibly legal process to the fickle winds of the political climate diminishes the normative power of international law. It is precisely the aim of an international rule of law to restrain the arbitrary use of power in international society; equally, it should prevent the exercise of such power being legitimated by dubious legal processes.

This is perhaps best borne out in statements accompanying the passage of a resolution not directly considered here. When the Council imposed sanctions on Libya for failing to hand over suspected terrorists, the US delegate stated that the resolution

makes it clear that neither Libya nor indeed any other State can seek to hide support for international terrorism behind traditional principles of international law and State practice.[394]

What, precisely, is replacing 'traditional principles of international law' remains unsaid. Two related trends can be identified, however.

The first is the arbitrariness of the current system. The repeated references to the 'uniqueness' of the situations in which the Council has acted over the past decade now appear disingenuous.[395] If anything was unique about Somalia, Rwanda, and Haiti it was that the United States and France decided to act *and* to seek Council authority to do so. At least in relation to Haiti there is evidence that a Russian veto was avoided only by an agreement to support a resolution on a CIS peacekeeping mission in Georgia.[396] Of course the nature of the international system will require such compromises, just as the absence of a standing UN army makes all operations dependent on the political will to send troops and money—the failings of the United Nations are indeed the failings of its member states. But the lack of consistency undermines faith in the United Nations as a whole.[397] One of many possible illustrations of this point is the case of Sudan. Civil war has raged there for 17 years, with an estimated two million casualties.[398] And yet the only resolutions passed by the Council in relation to Sudan concern its failure to extradite suspects in the unsuccessful attempt to assassinate President Mubarak of Egypt, which failure it determined to threaten international peace and security.[399]

---

[393] See Ch 2, Sect 2.2.1.

[394] S/PV.3033 (1992) 80, referring to SC Res 731 (1992). See also Brownlie, above n 3, 101.

[395] The Security Council resolutions on Somalia, Rwanda, and Haiti variously described the situations as 'unique' and thus exceptional.

[396] See Ch 5, Sect 2.1.          [397] Cf Berdal, above n 132, 71–2.

[398] See, eg, Editorial, 'Misguided Relief to Sudan', *NYT*, 6 Dec 1999.

[399] SC Res 1054 (1996).

The second trend is that this lack of coherence in the Security Council's mandate devalues the currency of international law. It is clear that the Council was intended to have a measure of discretion in carrying out its primary role in maintaining peace and security. Significantly, the relevant terms in Chapter VII are not defined in the Charter—the definition of aggression remains controversial[400]—and the question of whether its actions are subject to judicial review remains unclear. In light of the Council practice discussed in this Chapter, it would be easy to conclude that its discretion is absolute and that any attempt to reconcile practice with theory is futile.

But this would be to throw the normative baby out with the bathwater. What is perhaps most interesting about Council practice in the past decade is that it has become regarded as an important political aid in justifying the use of force. For the first time, the United States sought authorization to use force in the Western hemisphere; France was twice authorized to intervene in Africa; Nigeria twice sought belated recognition for its own operations through ECOMOG. Clearly, none of these actions was wholly disinterested, but in each case that interest was at least moulded into a form that gained support in the Security Council. At the same time, the repeated reference to the 'unique and exceptional' circumstances that justified such actions was perhaps recognition that to give explicit legal approval to a principle of humanitarian intervention might be to open a door that was better kept closed.[401]

The new world order was thus compromised by much older problems, though it would be simplistic merely to assert that bipolar paralysis gave way to unipolar unilateralism. If anything, Council practice of the period exhibited the promise and the danger of a more activist Organization tied to a legal framework still subject to the will of member states.

---

[400] See, eg, Rome Statute of the International Criminal Court, 17 July 1998, UN Doc A/CONF 183/9* (as corrected by the *procés-verbaux* of 10 Nov 1998 and 12 July 1999) art 5(2) (providing that the ICC will have jurisdiction over the crime of aggression once a definition is adopted in accordance with arts 121 and 123).

[401] Cf Adam Roberts, *Humanitarian Action in War: Aid Protection and Implementation in a Policy Vacuum* (Adelphi Paper 305; London: IISS, 1996) 26.

# 5

# Passing the Baton

## *The delegation of Security Council enforcement powers from Kuwait to Kosovo*

> The purpose of the enforcement action under Article 39 is not to maintain or restore the law, but to maintain, or restore peace, which is not necessarily identical with the law.
>
> Hans Kelsen, 1950[1]

By late October 1990 Iraq had occupied Kuwait for more than two months and a consensus was emerging between the United States and the USSR that some form of enforcement action might be authorized by the Security Council. In the course of negotiations, a senior US State Department official was quoted to the effect that, '[l]egally, our position and the position shared by others is that Article 51 provides a sufficient basis under international law for further action'. A Council resolution authorizing some specific military action would, however, 'provide a firmer political basis'.[2] There was little serious discussion of establishing an independent UN force; rather, the preferred action would put coalition forces under a kind of UN 'umbrella'. On a visit to Moscow on 8 November, US Secretary of State James Baker lobbied for such a resolution, citing President Mikhail Gorbachev's 1987 speech on enhancing the role of the United Nations.[3] Gorbachev suggested that the Council pass two resolutions: the first, adopted in late November, would authorize force after a six-week grace period; the second would provide the actual go-ahead. Baker proposed a single resolution with a grace period before it would become operative.[4] When he met the Soviet Foreign Minister Eduard Shevardnadze in Paris on 18 November, the United States believed it had the votes for a resolution but the USSR demurred;[5] among other concerns,

---

[1] Hans Kelsen, *The Law of the United Nations* (London: Stevens & Sons, 1950) 294.

[2] Thomas L Friedman, 'Allies Tell Baker Use of Force Needs UN Backing', *NYT*, 8 Nov 1990.

[3] Mikhail S Gorbachev, 'Reality and the Guarantees of a Secure World', in *FBIS Daily Report: Soviet Union*, 17 Sept 1987, 23–8, cited in David Malone, *Decision-Making in the UN Security Council: The Case of Haiti, 1990–1997* (Oxford: Clarendon Press, 1998) 8.

[4] Thomas L Friedman, 'How US Won Support to Use Mideast Forces', *NYT*, 2 Dec 1990; Michael R Beschloss and Strobe Talbott, *At the Highest Levels: The Inside Story of the End of the Cold War* (London: Little Brown, 1993) 282.

[5] Andrew Rosenthal, 'Bush Fails to Gain Soviet Agreement on Gulf Force Use', *NYT*, 20 Nov 1990.

Shevardnadze insisted that the actual word 'force' not be used. Baker came up with five different euphemisms, finally settling on the phrase 'all necessary means'.[6]

On 29 November 1990 resolution 678 (1990) was adopted by twelve votes to two (Cuba and Yemen) with China abstaining. In its operative paragraph, the Security Council

*Authorizes* Member States co-operating with the Government of Kuwait, unless Iraq on or before 15 January 1991 fully implements . . . the foregoing resolutions, to use all necessary means to uphold and implement resolution 660 (1990) and all subsequent relevant resolutions and to restore international peace and security in the area.[7]

The extraordinary breadth of the resolution was barely remarked upon during debate. Cuba and Iraq denounced it as illegal for its failure to refer to the relevant articles of Chapter vii,[8] but only Yemen expressed concern at the possible scope of 'restor[ing] international peace and security in the area'.[9]

Resolution 678 (1990) provided the template for most of the enforcement actions taken through the 1990s: it was dependent on the willingness of certain states to undertake (and fund) a military operation; it conferred a broad discretion on those states to determine when and how the enumerated goals might be achieved; it limited Council involvement to a vague request to 'keep the Security Council regularly informed';[10] and it failed to provide an endpoint for the mandate. These four elements came to typify the manner in which the authority to maintain peace and security was delegated by the body given primary responsibility in this area. Early questions about the procedural legality of this adaptation of the Council's role now appear moot in light of state practice over the past decade. The Council has delegated its Chapter vii powers to member states for a variety of objectives: to counter a use of force by a state or entities within a state; to carry out a naval interdiction; to enforce a Council-declared no-fly zone; and to ensure implementation of an agreement that the Council has deemed is necessary for the maintenance or restoration of peace.[11] Of central interest here is the extent to which Council actions over the course of the past decade in fact mark a trend away from the *substantive* provisions of the collective security system envisaged in the UN Charter—and, indeed, that envisaged in the 'new world order' rhetoric amid the euphoria that followed Operation Desert Storm, which drove Iraq from Kuwait in 1991.

---

[6] Beschloss and Talbott, above n 4, 284; David Hoffman, 'Six Weeks of Intense Consultations Led to UN Resolution', *Washington Post*, 2 Dec 1990.
[7] SC Res 678 (1990) para 2.              [8] S/PV.2963 (1990) 20-1 (Iraq), 58 (Cuba).
[9] Ibid 33 (Yemen).                        [10] SC Res 678 (1990) para 4.
[11] See Danesh Sarooshi, *The United Nations and the Development of Collective Security: The Delegation by the UN Security Council of its Chapter VII Powers* (Oxford: Clarendon Press, 1999) 167–246.

This Chapter argues that the weakening of the normative framework of the collective security system can be tracked in the progression from open-ended resolutions 'authorizing' unilateral action, to the retrospective validation of actions by regional arrangements and, finally, unilateral action claimed to be 'in support of' Council resolutions. First, it will be necessary to examine the legal and political bases for delegating Security Council enforcement powers. This provides a framework for the analysis of the normative consequences of such delegation. Section 2 then considers the effect that handing over effective responsibility for enforcement actions has on the initial decision to take such action and the increasingly explicit links with the self-interest of the acting state(s). Section 3 looks in more detail at the uncertainty that ambiguous or open-ended delegations create in practice. Finally, Section 4 considers two case studies of interventions that were claimed to be undertaken, at least in part, in support of Security Council resolutions: the no-fly zones in northern and southern Iraq policed by the United States, the United Kingdom, and (for a time) France; and NATO's Operation Allied Force in the Federal Republic of Yugoslavia (FRY).

The central argument advanced here is that the Council's practice of delegating its enforcement powers has depended more upon a coincidence of national interest than on procedural legality. It would be naïve to expect complete disinterestedness on the part of states exercising such delegated power. Nevertheless, the trend towards action in advance of Council authorization can, in part, be attributed to the reduction of delegation to a mere formality.

## 1. THE DELEGATION OF SECURITY COUNCIL ENFORCEMENT POWERS

The Security Council resolutions delegating its enforcement powers to states or regional arrangements uniformly use the term 'authorize'. This is misleading. Whereas an authorization implies the conferring of a limited power to exercise a function, delegation more properly denotes a broader discretion to use the power held by the delegator. As Danesh Sarooshi observes, this is an important distinction to maintain, even if it is not always clear in formal terms.[12] Though some of the delegations discussed in this Chapter were circumscribed by Council requirements as to the objectives, reporting requirements or time limits, the central characteristic has been the transferral of discretion in the exercise of Council powers to the acting state(s). This section discusses the emergence of delegation in Council practice and the modalities of delegation through the 1990s.

The provisions in the UN Charter concerning Security Council enforcement actions presume the existence of agreements with member states to

---

[12] Ibid 13.

make forces available to the Council 'on its call'.[13] Article 106, for example, provides for transitional security arrangements '[p]ending the coming into force of such special agreements referred to in Article 43 as in the opinion of the Security Council enable it to begin the exercise of its responsibilities under Article 42'.[14] Governments at the San Francisco Conference and many subsequent commentators on the Charter considered Article 43 agreements a condition precedent to collective military measures by the Security Council.[15]

Such agreements were never concluded.[16] Some sixteen years after the formation of the United Nations a number of states refused to pay for the UNEF and ONUC peacekeeping operations in the Middle East and the Congo, arguing *inter alia* that they involved military forces operating outside of Article 43 agreements and were therefore unconstitutional. In the *Certain Expenses* advisory opinion, the International Court of Justice held that these were not, in fact, enforcement actions under Chapter VII, but went on to outline a broad compass for Security Council action:

[A]n argument which insists that all measures taken for the maintenance of international peace and security must be financed through agreements concluded under Article 43, would seem to exclude the possibility that the Security Council might act under some other Article of the Charter. The Court cannot accept so limited a view of the powers of the Security Council under the Charter. It cannot be said that the Charter has left the Security Council impotent in the face of an emergency situation when agreements under Article 43 have not been concluded.[17]

This flexibility has been confirmed by subsequent practice and a strong argument may now be made that agreements under Article 43 are not a prerequisite to enforcement action under Article 42—merely to the ability legally to compel participation by member states at large.[18] On this reading, Article 42 also provides the basis for *voluntary* action by member states acting on Council authorization.[19]

---

[13] UN Charter, art 43(1). Such agreements were to be negotiated 'as soon as possible': art 43(3).

[14] UN Charter, art 106.

[15] See 12 UNCIO 508–12; Kelsen, above n 1, 756; Leland M Goodrich and Anne Patricia Simmons, *The United Nations and the Maintenance of International Peace and Security* (Washington, DC: Brookings, 1955) 398–405; Yoram Dinstein, *War, Aggression and Self-Defence* (2nd edn; Cambridge: Cambridge University Press, 1994) 296–7.

[16] See Ch 4, Sects 1.1.1–1.1.2.

[17] *Certain Expenses Case* [1962] ICJ Rep 151, 167.

[18] See, eg, John W Halderman, 'Legal Basis for United Nations Armed Forces' (1962) 56 *AJIL* 971; Rosalyn Higgins, *United Nations Peacekeeping 1946–1967: Documents and Commentary: Vol 2, Asia* (London: Oxford University Press, 1970) 176–7; Oscar Schachter, 'United Nations Law in the Gulf Conflict' (1991) 85 *AJIL* 452, 464; Rosalyn Higgins, 'The New United Nations and the Former Yugoslavia' (1993) 69 *International Affairs* 465, 468; Michael Bothe, 'Peace-Keeping', in Bruno Simma (ed), *The Charter of the United Nations: A Commentary* (Oxford: Oxford University Press, 1994) 565, 590–1.

[19] Cf Schachter, above n 18, 464–5.

At the time of the Gulf War, a number of writers persisted with the argument that the absence of Article 43 agreements deprived resolution 678 (1990) of any legal basis, with many preferring to locate the action of coalition states in the collective self-defence provisions of Article 51.[20] Devoid of legal significance, the resolution was regarded as more of a public relations exercise.[21] In light of the large number of such operations undertaken in the 1990s, such a distinction now appears untenable.[22] Most criticism of resolution 678 (1990) focused on the decision to delegate the enforcement powers of the Security Council, invoking either the letter or the spirit of the Charter. In addition to the requirement for Article 43 agreements, some writers noted that Articles 46 and 47 imply that enforcement actions should take place under the control of the Council and the Military Staff Committee.[23] Others argued that the primary responsibility for peace and security conferred upon the Council by Article 24 was incompatible with delegation,[24] and that in handing over control of the operation to the coalition forces, the Council 'eschewed direct UN responsibility *and* accountability for the military force that ultimately was deployed'.[25] These criticisms recall earlier disputes about the legal status of the Korean operation in 1950.[26] That case was further complicated by the Council's use of the word 'recommend' in the relevant resolution,[27] recalling the language of Article 39. The geopolitics of the Cold War ensured that the legal ambiguities of the Korean operation were left unresolved.[28]

The precise legal basis for delegation remains in dispute. One view is that, as a matter of the law of international institutions, the Council has competence to delegate Chapter VII powers to member states. This competence is located in the practice of the Council and other UN organs, and in an interpretation of Articles 42 and 53 of the Charter.[29] Sarooshi has argued that a

---

[20]  See, eg, Eugene V Rostow, 'Until What? Enforcement Action or Collective Self-Defense?' (1991) 85 *AJIL* 506; Schachter, above n 18, 459–60; Dinstein, above n 15, 272; D J Harris, *Cases and Materials on International Law* (5th edn; London: Sweet & Maxwell, 1998) 961–2.

[21]  Schachter, above n 18, 460. Cf above n 2.

[22]  Cf Kaiyan Homi Kaikobad, 'Self-Defence, Enforcement Action and the Gulf Wars: 1980–88 and 1990–91' (1992) 63 *British YBIL* 299, 353–63; John Quigley, 'The "Privatization" of Security Council Enforcement Action: A Threat to Multilateralism' (1996) 17 *Michigan JIL* 249, 269–70.

[23]  See, eg, Brian Urquhart, 'Learning from the Gulf', *New York Review*, 7 Mar 1991, 34.

[24]  See, eg, Michael Bothe, 'Les limites des pouvoirs du Conseil de sécurité', in René-Jean Dupuy (ed), *The Development of the Role of the Security Council: Peace-Keeping and Peace-Building* (Dordrecht: Martinus Nijhoff, 1993) 67, 73.

[25]  Burns H Weston, 'Security Council Resolution 678 and Persian Gulf Decision Making: Precarious Legitimacy' (1991) 85 *AJIl* 516, 517.

[26]  See, eg, Kelsen, above n 1, 756; Leland M Goodrich, Edvard Hambro, and Anne Patricia Simons, *Charter of the United Nations: Commentary and Documents* (3rd edn; New York: Columbia University Press, 1969) 315–16; Harris, above n 20, 955.

[27]  SC Res 82 (1950); SC Res 83 (1950); SC Res 84 (1950). Relevant sections of the resolutions are collected in Appendix 4.1.

[28]  For a discussion of Security Council actions in the Congo and Southern Rhodesia that approximated enforcement actions, see Ch 4, Sect 1.1.1.

[29]  See generally Sarooshi, above n 11, 142–66.

corollary of this position is that there are certain limits on the Security Council's power of delegation: a minimum degree of clarity, a requirement for some form of supervision on the part of the Council, and a requirement that the Council oblige member states to report on the way in which the delegated powers are being exercised.[30]

Secondly, it has been argued that the Council possesses—or has created—a general implied power under the Charter to authorize member states to use force.[31] This view is based on an 'effective' interpretation of the Charter and finds some support in the *Reparation* case.[32] It has the benefit of 'fitting' all purported delegations, but at the expense of any clear limitations on the Council's power to delegate.

Thirdly, it has been argued that Article 48 of the Charter, which provides that the 'action required to carry out the decisions of the Security Council for the maintenance of international peace and security shall be taken by all Members of the United Nations or by some of them, as the Security Council may determine', allows the Council to delegate its Chapter VII powers.[33] This interpretation has received little support. Article 48 refers only to the *execution* of decisions of the Council, which must find their basis in other provisions.[34] Its effect is to restate the obligation of members to carry out the decisions of the Council and to allow the Council flexibility in its mandate by giving it discretionary authority to decide which members shall be called upon to take action.[35]

[30] Sarooshi, above n 11, 155–63.

[31] See Thomas M Franck and Faiza Patel, 'UN Police Action in Lieu of War: "The Old Order Changeth"' (1991) 85 *AJIL* 63, 74; Oscar Schachter, 'Authorized Uses of Force by the United Nations and Regional Organizations', in Lori Fisler Damrosch and David J Scheffer (eds), *Law and Force in the New International Order* (Boulder: Westview, 1991) 65, 68; Weston, above n 25, 522 (referring to 'Article 42½'); Helmut Freudenschuss, 'Between Unilateralism and Collective Security: Authorizations of the Use of Force by the UN Security Council' (1994) 5 *European JIL* 492, 526; Giorgio Gaga, 'Use of Force Made or Authorized by the United Nations', in Christian Tomuschat (ed), *The United Nations at Age Fifty: A Legal Perspective* (The Hague: Kluwer Law International, 1995) 39, 41; Frederic L Kirgis, 'The Security Council's First Fifty Years' (1995) 89 *AJIL* 506, 521.

[32] See *Reparation Case* [1949] ICJ Rep 174, 179, 182: 'Under international law, the Organization must be deemed to have those powers which, though not expressly provided in the Charter, are conferred upon it by necessary implication as being essential to the performance of its duties.' See also the discussion of the *Certain Expenses* case: above n 17.

[33] UN Charter, art 48(1). See, eg, Marc Weller, 'The Kuwait Crisis: A Survey of Some Legal Issues' (1991) 3 *African JICL* 1, 25–6; Christopher Greenwood, 'The United Nations as Guarantor of International Peace and Security: Past, Present and Future—A United Kingdom View', in Tomuschat, above n 31, 59, 69–70. Cf Kelsen, above n 1, 756 (observing that, despite the apparent intention of the framers, the wording of Articles 39, 42, 47, and 48 'does not exclude the possibility of a decision of the Security Council to the effect that Members which have not concluded a special agreement under Article 43 shall take a definite enforcement action, or that Members which have concluded special agreements shall provide armed forces in excess of those which they have placed at the disposal of the Council in their special agreements').

[34] Brun-Otto Bryde, 'Articles 44–50', in Simma, above n 18, 640, 652.

[35] Goodrich, Hambro, and Simons, above n 26, 334.

The experience of the Security Council over the decade following resolution 678 (1990) has seen procedure evolve through practice: the delegation of Chapter VII powers now appears to have gained relatively broad acceptance, with few publicists seriously contesting its legitimacy after about 1996,[36] and very few states criticizing delegation in principle.[37] Such an organic interpretation of the UN Charter is not uncommon—Secretary-General Dag Hammarskjöld located peacekeeping in 'Chapter VI½' of the Charter, and the *Uniting for Peace* resolution was a creative response to Security Council deadlock.[38] But it is not an adequate response simply to conclude that the Council may play 'fast and loose' with the Charter, privileging success over legitimacy.[39] Rather, it is necessary to adopt a more nuanced critique of the practice of delegation. The greatest innovation of the UN Charter was the prohibition of the use of force by member states other than in self-defence, with the authority to use force in other situations reserved to the Security Council. The Covenant of the League of Nations, by contrast, merely gave its Council the power to advise members of the League on matters of collective security: the decision to act on any such advice lay ultimately with states themselves.[40] In many respects, current practice resembles this structure more than that originally envisaged in Chapter VII.[41] A central concern with such an application of the Charter, then, is the extent to which a liberal attitude to Security Council authority affects the more basic normative constraints on unilateral action.

A preliminary question that must be considered is where delegated enforcement action fits within the collective security regime of the UN Charter. In June 1992 Secretary-General Boutros Boutros-Ghali attempted to outline a framework within which the revitalized United Nations could play a more significant role in maintaining international peace and security. *An Agenda for Peace* defined four key areas in which the Organization could assist in the resolution and prevention of conflict:

---

[36] See, eg, Urquhart, above n 23 (criticizing SC Res 678 (1990)) and cf Brian Urquhart, 'How Not to Fight a Dictator', *New York Review*, 6 May 1999, 25 (referring to the Council's actions as 'exemplary and prompt').

[37] In addition to the criticism of SC Res 678 (1990) on Iraq, see also the criticism of SC Res 940 (1994) on Haiti: S/PV.3413 (1994) 5 (Cuba), 10 (China). The policy concerns attendant to handing over primary responsibility for peace and security are considered below.

[38] See Ch 4, Sect 1.1.2.

[39] Quigley, above n 22, 260. Cf David D Caron, 'The Legitimacy of the Collective Authority of the Security Council' (1993) 87 *AJIL* 552, 554 n 8; Richard A Falk, 'The United Nations and the Rule of Law' (1994) 4 *Transnational Law and Contemporary Problems* 611, 613 n 4.

[40] Covenant of the League of Nations, art 10: 'The Members of the League undertake to respect and preserve as against external aggression the territorial integrity and existing political independence of all Members of the League. In case of any such aggression or in case of any threat or danger of such aggression the Council shall advise upon the means by which this obligation shall be fulfilled.'

[41] Cf Quigley, above n 22, 261.

- *Preventive diplomacy*—action to prevent disputes from arising between parties, to prevent existing disputes from escalating into conflicts, and to limit the spread of conflicts when they occur.
- *Peacekeeping*—the deployment of a UN presence in the field, with the consent of the parties concerned, normally involving UN military and/or police personnel and frequently civilians as well.
- *Post-conflict peace-building*—action to identify and support structures that strengthen and solidify peace to avoid a relapse into conflict.
- *Peacemaking*—action to bring hostile parties to agreement, 'essentially through such peaceful means as those foreseen in Chapter VI of the Charter'.[42]

The first three areas of action were premised on the consent of the parties concerned and will not be directly considered here. 'Peacemaking', by contrast, was applicable to hostile parties and embraced a range of options, from adjudication by the ICJ and non-coercive humanitarian assistance, to sanctions and the use of military force by member states authorized by the Security Council or 'peace-enforcement units' operating under Article 43 agreements.[43] This schema did not reflect practice, however, and in the Secretary-General's March 1994 report on peacekeeping, peace-enforcement constituted an independent category,[44] as it did in the more conservative *Supplement to An Agenda for Peace* of January 1995.[45]

The search for an effective taxonomy is of more than academic interest. Clarity of mandate has been one of the primary concerns of 'Blue Helmets' operating under UN command and national troops under UN authorization—a major criticism of the Security Council has been the tendency for such mandates to relate more to the political climate in New York than the situation on the ground.[46] As the concern here is with the legality of the use of force, the focus will be on 'peace-enforcement' (here referred to simply as enforcement actions) and those situations in which peacekeeping adopts a more 'muscular' profile (variously described as 'extended' peacekeeping in Whitehall or 'aggravated' peacekeeping in the Pentagon[47]). The lack of coherence in the manner in which the Council delegated its enforcement powers in the period 1990–9 has spawned a cottage industry of analysis and critique. It is, however, useful to delineate some basic conceptual categories in

[42] An Agenda for Peace: Preventive Diplomacy, Peacemaking and Peace-keeping (Report of the Secretary-General pursuant to the statement adopted by the Summit Meeting of the Security Council on 31 Jan 1992), UN Doc A/47/277-S/24111 (1992) paras 20–1.

[43] Ibid paras 34–44.

[44] A/48/403-S/26450 (1994) para 4.

[45] Supplement to An Agenda for Peace: Position Paper of the Secretary-General on the Occasion of the Fiftieth Anniversary of the United Nations, UN Doc A/50/60-S/1995/1 (1995) paras 77–80.

[46] See below Sect 2.2.

[47] Thomas G Weiss, 'Rekindling Hope in UN Humanitarian Intervention', in Walter Clarke and Jeffrey Herbst (eds), *Learning from Somalia: The Lessons of Armed Humanitarian Intervention* (Boulder: Westview, 1997) 207, 211.

the different forms of delegation adopted by the Security Council. Broadly, five classes of action can be identified, which will be considered in turn:

   (i) Article 42 action by the Security Council using troops contributed pursuant to Article 43 agreements;

  (ii) action under the command of the Secretary-General;

  (iii) action by any state;

  (iv) action by certain nominated state(s); and

  (v) action by regional arrangement(s).

## 1.1. Action by the Security Council under Article 42

The failure to implement the collective security system as envisaged by the framers of the Charter is well documented.[48] In particular, agreements to place military forces at the disposal of the Security Council were never completed,[49] and the Military Staff Committee (MSC), which was to advise and assist the Security Council on the 'employment and command of forces placed at its disposal',[50] remains little more than a curiosity. Its published records indicate that the MSC has met once every two weeks since February 1946; in over fifty years, it has done nothing of substance since it reported to the Council in July 1948 that it was unable to complete the mandate given to it two years previously. Meetings presently last a couple of minutes.[51]

There are, occasionally, proposals to reinvigorate the MSC and conclude agreements under Article 43.[52] President Gorbachev suggested that the MSC be activated to manage the Council's response to Iraq's invasion of Kuwait;[53] resolution 665 (1990) requested the MSC to co-ordinate a naval 'interdiction' against Iraq, though its involvement was ultimately restricted to a few informal meetings for the exchange of information.[54] In *An Agenda for Peace* the Secretary-General recommended that the Security Council, supported by the MSC, 'initiate negotiations' towards Article 43 agreements.[55] By the time of

---

[48] See Ch 4, Sect 1.1.

[49] UN Charter, art 43. See Andrew Boyd, *Fifteen Men on a Powder Keg: A History of the UN Security Council* (London: Methuen, 1971) 78–81.

[50] UN Charter, art 47(1).

[51] Sydney D Bailey and Sam Daws, *The Procedure of the Security Council* (3rd edn; Oxford: Clarendon Press, 1998) 274. See also Boyd, above n 49, 80; Bryde, above n 34, 648.

[52] For an early example, see GA Res 2734(xxv) (1970) para 6.

[53] See Frank J Prial, 'Crisis Breathes Life into a Moribund UN Panel', *NYT*, 6 Sept 1990; Paul Lewis, 'Security Council's Military Panel Reviews Naval Efforts to Enforce Trade Embargo', *NYT*, 19 Sept 1990; Paul Lewis, 'Soviet Announces Shift on UN Staff Demanded by US', *NYT*, 4 June 1988.

[54] Bailey and Daws, above n 51, 280.

[55] Agenda for Peace, above n 42, para 43. See also Sean D Murphy, 'The Security Council, Legitimacy, and the Concept of Collective Security After the Cold War' (1994) 32 *Columbia JTL* 201, 275.

the *Supplement*, however, this was merely 'desirable in the long term'—to attempt to do so at the present time would be 'folly'.[56]

The relevant Charter provisions are hardly dead letters,[57] but the likeli-, hood of member states concluding such agreements in the foreseeable future is slim. In the words of one US officer, quoted during the gun-cocked withdrawal from Somalia in December 1993, the idea of US troops even *operating* under foreign command would be revived 'as soon as it snows in Mogadishu'.[58]

### 1.2. Action under the command of the Secretary-General

In the absence of a functioning collective security regime, peacekeeping became a substitute for Chapter VII action during the Cold War. With no provision for such operations in the Charter, peacekeeping was a pragmatic institutional response to the geopolitical climate in which the United Nations found itself.[59] Ultimate political control for such operations remains with the relevant principal organ (typically the Security Council[60]), but executive command is delegated to the Secretary-General.[61] The legality of such delegation by the Security Council was accepted by the ICJ in the *Certain Expenses* case,[62] and it is now established practice.[63]

As UN peacekeeping operations grew more complex in the 1990s, however, the line between peacekeeping and enforcement actions became blurred. In a

---

[56] Supplement to An Agenda for Peace, above n 45, para 77.

[57] Cf Schachter, above n 18, 464; Dinstein, above n 15, 297–9.

[58] Rick Atkinson, 'US to Leave Somalia with Its Guard up: Officers Say Lessons Learned in Perils of Urban Combat, Foreign Command', *Washington Post*, 8 Dec 1993. This is, of course, a misrepresentation of UNOSOM II—US troops remained at all times under US command, following US policy, but under a more robust UN mandate as determined by the Security Council. Blaming the UN for the death of Americans was more a rallying call for a return to isolationism than for US independence: see James L Woods, 'US Government Decisionmaking Processes During Humanitarian Operations in Somalia', in Clarke and Herbst, above n 47, 151, 167 (James L Woods served as chair of the US Office of the Secretary of Defence Somalia Task Force); Jonathan T Howe, 'Relations Between the United States and United Nations in Dealing with Somalia', in Clarke and Herbst, above n 47, 173, 185–6 (Jonathan T Howe was special representative of the Secretary-General in Somalia); Harry Johnston and Ted Dagne, 'Congress and the Somalia Crisis', in Clarke and Herbst, above n 47, 191, 202.

[59] See Ch 4, Sect 1.1.2.

[60] The First UN Emergency Force (UNEF I) (1956–67) and the UN Security Force in West New Guinea (West Irian) (UNSF: 1962–3) were established by General Assembly resolutions. See Ch 4, Sect 1.1.2.

[61] See Supplement to An Agenda for Peace, above n 45, para 38, distinguishing three levels of authority in respect of command and control over UN peacekeeping forces: '(a) Overall political direction, which belongs to the Security Council; (b) Executive direction and command, for which the Secretary-General is responsible; (c) Command in the field, which is entrusted by the Secretary-General to the chief of mission (special representative or force commander/chief military observer).'

[62] *Certain Expenses Case* [1962] ICJ Rep 151, 177.          [63] See Sarooshi, above n 11, 64.

departure from the principles of impartiality, consent and minimum force,[64] it became common for peacekeepers to be given more 'muscular' mandates while remaining under the operational control of the Secretary-General. UNPROFOR, for example, was initially established in February 1992 as a peace-keeping operation with the consent of the Yugoslav and other governments.[65] As the situation deteriorated, its mandate was expanded from monitoring demilitarization in certain 'United Nations Protected Areas' in Croatia to conducting more complex security operations through Croatia and Bosnia and Herzegovina. Then, in 1993, the Security Council established 'safe areas' around five Bosnian towns and the city of Sarajevo.[66] UNPROFOR was given an ambiguous mandate to protect them:

[The Security Council authorizes UNPROFOR] *acting in self-defence*, to take the neces-sary measures, including the use of force, in reply to bombardments against the safe areas by any of the parties or to armed incursion into them or in the event of any delib-erate obstruction in or around those areas to the freedom of movement of UNPROFOR or of protected humanitarian convoys.[67]

This exhibited an unusual interpretation of a right of 'self-defence', but recalled the expanding mandate given to ONUC forces in the Congo.[68] At the same time, while UNPROFOR operated on the ground an apparently general authorization was given to member states to take 'all necessary measures, through the use of air power' to support it in and around the safe areas from the air.[69] Though unclear in the resolution, the decision to initiate the use of air power was to be taken by the Secretary-General in consultation with the members of the Security Council.[70] This served to deter attacks in the short term, but when it was overrun by the Bosnian Serbs in 1995, the name of one of the safe areas, Srebrenica, became synonymous with the disjunction between Council rhetoric and resolve.[71]

Conventional wisdom concerning the fall of the Bosnian safe areas was that the international community had failed to learn the lessons of Somalia: that absolute impartiality was the keystone to a peacekeeping operation (ie,

---

[64] Mats R Berdal, *Whither UN Peacekeeping?* (Adelphi Paper 281; London: IISS, 1993) 3.
[65] SC Res 743 (1992).      [66] SC Res 819 (1993); SC Res 824 (1993).
[67] SC Res 836 (1993) para 9 (emphasis added). UNPROFOR's mandate was expanded in the fol-lowing terms: 'to enable it, in the safe areas referred to in resolution 824 (1993), to deter attacks against the safe areas, to monitor the cease-fire, to promote the withdrawal of military or para-military units other than those of the Government of the Republic of Bosnia and Herzegovina and to occupy some key points on the ground, in addition to participating in the delivery of humanitarian relief to the population as provided for in resolution 776 (1992)': ibid para 5.
[68] See above Ch 4, Sect 1.1.1.      [69] SC Res 836 (1993) para 10.
[70] S/25939 (1993). See Dick A Leurdijk, *The United Nations and NATO in Former Yugoslavia: Partners in International Cooperation* (The Hague: Netherlands Atlantic Commission, 1994) 16–17; Sarooshi, above n 11, 72–3.
[71] See Report of the Secretary-General pursuant to General Assembly resolution 53/35: The Fall of Srebrenica, UN Doc A/54/549 (1999).

the 'Mogadishu line' was crossed[72]), and that UN command provided an unworkable structure for the alternative—an enforcement action.[73] The apparent success of NATO air strikes in coercing the parties to negotiate at Dayton, Ohio in November 1995 reinforced this view, and the Dayton Peace Agreement was subsequently implemented and maintained by IFOR and SFOR—NATO-run operations authorized by but independent of the Security Council.[74]

Such wisdom gave rise to three policy changes. First, the strict dichotomy between peacekeeping and enforcement actions was reasserted, most notably by the Secretary-General in his *Supplement to An Agenda for Peace*.[75] Secondly, subsequent enforcement actions were kept under national and, importantly, *regional* control, rather than under that of the Council or the Secretary-General. Thirdly—and of particular importance to the situation in Kosovo in 1998–9[76]—Bosnia was taken as proof that superior air power could provide a 'clean' resolution to a messy conflict on the ground by coercing belligerents to negotiate. (This view overlooked the importance of Croatia's ground offensive in reversing Bosnian Serb gains and the effect that the prolonged ground war had had on the parties.[77])

### 1.3. Action by any state

The authorization granted by resolution 678 (1990) was general in form: addressed to 'Member States co-operating with the Government of Kuwait', it provided a broad mandate for the international community to respond to Iraqi aggression.[78] This was also the approach adopted in the first response to the humanitarian crisis in Bosnia and Herzegovina. Resolution 770 (1992) called upon 'States to take nationally or through regional agencies or arrangements all measures necessary' to facilitate delivery of humanitarian assistance in co-ordination with the United Nations.[79] Similarly, in resolutions 816 (1993) and 836 (1993), the Council's authorization was to states 'acting nationally or through regional organizations or arrangements'.[80]

---

[72] See below Sect 3.1.

[73] Michael Dobbs, 'Srebrenica Massacre's Uncertain Legacy: Slaughter by Serbs Last July Prodded NATO to Halt War, Yet Peace Remains Illusory in Bosnia', *Washington Post*, 7 July 1996. Cf Berdal, above n 64, 39–41 (discussing the difficulties of command and control in UN peacekeeping activities generally); Leurdijk, above n 70, 81.

[74] See below Sect 1.5.

[75] Supplement to An Agenda for Peace, above n 45, para 36. See also Shashi Tharoor, 'The Changing Face of Peace-Keeping and Peace-Enforcement' (1995) 19 *Fordham ILJ* 408.

[76] See below Sect 4.2.

[77] See, eg, Richard Holbrooke, *To End a War* (New York: Random House, 1998) 72–3.

[78] SC Res 678 (1990) para 2.                    [79] SC Res 770 (1992) para 2.

[80] SC Res 816 (1993) para 4; SC Res 836 (1993) para 10.

Two countervailing factors led to the abandonment of such a strategy. On the one hand, there was dissatisfaction with the breadth of the mandate that such an approach entailed; subsequent authorizations were generally more defined in their mandate and their reporting requirements. On the other, the experiences in Somalia and Bosnia led to a more explicit link between UN authorization and the preparedness of a state or states to act.

### 1.4. Action by nominated state(s)

The majority of Chapter VII enforcement actions in the period under consideration were delegated by the Security Council to certain nominated states or regional arrangements. The degree of specificity has varied, however.

### 1.4.1. *Authorization excluding (a) certain state(s)*

First, an authorization may be general in form but exclude a certain state or states. Resolution 678 (1990), for example, authorized 'Member States co-operating with the Government of Kuwait' to use all necessary means to restore peace and security—the apparent intention being to exclude Israel from the enforcement action. At the same time, this terminology also confused the issue as to whether the action was in fact enforcement or collective self-defence.[81]

### 1.4.2. *Authorization to participate in an operation led by a nominated state*

Secondly, an authorization may be addressed to member states in general but make their participation subject to the leadership of a nominated state. Though it is arguable whether or not it was an enforcement action, this is analogous to the resolution that put the Unified Command in Korea under US command and control in 1950.[82]

Operation Restore Hope (UNITAF) in Somalia (1992–93) was the first enforcement action of this type. Resolution 794 (1992) authorized

the Secretary-General and Member States cooperating to implement the offer referred to in paragraph 8 above to use all necessary means to establish as soon as possible a secure environment for humanitarian relief operations in Somalia.[83]

In language that bordered on the coy, paragraph 8 referred to 'the offer by a Member State described in the Secretary-General's letter to the Council of

---

[81] See above nn 20–1.

[82] See Ch 4, Sect 1.1.1. At the same time, Sarooshi argues that the Security Council delegated other powers to the Unified Command (such as the power to conclude a ceasefire) making it comparable to a subsidiary organ: see Sarooshi, above n 11, 111–19.

[83] SC Res 794 (1992) para 10.

29 November 1992'.[84] A subsequent provision authorized the Secretary-General and member states concerned to 'make the necessary arrangements for the unified command and control of the forces involved, which will reflect the offer referred to in paragraph 8 above'.[85] The effect was to hand over responsibility for the military operation to the United States.[86]

Resolution 940 (1994) on Haiti was still more discreet, simply authorizing 'Member States to form a multinational force under unified command and control'. Nevertheless, US preparedness to organize and lead the operation to reinstall Aristide was made clear in Council debate immediately after the resolution was adopted.[87] The resolutions concerning Canada's proposed operation in eastern Zaïre (1996) and the Italian-led multinational force in Albania (1997), by contrast, both welcomed the offer by a member state to take the lead in organizing and commanding the action.[88] The resolution authorizing the Australian-led multinational force in East Timor (1999) followed a similar model.[89]

### 1.4.3.  Authorization solely to nominated state(s)

Thirdly, a resolution may explicitly authorize a named state or states to undertake action on the Council's behalf. Such a practice is not without precedent—resolution 221 (1966) authorized the United Kingdom (named in the resolution) to use force to police the embargo on Southern Rhodesia, though whether this was in fact an enforcement action is debatable.[90]

Opération Turquoise by France (with Senegal) in Rwanda in 1994 is the only other action to have been undertaken on such a basis. Though such an authorization is not far removed from one in which a state is given leadership of an action, it was presumably the lack of even a suggestion of multilateralism that explains the failure to repeat this practice. An additional concern was that France was hardly the most appropriate state to intervene, given its role in arming and training the predominantly Hutu government forces.[91] These

---

[84]  SC Res 794 (1992) para 8, referring to S/24868.
[85]  Ibid para 12.                          [86]  See Ch 4, Sect 3.2.1.
[87]  S/PV.3413 (1994) 13 (statement by Madeleine Albright that 'the United States is prepared to organize and lead such a force').
[88]  SC Res 1080 (1996) para 4 (welcoming Canadian offer S/1996/941 to lead an operation in eastern Zaïre); SC Res 1101 (1997) para 3 (welcoming Italian offer S/1997/258 to lead operation in Albania). See Ch 4, Sects 3.2.3 and 3.2.4.
[89]  SC Res 1264 (1999) para 6 (welcoming the 'offers by Member States to organize, lead and contribute to the multinational force', with the Australian offer to lead (S/1999/975) welcomed in the preamble).
[90]  See Ch 4, Sect 1.1.1. See also Sarooshi, above n 11, 195–200.
[91]  John F Murphy, 'Force and Arms', in Oscar Schachter and Christopher C Joyner (eds), *United Nations Legal Order* (Cambridge: Cambridge University Press, 1995) 247, 248; Philip Gourevitch, *We Wish to Inform You that Tomorrow We Will Be Killed with Our Familiars* (London: Picador, 1999) 88–90, 154–5. See Ch 4, Sect 3.2.2.

reservations were reflected in the five abstentions to resolution 929 (1994) and statements made before and after the vote.[92]

## 1.5. Action by regional arrangements (or agencies)[93]

Finally, and in what may prove to be the most significant trend in Security Council practice, authorization has, on a number of occasions, been granted to regional arrangements. Delegation to a regional arrangement is less problematic than delegation to member states as it is specifically provided for in Chapter VIII of the Charter, Article 53(1) of which provides that:

The Security Council shall, where appropriate, utilize such regional arrangements or agencies for enforcement action under its authority. But no enforcement action shall be taken under regional arrangements or by regional agencies without the authorization of the Security Council.[94]

Though NATO has long resisted characterization as a regional arrangement[95] (which would require it to act only on the Council's authorization, rather than merely to report on measures taken in its capacity as a collective self-defence organization[96]), its 'out of area' actions will be included within this category.[97] Certainly, the resolutions concerning NATO suggest that the Council considers it to be a regional arrangement that may be entrusted with specific enforcement actions.[98]

Earlier resolutions on Bosnia had authorized member states to act nationally or '*through* regional arrangements',[99] but the first delegation to a regional arrangement *stricto sensu* was the IFOR operation that superseded UNPROFOR in Bosnia and Herzegovina. The Dayton Agreement—which had

---

[92] SC Res 929 (1994) adopted 10-0-5 (Brazil, China, New Zealand, Nigeria, Pakistan abstaining). See S/PV.3392 (1994).

[93] On the delegation of enforcement powers to regional arrangements generally, see Sarooshi, above n 11, 247–84 and sources there cited.

[94] UN Charter, art 53(1).

[95] See, eg, S/25996 (1993) 18, in which NATO presents itself as a 'collective defence organization' prepared to support peacekeeping activities on a case-by-case basis.

[96] UN Charter, art 51.

[97] The German Constitutional Court has held that NATO may be classified as a type of collective security system, and that German troops could participate in NATO actions directed at the implementation of Security Council resolutions: *Adria-, AWACS- und Somalia-Einsatze der Bundeswehr* (1994) 90 BVerfGE 286. See also Markus Zöckler, 'Germany in Collective Security Systems—Anything Goes?' (1995) 6 *European JIL* 274, 279. For an early argument that NATO may plausibly be considered a regional arrangement, see Hans Kelsen, 'Is the North Atlantic Treaty a Regional Arrangement?' (1951) 45 *AJIL* 162.

[98] George Ress, 'Article 53', in Simma, above n 18, 722, 730; Christine Gray, 'Regional Arrangements and the United Nations Collective Security System', in Hazel Fox (ed), *The Changing Constitution of the United Nations* (London: BIICL, 1997) 92, 113. *Contra* Bruno Simma, 'NATO, the UN and the Use of Force: Legal Aspects' (1999) 10 *European JIL* 1, 10.

[99] See above nn 79–80.

Just War or Just Peace?

been concluded under the threat of further NATO air strikes—reinforced the view that military rather than political mechanisms were necessary to enforce a peace agreement. This was specifically provided for at Dayton, with the parties 'invit[ing]' the Security Council to adopt the resolution to establish IFOR.[100] Resolution 1031 (1995), duly adopted, authorized member states 'acting through or in cooperation with the organization referred to in Annex 1–A of the Peace Agreement [sc NATO] . . . under unified command and control' to take 'all necessary measures to effect the implementation of and to ensure compliance with Annex 1-A of the Peace Agreement'.[101] As in the case of the US offer to lead troops into Somalia,[102] NATO was not explicitly mentioned in the text of the resolution, nor in resolution 1088 (1996) establishing SFOR as IFOR's legal successor.

Lesser authorizations have also been given to the Economic Community of West African States (ECOWAS) acting through the ECOWAS Cease-fire Monitoring Group (ECOMOG) in Western Africa. The retrospective validation of ECOMOG's 'peacekeeping' role in Liberia (1990–2) was passed with a preambular reference to Chapter VIII of the UN Charter, though Chapter VII was only invoked to impose an arms embargo.[103] In Sierra Leone (1997–8), ECOWAS was expressly authorized under Chapters VII and VIII to enforce the arms embargo against rebel forces.[104] Two months earlier, the Council specifically approved the 'peacekeeping' activities of the Inter-African Mission to Monitor the Implementation of the Bangui Agreements (MISAB) in the Central African Republic (CAR).[105] An ad hoc organization formed to supervise the Bangui Agreements, MISAB comprised troops from six countries in the region (Burkina Faso, Chad, Gabon, Mali, Senegal, and Togo).[106]

The ambiguous legal status accorded by the Security Council to NATO's actions in Kosovo is evidence of the strengths and weaknesses of such a regime. NATO was by then regarded as the United States' 'institution of choice' for defending Western values on 'Europe's doorstep'.[107] At the same time, Russia (among others) expressed its concern that an organization specifically set up in opposition to Russian interests was now asserting regional pre-eminence.[108] This tension was reflected in the Council resolutions on point: in October 1998 it endorsed agreements concluded under the threat of NATO air

[100] Dayton Agreement on Implementing the Federation of Bosnia and Herzegovina of 10 Nov 1995, UN Doc S/1995/1021 (1995), Annex 1A, art I(1)(a).
[101] SC Res 1031 (1995) paras 14–15.                                    [102] See above nn 83–6.
[103] SC Res 788 (1992). See Ch 4, Sect 3.1.3.
[104] SC Res 1132 (1997) para 8. See Ch 4, Sect 3.3.2.
[105] SC Res 1125 (1997) para 2. See Ch 4, Sect 3.1.5.
[106] UN Press Release SC/6407 (6 Aug 1997); Keesing's (1997) 41481.
[107] US Secretary of State Madeleine Albright, Press Conference on Kosovo, Brussels, 8 Oct 1998 <http://secretary.state.gov/www/statements/1998/981008.html>.
[108] See, eg, Thomas W Lippman, 'Russian Leader Cancels Trip in Protest', Washington Post, 24 Mar 1999.

strikes,[109] but failed to gain support for NATO to follow through with those threats.[110] The requirement that NATO troops be allowed freedom of movement throughout the whole of the FRY[111] was one of the main reasons given by the FRY for rejecting the Rambouillet Accords, and the composition of a 'peacekeeping' force was a major stumbling block in negotiations to stop the air strikes that followed.

In its new Strategic Concept, adopted in April 1999, NATO acknowledged the Security Council's 'primary responsibility for the maintenance of international peace and security'.[112] This was hailed by President Chirac as a 'triumph for French diplomacy'[113]—France had previously expressed concern about the lack of any clear legal basis for NATO's threatened action in Kosovo in late 1998.[114] Nevertheless, US officials reportedly said that the provision is 'virtually meaningless', because it does not require the alliance to obtain *explicit* UN Security Council approval for NATO military actions beyond its territory.[115]

### 1.6. Trends in delegation

The general trend of Security Council delegated actions in the 1990s, then, was towards intervention only when such action coincided with the preparedness of a regional power to act—NATO in Europe, France and ECOWAS in Western Africa, the United States in the Americas.[116] Evidence of such a trend has been shown in the *form* of authorizations, but this was accompanied by a more troubling shift in the practice of the Security Council away from debating international peace and security issues in open session, to granting its formal imprimatur to pre-arranged deals. Such practices depended on a level of political comity that ultimately foundered when national interests clashed over the appropriate response to the situation in Kosovo in 1998–9.[117]

---

[109] SC Res 1203 (1998) para 1.     [110] See Sect 4.2.

[111] Interim Agreement for Peace and Self-Government in Kosovo, signed at Rambouillet 23 Feb 1999, UN Doc S/1999/648 (1999), Appendix B, art 8.

[112] NATO Press Release (1999) 65 (24 Apr 1999) para 15.

[113] William Drozdiak and Thomas W Lippman, 'NATO Widens Security "Map"', *Washington Post*, 25 Apr 1999.

[114] Steven Erlanger, 'US to NATO: Widen Purpose to Fight Terror', *NYT*, 7 Dec 1998.

[115] William Drozdiak and Thomas W Lippman, 'NATO Widens Security "Map"', *Washington Post*, 25 Apr 1999.

[116] Australia's role in securing authorization to lead INTERFET in East Timor fits a similar model: see Ch 4, Sect 3.2.5.

[117] See below Sect 4.2.

## 2. THE WILLING AND THE ABLE

In the period under consideration, it became relatively common for the Security Council to authorize an enforcement action without formal debate, or with minimal statements that indicated that the true work was taking place outside the Council.[118] The Council is, of course, a political body and such manoeuvrings are a necessary part of its work. Nevertheless, two aspects of this procedural shift suggest that the Council delegated more than responsibility for the implementation of its decisions: the increasing dependence of Council action upon offers by member states to undertake or lead a given operation, and the changing role of the Secretary-General.

### 2.1.  Offers of acting states

The trend towards delegation has been compared to privatization of the Security Council's responsibility to maintain international peace and security.[119] Certainly, the Council has demonstrated a willingness to hand over control of enforcement actions to member states or regional arrangements, and its preparedness to invoke Chapter VII powers at all has been contingent on the political willingness of member states at least to impose sanctions.[120] This is commonly viewed as a realistic assessment of the capabilities of the United Nations. Secretary-General Boutros-Ghali observed that neither he nor the Security Council had the capacity to deploy, direct, command, and control such operations.[121] In the words of one analyst, the United Nations itself can no more conduct large-scale military operations than a trade association of hospitals can conduct heart surgery.[122]

The UNITAF operation in Somalia confirmed this view in the most graphic terms. Resolution 794 (1992) was not merely contingent on a US offer of troops—the first draft was written in the Pentagon and tailored to US Central Command (CENTCOM) concerns.[123] In a statement after the Security Council voted on the resolution, India's representative reflected on the fact that action was possible only because of the offer of the United States. Together with France and Morocco, India favoured

---

[118] Malone, above n 3, 13–15.

[119] Quigley, above n 22, 250.

[120] Peter H Kooijmans, 'The Enlargement of the Concept "Threat to the Peace"', in Dupuy, above n 24, 111, 112–13; N D White, *The United Nations and the Maintenance of International Peace and Security* (Manchester: Manchester University Press, 1990) 37. See further Ch 4.

[121] Supplement to An Agenda for Peace, above n 45, para 77.

[122] Michael Mandelbaum, 'The Reluctance to Intervene' (1994) 95 *Foreign Policy* 3, 11.

[123] Walter Clarke, 'Failed Visions and Uncertain Mandates in Somalia', in Clarke and Herbst, above n 47, 3, 9. Modifications were made in the course of Security Council debate, but the substance of both this and SC Res 814 (1993) were consistent with Pentagon demands: ibid.

an arrangement under which the United Nations would keep effective political command and control while leaving enough flexibility for the contributing States to retain on the ground the operational autonomy they had requested and which was understandable, given the circumstances. . . .

The present action should not, however, set a precedent for the future. We would expect that, should situations arise in the future requiring action under Chapter VII, it would be carried out in full conformity with the Charter provisions and in the spirit of the Secretary-General's report 'An Agenda for Peace'.[124]

Such hopes were misplaced. The action to protect Bosnian 'safe areas' in 1993 was authorized without a clear leadership role established in advance of the mandate, and was perceived to have failed, in part, for precisely that reason.[125] No action whatsoever would have been taken in response to the genocide in Rwanda had France not gone to the Council with a ready-made plan.[126] Similarly, the Council only proposed an enforcement action in Haiti when the United States had reversed its position to support and offer to lead such an action.[127] The process was repeated in eastern Zaïre (1996) and Albania (1997), where action followed Canadian and Italian offers to lead the respective actions.[128] And it seems probable that no action would have been taken in relation to the violence that followed East Timor's popular consultation on independence from Indonesia, had Australia not offered to lead a multinational force.[129]

This explicit conjunction of Security Council enforcement actions and national interest has exacerbated the politicization of Council voting. The inducements offered by the United States to members of the Security Council voting on resolution 678 (1990) are merely the most prominent example. These included promises of financial help to Colombia, Côte d'Ivoire, Ethiopia, and Zaïre, and agreements with the USSR to help keep Estonia, Latvia, and Lithuania out of the November 1990 Paris summit conference, and to persuade Kuwait and Saudi Arabia to provide it with hard currency. China's abstention appears to have been secured by agreements to lift trade sanctions in place since the June 1989 Tian'anmen Square massacre, and to support a World Bank loan of US$114.3m.[130] Yemen, one of the two states to vote against the resolution, had US$70 million in annual aid from the United States cut off[131]—minutes after the vote was taken, a senior US diplomat reportedly told the Yemeni representative: 'That was the most expensive no vote you ever cast.'[132] The other dissenting state (Cuba) was already the subject of extensive sanctions.

---

[124] S/PV.3145 (1992) 51 (India).　　　[125] See above Sect 1.2.
[126] See above Sect 1.4.3.　　　[127] See above n 87. See further Ch 4, Sect 3.3.1.
[128] See above n 88. See further Ch 4, Sects 3.2.3 (eastern Zaïre) and 3.2.4 (Albania).
[129] See Ch 4, Sect 3.2.5.　　　[130] Weston, above n 25, 523–5.
[131] Ibid 524.
[132] Thomas L Friedman, 'How US Won Support to Use Mideast Forces', *NYT*, 2 Dec 1990.

Similar horse-trading has been documented in relation to the Security Council's treatment of Haiti. David Malone writes that when an expanded mandate to provide international support for the restoration of democracy was first discussed in the Council, Russia threatened to veto it owing to lack of US support for the language Russia had proposed in a separate resolution welcoming a CIS peacekeeping mission in Georgia. He also suggests that Russia was disappointed that its support for France's Opération Turquoise had not paid more dividends. It is, he concludes,

impossible to determine the extent to which Russian objections to [the draft of resolution 940 (1994)] were bought off by specific promises of a more forthcoming US (and French) position on Georgia and Tajikistan. . . . Nevertheless, leading Russian, US, and French diplomats do not deny that linkages were loosely established at the time.[133]

It would be idealistic in the extreme to argue that national interest should not play a role in such actions. Unless the United Nations establishes its own armed forces it will remain dependent on national forces, which in turn are dependent on domestic political support. The problem, rather, is that as Council authorization has become viewed as a formal step towards legitimate intervention, its substantive role in decisions on international peace and security has been diminished correspondingly.

### 2.2. The changing role of the Secretary-General

The changing nature of the advice provided by the Secretary-General to the Security Council also reflects the Council's shift from substantive to formal oversight of enforcement actions. Increasingly, the Secretary-General's reports to the Council have served to recommend actions agreed in advance with one or more member states. Reflecting the move from debate in Council to politicking behind closed doors, this approach meant that reports were tailored to comply with the parameters acceptable to member states and to the permanent five (P5) in particular.[134]

In the case of Haiti, the Secretary-General reported to the Security Council that a UN-led operation was beyond the Organization's capacity.[135] Instead, he recommended another option that would also 'conform with the Charter, with past practice and with established principles':[136] authorizing a group of member states to carry out the operation. China abstained from resolution 940 (1994), stating that it was disconcerted by the practice of the Council

---

[133] Malone, above n 3, 107.                    [134] Ibid 14, citing confidential interviews.
[135] S/1994/828 (1994) paras 18–19, 25 (reporting that it would take too long to obtain the required personnel, given the principle that no single member state should contribute more than about one third of a peacekeeping force and the difficulties of approving a budget).
[136] Ibid para 20.

authorizing certain member states to use force;[137] Pakistan supported the resolution, but would have preferred a UN-led operation.[138] New Zealand also voted in favour of the resolution, but disputed the implications of the Secretary-General's report:

The resource and management difficulties that the United Nations faces are undeniable, but we believe they should be seen as challenges to be overcome, not as excuses for throwing in the towel and abrogating the responsibilities for international-dispute settlement under United Nations auspices which New Zealand and other Governments expect this Organization to fulfil.[139]

The Secretary-General is, of course, in a difficult position. In particular, the 1990s saw a divergence between the increased costs associated with UN peacekeeping activities and the commitment of the United States (among others) to fulfilling its funding obligations.[140] Boutros-Ghali's reappointment was blocked when he failed to satisfy US requirements in relation to UN reform.[141]

As the situation in Kosovo deteriorated, his replacement, Kofi Annan, faced the impossible task of maintaining a relevant role for the United Nations without alienating its major donors or being seen as complicit in NATO unilateralism. He settled on an uncomfortable fence. In January 1999 he stated in a press conference that the use of force in Kosovo might be 'unavoidable':

Normally the use of force in the past for these operations has required Security Council approval. The Council has not discussed this issue fully. There are expectations that there may be difficulties in the Council, one or two members may have difficulties embracing the use of force. But they have not really either vetoed it or not. I think that what I should say here is that given the situation on the ground, if it were to deteriorate very quickly, I think the Council will have to face up to this. We have had other situations where compelling situations on the ground have required the international community to act.[142]

This extraordinary statement was followed two days later by a speech at NATO headquarters in Brussels, in which he said that the past decade had left the international community with no illusions about the difficulty of halting internal conflicts: 'But nor have they left us with any illusions about the need to use force, when all other means have failed. We may be reaching that limit, once again, in the former Yugoslavia.'[143] This was reported as a *de facto*

---

[137] S/PV.3413 (1994) 10 (China).   [138] Ibid 26 (Pakistan).

[139] Ibid 22 (New Zealand).

[140] See generally Edward Newman, *The UN Secretary-General from the Cold War to the New Era* (London: Macmillan, 1998).

[141] Such, at least, were the reasons given by the United States: Newman, above n 140, 190. See now Boutros Boutros-Ghali, *Unvanquished: A US–UN Saga* (New York: Random House, 1999).

[142] UN Press Release SG/SM/6875 (26 Jan 1999).

[143] UN Press Release SG/SM/6878 (28 Jan 1999).

authorization to use force,[144] and on 30 January 1999, the North Atlantic Council reissued activation orders (ACTORDS) authorizing the NATO Secretary-General to launch air strikes if negotiations in Rambouillet, France, failed to resolve the dispute.[145]

When air strikes began, Secretary-General Annan could only note that, while the UN Charter 'assigns an important role to regional organizations' such as NATO, the Security Council 'should be involved in any decision to resort to the use of force'.[146] At the same time, he stressed his deep regret that

in spite of all the efforts made by the international community, the Yugoslav authorities have persisted in their rejection of a political settlement, which would have halted the bloodshed in Kosovo and secured an equitable peace for the population there. It is indeed tragic that diplomacy has failed, but there are times when the use of force may be legitimate in the pursuit of peace.[147]

This was interpreted as implicit endorsement of the action,[148] an assessment that gained support when he presented five conditions to end the hostilities in Kosovo during the third week of bombing. These included the FRY's acceptance of an international military presence to ensure a secure environment for the return of the refugees and the unimpeded delivery of humanitarian aid. He continued:

*Upon the acceptance by the Yugoslav authorities of these conditions,* I urge the leaders of the North Atlantic Alliance to suspend immediately the air bombardments upon the territory of the Federal Republic of Yugoslavia.[149]

This marked a fine line between pragmatism and endorsement of NATO's air campaign.

During the Cold War, the Secretary-General's role in peaceful change and conflict settlement was constrained and defined by Great Power politics. The post-Cold War situation has allowed greater scope for a proactive Secretary-General—notably in Africa, Central America, and the former USSR—but the position remains subject to political constraints that are as strong as before, if less predictable.[150] This is especially the case where enforcement actions are concerned. The danger is that in attempting to protect the relevance of both the office and the Organization, the Secretary-General becomes complicit in diluting their authority.

---

[144] Craig R Whitney, 'NATO Says It's Ready to Act to Stop Violence in Kosovo', *NYT*, 29 Jan 1999.

[145] NATO Press Release (1999)12 (30 Jan 1999).

[146] UN Press Release SG/SM/6938 (24 Mar 1999).

[147] Ibid.

[148] Judith Miller, 'The Secretary General Offers Implicit Endorsement of Raids', *NYT*, 25 Mar 1999.

[149] UN Press Release SG/SM/6952 (9 Apr 1999) (emphasis added).

[150] Newman, above n 140, 189–91.

### 3. EXTENT OF THE MANDATE

The diminished role of the Security Council in deciding *whether* to act has necessarily led to a diminution of its operational responsibility in three areas: (i) controlling *when* and *how* any such mandate should be carried out; (ii) monitoring the operations carried out in its name; and (iii) determining when those operations should conclude. This section considers these three areas and the hesitant steps taken by the Council to reassert its authority.

#### 3.1. The 'Mogadishu line'

> The suggestion that somehow we don't have a clear-cut mission, that the mission is fuzzy, is not accurate. I've heard some comments from some of my friends to that effect, and I would take strong exception to that notion. The mission is very clear. It is a humanitarian mission.
>
> US Secretary of Defense Dick Cheney, 1992[151]

The failure of the United Nations in Somalia—epitomized by the ignominious retreat of the last peacekeepers—coloured subsequent approaches to UN operations. Like Vietnam before it, Somalia became a 'syndrome', characterized as a naïve attempt to resolve a complex internal conflict in a marginal Third World state through benevolent intervention.[152] Rwanda was the first casualty of this malaise.[153] One of the central problems identified with the Somali intervention was the uncertain mandate of UN troops, as their role expanded from primarily humanitarian objectives to include disarmament and, in the wake of the killing of the Pakistani soldiers in June 1993, to an effective declaration of war against General Aideed's militia. In the course of UN operations in Bosnia, this form of mission creep became referred to as 'crossing the Mogadishu line'.[154]

This expression conflates a number of discrete issues: the consent of the target state, the (im)partiality of the intervening state(s), and their command structure and objectives. In practice, it has been used to justify reinforcing the division between peacekeeping and enforcement actions, and limiting UN

---

[151] Defense Department briefing at the Pentagon, 4 Dec 1992, quoted in Adam Roberts, 'Humanitarian War: Military Intervention and Human Rights' (1993) 69 *International Affairs* 429, 441.

[152] See Clarke, above n 123, 3; John Drysdale, 'Foreign Military Intervention in Somalia: The Root Cause of the Shift from UN Peacekeeping to Peacemaking and Its Consequences', in Clarke and Herbst, above n 47, 118, 133.

[153] See Ch 4, Sect 3.2.2.

[154] The term was coined by the then Commander of UNPROFOR, Lt-Gen Sir Michael Rose: 'Patience and Bloody Noses', *Guardian*, 30 Sept 1994.

command to the former. The result has been that states operating under Council authorization have been given a relatively free hand in determining the modality of the operation authorized.

Following the very broad scope of resolution 678 (1990), indicated earlier,[155] subsequent resolutions usually expressed broad, medium-term goals rather than specific objectives. Resolutions thus tied the Council's authorization to generalities such as a creating a 'secure environment', whether to permit delivery of humanitarian assistance (Somalia, Albania) or implementation of a peace agreement (Haiti). In situations where such an outcome was improbable, operative paragraphs referred to the even vaguer criteria of 'contributing to' or 'facilitating' humanitarian objectives (Rwanda, eastern Zaïre).

The resolutions on Bosnia and Herzegovina were a clear exception to this trend, setting objectives such as the protection of designated 'safe areas', and linking member state action and the later IFOR and SFOR operations to UNPROFOR objectives and the terms of the Dayton Agreement. As indicated above, Bosnia came to be viewed precisely as the exception that proved the rule.[156]

Resolutions on the CAR and Sierra Leone were more circumscribed still, but were adopted by the Council at times when their limited mandates were already being exceeded. Resolution 1125 (1997), which 'approved' MISAB's role in monitoring implementation of the Bangui Agreements, limited its Chapter VII authorization to ensuring the security and freedom of movement of MISAB personnel.[157] Resolution 1132 (1997) limited Chapter VII and VIII authorization to ECOWAS 'cooperating with the democratically-elected Government of Sierra Leone' to ensuring 'strict implementation' of the arms and petroleum embargo.[158] In each case, the relevant organization was operating well in advance of such authorization.[159] Finally, resolution 1264 (1999) on East Timor was even more limited, with the operative paragraph authorizing the establishment of a multinational force but stating that its mandate was 'pursuant to the request of the Government of Indonesia'.[160]

Despite this trend towards more restrictive authorizations, the question of *when* to intervene was thus left up to the acting state(s). Given the explicit linkage between the delegation of Council powers and offers of member states to act, this is hardly surprising. Of more concern is the lack of any clear limitation on *how* any such intervention must be conducted. Quite apart from the applicability of international humanitarian law, which raises issues of the *jus in bello* that are beyond the scope of the present work,[161] the very generality

---

[155] See above nn 7–10.
[156] See above nn 72–6.
[157] SC Res 1125 (1997) para 3.
[158] SC Res 1132 (1997) para 8.
[159] See Ch 4, Sect 3.1.5 (CAR), Sect 3.3.2 (Sierra Leone).
[160] SC Res 1264 (1999) para 3.
[161] Oscar Schachter has observed that it was a noteworthy feature of the Gulf War that no government in the coalition and no commander suggested that either the aggressor state or its inhabitants should be denied the protection of international law applicable in armed conflict: Schachter, above n 18, 465. Such suggestions had been argued (unsuccessfully) at Nuremberg:

of the objectives and the use of studied euphemisms such as 'all necessary means' or 'all measures necessary' gives a latitude of discretion to the state(s) interpreting the mandate. In those situations where the Council has given a more limited mandate (CAR, Sierra Leone), this has been interpreted as an official nod and a wink at the broader operations that were in fact taking place on the ground. Such was the interpretation of the earlier resolution on ECOWAS activities in Liberia,[162] and seems a likely gloss on resolution 1244 (1999) that followed NATO's air campaign against the FRY.[163]

One of the main consequences of basing a collective security regime on delegation is that states will only 'sign on' to actions over which they retain some control. If it is accepted that the United Nations will not in the near future have its own independent armed forces, this is inevitable. But relinquishing control over an operation need not entail divesting the Council of any substantive role in giving that operation its legitimacy. The response of the Council has been to modify the terms in which authorizations are given in order to retain some form of oversight—if only a requirement for regular reports—and to reserve the power to terminate a given authorization. Both these techniques arose gradually through the 1990s, and both have been only partial in their success.

## 3.2. Reporting requirements and Security Council oversight

What we know about the war . . . is what we hear from the three members of the Security Council which are involved—Britain, France and the United

Bernard D Meltzer, 'A Note on Some Aspects of the Nuremberg Debate' (1947) 14 *University of Chicago Law Review* 455, 461–2. In 1952 a committee of the American Society of International Law expressed doubts that international humanitarian law was fully applicable to UN forces, and concluded that the UN should 'select such of the laws of war as may seem to fit its purposes': (1952) 46 *ASIL Proc* 220. It has been assumed by most writers that states involved in enforcement actions remain bound by their individual obligations under the *jus in bello*: Derek W Bowett, *United Nations Forces: A Legal Study of United Nations Practice* (London: Stevens, 1964) 503–6; Schachter, above n 31, 76. This is presumably the case in the authorized actions considered in this Chapter, but it is less clear that they would be so bound if the Security Council deployed forces made available to it under Article 43 agreements. See generally Christopher Greenwood, 'Protection of Peacekeepers: The Legal Regime' (1996) 7 *Duke JCIL* 185; Julianne Peck, 'The UN and the Laws of War: How Can the World's Peacekeepers Be Held Accountable?' (1995) 21 *Syracuse JILC* 283; Brian D Tittemore, 'Belligerents in Blue Helmets: Applying International Humanitarian Law to United Nations Peace Operations' (1997) 33 *Stanford JIL* 61. See also 1971 Zagreb Resolution of the Institute of International Law on Conditions of Application of Humanitarian Rules of Armed Conflict to Hostilities in Which United Nations Forces May Be Engaged, in Adam Roberts and Richard Guelff, *Documents on the Laws of War* (2nd edn; Oxford: Clarendon Press, 1989) 371. See now Secretary-General's Bulletin: Observance by United Nations Forces of International Humanitarian Law, ST/SGB/1999/13 (1999), 38 ILM 1656.

[162] See Ch 4, Sect 3.1.3.
[163] In SC Res 1244 (1999), the Council, acting under Ch VII, welcomed the FRY's acceptance of the principles set out in the 6 May 1999 Meeting of G-8 Foreign Ministers (para 2) and authorized member states and 'relevant international organizations' to establish an international security presence in Kosovo (para 7).

States—which every two or three days report to the Council, after the actions have taken place.

The Council, which has authorized all this, [is informed] only after the military actions have taken place. As I am not a military expert I cannot evaluate how necessary are the military actions taking place now.

*Javier Pérez de Cuéllar, 1991*[164]

One of the few aspects of delegation that has been the subject of significant debate in the Council is the question of reporting requirements. Malaysia, after voting in favour of resolution 678 (1990), somewhat optimistically stated that 'these countries are fully accountable for their actions to the Council through a clear system of reporting and accountability, which is not adequately covered in [the] resolution'.[165]

India and Zimbabwe subsequently abstained from resolution 770 (1992) on Bosnia specifically because of the lack of Security Council control.[166] By contrast, the only resolution authorizing a Chapter VII enforcement action to be adopted unanimously was resolution 794 (1992) on Somalia—apparently due to the stricter control mechanisms incorporated into the resolution.[167] These included a more significant role for the Secretary-General, the creation of an ad hoc commission of Council members to report to the full Council on implementation of the resolution, and a requirement that the Secretary-General and, as appropriate, the states concerned report to the Council 'on a regular basis', the first such report to take place within 15 days.[168]

Later delegations attempted a compromise between accountability and the received truth that enforcement actions required a command structure that the United Nations could not provide. The diminished role of the Secretary-General thus led to requirements that states themselves report to the Council, sometimes 'through' the Secretary-General.[169] For Opération Turquoise in Rwanda, France itself was requested to report to the Council on a 'regular basis', the first report to be made within 15 days,[170] though there was still some dissatisfaction about the lack of Council oversight.[171] States participating in Operation Uphold Democracy in Haiti were also requested to make reports at 'regular intervals', the first within 7 days,[172] but the Council also established an advance team of the UN Mission in Haiti (UNMIH) to monitor operations of the multinational force.[173]

[164] Quoted in Leonard Doyle, 'UN "Has No Role in Running War"', *Independent*, 11 Feb 1991.
[165] S/PV.2963 (1990) 76 (Malaysia).        [166] S/PV.3106 (1992) 12 (India), 16–17 (Zimbabwe).
[167] S/PV.3145 (1992) 7-10 (Zimbabwe), 17 (China), 24 (Belgium), 32 (Austria).
[168] SC Res 794 (1992) paras 10–19.        [169] See, eg, SC Res 836 (1993) para 11 (Bosnia).
[170] SC Res 929 (1994) para 10.        [171] See, eg, S/PV.3392 (1994) 10 (Nigeria).
[172] SC Res 940 (1994) para 13. In fact US troops did not start to deploy for seven weeks.
[173] Ibid para 8.

This attempt to retain some form of independent verification of action taken in the Council's name was not repeated, however. Member states participating in IFOR and SFOR were requested to make monthly reports 'through the appropriate channels';[174] those taking part in the aborted Canadian-led operation in eastern Zaïre, MISAB's mission in the CAR, and the Italian-led action in Albania were to report fortnightly 'through the Secretary-General'.[175] ECOWAS (*not* its member states) was to report on its actions in Sierra Leone to a committee of the Security Council every thirty days.[176] The leadership of INTERFET in East Timor were required to report within 14 days and then 'periodically' to the Security Council through the Secretary-General.[177]

The increased obligations to report reflect a desire on the part of the Council to play a meaningful part in Chapter VII operations.[178] The absence of any obligation to consult *before* taking action, however, demonstrates the marginal nature of this role once operations commence. The Council's primary option for influencing policy in such a situation, then, is the threat that a given delegation might be revoked. In practice, however, this is more easily said than done.

### 3.3. The 'reverse veto'

As the coalition states commenced the air campaign that heralded Operation Desert Storm against Iraq in January and February 1991, a number of other states sought to bring about a last-minute peaceful resolution to the conflict. Under a plan proposed by the USSR, the trade embargo on Iraq would have been lifted once two-thirds of Iraqi troops left Kuwait, with remaining sanctions to be lifted when the withdrawal was complete. This was rejected by the United States and the United Kingdom, which asserted that they had the power to maintain sanctions for as long as they chose and to continue the war authorized by the Security Council until it adopted another resolution. And, as permanent members of the Council, they reserved the right to veto any such resolution.[179] The ground war commenced two days later.

David Caron has termed this use of the veto to block the modification or termination of an authorization the 'reverse veto',[180] tracing it back to disputes in the Council over the manner in which sanctions against the illegal

---

[174] SC Res 1031 (1995) para 25; SC Res 1088 (1996) para 26.
[175] SC Res 1080 (1996) para 11 (eastern Zaïre); SC Res 1125 (1997) para 6 (CAR); SC Res 1101 (1997) para 9 (Albania).
[176] SC Res 1132 (1997) para 9.         [177] SC Res 1264 (1999) para 12.
[178] Cf Sarooshi, above n 11, 159–63.
[179] Paul Lewis, 'US and Britain See UN Mandate to Maintain Curbs Against Iraq', *NYT*, 22 Feb 1991. See S/PV.2977 (1991) 301 (US), 313 (UK), 332 (Romania).
[180] Caron, above n 39, 577.

regime of Southern Rhodesia should be terminated. In 1979, concerned that the United Kingdom would unilaterally lift the sanctions imposed pursuant to Council resolutions, the President of the Committee on Sanctions had written to the Council emphasizing that 'only the Security Council, which had instituted the sanctions in the first place, had a right to lift them'.[181] When the Smith regime agreed to a British governor resuming full authority, the United Kingdom informed the Council that it viewed its Article 25 obligation to maintain the sanctions as having been discharged.[182] The African Group in the United Nations promptly declared this to be unacceptable and illegal.[183] The United States then also lifted its sanctions, causing the USSR to declare that 'these unilateral acts . . . represent a flagrant violation of the United Nations Charter, since only the Council can terminate the effect of decisions which it has taken'.[184] A matter of days later, the situation was resolved when the Council adopted a resolution terminating the sanctions.[185] Strangely, given the controversy over the previous weeks, the resolution was adopted without debate.[186] After the vote, Tanzania stressed that only such a Council resolution could terminate the sanctions.[187] The United Kingdom and the United States made more ambiguous statements noting the importance of the Council resolution, but leaving it unclear as to whether they continued to assert that they had been entitled to terminate the sanctions prior to the adoption of such a resolution.[188]

Since it was precisely these two states that later defended the use of the reverse veto during Desert Storm,[189] there is considerable support for the proposition that Council-mandated actions can only be terminated by subsequent Council resolution.[190] In practice, given the discretion with which a member of the P5 can exercise its veto power, this may have the effect of dramatically altering the terms on which a Council action is based. In May 1991, after the ground war had been concluded and a ceasefire resolution passed, Prime Minister John Major declared that the United Kingdom would veto any Council resolution designed to weaken sanctions in place against Iraq as long as Saddam Hussein remained in power,[191] a statement later echoed by

---

[181] S/13617 (1979).                [182] S/13688 (1979).                [183] S/13693 (1979).
[184] S/13702 (1979).
[185] SC Res 460 (1979) adopted 13-0-2 (Czechoslovakia and USSR abstaining).
[186] S/PV.2181 (1979) 1.                [187] Ibid 19 (Tanzania).
[188] Ibid 2 (UK),: 'Our view remains that the obligation to impose those sanctions fell away automatically with the return to legality of the colony. But we have been very conscious that many countries have attached great importance to the adoption by the Council of a resolution on this subject.' Cf S/PV 2181 (1979) 8 (US) (expressing its pleasure that 'the Council is calling upon Member States to terminate the measures taken against Southern Rhodesia . . . because the objective of those measures has been achieved. It was in recognition of that fact that the United States made its recent announcement regarding sanctions').
[189] See above n 179.                [190] Caron, above n 39, 582.
[191] Martin Fletcher and Michael Binyon, 'UN and Iraq Edge Towards Accord on Peace Force', *The Times*, 15 May 1991.

US Secretary of State James Baker.[192] The following month, in a letter to the President of the Security Council, the United Kingdom stated that it would use its veto power to block any resolution to lift sanctions against Iraq until it released two British nationals—one of whom had been gaoled for corruption in 1987.[193]

(Sarooshi has argued for an even stronger version of the reverse veto: that when a state agrees to take part in an enforcement action, it remains under an obligation to continue that action until the Council decides that the relevant objective has been obtained.[194] This position is untenable. Such an analysis may be appropriate to a sanctions regime—which prohibits action and may not be lifted unilaterally by a state—but can hardly require the continuation of military operations under the command and control of a state or states, even if ultimate *political* control remains vested in the Council. In addition, it simply does not reflect the terms according to which relevant Council resolutions have delegated elements of its powers.)

In fact the problem identified by Caron is considerably older than he suggests. Indeed, the failure to adopt subsequent resolutions has left not merely sanctions regimes but entire organizations in stasis. The most spectacular example of this is the UN Military Observer Group in India and Pakistan (UNMOGIP), established in 1948 to supervise the ceasefire between India and Pakistan in the state of Jammu and Kashmir.[195] Following the 1972 India–Pakistan agreement on a Line of Control in Kashmir, India asserted that UNMOGIP's mandate had lapsed. Pakistan disagreed and the Secretary-General held that UNMOGIP could only be terminated by a decision of the Security Council. No resolution has been passed on UNMOGIP since 1965, and it has been maintained with the same mandate and function.[196]

This problem has been avoided in other peacekeeping operations by the practice of limiting an authorization in time and providing an option for renewal of the mandate if so required. The UN Peace-Keeping Force in Cyprus (UNFICYP), for example, was established in 1964[197] with a mandate that has been extended at six-monthly intervals for the past 36 years.[198] This merely reverses the problem, of course—a veto may still be used prematurely to *end* an operation, though this has been seen as preferable to the paralysis of being unable to modify it at all.[199] (The one exception to this is the UN Iraq–Kuwait Observation Mission (UNIKOM).[200])

---

[192] Martin Fletcher and Michael Theodoulou, 'Baker Says Sanctions Must Stay as Long as Saddam Holds Power', *The Times*, 23 May 1991.

[193] S/22664 (1991). See James Bone, 'UK Links Sanctions to Fate of Prisoners', ibid 4 June 1991; Sarah Helm, 'Major Gives UN Warning on Sanctions Against Iraq', *Independent*, 5 June 1991.

[194] Sarooshi, above n 11, 151–2.   [195] SC Res 47 (1948).

[196] Bailey and Daws, above n 51, 483.   [197] SC Res 186 (1964).

[198] See, eg, SC Res 1283 (1999) extending UNFICYP's mandate until 15 June 2000.

[199] See Bailey and Daws, above n 51, 66. Cf the Chinese veto of UNPREDEP's mandate: below n 216.

[200] UNIKOM was established by SC Res 687 (1991) para 5. In SC Res 689 (1991) para 2, the

Such a practice was not adopted for the resolutions delegating enforcement actions in the early 1990s. In the first place, the various mandates entailed the achievement of an objective (however vaguely defined) rather than the maintenance of the status quo. Where a peacekeeping operation is implementing a political settlement on the ground, it may be appropriate to put a time limit on its involvement; once the decision had been made to use force, it would have seemed absurd to impose such a requirement on the coalition action against Iraq. Additionally, where a Council action is 'contracted out' to member states, this imposes no direct financial burden on the United Nations. The enforcement actions authorized by the Council in the 1990s were all funded either by the states concerned[201] or on a 'voluntary' basis.[202] Most importantly, however, the acting states simply would not have agreed to such a restriction.

In the case of the action against Iraq, no end point was specified for the mandate except an implication that it would expire when international peace and security in the area had been restored.[203] The resolutions on Somalia and Haiti were similarly open-ended, though they required the preparation of reports to enable the Council to authorize the transition from enforcement action to peacekeeping operation.[204] Resolution 836 (1993) authorizing air strikes to defend safe areas in Bosnia and Herzegovina also had no time limit, though it was implicitly linked to the UNPROFOR mandate.

During this period, the legitimacy of ongoing operations against Iraq was the subject of considerable dispute.[205] It seems probable that this contributed to the desire for certainty in the mandates issued in the Council's name. In 1994 France's Opération Turquoise in Rwanda (controversial in its own right) became the first enforcement action to be given a time-restricted mandate: the mission was 'limited to a period of two months . . . unless the Secretary-General determines at an earlier date that the expanded UNAMIR is able to carry out its mandate'.[206] Whether or not the Secretary-General could in fact have terminated the mission unilaterally was never put to the test; French troops duly departed after two months had passed.[207]

---

Council specifically noted that 'the decision to set up the observer unit was taken in paragraph 5 of resolution 687 (1991) and can only be terminated by a decision of the Council. The Council shall therefore review the question of termination or continuation every six months.' UNIKOM remains in force.

[201] See, eg, SC Res 929 (1994) para 2 (Rwanda); SC Res 940 (1994) para 4 (Haiti); SC Res 1080 (1996) para 9 (eastern Zaïre); SC Res 1125 (1997) para 5 (CAR); SC Res 1107 (1997) para 7 (Albania).
[202] See, eg, SC Res 665 (1990) para 3 and SC Res 678 (1990) para 3 (Iraq–Kuwait); SC Res 794 (1992) para 11 and SC Res 814 (1993) para 15 (Somalia); SC Res 770 (1992) and SC Res 1031 (1995) para 23 (Bosnia and Herzegovina).
[203] See above nn 7–9.
[204] SC Res 794 (1992) para 18 (Somalia); SC Res 940 (1994) para 8 (Haiti).
[205] See below Sect 4.1.        [206] SC Res 929 (1994) para 4.        [207] See Ch 4, Sect 3.2.2.

This marked a turning point in the nature of Council delegation of Chapter VII powers. IFOR was authorized for a year with provision for reports to enable the Council to determine whether to extend that authorization.[208] SFOR, which replaced it, was authorized for an initial eighteen-month period;[209] its mandate has since been renewed twice for further twelve-month periods.[210] Canada's aborted operation in eastern Zaïre was given a fixed date for its termination (4½ months), with provision for earlier termination by the Council on the basis of reports from the Secretary-General.[211] The two operations authorized in 1997—the Italian Operation Alba and the French-MISAB operation in the CAR—were authorized for a period of three months with the possibility of review on the basis of reports to be submitted to the Council.[212] INTERFET in East Timor had no time-limited mandate but was to be replaced by a peacekeeping force 'as soon as possible'.[213]

The resolutions on Sierra Leone appear to be an exception to this trend. In resolution 1132 (1997), the Council expressed its intention to terminate the measures taken against the military junta only when it relinquished power and made way for 'the restoration of the democratically-elected Government and a return to constitutional order'.[214] Nevertheless, the Chapter VIII authorization given to ECOWAS to 'ensure strict implementation' of the petroleum and arms embargo was not an authorization to use force. Although the action by its predominantly Nigerian forces was later welcomed by the Council, the resolution is of a type with other sanctions regimes that continue to require a terminating resolution.[215]

The requirement to seek the renewal of a mandate has thus emerged as the primary source of accountability in operations carried out in the Council's name. But it is a blunt instrument at best. In February 1999 China vetoed an extension of the UN Preventive Deployment Force (UNPREDEP) in the former Yugoslav Republic of Macedonia, stating that its mission had been completed and that regions such as Africa should have a higher claim to the United Nations's limited resources.[216] There was widespread speculation that the veto was in fact a response to Macedonia's diplomatic recognition of Taiwan.[217]

---

[208] SC Res 1031 (1995) para 21.
[209] SC Res 1088 (1996) para 18.
[210] SC Res 1174 (1998); SC Res 1247 (1999).
[211] SC Res 1080 (1996) para 8.
[212] SC Res 1101 (1997) para 6 (Albania); SC Res 1125 (1997) para 4 (CAR).
[213] SC Res 1264 (1999) para 10. Six weeks later the Council passed the resolution establishing the Transitional Administration UNTAET: SC Res 1272 (1999).
[214] SC Res 1132 (1997) paras 19, 1.
[215] See S/PRST/1998/5; SC Res 1162 (1998). Cf SC Res 1244 (1999) para 19, providing that the international civil and security presences in Kosovo were 'established for an initial period of 12 months, *to continue thereafter unless the Security Council decides otherwise*' (emphasis added).
[216] UN Press Release SC/6648 (25 Feb 1999). Draft resolution S/1999/201 not adopted 13-1-1 (China against, Russia abstaining).
[217] Paul Lewis, 'China Votes a UN Force out of Balkans', *NYT*, 26 Feb 1999. When China vetoed a resolution that would have sent peacekeepers to Guatemala in 1997, official statements

A number of alternative approaches have been suggested for dealing with the reverse veto. First, the Council could delegate oversight of a particular resolution to another body. This could be in the form of allowing an independent assessment to trigger a termination clause (an untested interpretation of the role given to the Secretary-General by resolution 929 (1994)[218]) or providing that another body may supervise implementation of a resolution.[219] Such was the approach adopted in resolution 687 (1991), when the Council created a Compensation Commission to address claims against Iraq arising from the Gulf War. In accordance with the Secretary-General's recommendation, the Governing Council of the Commission was composed of the fifteen members of the Security Council, with decisions to be taken by a majority of nine but without the application of a veto power.[220] In practice, however, this was more comparable to a sanctions committee, the establishment of which is now standard procedure when the Council imposes a sanctions regime.[221] In neither case could the subsidiary organ unilaterally terminate measures taken by the Council.

It is possible that the Council might in future delegate such a power to the Secretary-General or a subsidiary organ, but Caron goes one step further to state that the reverse veto could also be avoided through a 'modified voting procedure'. He suggests that a resolution imposing a sanctions regime could also provide that 'any decision to terminate any or all of the measures taken in [for example] paragraphs 1 through 9 of this resolution shall be made by an affirmative vote of [for example] twelve members'[222] and without the application of a veto. Though this has found some support in later writings,[223] Caron does not explain how such a manner and form provision avoids the clear wording of the UN Charter that non-procedural decisions of the Council require nine affirmative votes and the concurring votes of the P5.[224] His argument that a resolution with a termination date effectively 'waives . . . the veto'[225] confuses the power of veto over affirmative decisions taken by the Council with a more general veto over any action (or inaction) taken in its name. Similarly, the possibility of delegating subsequent decisions to a subsidiary organ with different voting procedures is not equivalent to applying those voting procedures to the Council itself.

made it clear that this was due to Guatemala's longstanding diplomatic recognition of Taiwan: Patrick E Tyler, 'China Asserts Taiwan's Ties To Guatemala Led to Veto', *NYT*, 12 Jan 1997. In 1996 it insisted on the downsizing of UNMIH when Haiti invited Taiwan's Vice-President to attend the inauguration of President Rene Preval: Barbara Crossette, 'Latin Nations at UN Insist China Change Stand on Haiti', *NYT*, 24 Feb 1996; Malone, above n 3, 12.

[218] See above nn 206–7.                    [219] Caron, above n 39, 584–5.
[220] S/22559 (1991); SC Res 692 (1991). See Caron, above n 39, 585.
[221] Bailey and Daws, above n 51, 365.       [222] Caron, above n 39, 586.
[223] See, eg, Jules Lobel and Michael Ratner, 'Bypassing the Security Council: Ambiguous Authorizations to Use Force, Cease-Fires and the Iraqi Inspection Regime' (1999) 93 *AJIL* 125, 143 n 77.
[224] UN Charter, art 27(3).                   [225] Caron, above n 39, 584.

Any such attempt to bind the Council in the exercise of its *political* functions—especially any procedural measure that would prevent a resolution adopted under normal voting procedures from having its desired effect—would exceed the powers of delegation recognized in the law of international institutions.[226] This may be contrasted with the decision in the *Administrative Tribunal* case that a principal UN organ can constitute a subsidiary *judicial* body whose decisions will be binding on the delegating organ.[227] This distinction was upheld in the jurisprudence of the International Criminal Tribunals for the Former Yugoslavia and Rwanda established by the Council under Chapter VII.[228]

Given the reluctance of acting states to submit to direct oversight by the United Nations and the wariness of some members of the Council of granting unlimited authorizations, it is probable that the need to obtain the periodic renewal of mandates will remain an important condition for the Council's continued legitimization of an enforcement action.

### 4. PASSING THE BATON

Enforcement action, duly authorized by the Security Council, is greatly preferable to the unilateral use of force. Such action is, however, a double-edged sword. It offers the Organization a capacity not otherwise available but carries with it the risk of potential damage to the credibility and stature of the United Nations. Once the Security Council authorizes such interventions, States may claim international legitimacy and approval for measures not initially envisaged by the Council.

Boutros Boutros-Ghali, 1996[229]

It was, perhaps, inevitable that the Security Council would be unable to live up to the rhetoric that followed the liberation of Kuwait. This must be distinguished from the simple assertion that the 'new world order' proclaimed by US President George Bush was beset by the same old problems, however. The currency and the language of foreign policy have changed radically since the end of the Cold War, with international law being accorded greater respect than at any point in its history. In counterpoint to the increased importance of legalism has been the emergence of 'humanitarianism' as a foreign policy

---

[226] See Sarooshi, above n 11, 36–41.

[227] *Administrative Tribunal Case* [1954] ICJ Rep 47, 56–8. See Sarooshi, above n 11, 8.

[228] See *Prosecutor v Tadic*, IT-94-1-AR72, Interlocutory Appeal on Jurisdiction (1995) para 38; *Blaskic Subpoena Case*, IT-95-14-PT (1997) para 23. See further Sarooshi, above n 11, 102–6.

[229] Boutros Boutros-Ghali, 'Introduction', *Blue Helmets* (3rd edn; New York: UN Department of Public Information, 1996) 3, 6. Cf Supplement to An Agenda for Peace, above n 45, para 80.

justification in its own right.[230] Though always tied ultimately to national interest (if only to domestic political concern about the plight of a certain group), it is this 'moral' concern that was said to lie behind many of the interventions documented in this and the preceding Chapter. And, echoing Grotian natural law principles, it was sometimes claimed that such concerns trumped other considerations of international law.

This tension between legal and moral legitimacy, and the relative weight accorded to each in the justification of foreign policy, can be seen most clearly in two actions that book-end the decade: the extended operations against Iraq that followed the ceasefire of April 1991, and the NATO operations against the FRY that commenced in March 1999.

### 4.1. Northern and southern Iraq, 1991–

> [T]here's another way for the bloodshed to stop, and that is for the Iraqi military and the Iraqi people to take matters into their own hands—to force Saddam Hussein, the dictator, to step aside, and to comply with the United Nations resolutions and then rejoin the family of peace-loving nations.
>
> George Bush, 15 February 1991[231]

> [D]o I think that the United States should bear guilt because of suggesting that the Iraqi people take matters into their own hands, with the implication being given by some that the United States would be there to support them militarily? That was not true. We never implied that.
>
> George Bush, 16 April 1991[232]

The circumstances leading up to the adoption of resolution 688 on 5 April 1991 have been considered in the previous Chapter.[233] Of central concern here is the alleged authority it gave for the United States, the United Kingdom, and France to conduct Operation Provide Comfort, and the establishment of the air exclusion zones ('no-fly zones') that remain in force.

### 4.1.1. *Operation Provide Comfort and the no-fly zones*

In the first three operative paragraphs of resolution 688 (1991), the Council condemned the repression of the Iraqi civilian population, demanded that Iraq end this oppression, and insisted that Iraq allow international humani-

---

[230] See Adam Roberts, *Humanitarian Action in War: Aid Protection and Implementation in a Policy Vacuum* (Adelphi Paper 305; London: IISS, 1996).

[231] 'Remarks to the American Association for the Advancement of Science', 15 Feb 1991, in [1991] 1 *Bush Papers* 145.

[232] 'Remarks on Assistance for Iraqi Refugees and a News Conference', 16 Apr 1991, in ibid 380.

[233] See Ch 4, Sect 3.1.1.

tarian organizations immediate access to all those in need of assistance in all parts of Iraq and make available all necessary facilities for their operations. The Council also *appealed* to all member states and to all humanitarian organizations 'to contribute to these humanitarian relief efforts'.[234] It is arguable that the strong language of the resolution was reminiscent of Chapter VII authorization,[235] but given the Council practice on explicitly adopting resolutions under that Chapter it is drawing a long bow indeed to argue that the coercive provisions of Chapter VII can be implied by the use of words like 'demand' and 'insist'. In any event, there was no indication that the resolution authorized enforcement action. None of the states voting for the resolution characterized it as doing so, although the United States did note that it planned to use military aircraft to drop food, blankets, clothing, tents, and other relief into northern Iraq.[236] On the same day that the Security Council passed resolution 688 (1991), US President George Bush announced plans to commence aid drops to Kurds in northern Iraq in co-operation with France and the United Kingdom,[237] at the same time emphasizing that the United States would not intervene militarily in the conflict.[238]

Turkey was one of the first states to propose the idea of safe havens for the Kurds.[239] On 7 April Turkish President Turgut Özal declared that '[w]e have to get [the Kurds] better land under UN control and to put those people in the Iraqi territory and take care of them'.[240] US Secretary of State James Baker affirmed the importance of the Kurds being free from threats and persecution, but reiterated the US position that it would not 'go down the slippery slope of being sucked into a civil war'.[241]

European governments were less reticent in their support for more direct action. France had long advocated a bolder response to the Kurdish crisis, but the first concrete proposal came from the United Kingdom. Speaking at the Luxembourg summit meeting of the European Community (EC) on 8 April 1991, Prime Minister John Major proposed the creation of UN-protected Kurdish enclaves in northern Iraq. The summit had been called by

[234] SC Res 688 (1991) paras 1–3, 6.
[235] Nigel S Rodley, 'Collective Intervention to Protect Human Rights and Civilian Populations: The Legal Framework', in Nigel S Rodley (ed), *To Loose the Bands of Wickedness: International Intervention in Defence of Human Rights* (London: Brassey's, 1992) 14, 31; Sean D Murphy, *Humanitarian Intervention: The United Nations in an Evolving World Order* (Philadelphia: University of Pennsylvania Press, 1996) 196–7.
[236] S/PV.2982 (1991) 58.
[237] 'Statement on Aid to Refugees', 5 Apr 1991, in [1991] 1 *Bush Papers* 331.
[238] 'Remarks at a Meeting with Hispanic Business Leaders and an Exchange with Reporters', 5 Apr 1991, in ibid 333.
[239] Austria reportedly called for the creation of a UN buffer zone in northern Iraq on 6 Apr 1991: *Keesing's* (1991) 38127.
[240] Donald Macintyre, 'Major Gambles for High Stakes in the Mountains of Kurdistan', *Independent*, 14 Apr 1991.
[241] Edward Lucas, Annika Savill, Will Bennett, and Anthony Bevins, 'US Shifts Policy on Kurds', *Independent*, 8 Apr 1991.

France to discuss the generally weak performance by the EC during the Gulf War; given the relative inaction by the United States on the Kurdish problem, Community leaders were pleased to be able to take the initiative on that issue. As one European official was reported to remark: 'The Kurds saved the summit so we must save the Kurds.'[242] Major stated that the proposal was intended to 'build on' resolutions 687 and 688: 'We believe the rubric exists within 688 to avoid the need for a separate resolution but clearly we will need to discuss that in New York.'[243]

The initial response of the United States to the proposed safe havens was lukewarm,[244] but it stressed its determination to protect the relief effort. On 10 April it instructed the Iraqi Government to cease all military activity north of the 36th parallel to enable relief supplies to be delivered unimpeded and to prevent attacks on Kurdish refugees.[245] The choice of this line excluded the oil-producing area around Kirkuk (a town claimed by Kurdish separatists), apparently in an attempt to avoid encouraging Kurdish secession from Iraq.[246]

As it became clear that relief efforts were severely restricted by the geography of the Turkey–Iraq border, President Bush announced a policy reversal on 16 April, and stated that, 'consistent with' resolution 688, US troops would enter northern Iraq to establish 'safe havens':

> I want to underscore that all we are doing is motivated by humanitarian concerns. We continue to expect the government of Iraq not to interfere in any way with this latest relief effort. The prohibition against any Iraqi fixed- or rotary-wing aircraft flying north of the 36th parallel thus remains in effect. . . .
>
> [S]ome might argue that this is an intervention into the internal affairs of Iraq. But I think the humanitarian concern, the refugee concern is so overwhelming that there will be a lot of understanding about this.[247]

Early efforts focused on the Turkey–Iraq border, in part due to Western reluctance to co-operate with Iran. This was despite the fact that Iran had by then received more Kurdish refugees than any other state and had spent as much as US$57 million on aid—far in excess of any other country at the time.[248]

---

[242] Lawrence Freedman and David Boren, ' "Safe Havens" for Kurds in Post-War Iraq', in Rodley, *To Loose the Bands of Wickedness*, above n 235, 43, 52–3.

[243] John Major, transcript of press conference in Luxembourg, 8 Apr 1991, in Marc Weller (ed), *Iraq and Kuwait: The Hostilities and Their Aftermath* (Cambridge International Documents Series, vol 3; Cambridge: Grotius Publications Ltd, 1993) 715.

[244] On 9 Apr, a White House spokesman said that the US had 'no position' on the question of Kurdish safe havens: *Keesing's* (1991) 38127.

[245] Elaine Sciolino, 'US Warns Against Attack by Iraq on Kurdish Refugees', *NYT*, 11 Apr 1991.

[246] *Keesing's* (1991) 38127; Freedman and Boren, above n 242, 53.

[247] 'Remarks on Assistance for Iraqi Refugees and a News Conference', 16 Apr 1991, in [1991] 1 *Bush Papers* 379, 381.

[248] Freedman and Boren, above n 242, 51.

On 18 April twelve military relief flights (9 US, 2 UK, 1 French) dropped 57.6 tons of relief supplies to refugees on the Turkey–Iraq border.[249] This coincided with the signing of a Memorandum of Understanding (MOU) between the United Nations and Iraq, allowing the United Nations to have a purely civilian 'humanitarian presence' throughout Iraq.[250] In less than a week nearly 6,000 tons of supplies had been dropped to the refugees. Towards the end of April, death rates among refugees had fallen from between 400 and 1,000 deaths per day to about 60.[251] By 24 April, approximately 2,000 US Marines and several hundred British and French troops were stationed on Iraqi soil.[252] At the peak of the operation over 20,000 forces from thirteen states were involved.[253]

By mid-July, most of the Kurdish refugees who had fled to Turkey in March had returned. With the withdrawal of coalition troops being used as a bargaining chip, Iraq consented to the presence of the 500-strong lightly armed UN Guard Contingent in Iraq (UNGCI), signing an Annex to the MOU on 25 May 1991.[254] The last allied soldiers departed Iraq on 15 July 1991, leaving in place a multinational rapid-deployment force in Turkey that temporarily bore the Damoclean title 'Operation Poised Hammer'.[255]

The United States and its allies continued to police the no-fly zone and on 26 August 1992 declared a second air exclusion zone in southern Iraq below the 32nd parallel. Ostensibly designed to protect the Shiites, the action was said to be justified by resolution 688 (1991), though it did not specifically mention southern Iraq.[256] This second zone was subsequently extended to the 33rd parallel in September 1996, a move that prompted France to announce its refusal to patrol the extended area,[257] and later to withdraw from patrols entirely.[258]

### 4.1.2. Legal rationales for the no-fly zones

No consistent legal rationale was given for the no-fly zones. Contradictory justifications were proposed by the United States, the United Kingdom, and

[249] Ibid 50.

[250] Memorandum of Understanding Between Iraq and the United Nations, 18 Apr 1991, UN Doc S/22513 (1991), 30 ILM 860.

[251] Freedman and Boren, above n 242, 51.

[252] Blaine Harden, 'US Expands Control of Refugee Zone', *Washington Post*, 24 Apr 1991.

[253] See Murphy, above n 235, 174 and sources there cited.

[254] Annex to the Memorandum of Understanding, 25 May 1991, UN Doc S/22663 (1991), 30 ILM 862; [1991] *UNYB* 206.

[255] Clyde Haberman, 'Allied Strike Force Aimed at Iraq Forms in Turkey', *NYT*, 25 July 1991.

[256] 'Remarks on Hurricane Andrew and the Situation in Iraq and an Exchange with Reporters', 26 Aug 1992, in [1992–3] 2 *Bush Papers* 1430; John Lancaster, 'Allies Declare "No-Fly" Zone in Iraq', *Washington Post*, 27 Aug 1992.

[257] Ben MacIntyre, 'France Refuses to Patrol Widened Iraq No-Fly Zone; Split Allies', *The Times*, 6 Sept 1996.

[258] Charles Truehart, 'French Military to Quit Patrols over N Iraq', *Washington Post*, 28 Dec 1996.

France, with ambiguous support being given by the Secretary-General. Moreover, none of these individual justifications—even taken on its own terms—was sufficient to justify the multitude of operations carried out against Iraq in the period 1991–9.

### (i)  Action 'consistent with' resolution 688 (1991)

On 11 April 1991 the US Senate passed resolution 99, recognizing a 'moral obligation to provide sustained humanitarian relief for Iraqi refugees' and calling upon President Bush

immediately to press the United Nations Security Council to adopt effective measures to assist Iraqi refugees as set forth in Resolution 688 and to enforce, pursuant to Chapter VII of the United Nations Charter, the demand in Resolution 688 that Iraq end its repression of the Iraqi civilian population.[259]

No such measures were introduced in the Council. This was largely attributed to the fear of a Chinese veto,[260] but Helmut Freudenschuss argues that there was no serious attempt to propose a Chapter VII resolution. He suggests that the reason for this was that from the outset the coalition simply did not intend to do anything serious about the plight of the Kurds. Later, when the objective was to transfer responsibility for the humanitarian effort to the United Nations, a Chapter VII resolution was not necessary. With regard to the creation of the second no-fly zone and subsequent air attacks, he notes that Council authorization might have set a precedent and 'tied hands with regard to other measures against Iraq which were not necessarily related to humanitarian concerns'.[261]

Nigel Rodley has observed that no Security Council member that voted in favour of resolution 688 (1991) publicly challenged the view that Operation Provide Comfort was 'consistent with' the resolution;[262] on the contrary, broad statements of support were given in the G7's London Economic Summit Political Declaration on Strengthening the International Order.[263]

---

[259]  US Senate Resolution 99 Concerning the Protection of Refugees in Iraq (1991) 137 Cong Rec S4377–01, 1991 WL 57485 (Cong Rec).

[260]  Peter Malanczuck, 'The Kurdish Crisis and Allied Intervention in the Aftermath of the Second Gulf War' (1991) 2 *European JIL* 114, 129; Schachter, above n 18, 469; Murphy, above n 235, 174.

[261]  Helmut Freudenschuss, 'Article 39 of the UN Charter Revisited: Threats to the Peace and the Recent Practice of the UN Security Council' (1993) 46 *Austrian JPIL* 1, 10.

[262]  Rodley, 'Collective Intervention', above n 235, 33.

[263]  London Economic Summit Political Declaration: Strengthening the International Order, 16 July 1991, reprinted in 'Summit in London', *NYT*, 17 July 1991: 'We note that the urgent and overwhelming nature of the humanitarian problem in Iraq caused by violent oppression by the Government required exceptional action by the international community, following UNSCR 688. We urge the UN and its affiliated agencies to be ready to consider similar action in the future if the circumstances require it.'

As the months wore into years, however, calls for a reassessment of the policy became more frequent.[264]

Throughout this period, the United States continued to assert its right to enforce the no-fly zones. Following an attack on Iraqi missile launchers in January 1993 by the United States, the United Kingdom, and France,[265] the White House issued a statement that the action was 'in response to Iraqi moves to reconstitute its surface-to-air missile systems in the region south of the 32nd parallel and to Iraq's openly proclaimed policy of challenging the no-fly zones'. It also announced that Iraq had been warned by the coalition on 6 January 'that further attempts to threaten flight operations conducted to monitor Iraqi compliance with SCR 688 would be dealt with forcefully and without warning'.[266]

This interpretation of resolution 688 (1991) is unpersuasive. As indicated earlier, it was the first of fourteen resolutions on Iraq *not* adopted under Chapter VII; statements made in the Security Council confirm that it was not understood to authorize an enforcement action such as the no-fly zones. This view is supported by the other justifications that were put forward at the time and subsequently.

### (ii) The continuing operation of resolution 678 (1990)

Following the January 1993 attack, which the United States had justified under resolution 688 (1991), the UN Secretary-General issued a statement that

the forces that carried out the raid have received a mandate from the Security Council, according to resolution 678, and the cause of the raid was the violation by Iraq of resolution 687 concerning the ceasefire. So, as Secretary-General of the United Nations, I can say that this action was taken and conforms to the resolutions of the Security Council and conforms to the Charter of the United Nations.[267]

This was unusual not least because it is unclear what status should be accorded to such a pronouncement by the Secretary-General[268]—or, indeed, why he should make such a statement at all. It was, moreover, inconsistent with the justifications proposed by the acting states (the United Kingdom claimed the incident was an act of self-defence,[269] France criticized the United States for exceeding its mandate in attacking the Iraqi nuclear weapons

---

[264] See, eg, Christine Gray, 'After the Ceasefire: Iraq, the Security Council and the Use of Force' (1994) 65 *British YBIL* 135, 168–9; Ben MacIntyre, 'France Refuses to Patrol Widened Iraq No-Fly Zone; Split Allies', *The Times*, 6 Sept 1996.

[265] *Keesing's* (1992) 39291; Gray, above n 264, 167.

[266] White House statement of 18 Jan 1993, USUN Press Release 6–(93) quoted in Freudenschuss, above n 261, 10.

[267] Secretary-General Boutros-Ghali, quoted in Freudenschuss, above n 261, 9; Gray, above n 264, 167.

[268] Gray, above n 264, 167.       [269] See Sect 4.1.2 (iv).

facility at Zafaraniyah[270]) and, by relying on the terms of the ceasefire resolution, the Secretary-General's statement omitted any reference to the plight
of Iraqi minorities that provided the *raison d'être* for the no-fly zones.[271]

Such a reading of resolutions 678 (1990) and 687 (1991) assumes that a violation of the latter allowed a resumption of the means authorized by the former, apparently recalling the pre-Charter position that serious violation of an
armistice by one party entitles the other party to resume hostilities.[272]
Whereas the earlier position made sense in a legal order in which war itself
was not prohibited, the post-Charter position on the legality of the use of
force (and, indeed, of armed reprisals) makes an argument that unilateral
recourse to force may be justified in such circumstances difficult to sustain.
This is especially true for circumstances in which the legitimacy of the use of
force that led to the ceasefire depends on the delegation of power by the
Security Council.[273] Resolution 678 (1990) authorized the use of all necessary
means to 'uphold and implement resolution 660 (1990) *and all subsequent
relevant resolutions*'.[274] Following the suspension of hostilities, the Council
adopted resolution 686 (1991) as a provisional ceasefire resolution, explicitly
recognizing that the authorization in resolution 678 (1990) remained valid for
the period required by Iraq to comply with its terms.[275] Resolution 687
(1991), by contrast, represented a 'formal ceasefire' effective upon Iraq's
*acceptance* of the provisions.[276] For the provisional ceasefire, the Council
affirmed that the previous resolutions 'continue to have full force and
effect';[277] the second resolution affirmed the previous resolutions 'except as
expressly changed below to achieve the goals of this resolution, including a
formal cease-fire'.[278] Indeed, China and India abstained from resolution 686
(1991) as they disagreed with the continuation of the resolution 678 (1990)
authorization to use force.[279] Both states later voted in favour of resolution
687 (1991).[280]

---

[270] *Keesing's* (1993) 39292.

[271] SC Res 687 (1991) did not, for example, refer to the Kurds: see Ch 4, Sect 3.1.1.

[272] Hague Convention [No IV] Respecting the Laws and Customs of War on Land, 18 Oct
1907, annexed Regulations, 36 Stat 2277, 1 Bevans 631, art 40. Given the provisions of Article
2(4) and Chapter VII of the Charter, it has been argued that this does not apply to an alleged violation of a *UN-imposed* ceasefire: see Lobel and Ratner, above n 70, 144 and sources there cited.

[273] See Sarooshi, above n 11, 231–2 (concluding that the no-fly zones cannot be justified as the
exercise of delegated Ch VII powers).

[274] SC Res 678 (1990) para 2.

[275] SC Res 686 (1991) para 4. The relevant terms were that Iraq: rescind its purported annexation of Kuwait; accept in principle its liability for damages suffered by Kuwait and third states;
release all prisoners; return Kuwaiti property; cease hostile or provocative acts; and provide
information on mines and chemical and biological weapons in Kuwait and areas of Iraq temporarily occupied by allied forces pursuant to SC Res 678 (1990): ibid paras 2–3.

[276] SC Res 687 (1991) para 33.          [277] SC Res 686 (1991) para 1.

[278] SC Res 687 (1991) para 1.          [279] S/PV.2978 (1991) 51 (China), 76 (India).

[280] SC Res 687 (1991) adopted 12-1-2 (Cuba against; Ecuador and Yemen abstaining).

Discussion in the Security Council over subsequent enforcement actions against Iraq centred on the protection of the Iraq–Kuwait border. An earlier draft of resolution 687 (1991) would have authorized the coalition states 'to use all necessary means' to guarantee the border.[281] India expressed its understanding that the resolution as adopted did not confer authority on any state to take unilateral action: 'Rather, the sponsors have explained to us that in the case of any threat or actual violation of the boundary in future the Security Council will meet to take, as appropriate, all necessary measures in accordance with the Charter.'[282] Russia agreed with this interpretation,[283] and the United Kingdom also made it clear that it was up to the Council to respond to any violation.[284]

Despite the foregoing, alleged violations of Iraq's obligation to submit to UNSCOM inspections constituted one aspect of the January 1993 strikes,[285] and were directly invoked by the United States and the United Kingdom to justify further air strikes in December 1998[286] that evolved into a low-level air campaign that continued into 2000. It is submitted that such alleged violations by Iraq—even where acknowledged as such by the Security Council[287]—were insufficient to legitimize the use of force by the two remaining coalition states. Significantly, the United Kingdom continued to seek a Council declaration that Iraq was in 'material breach' of resolution 687 (1991) and only began to argue that a further resolution was unnecessary when it became apparent that one would not be forthcoming.[288] In any event, it was never seriously argued that the no-fly zones themselves had their legal foundation in any violation of a Chapter VII resolution.

### (iii) Humanitarian intervention

David Scheffer has observed that the Bush Administration would have been more honest if it had based its action on a broad view of humanitarian intervention.[289] This was most closely approximated by the approach of the British Government: in an interview on BBC Radio, Foreign Secretary Douglas Hurd observed that not every action taken by a state has to be authorized by a specific provision in a UN resolution provided that international law is otherwise observed. And, he stated, '[i]nternational law

---

281 Freudenschuss, above n 31, 500.
282 S/PV.2981 (1991) 78 (India).
283 Ibid 101 (USSR).
284 Ibid 113 (UK).
285 See Lobel and Ratner, above n 70, 150–1.
286 Ibid 154.
287 In Jan 1993, the Council found that Iraqi actions constituted 'an unacceptable and material breach of the relevant provisions of resolution 687': S/25081 (1993) (Presidential statement); S/25091 (1993) (Presidential statement).
288 Lobel and Ratner, above n 70, 151 n 114.
289 David J Scheffer, 'Use of Force After the Cold War: Panama, Iraq, and the New World Order', in Louis Henkin (ed), *Right v Might: International Law and the Use of Force* (2nd edn; New York: Council on Foreign Relations, 1991) 109, 146–7. See also Ved P Nanda, 'Tragedies in Northern Iraq, Liberia, Yugoslavia, and Haiti—Revisiting the Validity of Humanitarian Intervention Under International Law' (1992) 20 *Denver JILP* 305, 306.

recognizes extreme humanitarian need'.[290] Nevertheless, he continued to rely
in part on the Security Council's authority, referring to the British, French,
and US action as being taken 'in support of' resolution 688 (1991).[291]

A more detailed legal opinion was presented by Foreign and Commonwealth Office Legal Counsel Anthony Aust at a hearing of the House of
Commons Foreign Affairs Committee. A written answer reiterated the argument that intervention could be justified 'in cases of extreme humanitarian
need', but again asserted that the no-fly zones were 'entirely consistent with
the objectives of [resolution] 688'.[292] Then in oral evidence the Legal Counsel
acknowledged that

Resolution 688, which applies not only to northern Iraq but to the whole of Iraq, was
not made under Chapter VII. Resolution 688 recognized that there was a severe human
rights and humanitarian situation in Iraq and, in particular, northern Iraq; but the
intervention in northern Iraq 'Provide Comfort' was in fact, not specifically mandated
by the United Nations, but the states taking action in northern Iraq did so in exercise
of the customary international law principle of humanitarian intervention.[293]

In any event, the no-fly zones were an unorthodox example of humanitarian intervention.[294] Established by the forces of three or four powers (depending on whether one includes Turkey, and later excludes France), for over eight
years they opposed airborne Iraqi incursions on the lines that had been drawn
in the sand at the 36th and the 32nd (later the 33rd) parallels, even as Turkey,
Iran, and eventually Iraq itself went in, or were invited in, on the ground to
support Kurdish factions they saw as friendly and fight those they regarded
as a threat.[295]

In so far as there is an argument that the initial relief effort was in fact justified on humanitarian grounds, a legal basis can be more easily found in the
MOU concluded between Iraq and the United Nations in April 1991,[296] as
humanitarian concerns alone could not serve to justify the many violations of
Iraqi sovereignty that took place in the following years. This distinction
between humanitarian *assistance* and intervention is implicit in Secretary-
General Javier Pérez de Cuéllar's 1991 Report on the United Nations:

[290] UK Foreign Secretary Douglas Hurd, BBC Radio interview, 19 Aug 1992, reprinted in
(1992) 63 *British YBIL* 824.
[291] Ibid. See also Douglas Hurd, 'A Year the World Lived Dangerously', *The Times*, 2 Aug
1991 (SC Res 688 (1991) created a significant precedent for mobilization if comparable conditions arise in the future).
[292] *Parliamentary Papers*, 1992–3, HC, Paper 235-iii, pp 58–9, reprinted in (1992) 63 *British
YBIL* 825–7.
[293] Anthony Aust, Legal Counsellor, FCO, statement before HC Foreign Affairs Committee, 2
Dec 1992, *Parliamentary Papers*, 1992–3, HC, Paper 235-iii, p 85, reprinted in (1992) 63 *British
YBIL* 827.
[294] Cf Roberts, above n 230, 42.
[295] See Christopher de Bellaigue, 'Justice and the Kurds', *New York Review*, 24 June 1999, 19,
22.
[296] See above n 250.

We need not impale ourselves on the horns of a dilemma between respect for sovereignty and the protection of human rights. . . . What is involved is not the right of intervention but the collective obligation of States to bring relief and redress in human rights emergencies.[297]

This would have limited the operation to air drops and other non-forcible assistance of a humanitarian character. It could not provide a basis for the ongoing no-fly zones and sporadic air strikes.

*(iv) Self-defence*

Interspersed with the various assertions of Security Council authorizations and humanitarian justifications was the occasional reference to a right of self-defence. Unlike the United States and the Secretary-General, the United Kingdom justified the January 1993 strikes as an act of self-defence against a threat to allied aircraft:

Iraq has been warned frequently not to interfere with allied aircraft in the zones. Such aircraft have the inherent right of self-defence against Iraqi threats to their safety. Attacks against Iraqi missile systems and associated command and control centres were necessary and proportionate responses in self-defence to such threats.[298]

To couch such an action in the language of self-defence is misleading, however, since the argument depends on coalition aircraft having the right to fly over Iraq in the first place.[299]

Self-defence was also invoked by the United States in June 1993 when it launched twenty-three cruise missiles against Iraq in response to an alleged assassination attempt on former President George Bush. The assassination attempt was said to have been foiled two months earlier, and President Clinton claimed that the air strike was a 'firm and commensurate' response.[300] There was no serious attempt to establish that the strike satisfied the requirements of necessity and proportionality to fall within the scope of self-defence.[301] The Security Council has consistently rejected such 'responses' as illegal reprisals,[302] which have also been declared illegal by the ICJ[303] and the General Assembly.[304] (Indeed, the US action may easily be

---

[297] [1991] *UNYB* 8.

[298] UK Parliamentary Debates, 25 Jan 1993, WA 514 (Mr Hogg).

[299] Gray, above n 264, 168.

[300] David von Drehle and R Jeffrey Smith, 'US Strikes Iraq for Plot to Kill Bush', *Washington Post*, 27 June 1993.

[301] *Nicaragua (Merits)* [1986] ICJ Rep 14, 94 para 176; *Nuclear Weapons* [1996] ICJ Rep 226, 245 para 41.

[302] See Derek W Bowett, 'Reprisals Involving Recourse to Armed Force' (1972) 66 *AJIL* 1, 10.

[303] *Corfu Channel Case* [1949] ICJ Rep 4, 35; *Nuclear Weapons* [1996] ICJ Rep 226, 246 para 46.

[304] Declaration on Friendly Relations, GA Res 2625(xxv) (1970): 'States have a duty to refrain from acts of reprisal involving the use of force.'

characterized as a reprisal. Unlike Israel, however, the United States has been loath to declare its actions as such.[305])

### 4.1.3. After the storm

Operation Provide Comfort saved many lives and established a fragile basis for Kurdish autonomy, but, as Adam Roberts observes, it is tempting to comment that 'not the least of its remarkable achievements was the degree of comfort it provided in the countries which organized it'.[306] The claim that 'the wind is breathing in the direction of collective humanitarian intervention'[307] greatly overstates the significance of resolution 688 (1991) and the action taken 'consistent with' its provisions. Though some commentators writing soon after its adoption regarded it as sanctioning intervention for humanitarian purposes,[308] with the benefit of hindsight it appears that it was, at best, an indecisive and highly ambiguous step by the Council.[309]

It was precisely this indecision and the weakening of Council oversight of enforcement action taken in its name that established the conditions for its ambiguous response to events in Kosovo in 1998, leading to the unilateral intervention by NATO the following year.

### 4.2. Kosovo, 1998–9[310]

Operation Allied Force against the FRY in response to events in Kosovo follows, in many ways, a natural progression from the other actions discussed in this Chapter. Security Council resolutions provided political (if not legal) support for increasingly militant rhetoric and, later, action that was determined outside its sessions; the Secretary-General of the United Nations gave his vague blessing to the intervention when it was too late to do anything else;

---

[305] Barry Levenfeld, 'Israel's Counter-Fedayeen Tactics in Lebanon: Self-Defense and Reprisal Under Modern International Law' (1982) 21 *Columbia JTL* 1, 40.

[306] Roberts, above n 151, 438.

[307] Rodley, 'Collective Intervention', above n 235, 40 (concluding that 'it may be difficult to keep it blowing in the absence of a threat to international peace and security manifested by palpable transborder consequences').

[308] See, eg, James A R Nafziger, 'Self-Determination and Humanitarian Intervention in a Community of Power' (1991) 20 *Denver JILP* 9, 38; Thomas G Weiss and Kurt M Campbell, 'Military Humanitarianism' (1991) 33 *Survival* 451; Kelly-Kate Pease and David P Forsythe, 'Humanitarian Intervention and International Law' (1993) 45 *Austrian JPIL* 1, 11.

[309] See, eg, Malanczuck, above n 260, 129; Scheffer, above n 289, 146; Freudenschuss, above n 261, 11; Roberts, above n 151, 437–8.

[310] See generally Mark Littman, *Kosovo: Law & Diplomacy* (London: Centre for Policy Studies, 1999); Marc Weller, *The Crisis in Kosovo, 1989–1999: From the Dissolution of Yugoslavia to Rambouillet and the Outbreak of Hostilities* (International Documents and Analysis vol 1; Linton: Book Systems Plus, 1999); Tim Judah, *Kosovo: War and Revenge* (New Haven: Yale University Press, 2000).

and acting states asserted a mix of legal and humanitarian justifications for their actions.

### 4.2.1. Origins of the conflict

Though there were more proximate causes, the roots of the conflict in Kosovo are commonly traced back to the defeat of Serbian Prince Lazar by Ottoman Turks in 1389. The province remained under Ottoman rule until 1912, when Serbia and the other independent Balkan states united to force the Turks out of their European territory. The Serbs were driven out of Kosovo during the First World War, but the formation of the 'Kingdom of Serbs, Croats, and Slovenes' in 1918 saw Kosovo return to Serbia. Rechristened 'Yugoslavia' in 1929—literally, the Southern Slav state—it was divided once more during the Second World War. Reconstituted in 1945 under Tito, the 'People's Federal Republic of Yugoslavia' consisted of six republics (Serbia, Montenegro, Croatia, Slovenia, Bosnia and Herzegovina, and Macedonia) and two autonomous regions within Serbia (Vojvodina and Kosovo). In 1974 Kosovo was granted full autonomy, giving it status approaching that of a constituent republic.[311]

It has been argued that the spark that ignited the Balkan wars was Serbian President Slobodan Milošević's decision to remove Kosovo's autonomy in 1989. This decision played on Serbian fears of ethnic domination in Kosovo and invoked the memory of the Serbs' defeat at the hands of the Turks six centuries earlier. Ethnic Albanian politicians declared their independence in July 1990, establishing parallel institutions that Serbia refused to recognize. Unrest continued through the decade, and though widely acknowledged to be one of the most sensitive areas in the Balkans, Kosovo was nevertheless left out of the Dayton Peace Agreement.[312] A notable exception to this was the warning issued by outgoing President Bush to President Milošević on 24 December 1992 that '[i]n the event of conflict in Kosovo caused by Serbian action, the United States will be prepared to employ military force against the Serbs in Kosovo and in Serbia proper'.[313]

### 4.2.2. Security Council response, March–October 1998

Events escalated in February and March 1998 with dozens of suspected Albanian separatists being killed by Serb police and vice versa.[314] On 31

---

[311] See generally Misha Glenny, *The Fall of Yugoslavia: The Third Balkan War* (3rd edn; London: Penguin, 1996); Amnesty International, *Kosovo: After Tragedy, Justice?* (London: Amnesty International, 1999); Greg Campbell, *The Road to Kosovo: A Balkan Diary* (Boulder: Westview Press, 1999).

[312] Holbrooke, above n 77, 357.

[313] David Binder, 'Bush Warns Serbs Not to Widen War', *NYT*, 28 Dec 1992. Cf David Owen, *Balkan Odyssey* (New York: Harcourt Brace, 1995) 392.

[314] Elaine Sciolino and Ethan Bronner, 'How a President, Distracted by Scandal, Entered Balkan War', *NYT*, 18 Apr 1999.

March 1998 the Security Council adopted resolution 1160 (1998) in which it condemned the use of excessive force by Serbian police and terrorist action by the Kosovo Liberation Army (KLA/UÇK), imposed an arms embargo, and expressed support for a solution based on the territorial integrity of the FRY with a greater degree of autonomy for the Kosovar Albanians. The resolution was adopted under Chapter VII, though without an explicit determination of a threat to international peace and security.[315] Fighting continued, with US-sponsored peace talks between FRY President Milošević and unofficial President of Kosovo, Ibrahim Rugova, breaking down in May.[316]

On 23 September 1998 the Security Council adopted resolution 1199 (1998), in which it 'affirm[ed] that the deterioration of the situation in Kosovo constitutes a threat to peace and security in the region' and, acting under Chapter VII, demanded a ceasefire and action to improve the humanitarian situation.[317] It further demanded that the FRY take the following concrete steps to implement the Contact Group statement of 12 June 1998: (a) cease all action by security forces; (b) enable effective monitoring by the EC Monitoring Mission; (c) facilitate the return of refugees and displaced persons and allow free and unimpeded access for humanitarian organizations and supplies; and (d) 'make rapid progress' towards finding a political solution.[318] Finally, the Council decided, 'should the concrete measures demanded in this resolution and resolution 1160 (1998) not be taken, to *consider further action* and additional measures to maintain or restore peace and stability in the region'.[319] The *New York Times* described this as a 'deliberate ambiguity' necessary to allow Russia to support the resolution.[320]

In the following week, reports of two massacres by Serbian forces of about thirty Kosovar Albanians[321] apparently strengthened NATO resolve to act. In a press conference on 8 October 1998, US Secretary of State Madeleine Albright said that the time had come for the Alliance to authorize military force if Milošević failed to comply with existing Council resolutions. When questioned as to the need for a further Security Council resolution, she replied that 'the United Nations has now spoken out on this subject a number of times'.[322] *The Times* of London captured the curious mix of law and politics that underpinned this view:

Diplomatic sources said yesterday that alliance members were *approaching consensus on the legal basis* for airstrikes. Although several countries, including Greece, Spain, Germany and Italy, had previously favoured seeking authorization from the United

---

[315] SC Res 1160 (1998).                                    [316] *Keesing's* (1998) 42301.
[317] SC Res 1199 (1998) preamble, paras 1–2.                [318] Ibid para 4.
[319] Ibid para 16 (emphasis added).
[320] Barbara Crossette, 'Security Council Tells Serbs to Stop Kosovo Offensive', *NYT*, 24 Oct 1998.
[321] Jane Perlez, 'New Massacres by Serb Forces in Kosovo Villages', *NYT*, 30 Sept 1998.
[322] US Secretary of State Madeleine Albright, Press Conference on Kosovo, Brussels, 8 Oct 1998 <http://secretary.state.gov/www/statements/1998/981008.html>.

Nations Security Council, they now realised that was no longer realistic because of Moscow's pledge to veto military action.[323]

On 13 October 1998 the North Atlantic Council issued activation orders (ACTORDS) for a phased air campaign in the FRY and limited air operations. NATO Secretary-General Solana stated that execution of the limited air operations would not begin for at least 96 hours in order to 'allow time for the negotiations to bear fruit'. He continued:

The Allies believe that in the particular circumstances with respect to the present crisis in Kosovo as described in UNSC Resolution 1199, there are legitimate grounds for the Alliance to threaten, and if necessary, to use force.[324]

An agreement was duly signed on 15 October 1998 by the FRY's Chief of General Staff and General Wesley Clark, NATO's Supreme Allied Commander, Europe (SACEUR), providing for the establishment of an air verification mission over Kosovo.[325] The next day, an agreement signed by the FRY Foreign Minister and the Chairman-in-Office of the OSCE provided for a verification mission in Kosovo, including undertakings by the FRY to comply with Security Council resolutions 1160 (1998) and 1199 (1998).[326]

These agreements were explicitly endorsed by the Council in resolution 1203 (1998) on 24 October 1998, though there was no reference to the threat of force that had led to the agreements, which might have rendered them void for coercion.[327] (This may be contrasted with the explicit endorsement of French and MISAB peacekeeping operations in the CAR.[328]) Nor was much said about the legality of the threat itself—as the ICJ held in the *Nuclear Weapons* advisory opinion, a signalled intention to use force if certain events occur would contravene Article 2(4) if the envisaged use of force would itself be illegal.[329]

There were differences of opinion as to what, precisely, was authorized by resolution 1203 (1998). In addition to demanding that both the FRY and the Kosovar Albanians comply with resolutions 1160 (1998) and 1199 (1998), and that they respect the OSCE verification mission, the Council noted that the OSCE was 'considering arrangements to be implemented in cooperation with other organizations' and affirmed that 'in the event of an emergency, *action*

---

[323] Michael Evans and Tom Walker, 'NATO Bombers on Alert for Order to Hit Serbs', *The Times*, 12 Oct 1998 (emphasis added).

[324] NATO Secretary-General Dr Javier Solana, Press Conference at NATO HQ in Brussels, 13 Oct 1998 <http://www.nato.int/docu/speech/1998/s981013b.htm>.

[325] S/1998/991, Annex. It was reported that Clark presented FRY officials with a three-page list detailing the military and police units that had to pull out of Kosovo to satisfy NATO: Steven Lee Myers, 'Reprieve By NATO Allows Milošević Another 10 Days', *NYT*, 17 Oct 1998.

[326] S/1998/978.

[327] SC Res 1203 (1998) para 1. Vienna Convention on the Law of Treaties 1969, art 52, provides that a treaty 'is void if its conclusion has been procured by the threat or use of force in violation of the principles of international law embodied in the Charter of the United Nations'.

[328] See above n 105.      [329] *Nuclear Weapons* [1996] ICJ Rep 226, 246 para 47.

*may be needed* to ensure [the verification mission's] safety and freedom of movement'.[330] This represented a watering down of the draft that had originally circulated during the Council's consultations, with the deletion of elements threatening or authorizing the use of force.[331]

In statements made after they abstained from voting on resolution 1203 (1998), both Russia and China—which had threatened to veto any resolution authorizing the use of force[332]—made it clear that they did not see the resolution as authorizing military intervention in the FRY.[333] The US representative, by contrast, made the following observations after the vote:

We must acknowledge that a credible threat of force was key to achieving the OSCE and NATO agreements and remains key to ensuring their full implementation. . . .

The NATO allies, in agreeing on 13 October to the use of force, made it clear that they had the authority, the will and the means to resolve this issue. We retain that authority.[334]

An unnamed US official was reported to the effect that the resolution was 'all NATO needed to punish Mr Milošević if he stepped out of line'.[335]

### 4.2.3. Operation Allied Force, March–June 1999

Resolution 1203 (1998) marked the Security Council's final substantive involvement in Kosovo until NATO's air operations ceased on 10 June 1999.[336] The issue simmered for some months until the massacre of forty-five civilians in Račak in January 1999 led to more sabre-rattling.[337] The comments of Secretary-General Annan at this time have been quoted above;[338] this was swiftly followed by a NATO warning that it remained prepared to take military action.[339] Negotiations in Rambouillet from 6 to 23 February, and in Paris from 15 to 18 March concluded with the FRY refusing to sign the agreement that required freedom of movement for NATO throughout the whole of the FRY

---

[330] SC Res 1203 (1998) para 9 (emphasis added).

[331] See the statement by the Chinese representative after the vote: S/PV.3937 (1998) 14-15 (China).

[332] It was reported that a phrase asserting the Council's right to take all 'appropriate steps' if the FRY violated its pledges had been dropped to avoid such a veto: Youssef M Ibrahim, 'UN Measure Skirts Outright Threat of Force Against Milosovic', *NYT*, 25 Oct 1998.

[333] S/PV.3937 (1998) 12 (Russia), 14-15 (China).                    [334] Ibid 15 (US).

[335] Youssef M Ibrahim, 'UN Measure Skirts Outright Threat of Force Against Milosevic', *NYT*, 25 Oct 1998.

[336] On 14 May 1999 the Security Council passed SC Res 1239 (1999) concerning assistance to refugees from the conflict. The only reference to the ongoing air operations was a paragraph urging 'all concerned' to work towards a political solution along the lines of that proposed by the Meeting of G-8 Foreign Ministers on 6 May 1999 (para 5).

[337] Craig R Whitney, 'NATO Says It's Ready to Act to Stop Violence in Kosovo', *NYT*, 29 Jan 1999.

[338] See above nn 142–9.

[339] Whitney, above n 337.

and a referendum on Kosovo's independence in three years.[340] The draft agreement included a clause comparable to the Dayton Agreement, in which the parties 'invited' NATO to constitute and lead a military force authorized under a Chapter VII Security Council resolution.[341] In the days before air strikes commenced, it was reported that the only matter on which the United States was prepared to compromise was on the name of the international force that would police the agreement.[342]

On 24 March 1999 NATO commenced air strikes against the FRY. NATO Secretary-General Solana stated that the military alliance acted because all diplomatic avenues had failed:

We are taking action following the Federal Republic of Yugoslavia Government's refusal of the International Community's demands:

• Acceptance of the interim political settlement, which has been negotiated at Rambouillet;
• Full observance of limits on the Serb Army and the Special Police Forces, agreed on 25 October;
• Ending of the excessive and disproportionate use of force in Kosovo.[343]

President Clinton emphasized US interests in preventing a potentially wider war if action were not taken now, and the humanitarian concerns that led the allies to act;[344] UK Prime Minister Blair stressed the need to protect Kosovar Albanian citizens[345] and argued that the choice was to do something or do nothing.[346]

In an emergency session of the Security Council on 24 March, Russia, China, Belarus, and India opposed the action as a violation of the Charter.[347] Of those states that supported the action, few asserted a clear legal basis for it. The United States,[348] Canada,[349] and France[350] stressed that the FRY was in violation of legal obligations imposed by resolutions 1199 (1998) and 1203 (1998). Germany, speaking as the Presidency of the European Union, stated

---

[340] Robert Fisk, Emma Daly, and Andrew Marshall, 'West Quits Kosovo and Prepares to Attack', *Independent*, 20 Mar 1999.

[341] Rambouillet Accords, above n 111, Ch 7, art I(1)(a). Cf above n 100.

[342] R Jeffrey Smith, 'Belgrade Rebuffs Final US Warning', *Washington Post*, 23 Mar 1999.

[343] NATO Press Release (1999) 040 (23 Mar 1999).

[344] President Clinton's Address on Airstrikes Against Yugoslavia, *NYT*, 24 Mar 1999.

[345] Text of British Prime Minister Tony Blair's Statement on Kosovo Bombing, *NYT*, 24 Mar 1999: 'We are taking this action for one very simple reason; to damage the Serb forces sufficiently to prevent Milošević from continuing to perpetuate his vile oppression against innocent Kosovar Albanian civilians.'

[346] Rachel Sylvester, 'The Blair Doctrine: This is an Ethical Fight', *Independent on Sunday*, 28 Mar 1999.

[347] S/PV.3988 (1999) 12-13 (China), 13 (Russia), 15 (Belarus), 15-16 (India).

[348] Ibid 4 (US): '[W]e believe that such action is necessary to respond to Belgrade's brutal persecution of Kosovar Albanians, violations of international law, excessive and indiscriminate use of force, refusal to negotiate to resolve the issue peacefully and recent military build-up in Kosovo—all of which foreshadow a humanitarian catastrophe of immense proportions.'

[349] Ibid 5-6 (Canada).       [350] Ibid 9 (France).

that the members of the EU were under a 'moral obligation' to prevent a humanitarian catastrophe in the middle of Europe.[351] Only the Netherlands[352] and the United Kingdom[353] argued that the action was a *legal* response to a humanitarian catastrophe. The UK delegate stated:

The action being taken is legal. It is justified as an exceptional measure to prevent an overwhelming humanitarian catastrophe. Under present circumstances in Kosovo, there is convincing evidence that such a catastrophe is imminent. Renewed acts of repression by the authorities of the Federal Republic of Yugoslavia would cause further loss of civilian life and would lead to displacement of the civilian population on a large scale and in hostile conditions.

Every means short of force has been tried to avert this situation. In these circumstances, and as an exceptional measure on grounds of overwhelming humanitarian necessity, military intervention is legally justifiable. The force now proposed is directed exclusively to averting a humanitarian catastrophe, and is the minimum judged necessary for that purpose.[354]

Other states variously expressed concern about the humanitarian situation and the failure of diplomacy to achieve a peaceful resolution to the crisis.[355] In a revealing statement, the Slovenian representative alluded to the studied ambiguity of earlier Council resolutions:

Of course, [the resolutions] could be clearer, and one might have hoped that such resolutions would develop more completely the responsibility of the Security Council for the maintenance of international peace and security. Those of us who participated in the drafting of those resolutions know very well that the original draft texts were intended to do precisely that, and that, because of differences of views among permanent members, it was not possible to provide in those resolutions a sufficiently complete framework to allow for the entire range of measures that might be necessary to address the situation in Kosovo with success. That is another example of an imperfect world.[356]

---

[351] S/PV.3988 (1999) 17 (Germany): 'On the threshold of the 21st century, Europe cannot tolerate a humanitarian catastrophe in its midst. It cannot be permitted that, in the middle of Europe, the predominant population of Kosovo is collectively deprived of its rights and subjected to grave human rights abuses. We, the countries of the European Union, are under a moral obligation to ensure that indiscriminate behaviour and violence, which became tangible in the massacre of Racak in January 1999, are not repeated. We have a duty to ensure the return to their homes of the hundreds of thousands of refugees and displaced persons.'

[352] Ibid 8 (Netherlands): 'The Secretary-General is right when he observes in his press statement that the Council should be involved in any decision to resort to the use of force. If, however, due to one or two permanent members' rigid interpretation of the concept of domestic jurisdiction, such a resolution is not attainable, we cannot sit back and simply let the humanitarian catastrophe occur. In such a situation we will act on the legal basis we have available, and what we have available in this case is more than adequate.

'... As stated by the Secretary-General, diplomacy has failed, but there are times when the use of force may be legitimate in the pursuit of peace. The Netherlands feels that this is such a time.'

[353] Ibid 11-12 (UK).                                    [354] Ibid 12 (UK).

[355] Ibid *passim*.                                        [356] Ibid 19-20 (Slovenia).

On 26 March 1999 a draft resolution demanding an end to the air strikes was rejected by twelve votes to three.[357] Russia, China, and Namibia supported the draft resolution; those voting against included five states that were NATO members.[358] Few states opposing the resolution advanced any legal basis for the action. The United Kingdom echoed its justification for the no-fly zones in Iraq, stating that military intervention was justified as an exceptional measure to prevent an overwhelming humanitarian catastrophe.[359] France and the Netherlands noted that previous resolutions had been adopted under Chapter VII of the Charter, implying that the coercive powers of the Council had been invoked.[360] For the most part, the resolution was simply seen as an inappropriate response to the situation. The US delegate stated before the vote that by rejecting the resolution, the Council would reaffirm the requirements it had put to the Government in Belgrade to cease their brutal attacks against the people of Kosovo and move towards peace.[361] Other states observed that the draft resolution took a selective view of the legal issues raised by the situation in Kosovo,[362] or asserted that the only person to benefit from such a resolution would be President Milošević.[363]

These sentiments were echoed in the proceedings brought by the FRY against ten NATO members in the ICJ. In the course of hearings on the FRY's requests for provisional measures, Belgium presented the most elaborate legal justification for the action, relying variously on Security Council resolutions, a doctrine of humanitarian intervention (as compatible with Article 2(4) of the UN Charter or based on historical precedent), and the argument of necessity.[364] The United States also emphasized the importance of Security Council resolutions,[365] and, together with four other delegations (Germany,[366] the Netherlands,[367] Spain,[368] and the United Kingdom[369]) made reference to the existence of a 'humanitarian catastrophe'.[370] Four delegations did not offer any clear legal justification (Canada, France, Italy, Portugal).

Belgium's arguments on humanitarian intervention have been considered in Chapter 2.[371] Its reference to the doctrine of necessity is also unpersuasive.

---

[357] S/1999/328 sponsored by Belarus, India, and Russia.

[358] NATO members: US, UK, France, Canada, and the Netherlands. Argentina, Bahrain, Brazil, Gabon, Gambia, Malaysia, and Slovenia also voted against the draft resolution: UN Press Release SC/6659 (26 Mar 1999).

[359] Ibid (UK).    [360] Ibid (France, Netherlands).    [361] Ibid (US).

[362] Ibid (Slovenia, Argentina, Malaysia, Bahrain).    [363] Ibid (Canada, Netherlands, UK).

[364] *Legality of Use of Force Case* (*Provisional Measures*) (ICJ, 1999) pleadings of Belgium, 10 May 1999, CR 99/15 (uncorrected translation).

[365] Ibid pleadings of the United States, 11 May 1999, CR 99/24, para 1.7.

[366] Ibid pleadings of Germany, 11 May 1999, CR 99/18, para 1.3.1.

[367] Ibid pleadings of the Netherlands, 11 May 1999, CR 99/20, para 40. Cf para 38 ('remind[ing]' the Court of certain Security Council resolutions).

[368] Ibid pleadings of Spain, 11 May 1999, CR 99/22, para 1.

[369] Ibid pleadings of the United Kingdom, 11 May 1999, CR 99/23, paras 17–18.

[370] Ibid pleadings of the United States, 11 May 1999, CR 99/24, para 1.7.

[371] See Ch 2, Introduction.

In the *Gabcíkovo-Nagymaros* case, the ICJ applied Article 33 of the ILC's 1980 Draft Articles on State Responsibility[372] as reflecting customary international law.[373] The Court restated the requirements of customary international law as follows:

[A state of necessity] must have been occasioned by an 'essential interest' of the State which is the author of the act conflicting with one of its international obligations; that interest must have been threatened by a 'grave and imminent peril'; the act being challenged must have been the 'only means' of safeguarding that interest; that act must not have 'seriously impair[ed] an essential interest' of the State towards which the obligation existed; and the State which is the author of that act must not have 'contributed to the occurrence of the state of necessity'.[374]

It seems unlikely that NATO's action would have satisfied any of these cumulative requirements. Aside from the question of whether Kosovar self-determination was an 'essential interest' of NATO's member states and the factual question of the peril that preceded the commencement of air strikes, the failure to pursue means other than air strikes militates against a successful claim of necessity. It also appears broadly accepted that NATO's approach to the Rambouillet negotiations 'contributed to' the need for military action.[375] Finally, and most clearly, it can scarcely be doubted that the 78-day air campaign 'seriously impair[ed] an essential interest' of the FRY.

From the review of the Security Council's response to the situation above, it is also clear that the resolutions passed cannot provide a legal basis for the action, lacking even the ambiguity of resolution 688 (1991) on Iraq. This was evident in the manner in which the resolutions were said to support the action: no state argued that the resolutions actually authorized an enforcement action, or that the resolutions on their own constituted a legal basis for the intervention; they were relied on instead to provide a political justification for military action.

The remaining argument concerned the unusual formula of avoiding a 'humanitarian catastrophe'. Though this phrase recalls the doctrine of humanitarian intervention, some care appears to have been taken to avoid invoking that doctrine by name. The formulation derives from UK justifications for the no-fly zones over Iraq,[376] although no legal pedigree was ever established for this.

For technical reasons deriving from the FRY's declaration of acceptance of the Court's jurisdiction, the ICJ declined the relief sought but remains seised of eight of the ten cases. It did not discuss the merits of the FRY's cases.[377]

---

[372] [1980] 2(2) *ILC YB* 34.
[373] *Gabcíkovo-Nagymaros Case* [1997] ICJ Rep 7, 36–8 paras 49–52.
[374] Ibid 37–8 para 52.
[375] See, eg, Thomas L Friedman, 'Kosovo's Three Wars', *NYT*, 6 Aug 1999. See Ch 6.
[376] See above nn 290, 292.
[377] *Legality of Use of Force Case (Provisional Measures)* (ICJ, 1999) order of 2 June 1999.

During the air campaign, many international lawyers remained conspicuously silent on the issue. Of those who commented on the air strikes, many couched their opinions in terms of 'traditional international law' that provided no basis for the action.[378] Criticism focused on the constitutional basis for such action by NATO,[379] the lack of clear Security Council authority,[380] and hesitation as to the correlation between aerial bombardments and NATO's asserted humanitarian motives.[381] Those who supported the action tended to present it as a lesser wrong than that alleged against the FRY.[382] The few international lawyers to defend the principle according to which NATO claimed to act included Michael Reisman,[383] who had argued for such a right since about 1973,[384] and Christopher Greenwood,[385] who later acted for the United Kingdom in the case brought by the FRY before the ICJ.

Subsequent analyses were more sanguine: the air campaign was (eventually) concluded and the Security Council continued to function—notwithstanding the destruction of the embassy of one P5 member by another.[386] This view was commonly premised on the idea that Kosovo was 'exceptional', perhaps in the way that the Korean operation came to be seen in the early years of the United Nations.[387]

### 4.2.4. The exception and the rule

Unusually among the NATO states, the German Federal Government in October 1998 explicitly referred to NATO's threats against the FRY as an

[378] Neil A Lewis, 'A Word Bolsters Case for Allied Intervention', *NYT*, 4 Apr 1999 (quoting Abraham Chayes).

[379] William Branigin and John M Goshko, 'Legality of Airstrikes Disputed in US, UN—China Condemns "Blatant Aggression" ', *Washington Post*, 27 Mar 1999 (quoting Thomas Moore).

[380] Simon Chesterman and Michael Byers, 'Has US Power Destroyed the UN?', *London Review of Books*, 29 Apr 1999, 29.

[381] Neil A Lewis, 'A Word Bolsters Case for Allied Intervention', *NYT*, 4 Apr 1999 (quoting Ruth Wedgwood).

[382] Ibid (quoting Thomas Franck, Diane Orentlicher).

[383] Ibid (quoting Michael Reisman).

[384] W Michael Reisman and Myres S McDougal, 'Humanitarian Intervention to Protect the Ibos', in Richard B Lillich (ed), *Humanitarian Intervention and the United Nations* (Charlottesville: University Press of Virginia, 1973) 167.

[385] Christopher Greenwood, 'Yes, But Is the War Legal?', *Observer*, 28 Mar 1999: 'International law is not static. In recent years, States have come, perhaps reluctantly, to accept that there is a right of humanitarian intervention when a government—or the factions in a civil war—create a human tragedy of such magnitude that it constitutes a threat to international peace. In such a case, if the Security Council does not take military action, then other states have a right to do so.' CF UK House of Commons, Foreign Affairs Committee, Fourth Report: Kosovo, HC 28-I, 7 June 2000, para 132 (concluding that, in oral evidence given before the Committee in 2000, 'Professor Greenwood was too ambitious in saying that a new customary right has developed').

[386] See John Sweeney, Jens Holsoe, and Ed Vulliamy, 'NATO Bombed Chinese Deliberately', *Observer*, 17 Oct 1999.

[387] Cf Thomas M Franck, 'Lessons of Kosovo' (1999) 93 *AJIL* 857.

instance of 'humanitarian intervention' and approved the position of the alliance—provided that it was made clear that this was not to become a precedent for further action.[388] Speaking two weeks before the air campaign commenced, Bruno Simma endorsed this position. He noted that 'only a thin red line separates NATO's action in Kosovo from international legality', but argued that it should remain exceptional.[389]

The desire to avoid setting a precedent was evident in many subsequent statements by NATO members. US Secretary of State Madeleine Albright stressed in a press conference after the air campaign that Kosovo was 'a unique situation *sui generis* in the region of the Balkans', concluding that it is important 'not to overdraw the various lessons that come out of it'.[390] Speaking in Chicago on 22 April, UK Prime Minister Tony Blair appeared to suggest that such interventions might become more routine, stating that '[t]he most pressing foreign policy problem we face is to identify the circumstances in which we should get actively involved in other people's conflicts'.[391] He subsequently retreated from this position, however, and emphasized the exceptional nature of the air campaign.[392] This was consistent with one of the more considered UK statements on the legal issues involved, by Baroness Symons in the House of Lords on 16 November 1998 and reaffirmed on 6 May 1999:

The prohibitions on the use of force contained in the UN Charter do not preclude the use of force by a state or group of states in self-defence in accordance with Article 51 or under the authorisation of the Security Council acting under Chapter VII of the Charter. There is no general doctrine of humanitarian necessity in international law. Cases have nevertheless arisen (as in northern Iraq in 1991) when, in the light of all the circumstances, a limited use of force was justifiable in support of purposes laid down by the Security Council but without the council's express authorisation when that was the only means to avert an immediate and overwhelming humanitarian catastrophe. Such cases would in the nature of things be exceptional and would depend on an objective assessment of the factual circumstances at the time and on the terms of the relevant decisions of the Security Council bearing on the situation in question.[393]

---

[388] Deutscher Bundestag, Plenarprotokoll 13/248, 16 Oct 1998, 23129, in Simma, above n 98, 13.

[389] Simma, above n 98, 22.

[390] US Secretary of State Madeleine Albright, Press Conference with Russian Foreign Minister Igor Ivanov, Singapore, 26 July 1999 <http://secretary.state.gov/www/statements/1999/990726b.html>.

[391] Colin Brown, 'Blair's Vision of Global Police', *Independent*, 23 Apr 1999. For a discussion of Blair's formula for intervention, see Ch 6, Sect 2, n 41.

[392] See, eg, UK Parliamentary Debates, Commons, 26 Apr 1999, col 30 (Prime Minister Blair).

[393] UK Parliamentary Debates, Lords, 16 Nov 1998, WA 140 (Baroness Symons); reaffirmed in UK Parliamentary Debates, Lords, 6 May 1999, col 904 (Baroness Symons). Cf Foreign Affairs Committee, above n 385, para 138: 'we conclude that NATO's military action, if of dubious legality in the current state of international law, was justified on moral grounds.'

It is not clear whether reference to the 'exceptional' nature of NATO's action is an admission that it violated international law and a plea for mitigation, or merely a reference to the frequency with which such actions might take place in future. The significance of such 'exceptions' will be considered in the next and final Chapter. For now it is enough to note that, as Chapters 4 and 5 have shown, 'exceptional' responses may very quickly become rules.[394]

CONCLUSION

> If the Council were to be fully faced with the issue, I am not sure whether there would be vetoes on the table or not. But we have to understand in recent history that wherever there have been compelling humanitarian situations, where the international community collectively has not acted, some neighbours have acted. Here for example I have in mind Viet Nam in Cambodia. And that did not destroy, I hope, the international system, and I think given the nature of the regime and what was happening there, the international community came to accept it.
>
> Kofi Annan, January 1999[395]

The progression from the euphoria of the new world order to the cautiously pragmatic approach to the role of the United Nations in the quote above casts a sobering light on the United Nations Decade of International Law (1990–9).[396] This Chapter has argued that the transition from Operation Desert Storm in Kuwait to Operation Allied Force in Kosovo is not, however, as great as it might at first appear.

The Security Council resolutions that authorized the coalition action against Iraq depended upon a broad international consensus, but also upon a coincidence with the national interests of those acting states. In a voluntary regime, this is perhaps inevitable. As subsequent enforcement actions showed, however, this coincidence of interests quickly resolved into a condition precedent to action. This was reflected most graphically in the changing role of the Secretariat, as the Secretary-General's reports to the Council increasingly reflected pre-arranged deals with the P5. In the lead up to and during Operation Allied Force—where there was no deal—this role as salesman seamlessly transformed into that of apologist.

The very smoothness of this transition from Council delegation to unilateralism in Kosovo shows that the veneer of multilateralism in Council actions in the early 1990s was even thinner than suspected at the time, but it also

---

[394] Cf Antonio Cassese, '*Ex iniuria ius oritur*: Are We Moving Towards International Legitimation of Forcible Humanitarian Countermeasures in the World Community?' (1999) 10 *European JIL* 23, 25.

[395] UN Press Release SG/SM/6875 (26 Jan 1999).      [396] GA Res 44/23 (1989).

demonstrates three important factors in the emerging international order. First, the action reflected the trend towards regionalism in matters of international peace and security. Secondly, Operation Allied Force was consistent with the view that the use of force—in particular, air strikes—was a decisive factor in averting or stopping internal conflicts. Thirdly, and most importantly, NATO's action demonstrated the effect of reducing Council authorization to a purely formal level: rather than operating as a source of legal authority, it was seen as one policy justification among others. Reference was made to action being taken 'in support of' or 'consistent with' Security Council resolutions, and it was on this basis that recourse to force swiftly became the preferred option to continued diplomacy.[397]

To note the failure to take seriously the provisions of the UN Charter is not simply to bemoan a lack of respect for international law, however. On the contrary, the formal requirements of the Charter encapsulate sound policy requirements that should precede action—even where that action may coincide with the interests of an acting state. Without defending the composition of the Security Council or the continued right of veto, the need to ensure the concurrence or acquiescence of nine members including those with a power of veto ensures that a substantial body of world opinion consents to a particular action.

If the role of the Security Council presently approximates that of the Council of the League of Nations, with power merely to recommend action to its members,[398] it is possible that an increasingly regionalized international system may yet come to resemble something slightly older—notably, the alliances of the nineteenth century under the Concert of Europe.[399] And, as the aftermath of the war in Kosovo may yet demonstrate, such alliances of convenience do not always remain so.

---

[397] Cf Jimmy Carter, 'Have We Forgotten the Path to Peace?', *NYT*, 27 May 1999.
[398] See above n 40.                              [399] See Ch 1, especially Sect 2.3.

# 6

## Just War or Just Peace?

### *Humanitarian intervention, inhumanitarian non-intervention, and other peace strategies*

And the central contradiction—the Iron Law of Humanitarian War—is this: *Humanitarian war requires means that are inherently inadequate to its ends.* This contradiction, on starkest display in Kosovo, establishes humanitarian war as an idea with a brief past and very little future.

Charles Krauthammer, 1999[1]

As disaster unfolded in East Timor in early September 1999, there was a curious transformation in the continuing public debate over NATO's air campaign against the Federal Republic of Yugoslavia (FRY) concerning its actions in Kosovo. Critics of NATO's intervention pointed to the inconsistency of such 'inhumanitarian non-intervention' in the case of East Timor. Supporters of the Kosovo action uneasily warned that the international community could not be everything to everyone. When intervention came, at the instigation of Australia in its self-proclaimed role as 'deputy' to the United States' sheriff, a sigh of relief was heaved by all: hypocrisy had been avoided.[2]

This dominant view assumed that the two situations and the international reaction were of a kind. They were not. In Kosovo, an escalating air campaign was designed to force the FRY to agree to significant restrictions on its sovereignty in favour of an oppressed minority. The action was taken without the authorization of the Security Council and in the face of protests from numerous states.[3] In East Timor, a multinational force was dispatched with the consent of all parties (bar the pro-Indonesian militias and sections of the Indonesian military) to enable the East Timorese people to realize their own sovereignty. However irrelevant Indonesia's consent might have been in a legal or moral sense, it is clear that nothing would have happened had Indonesian President B J Habibie not given it the go-ahead.[4]

This forced equation—which in essence meant that a Western-led coalition decided *not* to do nothing—highlights one of the policy issues at the heart of

---

[1] Charles Krauthammer, 'The Short, Unhappy Life of Humanitarian War' (1999) 57 *The National Interest* 5, 6.
[2] See, eg, David Watts, 'Howard's "Sheriff" Role Angers Asians', *The Times*, 27 Sept 1999. Prime Minister John Howard later stated that he had been misquoted.
[3] See Ch 5, Sect 4.2.                    [4] See Ch 4, Sect 3.2.5.

this book: the view that, when facing a humanitarian crisis with a military dimension, there is a choice between doing something and doing nothing, and that 'something' means the application of military force. In this concluding Chapter, the equation is used as the departure point for an exploration of three sets of implications of the analysis presented in Chapters 1 to 5. Section 1 considers the consequences that these assumptions have on states' approaches to dealing with humanitarian crises, and the distorting effect they have on the relationship between collective and unilateral interventions. This leads to a consideration in Section 2 of the legal question that underlies analysis of the various allegedly humanitarian interventions: how to reconcile such eccentric behaviour with the normative order of international law. In particular, is it possible and/or desirable to regularize such 'exceptional' behaviour, at least where it is perceived to have had beneficial consequences? Finally, Section 3 reconsiders the changing position of the United Nations over the past decade of 'interventionism'. It was argued in Chapter 5 that the current role of the United Nations in peace and security matters in some ways approximates that of the League of Nations; here, the focus will be on the normative consequences for an international rule of law more generally.[5]

## 1. DO SOMETHING OR DO NOTHING

Soon after NATO's air campaign against the FRY began in March 1999, UK Prime Minister Tony Blair emerged as the staunchest defender of the Alliance's actions.[6] A significant reason for this was the simplicity of the moral dilemma as he presented it: this was, he said, a case where the world had to do something or do nothing.[7] This misrepresented the situation on three counts. First, and most obviously, it was not the world but NATO that was acting. Despite the much-vaunted unanimity of the Alliance (reservations in the Czech Republic and Hungary, and massive unpopularity in Greece notwithstanding[8]), states representing over half the world's population—and three of its seven declared nuclear powers—spoke out strongly against the action.[9] Secondly, Blair's framing of the ethical quandary elided the question of whether the 'something' that NATO was prepared to do—air strikes from a

---

[5] Note that the term 'just peace' used in the title of this Chapter is not intended to refer to the traditional doctrines of the just peace, particularly as espoused by the Catholic Church. See generally Peter Matheson (ed), *Profile of Love: Towards a Theology of the Just Peace* (Belfast: Christian Journals, 1979); Frank Przetacznik, *The Catholic Concept of Genuine and Just Peace as a Basic Human Right* (Roman Catholic Studies; Lewiston: Edwin Mellen, 1991).

[6] See, eg, Warren Hoge, 'Blair Rallies Public Support After China Embassy Strike', *NYT*, 10 May 1999.

[7] Rachel Sylvester, 'The Blair Doctrine: This is an Ethical Fight', *Independent*, 28 Mar 1999.

[8] See, eg, Serge Schmemann, 'Storm Front: A New Collision of East and West', *NYT*, 4 Apr 1999; Alan Cowell, 'It's a Wonder this Alliance is Unified', *NYT*, 25 Apr 1999.

[9] See Ch 5, Sect 4.2.3.

minimum of 15,000 feet, later including the use of B-52s, cluster bombs, and depleted uranium ordnance—was in fact better than nothing. It is not proposed to enter into the gruesome calculus of evaluating the campaign by comparative casualty projections, but it is at least questionable that the undoubted human rights abuses that took place in Kosovo over the preceding 12 months (including terrorist activity by the KLA) justified the eleven-week bombing campaign. Thirdly, it dismissed the possibility of any diplomacy other than that which followed guns and bombs. This section will consider these three policy issues in turn.

## 1.1. Unilateral action and collective inaction

> Of the many organizations in the former Yugoslavia in the last five years, only NATO—that is, the United States—has been respected.
>
> Richard Holbrooke to US President Clinton, 1996[10]

NATO's claim to be acting for 'the world' in 1999 recalls the arguments for a right of unilateral intervention advanced during the Cold War and the era of Security Council paralysis. As indicated in Chapter 2, such arguments found only marginal support at the time; they would appear to be even more tenuous in light of the past decade of Security Council interventions.[11]

Underpinning the claim that unilateral action was necessary to avoid a veto by Russia or China was the assumption that any such veto would be cast out of mere contrariness. This was apparent even in the words of the UN Secretary-General.[12] It was never seriously contemplated that there might be genuine objections to the policies of NATO member states in their dealings with the FRY. While there is evidence that the veto continues to be used capriciously—notably by China in relation to diplomatic recognition of Taiwan[13]—caution should be exercised in further undermining the fragile consensus that emerged during the 1990s.

Concern about the subjective nature of the assessments that justify such interventions was a significant cause of the emergence of a right of non-intervention in the eighteenth century.[14] In large part this was due to the fear that any right of intervention might be abused, though an analogous concern is that it may be used unwisely. In this context, it is noteworthy that the FRY in March 1999 was the fourth state targeted by US air strikes in the space of eight months. In August 1998 the United States justified missile strikes on Sudan and Afghanistan as acts of self-defence connected with bombings at its embassies in Kenya and Tanzania two weeks earlier. In December 1998 it

---

[10] Richard Holbrooke, *To End a War* (New York: Random House, 1998) 339.
[11] See Ch 2, Sect 2.1.  [12] See Ch 5, Sect 2.2.
[13] See Ch 5, Sect 3.3, nn 216–17.  [14] See Ch 1, Sect 2.

justified air strikes against Iraq on the basis of seven-year-old Security Council resolutions. Without going into the merits of either action, a common theme is that the United States neither referred the matters to the Security Council, nor discussed them with other states (perhaps with the exception of the United Kingdom).[15] At the very least, such reluctance to utilize multilateral channels is a troubling gloss on the new interventionism of the Security Council in the 1990s.[16] As argued in Chapters 4 and 5, however, recourse to unilateral action may in fact be seen as a natural consequence of the transformation of the role of the Council from substantive to formal (and occasionally *ex post facto*) involvement in such actions.

### 1.2. Humanitarian war

The second policy issue considered here—whether doing 'something' is necessarily better than doing nothing—reduces to an ends-versus-means question with a normative and an empirical aspect. Underlying much of the debate over a right of unilateral humanitarian intervention is the question of whether sovereignty or human rights is paramount in international law. As argued in Chapter 2, *peace* is in fact the primary goal of the international order established after the Second World War, which was understood to be protected primarily through respect for the equality of states and the renunciation of war as an instrument of national policy. It is clear from the drafting history of Article 2(4) that no exceptions to this principle were contemplated, beyond the right of self-defence and duly authorized Security Council enforcement actions.

In addition to this normative conclusion, however, it is far from clear that the methods associated with humanitarian intervention, at least in its current incarnation, are compatible with the ends sought. The two major unilateral interventions of the 1990s considered in Chapter 5—Iraq (1991– ) and the FRY (1998–9)—were both fought in the name of stopping an oppressive ruler's policies against ethnic minorities within a sovereign state. Both interventions, however, were dogged by the conflicting views of allies and less than full domestic support; as a result they were fought from a great distance in order to minimize the possibility of friendly casualties. Such a policy increased the likelihood of civilian casualties within the target state, but also contributed to the inconclusive nature of the outcome in each incident. At the end of the

---

[15] See James Risen, 'Question of Evidence: To Bomb Sudan Plant, or Not: A Year Later, Debates Rankle', *NYT*, 27 Oct 1999; John M Broder with Barbara Crossette, 'On Two Fronts: With Advance Word on UN Report, Clinton Set Strikes in Motion on Sunday', *NYT*, 18 Dec 1998; Steven Lee Myers, 'In Intense but Little-Noticed Fight, Allies Have Bombed Iraq All Year', *NYT*, 13 Aug 1999.

[16] See Simon Chesterman and Michael Byers, 'Has US Power Destroyed the UN?', *London Review of Books*, 29 Apr 1999, 29.

decade, both the targeted rulers remained in power and neither ethnic conflict had been resolved.[17]

This is not to say that humanitarian interventions can never be successful. The three 'best case' interventions discussed in Chapter 2—East Pakistan/ Bangladesh (1971), Uganda (1978–9), and Kampuchea/Cambodia (1978–9)— all produced outcomes that are now broadly regarded as positive. As indicated in Chapter 2, however, the acting states in each of these incidents relied on justifications other than humanitarian intervention, most notably self-defence. The implications of this for customary international law have already been considered. Of interest here is the question of whether the existence of other motives actually helped in producing the end result. It is beyond the scope of the present work to examine the military strategies adopted in detail, though it is significant that in each case the action taken was in response to some form of aggression by the target state. In addition, in both Uganda and Kampuchea, the foreign intervention was undertaken alongside domestic opposition groups, while India recognized the independent state of Bangladesh three days after commencing hostilities with Pakistan. The prospect of a realistic alternative polity was not present in either northern and southern Iraq or Kosovo.

The objective success of an intervention does not necessarily affect its legal validity. Nevertheless, the disjunction between the ends and the means of interventions suggests the need for caution in embracing humanitarian intervention even as a realistic policy goal.[18]

## 1.3. Diplomacy and force

It was argued in Chapter 5 that one of the false lessons drawn from the Bosnian conflict was that superior air power largely explained the success of the Dayton negotiations.[19] This brinkmanship was repeated in relation to Kosovo in October 1998 and early 1999, but with two significant differences: there were not the same incentives on the ground for the two parties to agree to a political settlement, and NATO had openly allied itself with one of the negotiating teams. Reports from Rambouillet suggest that it was less of a negotiating round than an ultimatum to the FRY delegation—one of US Secretary of State Madeleine Albright's aides was quoted as stating that the

---

[17] The ECOWAS intervention in Liberia (1990–2) is sometimes included as a third example of state practice in support of a right of humanitarian intervention in the 1990s, but is more properly understood as intervention in a civil war. It also received retrospective validation by the Security Council far beyond that of operations in northern and southern Iraq or in the FRY. See Ch 4, Sect 3.1.3.

[18] See Adam Roberts, 'Humanitarian War: Military Intervention and Human Rights' (1993) 69 *International Affairs* 429.

[19] See Ch 5, Sect 1.2.

showdown at Rambouillet had 'only one purpose: to get the war started with the Europeans locked in'.[20] Indeed, a credible argument may be made that NATO commenced air strikes primarily because it had said that it would. Amid the talk of preserving NATO's 'credibility', a widely held view, articulated most bluntly by Henry Kissinger, was that whatever folly led NATO into battle 'victory is the only exit strategy'.[21]

There are, of course, times when it is necessary to back up humanitarian words with military deeds. Had the international community been willing to send troops into Rwanda in April 1994, it seems probable that tens if not hundreds of thousands of lives might have been saved.[22] But the equation of the international responses to East Timor and Kosovo suggests a basic misunderstanding of the flaws in Prime Minister Blair's justification of NATO's air war. The most important lesson to be learnt from Kosovo is not that tyrants can no longer oppress their people with impunity. The various leaders of brutal dictatorships around the world would probably differ on this point. Rather it is that there is an enormous cost associated with adopting a negotiating position that takes literally the cliché that diplomacy is the art of saying 'nice doggy, nice doggy' until one finds a rock. A one-sided war was fought in part because the FRY refused to agree to a referendum on Kosovo's independence and allow NATO troops freedom of movement through all of Yugoslavia. These provisions were dropped in the eventual settlement, suggesting that some compromise was indeed possible on issues that Western negotiators had said were 'non-negotiable'.[23]

This is connected with a second lesson: that there is a desperate need for more research on the prevention and amelioration of such crises. In Kosovo there had been warnings that the humanitarian crisis would escalate if NATO made good its threat to bomb. From relatively few refugees prior to the air strikes, up to 800,000 fled their homes after they began. Clearly, primary responsibility for the atrocities that took place lies with the individuals that committed and encouraged them. At the same time, however, NATO Supreme Commander Wesley Clark later said that such consequences of the NATO campaign were 'entirely predictable'.[24] This merely begs the question of why the

[20] Joseph Tichett, 'Main Winner: UN Support for EU', *IHT*, 11 June 1999. See also William G Hyland, *Clinton's World: Remaking American Foreign Policy* (Westport, CT: Praeger, 1999) 21–3.

[21] Henry Kissinger, 'Doing Injury to History', *Newsweek*, 5 Apr 1999. Cf Tony Blair's statement on 22 Apr 1999 that '[s]uccess is the only exit strategy I am prepared to consider': Ben Macintyre, 'Hawk Blair Stiffens US Resolve', *The Times*, 23 Apr 1999.

[22] See Human Rights Watch, *'Leave None to Tell the Story': Genocide in Rwanda* (New York: Human Rights Watch, 1999); Report of the Independent Inquiry into the Actions of the United Nations During the 1994 Genocide in Rwanda, UN Doc S/199/1257 (1999) Annex.

[23] See Ch 5, Sect 4.2.

[24] Francis X Clines and Steven Lee Myers, 'NATO Launches Daytime Strike', *NYT*, 27 Mar 1999.

NATO states were so unprepared for the humanitarian disaster that subsequently confronted them.[25]

In East Timor the warning signs were much more explicit. Evidence was available in May 1999 that pro-Indonesian groups planned to terrorize the population if the referendum found in favour of independence; the Australian press reported that weapons were being stockpiled, possibly in preparation for a violent takeover of much of the territory.[26] And yet the international community agreed to President Habibie's timetable that put the referendum in the middle of Indonesia's drawn-out presidential elections, and took the military's word for security measures in the region it had actively oppressed for 24 years. It is not clear whether this was the result of wilful blindness or naïveté. Megawati Sukarnoputri was one of the most prominent Indonesians to call for a delay in the referendum, with the result that her democratic credentials were called into question.[27] In the absence of a delay, one of the conditions of the international community giving its blessing to the referendum should have been the presence of significant numbers of peacekeepers in, or near, the region.

The term 'international community' is used advisedly. The events in East Timor were not attributable simply to the inaction of the United Nations, whose reaction to the ominous warning signs was to warn that the situation would be 'rather delicate' after the vote. The United Nations acts (and fails to act) in accordance with the wishes of its member states. There would have been no INTERFET had Australia not offered to lead it. At the same time, Australia must take significant blame for hoping against all reason that its major foreign policy 'thorn' could be removed as quickly and as painlessly as Habibie had promised.

Preventive diplomacy is difficult. In part this is because it is hard to know when it has been successful; paraphrasing Sherlock Holmes, it is difficult indeed to establish why a dog *didn't* bark on a given night. It may, at times, amount to purely intellectual navel-gazing. Nevertheless, such navel-gazing would have been more profitable than the chorus of self-congratulatory rhetoric to the effect that East Timor proved that the international community had made good the promise of Kosovo.[28]

---

[25] See, eg, Robert Fisk, 'Was It Rescue or Revenge?', *Independent*, 21 June 1999.

[26] See, eg, Lindsay Murdoch, 'Indonesian Forces Cheer Militia on Their Rampage', *Sydney Morning Herald*, 11 May 1999; Lindsay Murdoch, 'Amnesty Confirms Worst Fears of Voter Intimidation', ibid, 22 June 1999.

[27] John Aglionby, 'Megawati Puts UN Ballot in Jeopardy', ibid 17 May 1999. Cf Megawati Sukarnoputri, 'Blame It on Habibie', *Newsweek*, 20 Sept 1999.

[28] See, eg, President Bill Clinton, 'Three Resolutions for the New Millennium', *NYT*, 22 Sept 1999. Cf David Rieff, 'Wars Without End?', *NYT*, 23 Sept 1999. See also Christine M Chinkin, 'Kosovo: A "Good" or "Bad" War?' (1999) 93 *AJIL* 841.

## 2. THE EXCEPTION AND THE RULE

This book has argued that there is no 'right' of humanitarian intervention in either the UN Charter or customary international law. What, then, is to be made of the apparent toleration of certain incidents characterized as humanitarian intervention?

In the nineteen incidents of unilateral intervention considered in Chapters 2, 3, and 5, the international reaction ranged from widespread criticism, to equivocation, to tacit acceptance. These reactions were present even in the three 'best cases', discussed in Chapter 2. The ousting of Pol Pot received virtually no support; on the contrary, only a USSR veto blocked a Security Council resolution critical of the action, and Pol Pot's delegate continued to attend the United Nations as Kampuchea's representative for over a decade. In relation to East Pakistan, a USSR veto once again blocked a Security Council resolution calling on India to withdraw; the General Assembly subsequently adopted a similar resolution that stopped short of condemning India. Tanzania's intervention in Uganda arguably received more support than any other incident merely through the international community's silence.

A number of writers have attempted to explain the apparent inconsistency in such responses by reference to municipal law. Ian Brownlie, for example, has argued that, rather than construing such incidents as creating an exception to the prohibition of the use of force, a useful analogy may be drawn with the manner in which many legal systems deal with euthanasia:

[I]n such a case the possibility of abuse is recognized by the legal policy (that the activity is classified as unlawful) but . . . in very clear cases the law allows mitigation. The father who smothers his severely abnormal child after several years of devoted attention may not be sent to prison, but he is not immune from prosecution and punishment. In international relations a difficulty arises in that 'a discretion not to prosecute' is exercisable by States collectively and by organs of the United Nations, and in the context of *practice* of States, mitigation and acceptance in principle are not always easy to distinguish. However, the euthanasia parallel is useful since it indicates that moderation is allowed for in social systems even when the principle remains firm. Moderation in application does not display a legislative intent to cancel the principle so applied.[29]

Although the jurisprudential distinction between mitigation and acceptance in the international legal order is indeed problematic, a more fundamental objection may be ontological: in municipal law, such a discretion is exercised

---

[29] Ian Brownlie, 'Thoughts on Kind-Hearted Gunmen', in Richard B Lillich (ed), *Humanitarian Intervention and the United Nations* (Charlottesville: University Press of Virginia, 1973) 139, 146 (emphasis in original). See also Lillich, *Humanitarian Intervention*, above, 117–21 (Lillich, Freedman, Moore, *et al*); Tom J Farer, 'A Paradigm of Legitimate Intervention', in Lori Fisler Damrosch (ed), *Enforcing Restraint: Collective Intervention in Internal Conflicts* (New York: Council on Foreign Relations Press, 1993) 327.

within an organized legal structure; in international law, it appears tantamount to abdicating responsibility for a particular class of cases. A closer analogy to euthanasia may lie in recognition of an international wrong with only a nominal sanction, as in the case of the International Court of Justice's declaration against the United Kingdom for its intervention in the *Corfu Channel* case,[30] or Israel's apology to Argentina for the abduction of Adolf Eichmann.[31]

Nevertheless, the essence of this position—that certain acts are against the law, but that the decision of whether to condemn them is *outside* the law—corresponds to the more favourable incidents of alleged humanitarian intervention. Tanzania presented no legal justification for its intervention in Uganda (beyond the claim of self-defence), nor was it supported on legal grounds by any of the states that commented upon it. But neither was there the political will to condemn the action. East Pakistan reflected this view more closely: the reaction of the international community was sympathetic but consistent with the norm of non-intervention. In the case of Kampuchea, the sympathy registered only at the margins. Similarly, many of the equivocating commentators on Kosovo couched their positions with reference to 'traditional' international law.[32]

Clearly, if the demand for any such violation of an established norm becomes widespread then legal regulation of the 'exception' becomes more important. This is happening in the case of euthanasia, where advances in medical technology have increased the discretion of physicians in making end-of-life decisions; reliance on the blunt instrument of a possible homicide charge in such cases is an inadequate legal response.[33] In relation to humanitarian intervention the position is more complex. There *is* a mechanism for legal regulation of such military interventions—Chapter VII of the UN Charter. And yet it was precisely in the decade that saw this mechanism start to operate that calls for an independent right of humanitarian intervention became more strident.

Into this normative vacuum, various writers have proposed formulae for evaluating whether an intervention truly is 'humanitarian', either on a moral

[30] See Ch 2, Sect 2.1, n 60.
[31] After Eichmann was abducted, Argentina lodged a complaint with the Security Council, which passed a resolution stating that the sovereignty of Argentina had been infringed and requesting Israel to make appropriate reparation: S/4349 (1960); SC Res 138 (1960). 'Mindful' of the concern that Eichmann be brought to appropriate justice, it was clear that 'appropriate reparation' would not involve the physical return of Eichmann to Argentina. Indeed, the governments of Israel and Argentina subsequently issued a joint communiqué resolving to 'view as settled the incident which was caused in the wake of the action of citizens of Israel which violated the basic rights of the State of Argentina': Joint Communiqué of the Governments of Israel and Argentina, 3 Aug 1960, reprinted in 36 ILR 59.
[32] See Ch 5, Sect 4.2.3.
[33] See further Simon Chesterman, 'Last Rights: Euthanasia, the Sanctity of Life and the Law in the Netherlands and the Northern Territory of Australia' (1998) 47 *ICLQ* 362.

or a legal scale. These extend from Michael Levitin's charmingly simple (and utterly unworkable) 'liberation of Paris principle'—if the people throw flowers, the invasion is lawful; if they throw anything else, the invasion is unlawful[34]—through to detailed criteria for evaluating a given intervention. It is not necessary to discuss the various proposals in detail, but five common themes may be distilled from the literature:[35]

- First, the character of the human rights abuses on the part of the target state must be severe and immediate. Phrases such as 'shocking to the conscience of mankind'[36] are sometimes used, recalling the language of the General Assembly in its 1946 resolution on genocide.[37] Alternatives include 'immediate and extensive threat to fundamental human rights',[38] or 'widespread deprivations of internationally recognized human rights'.[39] (The extreme position that the undemocratic nature of a government alone justifies intervention was considered in Chapter 3.)
- Secondly, there must be no realistic peaceful alternative to intervention. Negotiations must have been attempted and have failed, and there must be no competent international body to which the situation could effectively be submitted. Some writers argue that this includes the exhaustion of economic sanctions as a means of stopping the human rights violations.[40]
- Thirdly, collective action must have failed. The Security Council must be unable to act, and must not have explicitly prohibited intervention. In addition, some writers express a preference for multilateral action, diversifying the intervening forces.[41]

---

[34] Michael J Levitin, 'The Law of Force and the Force of Law: Grenada, the Falklands, and Humanitarian Intervention' (1986) 27 *Harvard ILJ* 621, 654.

[35] These criteria are drawn from Richard B Lillich, 'Forcible Self-Help by States to Protect Human Rights' (1967) 53 *Iowa Law Review* 325, 347–51; John N Moore, *Law and the Indo-China War* (Princeton, NY: Princeton University Press, 1972) 186; Howard L Weisberg, 'The Congo Crisis 1964: A Case Study in Humanitarian Intervention' (1972) 12 *Virginia JIL* 261, 275–6; Jean-Pierre L Fonteyne, 'The Customary International Law Doctrine of Humanitarian Intervention: Its Current Validity Under the UN Charter' (1974) 4 *California Western ILJ* 203, 258–68; Wil D Verwey, 'Humanitarian Intervention Under International Law' (1985) 32 *Netherlands ILR* 357, 413–18; Gary Klintworth, *Vietnam's Intervention in Cambodia in International Law* (Canberra: AGPS, 1989) 52–3; David J Scheffer, 'Toward a Modern Doctrine of Humanitarian Intervention' (1992) 23 *University of Toledo Law Review* 253, 290–1; Farer, above n 29, 327; Richard B Lillich, 'Humanitarian Intervention Through the United Nations: Towards the Development of Criteria' (1993) 53 *Zeitschrift für ausländisches öffentliches Recht und Völkerrecht* 557, 562–3; Sean D Murphy, *Humanitarian Intervention: The United Nations in an Evolving World Order* (Philadelphia: University of Pennsylvania Press, 1996) 382–7; Jonathan I Charney, 'Anticipatory Humanitarian Intervention in Kosovo' (1999) 93 *AJIL* 834, 838–40.

[36] See, eg, International Commission of Jurists, *The Events in East Pakistan 1971* (1972) 95.

[37] GA Res 96(I) (1946) preamble. Cf *Reservations to the Genocide Convention* [1951] ICJ Rep 15, 23.

[38] Moore, above n 35, 186.          [39] Murphy, above n 35, 386.

[40] See, eg, Scheffer, above n 35, 291.

[41] See, eg, Fonteyne, above n 35, 266–7. Cf the position of writers at the end of the nineteenth century: see Ch 1, Sect 4.4.

- Fourthly, any unilateral action must be limited to the amount necessary to prevent further violations. The action must have a reasonable chance of success and do more good than harm. This may be considered in both the short and long term: an intervention that imperils the long-term political independence and territorial integrity of a state may fail on this criterion.
- Finally, there is frequently a requirement for the 'disinterestedness' or 'relative disinterestedness'[42] of the acting state. Some writers require only that the humanitarian objective be 'paramount'.[43]

Needless to say, none of the incidents considered in this book would satisfy all five requirements. Even the three 'best cases' fail on the last criteria: although humanitarian concerns appear to have been operative, in none were such concerns 'paramount' (and the acting states were far from disinterested). Indeed, at the height of the Kosovo campaign, Prime Minister Blair proposed his own five criteria, one of which was whether 'we' had national interests involved.[44]

Perhaps recognizing the futility of substantive criteria for evaluating the humanitarian criteria for intervention, some commentators have favoured establishing formal prerequisites. One such possibility would be to require the Security Council to make a preliminary determination as to the existence of a 'threat to international peace and security' or a 'humanitarian catastrophe' but allow individual states to determine the appropriate action that might be taken.[45] This is not so far from the current practice of the Security Council authorizing pre-planned actions, and the dissatisfaction of various states concerning such a dilution of the Council's role was considered in Chapter 5. In any case, it is questionable that such a formula would avoid the problem of the veto, as it would merely push the problem one procedural step back. States that might feel impelled to block a resolution authorizing the use of force would instead block resolutions that could trigger any such unilateral use of force. Doubly weakening the position of the Security Council in this way seems an unlikely mechanism for advancing respect for international law.

Geoffrey Robertson has recently suggested that a declaration by judges of the proposed International Criminal Court 'formally confirming its prosecutor's indictment of the head of the offending government'[46] might provide the

---

[42] Fonteyne, above n 35, 261.   [43] See, eg, Scheffer, above n 35, 291.

[44] Michael Evans, 'Conflict Opens "Way to New International Community": Blair's Mission', *The Times*, 23 Apr 1999. The five criteria were: Are we sure of our case? Have we exhausted all diplomatic options? Are there military options we can sensibly and prudently undertake? Are we prepared for the long term? And do we have national interests involved? Cf Vaclav Havel's statements that NATO's intervention was 'probably the first war that has not been waged in the name of "national interests," but rather in the name of principles and values': Vaclav Havel, 'Kosovo and the End of the Nation-State', *New York Review*, 10 June 1999, 4, 6.

[45] Anne-Marie Slaughter proposed this as a 'thought experiment' at Civilians in War: 100 Years After the Hague Peace Conference (New York, 23–4 Sept 1999).

[46] Geoffrey Robertson, *Crimes Against Humanity: The Struggle for Global Justice* (London: Allen Lane, 1999) 381.

trigger. Aside from the fact that no such Court presently exists, the suggestion that it might one day adopt such a role would undermine the chances of getting the necessary ratifications for its treaty to come into force. Assuming that it does come into force, however, would such declarations only be valid as against states parties to the treaty? And would they authorize intervention by *any* state? It seems undesirable that a new qualification on the prohibition of the use of force should be so uncertain. In addition, it is difficult to reconcile the notion of a permanent International Criminal Court with such a concept of vigilante justice.

In fact, all such criteria are doomed to redundancy. The very project assumes the possibility of an 'ideal' humanitarian intervention. That there has been no such ideal intervention is rarely taken into account. The impetus to develop some sort of normative regime is understandable but misplaced: the circumstances in which the law may be violated are not themselves susceptible to legal regulation. This is why the euthanasia analogy is misleading. End-of-life decisions must increasingly be made by doctors operating without legal guidelines; such decisions are being taken and must be taken. Each instance of humanitarian intervention—genuine or not—is an admission or a claim that the legal order itself has failed.

For this reason, an alternative municipal law situation is sometimes invoked: that of a person acting to prevent domestic violence in a situation where the police are unwilling or unable to act.[47] This is regarded as an appealing analogy as it appears to capture the moral dilemma facing the prospective intervenor—the clear wrong being done, the absence of alternatives—but it is unhelpful in attempts to develop normative constraints for the exercise of such acts. Apart from the problems attendant to constructing the victims of abuse as 'wife' or 'child',[48] the very identification of these parties as individuals will often be inappropriate. The interventions under consideration here are not reducible to a simple case of restraining A from harming B in the manner suggested by the analogy. In addition, these acts in domestic law are typically limited by the relationship to the established (if ineffective) legal regime: most such regimes provide for the right to use minimal force in defence of another person, and to exercise certain powers of arrest. Such criteria are simply inapplicable to international law.[49]

[47] See, eg, Anthony D'Amato, 'Nicaragua and International Law: The "Academic" and the "Real"' (1985) 79 *AJIL* 657, 660; Fernando R Tesón, *Humanitarian Intervention: An Inquiry into Law and Morality* (2nd edn; Dobbs Ferry, NY: Transnational Publishers, 1997) 88.

[48] Cf Ch 3, Conclusion.

[49] Cf *Legality of Use of Force Case* (Provisional Measures) (ICJ, 1999) order of 2 June 1999, dissenting opinion of Vice-President Weeramantry: 'In domestic law a court seeing violence between two litigating parties relating to the subject-matter of a pending action would, however righteous be the motive of one or other of the parties, have no hesitation in issuing an enjoining order restraining such violence. The rationale for such action is twofold: it is essential that the rights of parties be preserved intact pending their determination by the Court and it is essential that there be no escalation of the dispute pending litigation. The nature of the judicial function

The inability to articulate a coherent legal regime for illegal acts reinforces the more commonly voiced concern that any such doctrine might be abused.[50] State practice since the Second World War has seen interventions for all and sundry reasons; the question is whether, in the case of allegedly humanitarian interventions, it is better for this to be principled or unprincipled. This book argues for the latter position: it is *more* dangerous to hand states a 'right'— even of such a limited nature—than simply to assert the cardinal principle of the prohibition of the use of force and let states seek a political justification for a particular action if they find themselves in breach of that norm. The state practice discussed in this book suggests that states have not refrained from intervening for fear of condemnation; where there has been political support for the intervention that condemnation has been slight. On the contrary, the provision of additional justifications for intervention appears likely to increase the number of interventions undertaken in bad faith.

Implicit in many of the arguments for a right of humanitarian intervention is the suggestion that the present normative order is preventing interventions that should take place. This is simply not true. Interventions do not take place because states do not want them to take place. Fear of international condemnation did not prevent any state intervening in Rwanda: televised images of a downed US Ranger being dragged through the streets of Somalia did. States did not refrain from going to the assistance of the East Timorese until Indonesia gave its consent for *legal* reasons (legally Indonesia had no right to exercise sovereignty in East Timor at all). And, most obviously, NATO was not prevented from embarking on an air campaign over Kosovo because various states and publicists complained that this was a violation of the UN Charter. In fact the opposite is true. Interventions would be far *more* likely if any such norm were formalized, but state practice to date suggests that it is unlikely that these would be interventions where humanitarian concerns were 'paramount'.

In the event of an intervention alleged to be on humanitarian grounds, the better view is that such an intervention is illegal but that the international

---

is no different when it is transposed into the international plane, especially when the Court concerned is the principal judicial organ of the United Nations, functioning under a Charter which ranks the peaceful resolution of disputes among its prime Purposes and Principles.

'It is no argument to the contrary that the Court lacks the means to enforce its measures. The voice of the Court as the principal judicial organ of the United Nations may well be the one factor which, in certain situations, can tilt the balance in favour of a solution of disputes according to the law.'

[50] See, eg, Derek W Bowett, *Self-Defence in International Law* (Manchester: Manchester University Press, 1958) 104–5 (discussing protection of nationals); Ian Brownlie, *International Law and the Use of Force by States* (Oxford: Clarendon Press, 1963) 340–2; Richard A Falk, *Legal Order in a Violent World* (Princeton, NJ: Princeton University Press, 1968) 161; Panel Discussion, 'Biafra, Bengal, and Beyond: International Responsibility and Genocidal Conflict' (1972) 66 *ASIL Proc* 89, 96 (Henkin); Oscar Schachter, 'The Legality of Pro-Democratic Invasion' (1984) 78 *AJIL* 645, 649; Farer, above n 29, 324.

community may, in extreme circumstances, tolerate the delict. In judicial
terms this might translate to a finding of illegality but the imposition of only
a nominal penalty.[51] The substantive criteria outlined above may be useful in
evaluating the intervention at a political level, but such an explicitly political
analysis is more appropriate to criteria that establish an 'ideal' rather than a
formula for legality. Moreover, by affirming the prohibition of the use of
force, recourse to military intervention is maintained as an extreme, and last,
resort.

### 3. THE UN AND AN INTERNATIONAL RULE OF LAW

> The League of Nations died, I remind you, when its members no longer
> resisted the use of aggressive force. . . . [W]e have witnessed tonight an effort
> to rewrite the Charter, to sanction the use of force in international relations
> when it suits one's own purposes. This approach can only lead to chaos and
> to the disintegration of the United Nations.
>
> US representative on the Security Council, 1961[52]

At the beginning of the 1990s the United States, while proclaiming itself the
victor of the Cold War, magnanimously asserted that this provided an opportunity for the United Nations to fulfil its long-promised role as the guardian
of international peace and security. The Security Council saw new possibilities for action without the paralysing veto; Secretary-General Boutros
Boutros-Ghali laid out grand plans with *An Agenda for Peace*. In President
Bush's words, 'the rule of law would supplant the rule of the jungle'.[53]

The rhetoric was euphoric, utopian, and short-lived. As Chapters 4 and 5
have argued, international security issues continued to be resolved by reference to Great Power interests; notably, the role of the UN Security Council
was reduced to something akin to the League of Nations Council, with power
merely to give advice on matters of collective security. There is, now, a real
danger that the United Nations will be used only when it is geopolitically con-
venient or useful to do so. The Security Council in particular may be reduced
to what Richard Falk has described as a 'law-laundering service': a legitimiz-
ing mandate for the unilateral use of force, or (at best) the use of force by a

---

[51] See the discussion of the *Corfu Channel* and *Eichmann* cases above nn 30–1. In the *Legality
of Use of Force Case*, Vice-President Weeramantry dissented from the decision to refuse the
request for provisional measures, arguing that the Court should have issued provisional measures on *both* parties to desist from acts of violence and indicating that these measures were inter-
linked and to be given simultaneous application: *Legality of Use of Force Case* (Provisional
Measures) (ICJ, 1999) order of 2 June 1999, dissenting opinion of Vice-President Weeramantry.
[52] S/PV.988 (1961) paras 130–1 (US) (referring to UN inaction in the face of the Indian invasion of Goa).
[53] See Ch 4, Sect 1.2.

coalition of like-minded states.[54] This is suggestive of the earlier historical period considered in Chapter 1, where peace was contingent on the alliances of convenience that formed the Concert of Europe. In such a schema, the Secretary-General of the United Nations assumes the role of a sort of secular Pope, holding all influence and no power, ensconced in the bureaucracy of his temporal office.[55]

These analogies are extreme, but highlight the diminishing significance of the United Nations. Less than two months before NATO's air campaign against the FRY commenced, US Deputy Secretary of State Strobe Talbott gave a speech that suggested one of the ways in which multilateralism was changing at the end of the twentieth century. In what was, presumably, intended to be a positive evaluation of multilateral approaches to dealing with the situation in Kosovo, he praised the 'unprecedented and promising degree of synergy' that had developed between

five bodies—NATO, the EU, the OSCE, the United Nations and the Contact Group . . . By that I mean that these disparate but overlapping organizations have pooled their energies and strengths on behalf of an urgent common cause.[56]

In terms of the United Nations's specific contribution, he noted that 'the UN has lent its political and moral authority to the Kosovo effort'.[57] (No reference was made to the United Nations's *legal* authority.) As Bruno Simma has observed, the rhetorical point of placing the United Nations in the company of regional organizations and similar institutions may suggest (and be intended to suggest) that it should be regarded as existing on a similar hierarchical plain as these bodies. Taken one step further, this could be seen as implicitly relativizing the legal primacy of the UN Charter and the obligations it embodies.[58]

Any such development should be treated with great caution. Despite the reservations expressed in Chapters 4 and 5 concerning the nature of UN authorizations to use force, the decade of the 1990s is remarkable for the fact that recourse was had to international institutions at all: the United States sought authorization to intervene in the hemisphere previously demarcated as its own under the Monroe Doctrine; France sought leave to intervene in its former African colonies; Nigeria (belatedly) sought legitimacy for operations in its sphere of influence. The politics might well have been the same as those that beset the old world order, but they had assumed a very different form—

---

[54] Richard A Falk, 'The United Nations and the Rule of Law' (1994) 4 *Transnational Law and Contemporary Problems* 611, 628.

[55] Cf Amos S Hershey, *The Essentials of International Public Law* (New York: Macmillan, 1918) 95–6.

[56] Strobe Talbott, address delivered in Bonn, 4 Feb 1999, quoted in Bruno Simma, 'NATO, the UN and the Use of Force: Legal Aspects' (1999) 10 *European JIL* 1, 11, 18.

[57] Ibid 11.

[58] Simma, above n 56, 18. Cf UN Charter, art 103.

it was the abandonment of even this form that made Kosovo all the more dangerous a precedent.

Writing on the development of the rule of law in eighteenth-century England, the Marxist historian E P Thompson noted that the law certainly had the effect of systematizing and reifying inequality between the classes. This was consistent with the view of law as part of the superstructure of society in traditional (and highly schematic) Marxism. But at the same time, he argued, it 'mediated these class relations through legal forms, which imposed, again and again, inhibitions upon the actions of the rulers'. For this reason, he termed the rule of law an 'unqualified human good'.[59] Similarly, the position adopted here is that the danger of an international rule of law being subverted to legitimating the interests of Great Powers is still preferable to the unregulated exercise of that power. Even though Security Council resolutions authorizing interventions might have been drafted in the war rooms of states preparing military action, adopted in votes of questionable impartiality, and implemented by states of dubious disinterestedness, such limitations do less damage to the international legal order than the abandonment of the multilateral institutions set in place after the Second World War that characterized NATO's 1999 intervention in the FRY.

## CONCLUSION

In one of the war crimes trials brought in the US Zone of Germany under Control Council Law No 10,[60] Brigadier General Telford Taylor, Chief of Counsel for the United States, was proposing a juridical basis for the count of crimes against humanity. Such charges had not played an important part in the judgment of the International Military Tribunal, which, he said, had 'emptied them of their substance'.[61] Taylor argued that the concept of crimes against humanity first found articulation in the works of Grotius, whose concept of the 'just war' allowed for armed intervention to put an end to inhumane atrocities against civilian populations, and he cited a number of such

[59] E P Thompson, *Whigs and Hunters: The Origin of the Black Act* (Harmondsworth: Penguin, 1977) 264.

[60] Control Council Law No 10 was a hybrid of international law and national law, empowering the Allies in the European theatre to prosecute Germans and others in their respective zones of occupation: see M Cherif Bassiouni, *Crimes Against Humanity in International Criminal Law* (2nd edn; The Hague: Kluwer, 1999) 3.

[61] *Flick Case* (1947) 6 CCL 10 Trials 3, 87 (Telford Taylor for the Prosecution), quoting a lecture delivered by Donnedieu de Vabres in Mar 1947: '*Il les a vidées de leur substance.*' Taylor continued, quoting from the same lecture: 'It is, no doubt, considerations such as these which led the distinguished French member of the International Military Tribunal to look upon crimes against humanity with such a jaundiced eye. "When he wanted to seize the Sudetenland or Danzig, he charged the Czechs and the Poles with crimes against humanity. Such charges give a pretext which leads to interference in international affairs of other countries." ' Ibid 90.

interventions from the nineteenth century. There could be no doubt, he stated, that murderous prosecutions and massacres of civilian population groups were clearly contrary to the law of nations long before the First World War. And, on occasion, nations had resorted to military intervention to put a stop to such atrocities.[62] Nevertheless, he continued,

unilateral sanctions of this kind today are ineffective if confined to words and dangerous if military measures are resorted to. Intervention may well have been an appropriate sanction in the nineteenth century, when the fearful resources of modern warfare were unknown, and particularly when resorted to by a strong nation in behalf of minorities persecuted by a much weaker nation. Indeed, lacking some vehicle for true collective action, interventions were probably the only possible sanction. But they are outmoded, and cannot be resorted to in these times either safely or effectively.[63]

This book began by stating that the question of the legality of humanitarian intervention was, at first blush, a simple one. Article 2(4) of the UN Charter clearly prohibits the use of force, with the only exceptions being self-defence and enforcement actions authorized by the Security Council. As Taylor pointed out, however, there were long-standing arguments that a right of unilateral intervention pre-existed that Charter. Chapter 1 examined the genealogy of this right, disputing the claim that the doctrine was a 'right' in any meaningful sense of that word. In an era where war itself was not outlawed, the only consensus appears to have been that international law could neither sanction nor ignore actions that 'shock the conscience of mankind'.

With the passage of the UN Charter, and for the reasons alluded to by Taylor, the continued existence of any such right seemed unlikely. Chapter 2 considered the various attempts to justify the existence (or continued existence) of a doctrine of humanitarian intervention, either through a loophole in Article 2(4) or under customary international law. None of these arguments was found to have merit, either in principle or in the practice of states. Chapter 3 then looked at an alternative argument that certain 'illegitimate' regimes lose the attributes of sovereignty and thereby are not protected by the prohibition of the use of force. This was also found to be unpersuasive, with the more general observation that such attempts to impose 'legitimate' or 'authentic' regimes from without have in practice been used to install 'friendly' or 'compliant' regimes. There is, in short, minimal state practice and virtually no *opinio juris* that supports a general right of humanitarian intervention.

Chapter 4 turned to the collective security structure that was created after the Second World War but soon paralysed by the Cold War. The thawing of

---

[62] Ibid 87–9 (Telford Taylor for the Prosecution). Cf 19 Trial of the Major War Criminals Before the International Military Tribunal 472: 'The fact is that the right of humanitarian intervention by war is not a novelty in international law—can intervention by judicial process then be illegal?' (statement of Sir Hartley Shawcross for the Prosecution).
[63] *Flick Case* (1947) 6 CCL 10 Trials 3, 89–90 (Telford Taylor for the Prosecution).

US–Soviet relations in the late 1980s made possible the explosion of Security Council activism in the 1990s, notable for the plasticity of the circumstances in which the Council was prepared to assert its primary responsibility for international peace and security, and the contingency of its actions on the willingness of states to carry them out. The latter point was explored further in Chapter 5, which argued that the trend towards 'authorizing' states to act in the Council's name reduced its role from substantive to formal, until such 'authorization' became merely one policy justification among others.

This concluding Chapter has sketched out some of the implications of the analysis undertaken in the preceding five chapters. Central to most arguments in favour of a right of humanitarian intervention is a moral position that, in the face of atrocity, one cannot simply do nothing. The corollary is then drawn that international law should recognize and affirm this moral imperative. And, in the absence of legal authorization, that one may nevertheless act as morality dictates. This book argues that these three propositions are a recipe for bad policy, bad law, and a bad international order. They are also badly founded in logic, as they rest on the premiss that a humanitarian crisis with a military dimension presents the dilemma of doing 'something' or doing nothing: the just war or just peace.

For the dichotomy of the just war or just peace is a false, misleading, and dangerous one. It is false in that it implies that humanitarian intervention is morally, if not legally, valid because the ends sought justify the means employed. As this book has shown, in practice these ends are never so clear and the means are rarely so closely bound to them. The dichotomy is misleading because it suggests that normative constraints currently prevent states from intervening on humanitarian grounds. Not only is there no evidence of such reluctance, precisely the contrary is true: states have demonstrated their willingness to intervene on any number of dubious bases—the question, rather, is whether a further and necessarily subjective legal basis should be given for future interventions. Finally, the dichotomy is dangerous because it obscures the fact that *unilateral enforcement is not a substitute for but the opposite of collective action*: as unilateral assertions of humanitarianism come to displace multilateral institutional legality, so the normative restraints on the recourse to force weaken. The resulting fragmentation and regionalization of the international security system thus makes it reliant, once again, on the eirenic munificence of the modern Great Power(s). And, as international law is deprivileged to become just one policy justification among others, so fade the hopes of mediating those Great Power relations through an international rule of law.

# Appendices

## 1. CHAPTER VII RESOLUTIONS, 1946–89

**24 resolutions**

| | |
|---|---|
| Palestine | 54 (1948); *62 (1948) |
| Korea | †82 (1950); †83 (1950); †84 (1950) |
| Congo | *146 (1960); †161 (1961); †169 (1961) |
| Southern Rhodesia | †217 (1965); †221 (1966); *232 (1966); 253 (1968); 277 (1970); 288 (1970); 314 (1972); *386 (1976); 388 (1976); 409 (1977) |
| East Pakistan | †307 (1971) |
| Cyprus | †353 (1974) |
| South Africa | 418 (1977); †421 (1977) |
| Falkland Islands (Islas Malvinas) | †502 (1982) |
| Iran–Iraq | *598 (1987) |

## 2. CHAPTER VII RESOLUTIONS, 1990–9

**166 resolutions**

| | |
|---|---|
| Iraq–Kuwait | *660 (1990); 661 (1990); 664 (1990); ‡665 (1990); 666 (1990); 667 (1990); *669 (1990); 670 (1990); 674 (1990); 677 (1990); 678 (1990); 686 (1991); 687 (1991); 689 (1991); 692 (1991); 699 (1991); 700 (1991); 705 (1991); 706 (1991); 707 (1991); 712 (1991); 715 (1991); 778 (1992); 806 (1993); 833 (1993); 899 (1994); 949 (1994); 986 (1995); 1051 (1996); 1060 (1996); 1111 (1997); 1115 (1997); 1129 (1997); 1134 (1997); 1137 (1997); 1143 (1997); 1153 (1998); 1154 (1998); 1158 (1998); 1175 (1998); 1194 (1998); 1205 (1998); 1210 (1998); 1242 (1999); 1266 (1999); 1275 (1999); 1280 (1999); 1281 (1999); 1284 (1999) |
| Former Yugoslavia/ FRY | 713 (1991); 724 (1991); 757 (1992); 760 (1992); 771 (1992); 787 (1992); 827 (1993); 908 (1994); 914 (1994); 947 (1994); 967 (1994); 992 (1995); 1074 (1996); 1166 (1998); 1207 (1998) |

* Resolution refers to a specific article in Chapter VII, but not explicitly to Chapter VII itself.
† Resolution uses wording that contains only an implicit reference to Chapter VII.
‡ Resolution refers to a previous Chapter VII resolution in its preamble.

| | |
|---|---|
| Bosnia and Herzegovina | 770 (1992); 816 (1993); 819 (1993); 820 (1993); 824 (1993); 836 (1993); 844 (1993); 859 (1993); 900 (1994); 913 (1994); 941 (1994); 942 (1994); 943 (1994); 958 (1994); 970 (1995); 982 (1995); 987 (1995); 988 (1995); 998 (1995); 1003 (1995); 1004 (1995); 1015 (1995); 1021 (1995); 1022 (1995); 1026 (1995); 1031 (1995); 1088 (1996); 1174 (1998); 1247 (1999) |
| Croatia | 807 (1993); 815 (1993); 847 (1993); 869 (1993); 870 (1993); 871 (1993); 981 (1995); 990 (1995); 994 (1995); 1009 (1995); 1025 (1995); 1037 (1996); 1079 (1996); 1120 (1997) |
| FRY (Kosovo) | 1160 (1998); 1199 (1998); 1203 (1998); 1244 (1999) |
| Somalia | 733 (1992); 794 (1992); 814 (1993); 837 (1993); 878 (1993); 886 (1993); 897 (1994); 923 (1994); 954 (1994); |
| Libya (Lockerbie) | 748 (1992); 883 (1993); 910 (1994); 915 (1994); 1192 (1998) |
| Liberia | 788 (1992); 813 (1993) |
| Haiti | 841 (1993); 861 (1993); 873 (1993); 875 (1993); 917 (1994); 940 (1994); 944 (1994) |
| Angola | 864 (1993); 1221 (1999); 1237 (1999) |
| Rwanda | 918 (1994); 929 (1994); 955 (1994); 1005 (1995); 1011 (1995); 1165 (1998) |
| South Africa (end of sanctions) | 919 (1994) |
| Sudan (Mubarak assassination attempt) | 1054 (1996); 1070 (1996) |
| Eastern Zaïre | 1080 (1996) |
| Albania | 1101 (1997); 1114 (1997) |
| Central African Republic | 1125 (1997); 1136 (1997); 1152 (1998); 1155 (1998); 1159 (1998) |
| Angola | 1127 (1997); 1130 (1997); 1135 (1997); 1173 (1998); 1176 (1998) |
| Sierra Leone | 1132 (1997); 1156 (1998); 1171 (1998); 1270 (1999) |
| East Timor | 1264 (1999); 1272 (1999) |
| Afghanistan (Usama bin Laden) | 1267 (1999) |

## 3. SECURITY COUNCIL DETERMINATIONS OF THREATS TO INTERNATIONAL PEACE AND SECURITY, 1990–9

SITUATION        RESOLUTION   SECURITY COUNCIL DETERMINATION

## I 'Determining'

Iraq–Kuwait    660 (1990)    '*Determining* that there exists a breach of international peace and security as regards the Iraqi invasion of Kuwait'

| | | |
|---|---|---|
| Libya | 748 (1992) | '*Determining* . . . that the failure by the Libyan Government to demonstrate by concrete actions its renunciation of terrorism and in particular its continued failure to respond fully and effectively to the requests in resolution 731 (1992) constitute a threat to international peace and security' |
| Liberia | 788 (1992) | '*Determining* that the deterioration of the situation in Liberia constitutes a threat to international peace and security' |
| Somalia | 794 (1992) | '*Determining* that the magnitude of the human tragedy caused by the conflict in Somalia . . . constitutes a threat to international peace and security' |
| Haiti | 841 (1993) | '*Determining* that, in these unique and exceptional circumstances, the continuation of this situation threatens international peace and security in the region' |
| Angola | 864 (1993) | '*Determining* that, as a result of UNITA's military actions, the situation in Angola constitutes a threat to international peace and security' |
| Rwanda | 918 (1994) | '*Determining* that the situation in Rwanda constitutes a threat to peace and security in the region' |
| Rwanda | 929 (1994) | '*Determining* that the magnitude of the humanitarian crisis in Rwanda constitutes a threat to peace and security in the region' |
| Sudan | 1054 (1996) | '*Determining* that the non-compliance by the Government of Sudan with the requests set out in paragraph 4 of resolution 1044 (1996) constitutes a threat to international peace and security' |
| Eastern Zaïre | *1078 (1996) | '*Determining* that the magnitude of the present humanitarian crisis in eastern Zaïre constitutes a threat to peace and security in the region' |
| Eastern Zaïre | 1080 (1996) | '*Determining* that the present situation in eastern Zaïre constitutes a threat to international peace and security in the region' |
| Albania | 1101 (1997) | '*Determining* that the present situation of crisis in Albania constitutes a threat to peace and security in the region' |
| Central African Republic | 1125 (1997) | '*Determining* that the situation in the Central African Republic continues to constitute a threat to international peace and security in the region' |
| Angola | 1127 (1997) | '*Determining* that the resulting situation in Angola constitutes a threat to international peace and security in the region' |
| Sierra Leone | 1132 (1997) | '*Determining* that the situation in Sierra Leone constitutes a threat to international peace and security in the region' |
| East Timor | 1264 (1999) | '*Determining* that the present situation in East Timor constitutes a threat to peace and security' |

\* Resolution was not adopted under Chapter VII.

Afghanistan    1267 (1999)    '*Determining* that the failure of the Taliban authorities to respond to the demands in paragraph 13 of resolution 1214 (1998) constitutes a threat to international peace and security'

## II 'Concerned'

Iraq (Kurdish    *688 (1991)    '*Gravely concerned* by the repression of the Iraqi civilian population in many parts of Iraq, including most recently in Kurdish-populated areas, which led to a massive flow of refugees towards and across international frontiers and to cross-border incursions, which threaten international peace and security in the region'

Former    713 (1991)    '*Concerned* that the continuation of this situation constitutes a threat to international peace and security'
Yugoslavia

Somalia    733 (1992)    '*Concerned* that the continuation of this situation constitutes . . . a threat to international peace and security'

## III 'Recognizing'

Bosnia and    770 (1992)    '*Recognizing* that the situation in Bosnia and Herzegovina constitutes a threat to international peace and security'
Herzegovina

* Resolution was not adopted under Chapter VII.

# 4. SECURITY COUNCIL AUTHORIZATIONS TO USE FORCE

## 4.1. Authorizations to use 'all necessary means' or equivalent

| Action | SC Res | Terms of authorization | Duration | Reporting requirements | Financing arrangements |
|---|---|---|---|---|---|
| Unified Command in Korea (1950) | 83 (1950) | '*Recommends* that the Members of the United Nations furnish **such assistance** to the Republic of Korea **as may be necessary** to repel the armed attack . . .' [operative para] | — | — | — |
| Unified Command in Korea (1950) | 84 (1950) | '*Recommends* that all Members providing military forces and other assistance . . . make such forces and other assistance available to a unified command under the United States of America . . . '*Authorizes* the unified command at its discretion to use the United Nations flag in the course of operations against North Korean forces concurrently with the flags of the various nations participating' [paras 3, 5] | — | '*Requests* the **United States** to provide the Security Council with reports as appropriate on the course of action taken under the unified command' [para 6] | |

| Action | SC Res | Terms of authorization | Duration | Reporting requirements | Financing arrangements |
|---|---|---|---|---|---|
| Iraq and Kuwait— Operations Desert Shield and Desert Storm (1990–1) | 678 (1990) | '*Authorizes* Member States co-operating with the Government of Kuwait . . . to use **all necessary means** to uphold and implement resolution 660 (1990) and all subsequent relevant resolutions and to restore international peace and security in the area' [para 2] | — | '*Requests* the **States concerned** to keep the Security Council **regularly** informed on the progress of actions undertaken' [para 4] | General request for other States to provide assistance [para 3] |
| Somalia— Operation Restore Hope (UNITAF) (1992–3) | 794 (1992) | '*Authorizes* the Secretary-General and Member States cooperating to implement [the US offer] to use **all necessary means** to establish as soon as possible a secure environment for humanitarian relief operations in Somalia . . . under unified command and control' [paras 10, 8, 12] | *Requires* reports to 'enable the Council to make the necessary decision for a prompt transition to continued peacekeeping operations' [para 18] | '*Requests* the **Secretary-General and, as appropriate, the States concerned** to report to the Council on a regular basis, the first such report to be made no later than **fifteen days** after the adoption of this resolution' [para 18] | '*Calls on* all Member States which are in a position to do so to provide military forces and to make additional contributions, in cash or in kind' [para 11] |
| Rwanda— Opération Turquoise in south-west Rwanda (1994) | 929 (1994) | '*Authorizes* [France and Senegal] cooperating with the Secretary-General' to establish a temporary operation aimed at 'contributing, in an impartial | The mission 'will be limited to a period of **two months** . . . unless the Secretary- | '*Requests* the **States concerned and the Secretary-General, as appropriate**, to report to the Council on a regular basis, the | 'on the understanding that the costs of implementing the offer will be borne by' France and Senegal [para 2] |

| | | | | |
|---|---|---|---|---|
| | | way, to the security and protection of displaced persons, refugees and civilians at risk in Rwanda' . . . using **all necessary means** to achieve the humanitarian objectives set out in SC Res 925 (1994) para 4, these being:<br>'(a) Contribute to the security and protection of displaced persons, refugees and civilians at risk in Rwanda, including through the establishment and maintenance, where feasible, of secure humanitarian areas; and<br>'(b) Provide security and support for the distribution of relief supplies and humanitarian relief operations' [paras 3, 2] | General determines at an earlier date that the expanded UNAMIR is able to carry out its mandate' [para 4] | first such report to be made no later than **fifteen days** after the adoption of this resolution, on the implementation of this operation and the progress made towards the fulfilment of the objectives' [para 10] |
| Haiti—Operation Uphold Democracy (1994–5) | 940 (1994) | '*Authorizes* Member States to form a multinational force under unified command and control and, in this framework, to use **all necessary means** to facilitate the departure from Haiti of the military leadership, consistent with the Governors Island Agreement, the prompt return of the | '*Decides* that the multinational force will terminate its mission and UNMIH will assume the full range of its functions . . . when a secure | '*Requests* the **Member States** . . . to report to the Council at regular intervals, the first such report to be made not later than **seven days** following the deployment of the multinational force'<br>An advance team of |
| | | | | 'on the understanding that the cost of implementing this temporary operation will be borne by the participating Member States' [para 4] |

| Action | SC Res | Terms of authorization | Duration | Reporting requirements | Financing arrangements |
|---|---|---|---|---|---|
| | | legitimately elected President and the restoration of the legitimate authorities of the Government of Haiti, and to establish and maintain a secure and stable environment that will permit implementation of the Governors Island Agreement' [para 4] | and stable environment has been established . . .; the determination will be made by the Security Council, taking into account recommendations from the Member States of the multi-national force' [para 8] | UNMIH 'carry out the monitoring of the operations of the multi-national force' [paras 13, 8] | |
| Bosnia and Herzegovina— IFOR (1995) | 1031 (1995) | 'Authorizes the Member States acting through or in cooperation with the organization referred to in Annex 1-A of the Peace Agreement [NATO] to establish a multinational implementation force (IFOR) under unified command and control in order to fulfil the role specified in Annex 1-A and Annex 2 of the Peace Agreement; 'Authorizes the Member States acting under paragraph 14 | 'Decides, with a view to terminating the authorization granted in paragraphs 14 to 17 above one year after the transfer of authority from UNPROFOR to IFOR, to review by that date and to take a decision whether | 'Requests the Member States acting through or in cooperation with the organization referred to in Annex 1-A of the Peace Agreement [sc NATO] to report to the Council, through the appropriate channels and at least at monthly intervals, the first such report be made not later than 10 days | 'Invites all States, in particular those in the region, to provide appropriate support and facilities, including transit facilities, for the Member States acting under paragraph 14 above' [para 23] |

above to take **all necessary measures** to effect the implementation of and to ensure compliance with Annex 1-A of the Peace Agreement, *stresses* that the parties shall be held equally responsible for compliance with that Annex, and shall be equally subject to **such enforcement action by IFOR as may be necessary** to ensure implementation of that Annex and the protection of IFOR, and *takes note* that the parties have consented to IFOR's taking such measures' [paras 14, 15]

that authorization should continue, based upon the recommendations from the States participating in IFOR and from the High Representative through the Secretary-General' [para 21]

following the adoption of this resolution' [para 25]

Bosnia and Herzegovina—SFOR (1996)

1088 (1996)

'*Authorizes* the Member States acting through or in cooperation with [NATO] to establish for a planned period of 18 months a multinational stabilization force (SFOR) as the legal successor to IFOR under unified command and control in order to fulfil the role specified in Annex 1-A and Annex 2 of the Peace Agreement;
'*Authorizes* the Member States acting under paragraph 18 above to take **all necessary measures** to effect the

**18 months**, extended for a further 12 months by SC Res 1174 (1998) of 15 June 1998, and SC Res 1247 (1999) of 18 June 1999

'*Requests* the **Member States acting through or in cooperation with the organization referred to in Annex 1-A of the Peace Agreement** [*sc* NATO] to report to the Council, through the appropriate channels and at least at monthly intervals' [para 26]

'*Invites* all States, in particular those in the region, to continue to provide appropriate support and facilities, including transit facilities, for the Member States acting under paragraph 18 above' [para 24]

| Action | SC Res | Terms of authorization | Duration | Reporting requirements | Financing arrangements |
|--------|--------|------------------------|----------|------------------------|------------------------|
| | | implementation of and to ensure compliance with Annex 1-A of the Peace Agreement, *stresses* that the parties shall continue to be held equally responsible for compliance with that Annex and shall be equally subject to **such enforcement action by SFOR as may be necessary** to ensure implementation of that Annex and the protection of SFOR, and *takes note* that the parties have consented to SFOR's taking such measures;<br><br>'*Authorizes* Member States to take **all necessary measures**, at the request of SFOR, either in defence of SFOR or to assist the force in carrying out its mission, and *recognizes* the right of the force to take **all necessary measures to defend itself** from attack or threat of attack;<br><br>'*Authorizes* the Member States acting under paragraph 18 above, in accordance with Annex 1-A of the Peace Agreement, to take **all necessary measures** to ensure compliance | | | |

| | | | | | |
|---|---|---|---|---|---|
| | | with the rules and procedures, to be established by the Commander of SFOR, governing command and control of airspace over Bosnia and Herzegovina with respect to all civilian and military air traffic' [paras 18–21] | | | |
| Eastern Zaïre—Canadian-led operation (1996) (never implemented) | 1080 (1996) | '*Authorizes* [Member States led by Canada] cooperating with the Secretary-General to conduct the operation . . . to achieve, by using **all necessary means**, the humanitarian objectives', being: 'to facilitate the immediate return of humanitarian organizations and the effective delivery by civilian relief organizations of humanitarian aid to alleviate the immediate suffering of displaced persons, refugees and civilians at risk in eastern Zaïre, and to facilitate the voluntary, orderly repatriation of refugees by the United Nations High Commissioner for Refugees as well as the voluntary return of displaced persons' [paras 3–5] | '*Decides* that the operation shall terminate on **31 March 1997**, unless the Council, on the basis of a report of the Secretary-General, determines that the objectives of the operation have been fulfilled earlier' [para 8] | '*Requests* the **Member States** participating in the multinational force to provide periodic reports **at least twice monthly**, through the Secretary-General, to the Council, the first such report to be made no later than 21 days after the adoption of this resolution' [para 11] | '*Decides* that the cost of implementing this temporary operation will be borne by the participating Member States and other voluntary contributions' [para 9] |

| Action | SC Res | Terms of authorization | Duration | Reporting requirements | Financing arrangements |
|---|---|---|---|---|---|
| FRY—NATO-led KFOR operations (1999–) | 1244 (1999) | 'Authorizes Member States and relevant international organizations to establish the international security presence in Kosovo as set out in point 4 of annex 2 with **all necessary means** to fulfil' the following responsibilities: (a) deterring renewed hostilities; (b) demilitarizing the KLA; (c) establishing a secure environment; (d) ensuring public safety and order; (e) supervising demining; (f) supporting the work of the international civil presence; (g) conducting border monitoring duties; (h) ensuring the protection and freedom of movement of itself, the international civil presence, and other international organizations' [paras 7, 9] | '*Decides* that the international civil and security presences are established for an initial period of **12 months**, to continue thereafter unless the Security Council decides otherwise' [para 19] | '*Requests* the **Secretary-General** to report to the Council at regular intervals on the implementation of this resolution, including reports from the leaderships of the international civil and security presences, the first reports to be submitted within **30 days** of the adoption of this resolution' [para 20] | Encouragement for member states to contribute to economic and social reconstruction [para 13] |
| East Timor—INTERFET (1999) | 1264 (1999) | '*Authorizes* the establishment of a multinational force under a unified command structure, pursuant to the request of the Government of Indonesia conveyed to the Secretary-General on 12 September 1999, | '*Agrees* that the multinational force should collectively be deployed in East Timor until **replaced as soon** | '*Requests* the leadership of the multinational force to provide periodic reports on progress towards the implementation of its mandate through the | '*Stresses* that the expenses for the force will be borne by the participating Member States concerned and *requests* the Secretary-General to establish a |

| Action | SC Res | Terms of authorization | Duration | Reporting requirements | Financing arrangements |
|---|---|---|---|---|---|
| | | with the following tasks: to restore peace and security in East Timor, to protect and support UNAMET in carrying out its tasks and, within force capabilities, to facilitate humanitarian assistance operations, and *authorizes* the States participating in the multinational force to take **all necessary measures** to fulfil this mandate' [para 3] | as possible by a United Nations peacekeeping operation, and *invites* the Secretary-General to make prompt recommendations on a peacekeeping operation to the Security Council' [para 10] | Secretary-General to the Council, the first such report to be made within **14 days** of the adoption of this resolution' [para 12] | trust fund through which contributions could be channelled to the States or operations concerned' [para 9] |

### 4.2. Limited authorizations to use force

| Action | SC Res | Terms of authorization | Duration | Reporting requirements | Financing arrangements |
|---|---|---|---|---|---|
| Southern Rhodesia (1966) | 221 (1966) | '*Calls upon* the Government of the United Kingdom . . . to prevent, **by the use of force if necessary**, the arrival at Beira of vessels reasonably believed to be carrying oil destined for Southern Rhodesia, and empowers the United Kingdom to arrest and detain the tanker known as the *Joanna V* upon her departure from Beira in the event her oil cargo is discharged there' [para 5] | — | — | — |

| Action | SC Res | Terms of authorization | Duration | Reporting requirements | Financing arrangements |
|---|---|---|---|---|---|
| Iraq and Kuwait—naval blockade (1990) | 665 (1990)* | 'Calls upon those Member States cooperating with the Government of Kuwait which are deploying maritime forces to the area to use **such measures commensurate to the specific circumstances as may be necessary** under the authority of the Security Council to halt all inward and outward maritime shipping in order to inspect and verify their cargoes and destinations and to ensure strict implementation of the provisions related to such shipping laid down in resolution 661 (1990)' [para 1] | — | '*Requests* the **States concerned** to co-ordinate their actions ... using as appropriate mechanisms of the **Military Staff Committee** and after consultation with the Secretary-General to submit reports to the Security Council ... to facilitate the monitoring of the implementation of this resolution' [para 4] | General request for other States to provide assistance [para 3] |
| Bosnia and Herzegovina (1992) | 770 (1992) | '*Calls upon* **States** to take nationally or through regional agencies or arrangements **all measures necessary** to facilitate in coordination with the United Nations the delivery by relevant United Nations humanitarian organizations and others of humanitarian assistance to Sarajevo and wherever needed in other parts of Bosnia and Herzegovina' [para 2] | — | '*Calls upon* **States** to report to the Secretary-General on measures they are taking in coordination with the United Nations to carry out this resolution' [para 4] | General request for appropriate support |

| | | | | | |
|---|---|---|---|---|---|
| Bosnia and Herzegovina—UNPROFOR (1993–5) | 836 (1993) | 'Decides that . . . Member States, acting nationally or through regional organizations or arrangements, may take, under the authority of the Security Council and subject to close coordination with the Secretary-General and UNPROFOR, **all necessary measures**, through the use of air power, in and around the safe areas in the Republic of Bosnia and Herzegovina, to support UNPROFOR in the performance of its mandate' [para 10] (see also para 9, below) | — | 'Requests the **Member States concerned, the Secretary-General and** UNPROFOR to coordinate closely . . . and to report to the Council through the Secretary-General; 'Invites the Secretary-General to report to the Council, for decision, if possible within **seven days**' [paras 11, 12] | — |
| Albania—Italian-led multinational force (1997) | 1101 (1997) | 'Authorizes [Member States led by Italy] participating in the multinational protection force to conduct the operation in a neutral and impartial way' (i) 'to establish a temporary and limited multinational protection force to facilitate the safe and prompt delivery of | 'Decides that the operation will be limited to a period of **three months** from the adoption of the present resolution, at which time the Council will | 'Requests the **Member States** participating in the multinational protection force to provide periodic reports, **at least every two weeks**, through the Secretary-General, to the Council, the first such | 'Decides that the cost of implementing this temporary operation will be borne by the participating Member] States' [para 7] |

* SC Res 665 (1990) was not explicitly adopted under Chapter VII of the UN Charter. Its second preambular paragraph does note, however, that the Council 'decided in resolution 661 (1990) to impose economic sanctions under Chapter VII of the Charter of the United Nations'.

| Action | SC Res | Terms of authorization | Duration | Reporting requirements | Financing arrangements |
|---|---|---|---|---|---|
| | | humanitarian assistance, and to help create a secure environment for the missions of international organizations in Albania, including those providing humanitarian assistance' and (ii) 'acting under Chapter VII of the Charter of the United Nations, *further authorizes* these Member States to ensure the security and freedom of movement of the personnel of the said multinational protection force' [paras 2–4] | assess the situation on the basis of the reports referred to in paragraph 9' [para 6] | report to be made no later than 14 days after the adoption of this resolution, *inter alia* specifying the parameters and modalities of the operation on the basis of consultations between those Member States and the Government of Albania' [para 9] | |

## 4.3. 'Muscular' peacekeeping operations

| Action | SC Res | Terms of authorization | Duration | Reporting requirements | Financing arrangements |
|---|---|---|---|---|---|
| Congo—ONUC (1960–4) | 161A (1961) | '*Authorizes* the Secretary-General to take **vigorous action, including the use of the requisite measure of force, if necessary**, for the immediate apprehension, detention pending legal action and/or | — | — | — |

deportation of all foreign military and paramilitary personnel and political advisers not under the United Nations Command, and mercentaries'

'*Further requests* the Secretary-General to take **all necessary measures** to prevent the entry or return of such elements under whatever guise, and also of arms, equipment or other material in support of such activities' [paras 4, 5]

| | | |
|---|---|---|
| Bosnia and Herzegovina— UNPROFOR (1993–95) | 836 (1993) | '*Decides* to extend . . . the mandate of UNPROFOR in order to enable it . . . to deter attacks against the safe areas, to monitor the cease-fire, to promote the withdrawal of military or paramilitary units other than those of the Government of the Republic of Bosnia and Herzegovina and to occupy some key points on the ground, in addition to participating in the delivery of humanitarian relief to the population' [para 5] <br> '*Authorizes* UNPROFOR . . . **acting in self-defence, to take the necessary measures, including** |

| Action | SC Res | Terms of authorization | Duration | Reporting requirements | Financing arrangements |
|---|---|---|---|---|---|
| | | **the use of force**, in reply to bombardments against the safe areas by any of the parties or to armed incursion into them or in the event of any deliberate obstruction in or around those areas to the freedom of movement of UNPROFOR or of protected humanitarian convoys [para 9] (see also para 10, above) | | | |
| Somalia— UNOSOM II | 837 (1993) | '*Reaffirms* that the Secretary-General is authorized under resolution 814 (1993) to take **all necessary measures** against those responsible for the armed attacks . . . to establish the effective authority of UNOSOM II throughout Somalia, including to secure the investigation of their actions and their arrest and detention for prosecution, trial and punishment' [para 5] | — | '*Requests* the **Secretary-General** to submit a report to the Council on the implementation of the present resolution, if possible within seven days from the date of its adoption' [para 9] | '*Urges* Member States to contribute, on an emergency basis, military support and transportation . . . to provide UNOSOM II the capability appropriately to confront and deter armed attacks directed against it in the accomplishment of its mandate' [para 8] |

**4.4. Ex post facto or questionable authorizations**

| Action | SC Res | Terms of authorization (lato sensu) | Duration | Reporting requirements | Financing arrangements |
|---|---|---|---|---|---|
| Liberia (1990–2) | 788 (1992) | 'Commends ECOWAS for its efforts to restore peace, security and stability in Liberia' [para 1] | — | — | — |
| Central African Republic—MISAB and French operations (1997–8) | 1125 (1997) | 'Approves the continued conduct by Member States participating in MISAB of the operation in a neutral and impartial way to achieve its objective to facilitate the return to peace and security by monitoring the implementation of the Bangui Agreements in the Central African Republic as stipulated in the mandate of MISAB (S/1997/561, Appendix I), including through the supervision of the surrendering of arms of former mutineers, militias and all other persons unlawfully bearing arms; 'Acting under Chapter VII of the Charter of the United Nations, authorizes the Member States participating in MISAB and those States providing logistical support [ie, France] to ensure the security and freedom of movement of their personnel' [paras 2–3] | 'Decides that the authorization referred to in paragraph 3 above will be limited to an initial period of **three months** from the adoption of this resolution, at which time the Council will assess the situation on the basis of the reports referred to in paragraph 6 below' [para 4] | 'Requests the Member States participating in MISAB to provide periodic reports **at least every two weeks** through the Secretary-General, the first report to be made within 14 days after the adoption of this resolution' [para 6] | 'Stresses that the expenses and logistical support for the force will be borne on a voluntary basis in accordance with article 11 of the mandate of MISAB' [para 5] |

| Action | SC Res | Terms of authorization (lato sensu) | Duration | Reporting requirements | Financing arrangements |
|---|---|---|---|---|---|
| Sierra Leone—ECOWAS operations (1997) | 1132 (1997) | 'Acting also under Chapter VIII of the Charter of the United Nations, *authorizes* ECOWAS, cooperating with the democratically-elected Government of Sierra Leone, to ensure strict implementation of the provisions of this resolution relating to the supply of petroleum and petroleum products, and arms and related *matériel* of all types, including, where necessary and in conformity with applicable international standards, by halting inward maritime shipping in order to inspect and verify their cargoes and destinations, and *calls upon* all States to cooperate with ECOWAS in this regard' [para 8] | 'Expresses its intention to terminate the measures set out in paragraphs 5 and 6 above when the demand in paragraph 1 above has been complied with' [para 19] [travel ban and embargoes until military junta steps down] | 'Requests ECOWAS to report **every 30 days** to the Committee established under paragraph 10 below on all activities undertaken pursuant to paragraph 8 above' [para 9] | 'Urges all States to provide technical and logistical support to assist ECOWAS to carry out its responsibilities in the implementation of this resolution' [para 18] |
| FRY—Kosovo (1998) | 1199 (1998) | 'Demands that all parties, groups and individuals immediately cease hostilities and maintain a ceasefire in Kosovo . . . which would . . . reduce the risks of a **humanitarian catastrophe**; | 'Decides, should the concrete measures demanded in this resolution and resolution 1160 (1998) not be taken, **to consider** | 'Requests the Secretary-General to provide regular reports to the Council as necessary on his assessment of compliance with this resolution by the | — |

| | | **further action and additional measures** to maintain or restore peace and stability in the region' [para 16] | authorities of the Federal Republic of Yugoslavia and all elements in the Kosovo Albanian community, including through his regular reports on compliance with resolution 1160 (1998)' [para 15] |
|---|---|---|---|
| FRY—KOSOVO (1998) | 1203 (1998) | | — |

'*Demands also* that the authorities of the Federal Republic of Yugoslavia and the Kosovo Albanian leadership take immediate steps to improve the humanitarian situation and to avert the impending **humanitarian catastrophe**' [paras 1–2]

'*Endorses* and supports the agreements signed in Belgrade on 16 October 1998 between the Federal Republic of Yugoslavia and the OSCE, and on 15 October 1998 between the Federal Republic of Yugoslavia and NATO, concerning the verification of compliance by the Federal Republic of Yugoslavia and all others concerned in Kosovo with the requirements of its resolution 1199 (1998), and *demands* the full and prompt implementation of these agreements by the Federal Republic of Yugoslavia' [para 1]

'*Demands* that the Federal Republic of Yugoslavia comply fully and swiftly with resolutions 1160 (1998) and

'*Requests* the Secretary-General, acting in consultation with the parties concerned with the agreements referred to in paragraph 1 above, to report regularly to the Council regarding implementation of this resolution' [para 16]

| Action | SC Res | Terms of authorization (lato sensu) | Duration | Reporting requirements | Financing arrangements |
|---|---|---|---|---|---|
| | | 1199 (1998) and cooperate fully with the OSCE Verification Mission in Kosovo and the NATO Air Verification Mission over Kosovo according to the terms of the agreements referred to in paragraph 1 above' [para 3]<br><br>'*Welcomes* in this context the commitment of the Federal Republic of Yugoslavia to guarantee the safety and security of the Verification Missions as contained in the agreements referred to in paragraph 1 above, *notes* that, to this end, the OSCE is considering arrangements to be implemented in cooperation with other organizations, and *affirms* that, **in the event of an emergency, action may be needed** to ensure their safety and freedom of movement as envisaged in the agreements referred to in paragraph 1 above' [para 9] | | | |

| FRY—Operation Allied Force (1999) | 1239 (1999) | '*Emphasizes* that the humanitarian situation will continue to deteriorate in the absence of a political solution to the crisis consistent with the principles adopted by the Foreign Ministers of Canada, France, Germany, Italy, Japan, the Russian Federation, the United Kingdom of Great Britain and Northern Ireland and the United States of America on 6 May 1999 (S/1999/516), and *urges* all concerned to work towards this aim' [para 5] |
| --- | --- | --- |

# Bibliography

Abiew, Francis Kofi, *The Evolution of the Doctrine and Practice of Humanitarian Intervention* (The Hague: Kluwer Law International, 1999)

Abi-Saab, G, *The United Nations Operation in the Congo 1960–1964* (Oxford: Oxford University Press, 1978)

Adelman, Howard, 'Humanitarian Intervention: The Case of the Kurds' (1992) 4 *International Journal of Refugee Law* 4

Ake, Claude, 'The Unique Case of African Democracy' (1993) 69 *International Affairs* 239

Akehurst, Michael, 'Custom as a Source of International Law' (1974) 47 *British YBIL* 1

—— 'Humanitarian Intervention', in Hedley Bull (ed), *Intervention in World Politics* (Oxford: Clarendon Press, 1984) 95

—— 'Letter' (1986) 80 *AJIL* 147

—— *A Modern Introduction to International Law* (Peter Malanczuk (ed); 7th edn; London: Routledge, 1997)

Alao, Abiodun, *The Burden of Collective Goodwill: The International Involvement in the Liberian Civil War* (Aldershot: Ashgate, 1998)

Amnesty International, *Kosovo: After Tragedy, Justice?* (London: Amnesty International, 1999)

Amos, Sheldon, *Lectures on International Law* (London: Stevens and Sons, 1874)

Annan, Kofi, 'Peace-Keeping in Situations of Civil War' (1994) 26 *NYUJILP* 623

Arend, Anthony C, and Robert J Beck, *International Law and the Use of Force: Beyond the UN Charter Paradigm* (London: Routledge, 1993)

Association of the Bar of the City of New York, *The Use of Armed Force in International Affairs: The Case of Panama* (*Report of The Committee on International Arms Control and Security Affairs and The Committee on International Law*) (1992)

Avirgan, Tony, and Martha Honey, *War in Uganda: The Legacy of Idi Amin* (Westport, CT: Lawrence Hill, 1982)

Ayala, Balthazar, *De jure et officiis bellicis et disciplina militari libri III* ([1582] Classics of International Law; Bate trans; Washington, DC: Carnegie Institution, 1912)

Bailey, Sydney D, and Sam Daws, *The Procedure of the Security Council* (3rd edn; Oxford: Clarendon Press, 1998)

Bassiouni, M Cherif, *Crimes Against Humanity in International Criminal Law* (2nd edn; The Hague: Kluwer, 1999)

Beck, Robert J, 'International Law and the Decision to Invade Grenada: A Ten-Year Retrospective' (1993) 33 *Virginia JIL* 765

Bedjaoui, Mohammed, *The New World Order and the Security Council: Testing the Legality of its Acts* (Dordrecht: Martinus Nijhoff, 1994)

Belli, Pierino, *De re militari et bello tractatus* ([1563] Classics of International Law; Cavaglieri trans; Oxford: Clarendon Press, 1936)

Berdal, Mats R, *Whither UN Peacekeeping?* (Adelphi Paper 281; London: IISS, 1993)

—— 'The Security Council, Peacekeeping and Internal Conflict After the Cold War' (1996) 7 *Duke JCIL* 71

Bernard, Montague, *On the Principle of Non-Intervention* (Oxford: J H & J Parker, 1860)

Bernhardt, Rudolf, *Encyclopedia of Public International Law* (Amsterdam: Elsevier, 1995)

Berry, Nicholas O, 'The Conflict Between United States Intervention and Promoting Democracy in the Third World' (1987) 60 *Temple Law Quarterly* 1015

Beschloss, Michael R, and Strobe Talbott, *At the Highest Levels: The Inside Story of the End of the Cold War* (London: Little Brown, 1993)

Betts, Richard K, 'The Delusion of Impartial Intervention' (1994) 73(6) *Foreign Affairs* 20

Bilder, Richard, *et al*, 'United States Attitudes On the Role of the United Nations Regarding the Maintenance and the Restoration of Peace [Panel Discussion]' (1996) 26 *Georgia JICL* 9

Bills, David, 'International Human Rights and Humanitarian Intervention: The Ramifications of Reform On the United Nations Security Council' (1996) 31 *Texas ILJ* 107

Bloed, Arie, 'A New CSCE Human Rights "Catalogue": The Copenhagen Meeting of the Conference on the Human Dimension of the CSCE', in Arie Bloed and Pieter van Dijk (eds), *The Human Dimension of the Helsinki Process: The Vienna Follow-up Meeting and Its Aftermath* (Dordrecht: Martinus Nijhoff, 1991) 54

—— (ed), *The Conference on Security and Co-operation in Europe: Analysis and Basic Documents, 1972–1993* (Dordrecht: Kluwer, 1993)

Bluntschli, M, *Le droit international codifié* (Paris: Librairie de Guillaumin, 1870)

Bodin, Jean, *The Six Books of a Commonweale* ([1577] A facsimile reprint of the English translation of 1606, corrected and supplemented in the light of a new comparison with the French and Latin texts; McRae trans; Cambridge, MA: Harvard University Press, 1962)

Bogen, David S, 'The Law of Humanitarian Intervention: United States Policy in Cuba (1898) and in the Dominican Republic (1965)' (1966) 7 *Harvard International Law Club Journal* 296

Borchard, Edwin Montefiore, *The Diplomatic Protection of Citizens Abroad* (New York: Banks Law, 1928)

Bothe, Michael, 'Les limites des pouvoirs du Conseil de sécurité', in René-Jean Dupuy (ed), *The Development of the Role of the Security Council: Peace-Keeping and Peace-Building* (Dordrecht: Martinus Nijhoff, 1993) 67

—— 'Peace-Keeping', in Bruno Simma (ed), *The Charter of the United Nations: A Commentary* (Oxford: Oxford University Press, 1994) 565

Boutros-Ghali, Boutros, 'Beyond Peacekeeping' (1992) 25 *NYUJILP* 113

—— 'Maintaining International Peace and Security: The United Nations As Forum and Focal Point' (1993) 16 *Loyola of Los Angeles ICLJ* 1

—— 'Introduction', in *Blue Helmets* (3rd edn; New York: UN Department of Public Information, 1996) 3

—— *Unvanquished: A US–UN Saga* (New York: Random House, 1999)

Bowden, Mark, *Black Hawk Down: A Story of Modern War* (New York: Atlantic Monthly Press, 1999)

Bowett, Derek W, 'The Use of Force in the Protection of Nationals' (1957) 43 *Grotius Society* 111
—— *Self-Defence in International Law* (Manchester: Manchester University Press, 1958)
—— *United Nations Forces: A Legal Study of United Nations Practice* (London: Stevens, 1964)
—— 'Reprisals Involving Recourse to Armed Force' (1972) 66 *AJIL* 1
—— 'The Use of Force for the Protection of Nationals Abroad', in Antonio Cassese (ed), *The Current Legal Regulation of the Use of Force* (Dordrecht: Martinus Nijhoff, 1986) 39
Bowring, Bill, 'The "*Droit et Devoir d'Ingerence*": A Timely New Remedy for Africa?' (1995) 7 *African JICL* 493
Boyd, Andrew, *Fifteen Men on a Powder Keg: A History of the UN Security Council* (London: Methuen, 1971)
Boyle, Francis A, 'The Entebbe Hostages Crisis' (1982) 29 *Netherlands ILR* 32
Bridgland, Fred, *The War for Africa: Twelve Months That Transformed a Continent* (Rivonia: Ashanti, 1990)
Brierly, J L, *The Law of Nations: An Introduction into the International Law of Peace* (Oxford: Clarendon Press, 1928)
—— *The Law of Nations: An Introduction into the International Law of Peace* (4th edn; Oxford: Clarendon Press, 1949)
—— *The Law of Nations* (C H M Waldock (ed); 6th edn; Oxford: Oxford University Press, 1963)
Brissaud, Jean, *A History of French Public Law* (Garner trans; London: John Murray, 1915)
Brown, Michael E, Sean M Lynn Jones, and Steven E Miller, *Debating the Democratic Peace* (Cambridge, MA: MIT Press, 1996)
Brown, Philip Marshall, 'Japanese Interpretation of the Kellogg Pact' (1933) 27 *AJIL* 100
Brownlie, Ian, *International Law and the Use of Force by States* (Oxford: Clarendon Press, 1963)
—— 'Thoughts on Kind-Hearted Gunmen', in Richard B Lillich (ed), *Humanitarian Intervention and the United Nations* (Charlottesville: University Press of Virginia, 1973) 139
—— 'Humanitarian Intervention', in John N Moore (ed), *Law and Civil War in the Modern World* (Baltimore, Maryland: Johns Hopkins University Press, 1974) 217
—— 'Causes of Action in the Law of Nations' (1981) 50 *British YBIL* 13
—— 'Recognition in Theory and Practice' (1982) 53 *British YBIL* 197
—— 'The United Nations Charter and the Use of Force, 1945–1985', in Antonio Cassese (ed), *The Current Legal Regulation of the Use of Force* (Dordrecht: Martinus Nijhoff, 1986) 491
—— 'The Relation of Law and Power', in Bin Cheng and E D Brown (eds), *Contemporary Problems of International Law: Essays in Honour of Georg Schwarzenberger on His Eightieth Birthday* (London: Stevens, 1988) 19
—— 'The Principle of Non-Use of Force in Contemporary International Law', in William E Butler (ed), *The Non-Use of Force in International Law* (Dordrecht: Martinus Nijhoff, 1989) 17
—— 'The Decisions of Political Organs of the United Nations and the Rule of Law',

in Ronald St John Macdonald (ed), *Essays in Honour of Wang Tieya* (Dordrecht: Martinus Nijhoff, 1994) 91

—— *Principles of Public International Law* (5th edn; Oxford: Clarendon Press, 1998)

—— Christine Chinkin, Christopher Greenwood, and Vaughan Lowe, 'Kosovo: House of Commons Foreign Affairs Committee 4th Report, June 2000: Memoranda' (2000) 49 *International and Comparative Law Quarterly*, 876.

Bryde, Brun-Otto, 'Articles 44–50', in Bruno Simma (ed), *The Charter of the United Nations: A Commentary* (Oxford: Oxford University Press, 1994) 640

Buergenthal, Thomas, 'The Copenhagen CSCE Meeting: A New Public Order for Europe' (1990) 11 *Human Rights Law Journal* 217

Bull, Hedley, *The Anarchical Society: A Study of Order in World Politics* (London: Macmillan, 1977)

—— 'The Importance of Grotius in the Study of International Relations', in Hedley Bull, Benedict Kingsbury, and Adam Roberts (eds), *Hugo Grotius and International Relations* (Oxford: Clarendon Press, 1990) 65

Butler, Geoffrey, and Simon Maccoby, *The Development of International Law* (London: Longmans Green & Co, 1928)

Byers, Michael, *Custom, Power and the Power of Rules: International Relations and Customary International Law* (Cambridge: Cambridge University Press, 1999)

Bynkershoek, Cornelius van, *Quaestionum juris publici libri duo* ([1737] Oxford: Clarendon Press, 1930)

Calvo, Charles, *Le droit international: théorique et pratique* (Arthur Rousseau (ed); 5th edn; Paris: Librairie nouvelle de Droit et de Jurisprudence, 1896)

Campbell, Greg, *The Road to Kosovo: A Balkan Diary* (Boulder, CO: Westview Press, 1999)

Caron, David D, 'The Legitimacy of the Collective Authority of the Security Council' (1993) 87 *AJIL* 552

Cassese, Antonio (ed), *The Current Legal Regulation of the Use of Force* (Dordrecht: Martinus Nijhoff, 1986)

—— *International Law in a Divided World* (Oxford: Clarendon Press, 1986)

—— *Self-Determination of Peoples: A Legal Reappraisal* (Hersch Lauterpacht Memorial Lectures; Cambridge: Cambridge University Press, 1995)

—— '*Ex iniuria ius oritur*: Are We Moving Towards International Legitimation of Forcible Humanitarian Countermeasures in the World Community?' (1999) 10 *European JIL* 23

Chadrahasan, Nirmala, 'Use of Force to Ensure Humanitarian Relief—A South Asian Precedent Examined' (1993) 42 *ICLQ* 664

Charney, Jonathan I, 'Anticipatory Humanitarian Intervention in Kosovo' (1999) 93 *AJIL* 834

Chatterjee, S K, 'Some Legal Problems of Support Role in International Law: Tanzania and Uganda' (1981) 30 *ICLQ* 755

Chesterman, Simon, 'Law, Subject and Subjectivity in International Relations: International Law and the Postcolony' (1996) 20 *Melbourne University Law Review* 979

—— 'Human Rights as Subjectivity: The Age of Rights and the Politics of Culture' (1998) 27(1) *Millennium: Journal of International Studies* 97

—— 'Last Rights: Euthanasia, the Sanctity of Life and the Law in the Netherlands and the Northern Territory of Australia' (1998) 47 *ICLQ* 362

Chesterman, Simon, 'Rethinking Panama: International Law and the US Invasion of Panama, 1989', in Guy S Goodwin-Gill and Stefan A Talmon (eds), *The Reality of International Law: Essays in Honour of Ian Brownlie* (Oxford: Oxford University Press, 1999) 57

—— and Michael Byers, 'Has US Power Destroyed the UN?', *London Review of Books*, 29 April 1999, 29

Chinkin, Christine M, 'Kosovo: A "Good" or "Bad" War?' (1999) 93 *AJIL* 841

Chomsky, Noam, *The New Military Humanism: Lessons from Kosovo* (London: Pluto Press, 1999)

Chopra, Jarat, and Thomas G Weiss, 'Sovereignty is No Longer Sacrosanct: Codifying Humanitarian Intervention' (1992) 6 *Ethics and International Affairs* 95

Chowdhury, Subrata Roy, *The Genesis of Bangladesh: A Study in International Legal Norms and Permissive Conscience* (London: Asia Publishing House, 1972)

Christenson, G A, 'The World Court and *Jus Cogens*' (1987) 81 *AJIL* 93

Clark, Roger S, 'Humanitarian Intervention: Help to Your Friends and State Practice' (1983) 13 *Georgia JICL* 211

Clarke, Walter, 'Failed Visions and Uncertain Mandates in Somalia', in Walter Clarke and Jeffrey Herbst (eds), *Learning from Somalia: The Lessons of Armed Humanitarian Intervention* (Boulder: Westview, 1997) 3

—— and Jeffrey Herbst (eds), *Learning from Somalia: The Lessons of Armed Humanitarian Intervention* (Boulder: Westview, 1997)

Claude, Inis, 'Collective Legitimization as a Political Function of the United Nations' (1966) 20 *International Organization* 367

Combacau, Jean, *Le pouvoir de sanction de l'ONU: Étude théorique de la coercition non militaire* (Paris: A Pedone, 1974)

Conniff, Michael L, *Panama and the United States: The Forced Alliance* (Athens, GA: University of Georgia Press, 1991)

Crawford, James, 'The Criteria for Statehood in International Law' (1976) 48 *British YBIL* 93

—— 'Democracy and International Law' (1993) 44 *British YBIL* 113

Crawford, Susan M, 'UN Humanitarian Intervention in Somalia' (1993) 3 *Transnational Law and Contemporary Problems* 273

Crawley, C W, *The Question of Greek Independence: A Study of British Policy in the Near East, 1821–1833* (Cambridge: Cambridge University Press, 1930)

Creasy, Edward S, *First Platform of International Law* (London: John van Voorst, 1876)

D'Amato, Anthony, *The Concept of Custom in International Law* (Ithaca: Cornell University Press, 1971)

—— 'Nicaragua and International Law: The "Academic" and the "Real"' (1985) 79 *AJIL* 657

—— 'Reply to letter of Michael Akehurst' (1986) 80 *AJIL* 148

—— *International Law: Process and Prospect* (Dobbs Ferry, NY: Transnational, 1987)

—— 'The Invasion of Panama was a Lawful Response to Tyranny' (1990) 84 *AJIL* 516

—— *International Law: Process and Prospect* (rev edn; Irvington, NY: Transnational, 1995)

da Legnano, Giovanni, *Tractatus de bello, de represaliis et de duello* ([1447] Classics of International Law; Brierly trans; Washington, DC: Carnegie Institution, 1917)

Dahm, G, 'Das Verbot der Gewaltanwendung nach Art 2(4) der UNO-Charta und die Selbsthilfe gegenüber Völkerrechtsverletzungen, die keinen bewaffneten Angriff enthalten' (1962) 11 *Jahrbuch für Internationales Recht* 48

Dakin, Douglas, *The Greek struggle in Macedonia, 1897–1913* (Thessaloniki: Institute for Balkan Studies, 1966)

Dam, Kenneth W, 'Statement Before the House Committee on Foreign Affairs, 2 November 1983' (1984) 78 *AJIL* 200

Damrosch, Lori Fisler, 'Politics Across Borders: Nonintervention and Nonforcible Influence over Domestic Affairs' (1989) 83 *AJIL* 31

—— 'Commentary on Collective Military Intervention to Enforce Human Rights', in Lori Fisler Damrosch and David J Scheffer (eds), *Law and Force in the New International Order* (Boulder: Westview, 1991) 185

—— 'International Human Rights Law in Soviet and American Courts' (1991) 100 *Yale LJ* 2315

—— 'The Role of the Great Powers in United Nations Peace-Keeping' (1993) 18 *Yale JIL* 429

Danilenko, Gennady, *Law-Making in the International Community* (Dordrecht: Martinus Nijhoff, 1993)

Davies, Norman, *Europe: A History* (London: Pimlico, 1997)

Davies, Peter, 'The EC/Canadian Dispute in the Northwest Atlantic' (1995) 44 *ICLQ* 927

—— and Catherine Redgwell, 'The International Legal Regulation of Straddling Fishing Stocks' (1996) 67 *British YBIL* 199

de Bellaigue, Christopher, 'Justice and the Kurds', *New York Review*, 24 June 1999, 19

Decalo, Samuel, *Psychoses of Power: African Personal Dictatorships* (2nd edn; Gainesville, FL: Florida Academic Press, 1997)

Delbrück, Jost, 'A Fresh Look at Humanitarian Intervention Under the Authority of the United Nations' (1992) 67 *Indiana LJ* 887

DeMuth, Christopher C, *The Reagan Doctrine and Beyond* (Washington, DC: American Enterprise Institute for Public Policy Research, 1988)

Dickinson, Edwin DeWitt, *The Equality of States in International Law* (Cambridge, MA: Harvard University Press, 1920)

Dinstein, Yoram, *War, Aggression and Self-Defence* (2nd edn; Cambridge: Cambridge University Press, 1994)

Donnelly, Jack, 'Human Rights, Humanitarian Intervention and American Foreign Policy: Law, Morality and Politics' (1984) 37 *Journal of International Affairs* 311

Donoho, Douglas Lee, 'Evolution or Expediency: The United Nations Response to the Disruption of Democracy' (1996) 29 *Cornell LJ* 329

Doppelt, Gerald, 'Walzer's Theory of Morality in International Relations' (1978) 8 *Philosophy and Public Affairs* 3

Dowty, Alan, and Gil Loescher, 'Refugee Flows as Grounds for International Action', in Michael Brown, Owen R Coté, Jr, Sean M Lynn Jones, and Steven E Miller (eds), *Nationalism and Ethnic Conflict: An International Security Reader* (Cambridge, MA: MIT Press, 1997) 305

Drysdale, John, *Whatever Happened to Somalia* (London: Haan Associates, 1994)

Drysdale, John, 'Foreign Military Intervention in Somalia: The Root Cause of the Shift from UN Peacekeeping to Peacemaking and Its Consequences', in Walter Clarke and Jeffrey Herbst (eds), *Learning from Somalia: The Lessons of Armed Humanitarian Intervention* (Boulder: Westview, 1997) 118

Dupuy, René-Jean (ed), *The Development of the Role of the Security Council: Peace-Keeping and Peace-Building* (Académie de droit international de la Haye, Colloque 1992; Dordrecht: Martinus Nijhoff, 1993)

Dworkin, Ronald, *Law's Empire* (London: Fontana, 1986)

Eagleton, Clyde, 'Self-Determination in the United Nations' (1953) 47 *AJIL* 88

Eppstein, John, *The Catholic Tradition of the Law of Nations* (London: Burns Oates & Washbourne, 1935)

Evans, Cedric E, 'The Concept of "Threat to Peace" And Humanitarian Concerns: Probing the Limits of Chapter VII of the UN Charter' (1995) 5 *Transnational Law and Contemporary Problems* 213

Evans, Glynne, *Responding to Crises in the African Great Lakes* (Adelphi Paper 311; London: IISS, 1997)

Falk, Richard A, *Legal Order in a Violent World* (Princeton, NJ: Princeton University Press, 1968)

—— (ed), *The Vietnam War and International Law* (Princeton, NJ: Princeton University Press 1968–76)

—— (ed), *The International Law of Civil War* (Baltimore: Johns Hopkins Press, 1971)

—— 'The United Nations and the Rule of Law' (1994) 4 *Transnational Law and Contemporary Problems* 611

—— 'The Complexities of Humanitarian Intervention: A New World Order Challenge' (1996) 17 *Michigan JIL* 491

—— 'Kosovo, World Order, and the Future of International Law' (1999) 93 *AJIL* 847

Farer, Tom J, 'Intervention in Civil Wars: A Modest Proposal' (1967) 67 *Columbia Law Review* 266

—— 'Harnessing Rogue Elephants: A Short Discourse on Foreign Intervention in Civil Strife' (1969) 82 *Harvard Law Review* 511

—— 'Humanitarian Intervention: The View from Charlottesville', in Richard B Lillich (ed), *Humanitarian Intervention and the United Nations* (Charlottesville: University Press of Virginia, 1973) 149

—— 'The Regulation of Foreign Intervention in Civil Armed Conflict' (1974) 142 *RCADI* 291

—— 'Panama: Beyond the Charter Paradigm' (1990) 84 *AJIL* 503

—— 'Human Rights in Law's Empire: The Jurisprudence War' (1991) 85 *AJIL* 117

—— 'Collectively Defending Democracy in a World of Sovereign States: The Western Hemisphere's Prospect' (1993) 15 *Human Rights Quarterly* 716

—— 'A Paradigm of Legitimate Intervention', in Lori Fisler Damrosch (ed), *Enforcing Restraint: Collective Intervention in Internal Conflicts* (New York: Council on Foreign Relations Press, 1993) 334

Fenwick, Charles G, 'Intervention: Individual and Collective' (1945) 39 *AJIL* 645

—— 'The Dominican Republic: Intervention or Collective Self-Defense' (1966) 60 *AJIL* 64

Ferrell, Robert H, *American Diplomacy: A History* (3rd edn; New York: Norton, 1975)

Fielding, Lois E, 'Taking the Next Step in the Development of New Human Rights: The Emerging Right of Humanitarian Assistance to Restore Democracy' (1995) 5 *Duke JCIL* 329

—— 'Taking a Closer Look at Threats to Peace: The Power of the Security Council to Address Humanitarian Crises' (1996) 73 *University of Detroit Mercy Law Review* 551

Fiore, Pasquale, *International Law Codified and Its Legal Sanction* (Borchard trans; 5th edn; New York: Baker Voorhis & Co, 1918)

Fisher, H A L, *A History of Europe* (rev edn; London: Eyre and Spottiswoode, 1943)

Fonteyne, Jean-Pierre L, 'The Customary International Law Doctrine of Humanitarian Intervention: Its Current Validity Under the UN Charter' (1974) 4 *California Western ILJ* 203

Foulke, Roland R, *A Treatise on International Law* (Philadelphia: John C Winston, 1920)

Fox, Gregory H, 'The Right to Political Participation in International Law' (1992) 17 *Yale JIL* 539

—— 'International Law and Civil Wars' (1994) 26 *NYUJILP* 633

—— and Brad R Roth (eds), *Democratic Governance and International Law* (Cambridge: Cambridge University Press, 2000)

Fox, Hazel (ed), *The Changing Constitution of the United Nations* (London: BIICL, 1997)

Franck, Thomas M, 'Who Killed Article 2(4)?' (1970) 64 *AJIL* 809

—— 'Of Gnats and Camels: Is There a Double Standard at the United Nations?' (1984) 78 *AJIL* 811

—— 'The Emerging Right to Democratic Governance' (1992) 86 *AJIL* 46

—— 'The Security Council and "Threats to the Peace": Some Remarks on Remarkable Recent Developments', in René-Jean Dupuy (ed), *The Development of the Role of the Security Council: Peace-Keeping and Peace-Building* (Dordrecht: Martinus Nijhoff, 1993) 83

—— 'The Democratic Entitlement' (1995) 29 *University of Richmond Law Review* 1

—— 'Lessons of Kosovo' (1999) 93 *AJIL* 857

—— 'Legitimacy and the Democratic Entitlement', in Gregory H Fox and Brad R Roth (eds), *Democratic Governance and International Law* (Cambridge: Cambridge University Press, 2000) 25

—— and Faiza Patel, 'UN Police Action in Lieu of War: "The Old Order Changeth"' (1991) 85 *AJIL* 63

—— and Nigel S Rodley, 'After Bangladesh: The Law of Humanitarian Intervention by Military Force' (1973) 67 *AJIL* 275

Freedman, Lawrence, and David Boren, '"Safe Havens" for Kurds in Post-War Iraq', in Nigel S Rodley (ed), *To Loose the Bands of Wickedness: International Intervention in Defence of Human Rights* (London: Brassey's, 1992) 43

Freudenschuss, Helmut, 'Article 39 of the UN Charter Revisited: Threats to the Peace and the Recent Practice of the UN Security Council' (1993) 46 *Austrian JPIL* 1

—— 'Between Unilateralism and Collective Security: Authorizations of the Use of Force by the UN Security Council' (1994) 5 *European JIL* 492

Frowein, Jochen Abr, 'Articles 39–43', in Bruno Simma (ed), *The Charter of the United Nations: A Commentary* (Oxford: Oxford University Press, 1994) 617

Gaga, Giorgio, 'Use of Force Made or Authorized by the United Nations', in Christian Tomuschat (ed), *The United Nations at Age Fifty: A Legal Perspective* (The Hague: Kluwer Law International, 1995) 39

Gallant, Judy A, 'Humanitarian Intervention and Security Council Resolution 688: A Reappraisal in Light of a Changing World Order' (1992) 7 *American University JILP* 881

Gandhi, M K, *Non-Violence in Peace and War* (2 vols; Ahmedabad: Navajivan Publishing House, 1942)

Ganji, Manouchehr, *International Protection of Human Rights* (Paris: Minard, 1962)

Gardam, Judith Gail, 'Legal Restraints On Security Council Military Enforcement Action' (1996) 17 *Michigan JIL* 285

Gayim, Eyassu, *The Principle of Self-Determination* (Oslo: Norwegian Institute of Human Rights, 1990)

Gentili, Alberico, *De jure belli* ([1612] Classics of International Law; Rolfe trans; Oxford: Clarendon Press, 1933)

Glennon, Michael J, 'Sovereignty and Community After Haiti: Rethinking the Collective Use of Force' (1995) 89 *AJIL* 70

Glenny, Misha, *The Fall of Yugoslavia: The Third Balkan War* (3rd edn; London: Penguin, 1996)

Gooch, G P, and Harold William Vazeille Temperly (eds), *British Documents on the Origins of the War 1898–1914* (London: HMSO, 1926)

Goodrich, Leland M, and Edvard Hambro, *Charter of the United Nations: Commentary and Documents* (1st edn; Boston: World Peace Foundation, 1946)

—— and Edvard Hambro, *Charter of the United Nations: Commentary and Documents* (2nd edn; London: Stevens & Sons, 1949)

——, Edvard Hambro, and Anne Patricia Simons, *Charter of the United Nations: Commentary and Documents* (3rd edn; New York: Columbia University Press, 1969)

—— and Anne Patricia Simons, *The United Nations and the Maintenance of International Peace and Security* (Washington, DC: Brookings, 1955)

Goodwin-Gill, Guy, 'Case and Comment: The Haitian Refoulement Case' (1994) 6 *International Journal of Refugee Law* 69

—— and Stefan A Talmon (eds), *The Reality of International Law: Essays in Honour of Ian Brownlie* (Oxford: Oxford University Press, 1999)

Gordon, Edward, *et al*, 'International Law and the United States Action in Grenada: A Report' (1984) 18 *International Lawyer* 331

Gordon, Ruth, 'United Nations Intervention in Internal Conflicts: Iraq, Somalia, And Beyond' (1994) 15 *Michigan JIL* 519

Gourevitch, Philip, *We Wish to Inform You that Tomorrow We Will Be Killed with Our Families* (London: Picador, 1999)

Gowlland-Debbas, Vera, *Collective Responses to Illegal Acts in International Law: United Nations Actions in the Question of Southern Rhodesia* (Dordrecht: Martinus Nijhoff, 1990)

—— 'Security Council Enforcement Action and Issues of State Responsibility' (1994) 43 *ICLQ* 55

Gray, Christine, 'After the Ceasefire: Iraq, the Security Council and the Use of Force' (1994) 65 *British YBIL* 135

—— 'Host-State Consent and United Nations Peacekeeping In Yugoslavia' (1996) 7 *Duke JCIL* 241

—— 'Regional Arrangements and the United Nations Collective Security System', in Hazel Fox (ed), *The Changing Constitution of the United Nations* (London: BIICL, 1997) 92

Greenwood, Christopher, 'Legal Constraints on UN Military Operations', *IISS Strategic Comments*, 22 March 1995

—— 'The United Nations as Guarantor of International Peace and Security: Past, Present and Future—A United Kingdom View', in Christian Tomuschat (ed), *The United Nations at Age Fifty: A Legal Perspective* (The Hague: Kluwer Law International, 1995) 59

—— 'Protection of Peacekeepers: The Legal Regime' (1996) 7 *Duke JCIL* 185

Greig, D W, *International Law* (2nd edn; London: Butterworths, 1976)

Gross, Leo, 'Voting in the Security Council: Abstention from Voting and Absence from Meetings' (1951) 60 *Yale LJ* 209

—— 'Voting in the Security Council: Abstention in the Post-1965 Amendment Phase and its Impact on Article 25 of the Charter' (1968) 62 *AJIL* 315

Grotius, Hugo, *De iure belli ac pacis libri tres* ([1646] Classics of International Law; Kelsey trans; Oxford: Clarendon Press, 1925)

—— *De iure praedae commentarius* ([1604] Classics of International Law; Williams trans; Oxford: Clarendon Press, 1950)

Guicherd, Catherine, 'International Law and the War in Kosovo' (1999) 41(2) *Survival* 19

Halberstam, Malvina, 'The Copenhagen Document: Intervention in Support of Democracy' (1993) 34 *Harvard ILJ* 163

—— 'The Right to Self-Defense Once the Security Council Takes Action' (1996) 17 *Michigan JIL* 229

Halderman, John W, 'Legal Basis for United Nations Armed Forces' (1962) 56 *AJIL* 971

Hall, William Edward, *International Law* (1st edn; Oxford: Clarendon Press, 1880)

—— *Treatise on International Law* (2nd edn; Oxford: Clarendon Press, 1884)

Halleck, H W, *International Law; or, Rules Regulating the Intercourse of States in Peace and War* (1st edn; San Francisco: H Bancroft & Co, 1861)

—— *Halleck's International Law* (Sherston Baker (ed); 4th edn; London: Kegan Paul Trench Trubner & Co, 1908)

Harcourt, William Vernon, *Letters by Historicus on Some Questions of International Law: Reprinted from 'The Times' with Considerable Additions* (London: Macmillan, 1863)

Harper, Keith, 'Does the United Nations Security Council Have the Competence to Act as Court and Legislature?' (1994) 27 *NYUJILP* 103

Harris, D J, *Cases and Materials on International Law* (4th edn; London: Sweet & Maxwell, 1991)

—— *Cases and Materials on International Law* (5th edn; London: Sweet & Maxwell, 1998)

Harris, John (ed), *The Politics of Humanitarian Intervention* (London: Pinter for Save the Children Fund, 1995)

Havel, Vaclav, 'Kosovo and the End of the Nation-State', *New York Review*, 10 June 1999, 4

Heffter, A G, *Le droit international public de l'Europe* ([1844] Bergson trans; Berlin: E H Schroeder, 1857)

Hegel, G W F, *Hegel's Philosophy of Right* ([1821] Knox trans; Oxford: Oxford University Press, 1967)

Heineccius, Johann Gottlieb, *Elementa juris naturae et gentium* (Turnbull trans; London: J Noon, 1741)

Hemleben, Sylvester John, *Plans for World Peace Through Six Centuries* (Chicago: University of Chicago Press, 1943)

Henkin, Louis, 'The Reports of the Death of Article 2(4) Are Greatly Exaggerated' (1971) 65 *AJIL* 547

—— *How Nations Behave: Law and Foreign Policy* (2nd edn; New York: Columbia University Press, 1979)

—— 'The Use of Force: Law and US Policy', in Louis Henkin (ed), *Right v Might: International Law and the Use of Force* (New York: Council on Foreign Relations, 1989) 37

—— 'The Invasion of Panama Under International Law: A Gross Violation' (1991) 29 *Columbia JTL* 293

—— 'Kosovo and the Law of "Humanitarian Intervention"' (1999) 93 *AJIL* 824

Henrikson, Alan K, 'The United Nations and Regional Organizations: "King Links" of a "Global Chain"' (1996) 7 *Duke JCIL* 35

Herdegen, Matthias J, 'The "Constitutionalization" of the UN Security System' (1994) 27 *Vanderbilt JTL* 135

Hershey, Amos S, 'The Calvo and Drago Doctrines' (1907) 1 *AJIL* 26

—— *The Essentials of International Public Law* (New York: Macmillan, 1918)

Hertslet, Edward, *The Map of Europe by Treaty* (London: Butterworths, 1875)

Hicks, Frederick Charles, 'The Equality of States and the Hague Conferences' (1908) 2 *AJIL* 530

Higgins, A Pearce, *Studies in International Law and Relations* (Cambridge: Cambridge University Press, 1928)

Higgins, Rosalyn, *The Development of International Law Through the Political Organs of the United Nations* (London: Oxford University Press, 1963)

—— *United Nations Peacekeeping 1946–1967: Documents and Commentary: Vol 1, The Middle East* (London: Oxford University Press, 1969)

—— *United Nations Peacekeeping 1946–1967: Documents and Commentary: Vol 2, Asia* (London: Oxford University Press, 1970)

—— *United Nations Peacekeeping 1946–1967: Documents and Commentary: Vol 3, Africa* (London: Oxford University Press, 1980)

—— *United Nations Peacekeeping: Documents and Commentary: Vol 4, Europe 1946–1979* (London: Oxford University Press, 1981)

—— 'The New United Nations and the Former Yugoslavia' (1993) 69 *International Affairs* 465

—— *Problems and Process: International Law and How We Use It* (Oxford: Clarendon Press, 1994)

—— 'The United Nations Role in Maintaining International Peace: The Lessons of the First Fifty Years' (1996) 16 *New York Law School JICL* 135

Hobbes, Thomas, *Leviathan* ([1651] London: Dent, 1914)

—— *De Cive* ([1647] Oxford: Clarendon Press, 1983)

Hohfeld, Wesley Newcomb, *Fundamental Legal Conceptions as Applied in Judicial Reasoning and Other Legal Essays* (Walter Wheeler Cook (ed); New Haven: Yale University Press, 1923)

Holbrooke, Richard, *To End a War* (New York: Random House, 1998)

Holland, Thomas Erskine, *Lectures on International Law* (London: Sweet & Maxwell, 1933)

Howe, Jonathan T, 'Relations Between the United States and United Nations in Dealing with Somalia', in Walter Clarke and Jeffrey Herbst (eds), *Learning from Somalia: The Lessons of Armed Humanitarian Intervention* (Boulder: Westview, 1997) 173

Hsiung, James C, *Anarchy and Order: The Interplay of Politics and Law in International Relations* (Boulder: Lynne Rienner, 1997)

Huband, Mark, *The Liberian Civil War* (London: Frank Cass, 1998)

Human Rights Watch, *'Leave None to Tell the Story': Genocide in Rwanda* (New York: Human Rights Watch, 1999)

Humphrey, John P, 'Foreword', in Richard B Lillich (ed), *Humanitarian Intervention and the United Nations* (Charlottesville: University Press of Virginia, 1973) vii

Hutchinson, Mark R, 'Restoring Hope: UN Security Council Resolutions for Somalia and an Expanded Doctrine of Humanitarian Intervention' (1993) 34 *Harvard ILJ* 624

Hyde, Charles, *International Law* (2nd edn; Boston: Little Brown, 1947)

Hyland, William G, *Clinton's World: Remaking American Foreign Policy* (Westport, CT: Praeger, 1999)

Inter-American Institute of International Legal Studies, *The Inter-American System: Its Development and Strengthening* (Dobbs Ferry, NY: Oceana, 1966)

International Commission of Jurists, *The Events in East Pakistan 1971* (1972)

International Committee of the Red Cross, 'Report on the Protection of War Victims' (1993) 296 *International Review of the Red Cross* 391

Irving, Karl J, 'The United Nations and Democratic Intervention: Is "Swords Into Ballot Boxes" Enough?' (1996) 25 *Denver JILP* 41

Jessup, Philip C, *A Modern Law of Nations* (New York: Macmillan, 1949)

Jhabvala, Farrokh, 'Unilateral Humanitarian Intervention: Some Conceptual Problems', in Rafael Gutiérrez Girardot, Helmut Ridder, Manohar Lal Sarin, and Theo Schiller (eds), *New Directions in International Law: Essays in Honour of Wolfgang Abendroth* (Frankfurt/New York: Campus Verlag, 1982) 459

Jiménez de Aréchaga, Eduardo, 'International Law in the Part Third of a Century' (1978) 159 *RCADI* 1

Johnston, Harry, and Ted Dagne, 'Congress and the Somalia Crisis', in Walter Clarke and Jeffrey Herbst (eds), *Learning from Somalia: The Lessons of Armed Humanitarian Intervention* (Boulder: Westview, 1997) 191

Judah, Tim, *Kosovo: War and Revenge* (New Haven: Yale University Press, 2000)

Kaikobad, Kaiyan Homi, 'Self-Defence, Enforcement Action and the Gulf Wars: 1980–88 and 1990–91' (1992) 63 *British YBIL* 299

Kant, Immanuel, *Practical Philosophy* ([1795] Gregor trans; Cambridge: Cambridge UP, 1996)

Kelsen, Hans, 'Collective Security and Collective Self-Defense Under the Charter of the United Nations' (1948) 42 *AJIL* 783

—— *The Law of the United Nations* (London: Stevens & Sons, 1950)

Kelsen, Hans, 'Is the North Atlantic Treaty a Regional Arrangement?' (1951) 45 *AJIL* 162

Kent, James, *Kent's Commentary on International Law* (J T Abdy (ed); 1st edn; Cambridge: Deighton Bell & Co, 1866)

Khadduri, Majid, *War and Peace in the Law of Islam* (Baltimore: Johns Hopkins, 1955)

Kirgis, Frederic L, 'The Security Council's First Fifty Years' (1995) 89 *AJIL* 506

Kirkpatrick, Jeane J, and Allan Gerson, 'The Reagan Doctrine, Human Rights, and International Law', in Louis Henkin (ed), *Right v Might: International Law and the Use of Force* (New York: Council on Foreign Relations, 1989) 19

Klintworth, Gary, *Vietnam's Intervention in Cambodia in International Law* (Canberra: AGPS, 1989)

Kontou, Nancy, *The Termination and Revision of Treaties in the Light of New Customary International Law* (Oxford: Clarendon Press, 1994)

Kooijmans, Peter H, 'The Enlargement of the Concept "Threat to the Peace"', in René-Jean Dupuy (ed), *The Development of the Role of the Security Council: Peace-Keeping and Peace-Building* (Dordrecht: Martinus Nijhoff, 1993) 111

Koskenniemi, Martti, *From Apologia to Utopia: The Structure of International Legal Argument* (Helsinki: Lakimiesliiton Kustannus, 1989)

—— 'The Police in the Temple: Order, Justice and the UN: A Dialectical View' (1995) 6 *European JIL* 325

—— 'The Place of Law in Collective Security' (1996) 17 *Michigan JIL* 455

Krauthammer, Charles, 'The Short, Unhappy Life of Humanitarian War' (1999) 57 *The National Interest* 5

Kritsiotis, Dino, 'Reappraising Policy Objections to Humanitarian Intervention' (1998) 19 *Michigan JIL* 1005

Lachs, Manfred, 'The Development and General Trends of International Law in Our Time' (1980) 169 *RCADI* 9

Lauterpacht, Elihu, 'The Legal Effects of Illegal Acts of International Organizations', in *Cambridge Essays in International Law: Essays in Honour of Lord McNair* (London: Stevens, 1965) 88

Lauterpacht, Hersch, 'The Grotian Tradition in International Law' (1946) 23 *British YBIL* 1

—— *International Law and Human Rights* (London: Stevens & Sons, 1950)

—— *The Development of International Law by the International Court* (London: Stevens, 1958)

Lawrence, T J, *The Principles of International Law* (London: Macmillan, 1895)

—— *A Handbook of Public International Law* (Percy H Winfield (ed); 11th edn; London: Macmillan, 1938)

Leurdijk, Dick A, *The United Nations and NATO in Former Yugoslavia: Partners in International Cooperation* (The Hague: Netherlands Atlantic Commission, 1994)

Levenfeld, Barry, 'Israel's Counter-Fedayeen Tactics in Lebanon: Self-Defense and Reprisal Under Modern International Law' (1982) 21 *Columbia JTL* 1

Levitin, Michael J, 'The Law of Force and the Force of Law: Grenada, the Falklands, and Humanitarian Intervention' (1986) 27 *Harvard ILJ* 621

Lillich, Richard B, 'Forcible Self-Help by States to Protect Human Rights' (1967) 53 *Iowa Law Review* 325

—— 'Intervention to Protect Human Rights' (1969) 15 *McGill LJ* 205

—— (ed), *Humanitarian Intervention and the United Nations* (Charlottesville: University Press of Virginia, 1973)

—— 'Humanitarian Intervention: A Reply to Ian Brownlie and a Plea for Constructive Alternatives', in John N Moore (ed), *Law and Civil War in the Modern World* (Baltimore, Maryland: Johns Hopkins University Press, 1974) 229

—— 'Forcible Protection of Nationals Abroad: The Liberian "Incident" of 1990' (1992) 35 *German Yearbook of International Law* 205

—— 'Humanitarian Intervention Through the United Nations: Towards the Development of Criteria' (1993) 53 *Zeitschrift für ausländisches öffentliches Recht und Völkerrecht* 557

—— 'The Role of the UN Security Council in Protecting Human Rights in Crisis Situations: UN Humanitarian Intervention in the Post-Cold War World' (1995) 3 *Tulane JICL* 1

—— 'Kant and the Current Debate over Humanitarian Intervention' (1997) 6 *Journal of Transnational Law and Policy* 397

Lingelbach, W E, 'The Doctrine and Practice of Intervention in Europe' (1900) 16 *Annals of the American Academy of Political and Social Science* 1

Littman, Mark, *Kosovo: Law & Diplomacy* (London: Centre for Policy Studies, 1999)

Lobel, Jules, and Michael Ratner, 'Bypassing the Security Council: Ambiguous Authorizations to Use Force, Cease-Fires and the Iraqi Inspection Regime' (1999) 93 *AJIL* 125

Lowe, Vaughan, and Malgosia Fitzmaurice (eds), *Fifty Years of the International Court of Justice: Essays in Honour of Sir Robert Jennings* (Cambridge: Grotius, 1996)

Lowenthal, Abraham F, *The Dominican Intervention* (Cambridge, MA: Harvard University Press, 1972)

Luban, David, 'Just War and Human Rights' (1979) 9 *Philosophy and Public Affairs* 160

Macfarlane, L J, *The Theory and Practice of Human Rights* (London: Temple Smith, 1985)

Macpherson, C B, *The Political Theory of Possessive Individualism: Hobbes to Locke* (Oxford: Clarendon Press, 1962)

Mahan, A T, *Some Neglected Aspects of War* (Boston: Little Brown, 1907)

Malanczuck, Peter, 'The Kurdish Crisis and Allied Intervention in the Aftermath of the Second Gulf War' (1991) 2 *European JIL* 114

—— *Humanitarian Intervention and the Legitimacy of the Use of Force* (Dordrecht: Martinus Nijhoff, 1993)

Malone, David, *Decision-Making in the UN Security Council: The Case of Haiti, 1990–1997* (Oxford: Clarendon Press, 1998)

Mandelbaum, Michael, 'The Reluctance to Intervene' (1994) 95 *Foreign Policy* 3

Manning, William Oke, *Commentaries on the Law of Nations* (Sheldon Amos (ed); London: Sweet, 1875)

Mansfield, Edward D, and Jack Snyder, 'Democratization and the Danger of War', in Michael E Brown, Sean M Lynn Jones, and Steven E Miller (eds), *Debating the Democratic Peace* (Cambridge, MA: MIT Press, 1996) 301

Mayall, James (ed), *The New Interventionism 1991–1994: United Nations Experience in Cambodia, Former Yugoslavia and Somalia* (Cambridge: Cambridge University Press, 1996)

McDougal, Myres S, 'Authority to Use Force on the High Seas' (1980) 61 *International Law Studies* 551

——, Harold D Lasswell, and Lung-chu Chen, *Human Rights and World Public Order: The Basic Policies of an International Law of Human Dignity* (New Haven and London: Yale University Press, 1980)

—— and W Michael Reisman, 'Rhodesia and the United Nations: The Lawfulness of International Concern' (1968) 62 *AJIL* 1

McNemar, Donald W, 'The Postindependence War in the Congo', in Richard A Falk (ed), *The International Law of Civil War* (Baltimore: Johns Hopkins Press, 1971) 244

Meltzer, Bernard D, 'A Note on Some Aspects of the Nuremberg Debate' (1947) 14 *University of Chicago Law Review* 455

Melvern, Linda, *The Ultimate Crime: Who Betrayed the UN and Why* (London: Allison & Busby, 1995)

Meron, Theodor, *Human Rights and Humanitarian Norms as Customary Law* (Oxford: Clarendon Press, 1989)

Minear, Larry, Colin Scott, and Thomas G Weiss, *The News Media, Civil War, and Humanitarian Action* (Boulder: Lynne Rienner, 1996)

Mohr, M, 'The ILC's Distinction Between "International Crimes" and "International Delicts" and Its Implications', in Marina Spinedi and Bruno Simma (eds), *United Nations Codification of State Responsibility* (New York: Oceana, 1987) 115

Moore, John Basset, *A Digest of International Law* (Washington, DC: Government Printing Office, 1906)

—— *The Principles of American Diplomacy* (New York: Harper and Brothers, 1918)

—— 'Some Essentials of League for Peace', in Stephen Pierce Duggan (ed), *The League of Nations: The Principle and the Practice* (Boston: Atlantic Monthly Press, 1919)

Moore, John N, *Law and the Indo-China War* (Princeton, NY: Princeton University Press, 1972)

—— (ed), *Law and Civil War in the Modern World* (Baltimore, Maryland: Johns Hopkins University Press, 1974)

—— 'Grenada and the International Double Standard' (1984) 78 *AJIL* 145

Morgan, H Wayne, *William McKinley and His America* (Syracuse, NY: Syracuse University Press, 1963)

Mowat, R B, *A History of European Diplomacy, 1815–1914* (London: Edward Arnold, 1923)

Mrazek, Josef, 'Prohibition on the Use and Threat of Force: Self-Defence and Self-Help in International Law' (1989) 27 *Canadian Yearbook of International Law* 81

Mullerson, Rein, 'Self-Defense in the Contemporary World', in Lori Fisler Damrosch and David J Scheffer (eds), *Law and Force in the New International Order* (Boulder: Westview, 1991) 13

Murphy, John F, 'State Self-Help and Problems of Public International Law', in Alona E Evans and John F Murphy (eds), *Legal Aspects of International Terrorism* (Lexington, MA: Lexington, 1978) 553

—— 'Force and Arms', in Oscar Schachter and Christopher C Joyner (eds), *United Nations Legal Order* (Cambridge: Cambridge University Press, 1995) 247

Murphy, Sean D, 'The Security Council, Legitimacy, And the Concept of Collective Security After the Cold War' (1994) 32 *Columbia JTL* 201

—— *Humanitarian Intervention: The United Nations in an Evolving World Order* (Philadelphia: University of Pennsylvania Press, 1996)

—— 'Democratic Legitimacy and the Recognition of States and Governments', in Gregory H Fox and Brad R Roth (eds), *Democratic Governance and International Law* (Cambridge: Cambridge University Press, 2000) 123

Nafziger, James A R, 'Self-Determination and Humanitarian Intervention in a Community of Power' (1991) 20 *Denver JILP* 9

—— 'Humanitarian Intervention in a Community of Power—Part II' (1994) 22 *Denver JILP* 219

Nanda, Ved P, 'The United States' Action in the 1965 Dominican Crisis: Impact on World Order—Part I' (1966) 43 *Denver LJ* 439

—— 'Self-Determination in International Law: The Tragic Tale of Two Cities— Islamabad (West Pakistan) and Dacca (East Pakistan)' (1972) 66 *AJIL* 321

—— 'The Validity of United States Intervention in Panama Under International Law' (1990) 84 *AJIL* 494

—— 'Tragedies in Northern Iraq, Liberia, Yugoslavia, and Haiti—Revisiting the Validity of Humanitarian Intervention Under International Law' (1992) 20 *Denver JILP* 305

Natsios, Andrew S, 'Humanitarian Relief Intervention in Somalia: The Economics of Chaos', in Walter Clarke and Jeffrey Herbst (eds), *Learning from Somalia: The Lessons of Armed Humanitarian Intervention* (Boulder: Westview, 1997) 77

Newman, Edward, *The UN Secretary-General from the Cold War to the New Era* (London: Macmillan, 1998)

Nincic, Djura, *The Problem of Sovereignty in the Charter and in the Practice of the United Nations* (The Hague: Martinus Nijhoff, 1970)

Nolte, Georg, *Eingreifen auf Einladung—Zur völkerrechtlichen Zulässigkeit des Einsatzes fremder Truppen im internen Konflikt auf Einladung der Regierung (Intervention upon Invitation: Use of Force by Foreign Troops in Internal Conflicts at the Invitation of a Government under International Law (English Summary))* (Berlin: Springer Verlag, 1999)

Nowrojee, Binaifer, 'Joining Forces: United Nations and Regional Peace-keeping: Lessons from Liberia' (1995) 8 *Harvard Human Rights Journal* 129

Nowrot, Karsten, and Emily W Schabacker, 'The Use of Force to Restore Democracy: International Legal Implications of the ECOWAS Intervention in Sierra Leone' (1998) 14 *American University International Law Review* 321

Nussbaum, Arthur, *A Concise History of the Law of Nations* (rev edn; New York: Macmillan, 1962)

O'Connell, Mary Ellen, 'Regulating the Use of Force In the 21st Century: The Continuing Importance of State Autonomy' (1997) 36 *Columbia JTL* 473

Ofodile, Anthony Chukwuka, 'The Legality of ECOWAS Intervention in Liberia' (1994) 32 *Columbia JTL* 381

Oppenheim, Lassa Francis Lawrence, *International Law* (New York: Longmans Green & Co, 1905)

Oppenheim, Lassa Francis Lawrence, *International Law* (Hersch Lauterpacht (ed); 7th edn; London: Longmans, 1952)
—— *International Law* (Hersch Lauterpacht (ed); 8th edn; London: Longman, 1955)
—— *International Law* (Robert Jennings and Arthur Watts (eds); 9th edn; London: Longman, 1996)
Orford, Anne, 'Locating the International: Military and Monetary Interventions After the Cold War' (1997) 38 *Harvard ILJ* 443
Osinbajo, Yemi, 'Legality in a Collapsed State: The Somali Experience' (1996) 45 *ICLQ* 910
Österdahl, Inger, *Threat to the Peace: The Interpretation by the Security Council of Article 39 of the UN Charter* (Studies in International Law, vol 13; Uppsala: Iustus Forlag, 1998)
Owen, David, *Balkan Odyssey* (New York: Harcourt Brace, 1995)
Palit, D K, *The Lightning Campaign: The Indo-Pakistan War, 1971* (New Delhi: Lancer, 1998)
Parsons, Anthony, *From Cold War to Hot Peace: UN Interventions 1947–1994* (London: Michael Joseph, 1995)
Patil, Anjali V, *The UN Veto in World Affairs 1946–1990: A Complete Record and Case Histories of the Security Council's Veto* (London: Mansell, 1992)
Pease, Kelly K, and David P Forsythe, 'Human Rights, Humanitarian Intervention, and World Politics' (1993) 15 *Human Rights Quarterly* 290
—— and David P Forsythe, 'Humanitarian Intervention and International Law' (1993) 45 *Austrian JPIL* 1
Peck, Julianne, 'The UN and the Laws of War: How Can the World's Peacekeepers Be Held Accountable?' (1995) 21 *Syracuse JILC* 283
Phillimore, Robert, *Commentaries upon International Law* (3rd edn; London: Butterworths, 1879)
—— *Commentaries upon International Law* (London: Benning & Co, 1954)
Phillips, W Alison, *The War of Greek Independence* (London: Smith Elder & Co, 1897)
Pogany, Istvan, 'Humanitarian Intervention in International Law: The French Intervention in Syria Re-Examined' (1986) 35 *ICLQ* 182
Pomeroy, John Norton, *Lecture on International Law in Time of Peace* (Theodore Salisbury Woolsey (ed); Cambridge, MA: Riverside Press, 1886)
Popper, Karl, *The Open Society and Its Enemies* (London: Routledge & Kegan Paul, 1966)
Potter, David, *et al*, *Democratization* (Malden, MA: Polity Press/Open University, 1997)
Prunier, Gérard, *The Rwanda Crisis: History of a Genocide* (New York: Columbia University Press, 1997)
Pufendorf, Samuel, *De jure naturae et gentium libri octo* ([1688] Classics of International Law; Oxford: Clarendon Press, 1934)
Quigley, John, 'The "Privatization" of Security Council Enforcement Action: A Threat to Multilateralism' (1996) 17 *Michigan JIL* 249
Rachel, Samuel, *De jure naturae et gentium dissertationes* ([1676] Washington, DC: Carnegie Institution, 1916)
Randelzhofer, Albrecht, 'Article 2(4)', in Bruno Simma (ed), *The Charter of the United Nations: A Commentary* (Oxford: Oxford University Press, 1994) 106

Ratner, Steven, 'Drawing a Better Line: Uti Possidetis Juris Today' (1996) 90 *AJIL* 590

Reddie, James, *Inquiries in International Law: Public and Private* (2nd edn; Edinburgh: William Blackwood and Sons, 1851)

Redslob, Robert, 'La doctrine idéaliste du droit des gens: proclamée par la révolution Française et par le philosophe Emmanuel Kant' (1921) 28 *RGDIP* 441

Reisman, W Michael, 'Coercion and Self-Determination: Construing Charter Art 2(4)' (1984) 78 *AJIL* 642

—— 'International Incidents: Introduction to a New Genre in the Study of International Law' (1984) 10 *Yale JIL* 1

—— 'Old Wine in New Bottles: The Reagan and Brezhnev Doctrines in Contemporary International Law and Practice' (1988) 13 *Yale JIL* 171

—— 'Sovereignty and Human Rights in Contemporary International Law' (1990) 84 *AJIL* 866

—— 'The Constitutional Crisis in the United Nations' (1993) 87 *AJIL* 83

—— 'Peacemaking' (1993) 18 *Yale JIL* 415

—— 'Preparing to Wage Peace: Towards the Creation of an International Peacemaking Command and Staff College' (1994) 88 *AJIL* 76

—— 'Haiti and the Validity of International Action' (1995) 89 *AJIL* 82

—— 'Humanitarian Intervention and Fledgling Democracies' (1995) 18 *Fordham ILJ* 794

—— 'Legal Responses to Genocide and Other Massive Violations of Human Rights' (1996) 59(4) *Law and Contemporary Problems* 75

—— 'Hollow Victory: Humanitarian Intervention and Protection of Minorities' (1997) 91 *ASIL Proc* 431

—— 'Stopping Wars and Making Peace: Reflections on the Ideology and Practice of Conflict Termination in Contemporary World Politics' (1998) 6 *Tulane JICL* 5

—— 'Kosovo's Antinomies' (1999) 93 *AJIL* 860

—— 'Sovereignty and Human Rights in Contemporary International Law', in Gregory H Fox and Brad R Roth (eds), *Democratic Governance and International Law* (Cambridge: Cambridge University Press, 2000) 239

—— and Myres S McDougal, 'Humanitarian Intervention to Protect the Ibos', in Richard B Lillich (ed), *Humanitarian Intervention and the United Nations* (Charlottesville: University Press of Virginia, 1973) 167

Reppas, Michael J, 'The Lawfulness of Humanitarian Intervention' (1997) 9 *St Thomas Law Review* 463

Ress, Georg, 'Article 53', in Bruno Simma (ed), *The Charter of the United Nations: A Commentary* (Oxford: Oxford University Press, 1994) 722

Reyhan, Patricia Y, 'Genocidal Violence in Burundi: Should International Law Prohibit Domestic Humanitarian Intervention?' (1997) 60 *Albany Law Review* 771

Ridley, Jasper, *Lord Palmerston* (London: Constable, 1971)

Roberts, Adam, 'Humanitarian War: Military Intervention and Human Rights' (1993) 69 *International Affairs* 429

—— *Humanitarian Action in War: Aid Protection and Implementation in a Policy Vacuum* (Adelphi Paper 305; London: IISS, 1996)

—— and Richard Guelff, *Documents on the Laws of War* (2nd edn; Oxford: Clarendon Press, 1989)

Robertson, Geoffrey, *Crimes Against Humanity: The Struggle for Global Justice* (London: Allen Lane, 1999)

Robinson, Davis R, 'Letter dated 10 February 1984, addressed to Professor Edward Gordon, Chairman of the Committee on Grenada of the American Bar Association's Section on International Law and Practice' (1984) 78 *AJIL* 661

Rodley, Nigel S, 'Human Rights and Humanitarian Intervention: The Case Law of the World Court' (1989) 38 *ICLQ* 321

—— 'Collective Intervention to Protect Human Rights and Civilian Populations: The Legal Framework', in Nigel S Rodley (ed), *To Loose the Bands of Wickedness: International Intervention in Defence of Human Rights* (London: Brassey's, 1992) 14

Röling, B V A, 'Are Grotius' Ideas Obsolete in an Expanded World?', in Hedley Bull, Benedict Kingsbury, and Adam Roberts (eds), *Hugo Grotius and International Relations* (Oxford: Clarendon Press, 1990)

Ronzitti, Natalino, *Rescuing Nationals Abroad Through Military Coercion and Intervention on Grounds of Humanity* (Dordrecht: Martinus Nijhoff, 1985)

—— 'Use of Force, *Jus Cogens* and State Consent', in Antonio Cassese (ed), *The Current Legal Regulation of the Use of Force* (Dordrecht: Martinus Nijhoff, 1986) 147

Rosner, Gabriella, *The United Nations Emergency Force* (Columbia University Studies in International Organization; New York: Columbia University Press, 1963)

Rostow, Eugene V, 'Until What? Enforcement Action or Collective Self-Defense?' (1991) 85 *AJIL* 506

Rotberg, Robert I, and Thomas G Weiss (eds), *From Massacres to Genocide: The Media, Public Policy, and Humanitarian Crises* (Washington, DC: Brookings Institution, 1996)

Roth, Brad R, *Governmental Illegitimacy in International Law* (Oxford: Clarendon Press, 1999)

—— 'The Illegality of "Pro-Democratic" Invasion Pacts', in Gregory H Fox and Brad R Roth (eds), *Democratic Governance and International Law* (Cambridge: Cambridge University Press, 2000) 328

Rougier, Antoine, 'La théorie de l'intervention d'humanité' (1910) 17 *RGDIP* 468

Rousseau, Charles, 'Chronique des faits internationaux' (1980) 83 *RGDIP* 351

Ruggie, John Gerard, 'Territoriality and Beyond: Problematizing Modernity in International Relations' (1993) 47 *International Organization* 139

Sapru, Tara, 'Into the Heart of Darkness: The Case Against the Foray of the Security Council Tribunal into the Rwandan Crisis' (1997) 32 *Texas ILJ* 329

Sarooshi, Danesh, *The United Nations and the Development of Collective Security: The Delegation by the UN Security Council of its Chapter VII Powers* (Oxford: Clarendon Press, 1999)

Schachter, Oscar, 'The Place of Law in the United Nations' [1950] *Annual Review of UN Affairs* 203

—— 'The United Nations and Internal Conflict', in John Norton Moore (ed), *Law and Civil War in the Modern World* (Baltimore: Johns Hopkins University Press, 1974) 401

—— 'The Legality of Pro-Democratic Invasion' (1984) 78 *AJIL* 645

—— 'The Right of States to Use Armed Force' (1984) 82 *Michigan Law Review* 1620

—— 'Authorized Uses of Force by the United Nations and Regional Organizations', in Lori Fisler Damrosch and David J Scheffer (eds), *Law and Force in the New International Order* (Boulder: Westview, 1991) 65

—— 'Is There a Right to Overthrow an Illegitimate Regime?', in *Le droit international au service de la paix, de la justice du développement: mélanges Michel Virally* (Paris: A Pedone, 1991) 423

—— 'United Nations Law in the Gulf Conflict' (1991) 85 *AJIL* 452

Scheffer, David J, 'Use of Force After the Cold War: Panama, Iraq, and the New World Order', in Louis Henkin (ed), *Right v Might: International Law and the Use of Force* (2nd edn; New York: Council on Foreign Relations, 1991) 109

—— 'Toward a Modern Doctrine of Humanitarian Intervention' (1992) 23 *University of Toledo Law Review* 253

Schwebel, Stephen M, 'Aggression, Intervention and Self-Defence' (1972) 136 *RCADI* 411

—— 'The Roles of the Security Council and the International Court of Justice in the Application of International Humanitarian Law' (1995) 27 *NYUJILP* 731

Senior, Nassau William, 'Book Review: Wheaton's International Law' (1843) 156 *Edinburgh Review* 334

Seyersted, Finn, 'United Nations Forces: Some Legal Problems' (1961) 37 *British YBIL* 351

Sharp, Walter G, 'Protecting the Avatars of International Peace and Security' (1996) 7 *Duke JCIL* 93

Shaw, Malcolm N, 'The Heritage of States: The Principle of *Uti Possidetis Juris* Today' (1996) 67 *British YBIL* 75

—— *International Law* (4th edn; Cambridge: Cambridge University Press, 1997)

Simma, Bruna, 'Article 27', in Bruno Simma (ed), *The Charter of the United Nations: A Commentary* (Oxford: Oxford University Press, 1994) 430

—— (ed), *The Charter of the United Nations: A Commentary* (Oxford: Oxford University Press, 1994)

—— 'NATO, the UN and the Use of Force: Legal Aspects' (1999) 10 *European JIL* 1

Skubiszewski, Krzysztof, 'The International Court of Justice and the Security Council', in Vaughan Lowe and Malgosia Fitzmaurice (eds), *Fifty Years of the International Court of Justice: Essays in Honour of Sir Robert Jennings* (Cambridge: Grotius, 1996) 606

Smith, F E, *International Law* (J Wylie (ed); 4th edn; London: J M Dent, 1911)

Smith, Tony, 'In Defense of Intervention' (1994) 73(6) *Foreign Affairs* 34

Sofaer, Abraham D, 'The Legality of the United States Action in Panama' (1991) 29 *Columbia JTL* 281

Sohn, Louis B, and Thomas Buergenthal, *International Protection of Human Rights* (Indianapolis: Bobbs-Merrill, 1973)

Stapleton, Augustus Granville, *Intervention and Non-Intervention: The Foreign Policy of Great Britain from 1790 to 1865* (London: J Murray, 1866)

Starke, J G, 'Human Rights and International Law', in Eugene Kamenka and Alice Erh-Soon Tay (eds), *Human Rights* (London: Edward Arnold, 1978) 113

Steiner, Henry J, and Philip Alston, *International Human Rights in Context: Law, Politics, Morals* (Oxford: Clarendon Press, 1996)

Stone, Julius, *Aggression and World Order* (London: Stevens, 1958)

Stone, Julius, *Legal Controls of International Conflict* (rev edn; Sydney: Maitland, 1959)

Stowell, Ellery C, *Intervention in International Law* (Washington, DC: John Byrne & Co, 1921)

Straus, Oscar S, 'Humanitarian Diplomacy of the United States' (1912) 6 *ASIL Proc* 45

Suárez, Francisco, *Selections from Three Works* (Oxford: Clarendon Press, 1944)

Suy, Erik, 'Peace-Keeping Operations', in René-Jean Dupuy (ed), *Handbook on International Organizations* (Dordrecht: Martinus Nijhoff, 1988) 379

Talmon, Stefan, 'Recognition of Governments: An Analysis of the New British Policy and Practice' (1992) 53 *British YBIL* 231

—— *Recognition of Governments in International Law: With Particular Reference to Governments in Exile* (Oxford: Clarendon Press, 1998)

Tesón, Fernando R, *Humanitarian Intervention: An Inquiry into Law and Morality* (Dobbs Ferry, NY: Transnational, 1988)

—— 'The Kantian Theory of International Law' (1992) 92 *Columbia Law Review* 53

—— 'Collective Humanitarian Intervention' (1996) 17 *Michigan JIL* 323

—— *Humanitarian Intervention: An Inquiry into Law and Morality* (2nd edn; Dobbs Ferry, NY: Transnational Publishers, 1997)

Textor, Johann Wolfgang, *Synopsis juris gentium* ([1680] Washington, DC: Carnegie Institution, 1916)

Tharoor, Shashi, 'The Changing Face of Peace-Keeping and Peace-Enforcement' (1995) 19 *Fordham ILJ* 408

Thiele, Terry Vernon, 'Norms of Intervention in a Decolonized World' (1978) 11 *NYUJILP* 141

Thomas, A J, and Ann Van Wynen Thomas, *The Dominican Republic Crisis 1965* (Background Paper and Proceedings of the Ninth Hammarskjöld Forum; Dobbs Ferry: Oceana, 1967)

Thomas, Ann Van Wynen, and A J Thomas, *Non-Intervention: The Law and Its Import in the Americas* (Dallas: Southern Methodist University Press, 1956)

Thompson, E P, *Whigs and Hunters: The Origin of the Black Act* (Harmondsworth: Penguin, 1977)

Tittemore, Brian D, 'Belligerents in Blue Helmets: Applying International Humanitarian Law to United Nations Peace Operations' (1997) 33 *Stanford JIL* 61

Tomuschat, Christian (ed), *The United Nations at Age Fifty: A Legal Perspective* (The Hague: Kluwer Law International, 1995)

Tunkin, G I, *Theory of International Law* (London: George Allen & Unwin, 1974)

Türk, Danilo, 'The Dangers of Failed States and a Failed Peace in the Post Cold War Era' (1995) 27 *NYUJILP* 625

Umozurike, U O, *Self-Determination in International Law* (Hamden, CT: Shoe String Press, 1972)

—— 'Tanzania's Intervention in Uganda' (1982) 20 *Archiv des Völkerrecht* 301

Urquhart, Brian, 'Learning from the Gulf', *New York Review*, 7 March 1991, 34

—— 'How Not to Fight a Dictator', *New York Review*, 6 May 1999, 25

Valenta, Jiri, *Soviet Intervention in Czechoslovakia: Anatomy of a Decision* (rev edn; Baltimore: Johns Hopkins University Press, 1991)

Vattel, Emmerich de, *The Law of Nations: Principles of the Law of Nature, Applied to the Conduct and Affairs of Nations and Sovereigns* ([1758] Classics of International Law; Fenwick trans; Washington, DC: Carnegie Institution, 1916)

Verwey, Wil D, 'Humanitarian Intervention Under International Law' (1985) 32 *Netherlands ILR* 357

—— 'Humanitarian Intervention', in Antonio Cassese (ed), *The Current Legal Regulation of the Use of Force* (Dordrecht: Martinus Nijhoff, 1986) 57

Verzijl, J H W, *International Law in Historical Perspective* (Leyden: A W Sijthoff, 1968)

Victoria, Fanciscus de, *De Indis et iure belli relectiones* ([1557] Classics of International Law; Washington, DC: Carnegie Institution, 1917)

Visscher, Charles de, *Theory and Reality in Public International Law* (Corbett trans; rev edn; Princeton, NJ: Princeton University Press, 1968)

von Elbe, Joachim, 'The Evolution of the Concept of the Just War in International Law' (1939) 33 *AJIL* 665

von Glahn, Gerhard, *Law Among Nations* (2nd edn; London: Macmillan, 1970)

—— *Law Among Nations* (6th edn; London: Macmillan, 1992)

Waldock, C H M, 'The Regulation of the Use of Force by Individual States in International Law' (1952) 81 *RCADI* 451

Walker, Thomas Alfred, *The Science of International Law* (London: Clay and Sons, 1893)

Walzer, Michael, 'On the Role of Symbolism in Political Thought' (1967) 82 *Political Science Quarterly* 191

—— 'World War II: Why Was This War Different?' (1971) 1 *Philosophy and Public Affairs* 3

—— 'The Moral Standing of States' (1978) 9 *Philosophy and Public Affairs* 209

—— *Just and Unjust Wars: A Moral Argument with Historical Illustrations* (2nd edn; New York: Basic Books, 1992)

Wani, 'Humanitarian Intervention and the Tanzania–Uganda War' (1980) 3 *Horn of Africa* 18

Warbrick, Colin, 'The New British Policy on Recognition of Governments' (1981) 30 *ICLQ* 568

Wedgwood, Ruth, 'The Use of Armed Force in International Affairs: Self-Defense and the Panama Invasion' (1991) 29 *Columbia JTL* 609

—— 'NATO's Campaign in Yugoslavia' (1999) 93 *AJIL* 828

Weisberg, Howard L, 'The Congo Crisis 1964: A Case Study in Humanitarian Intervention' (1972) 12 *Virginia JIL* 261

Weiss, Thomas G, 'Rekindling Hope in UN Humanitarian Intervention', in Walter Clarke and Jeffrey Herbst (eds), *Learning from Somalia: The Lessons of Armed Humanitarian Intervention* (Boulder: Westview, 1997) 207

—— and Kurt M Campbell, 'Military Humanitarianism' (1991) 33 *Survival* 451

Weller, Marc, 'The Kuwait Crisis: A Survey of Some Legal Issues' (1991) 3 *African JICL* 1

—— (ed), *Iraq and Kuwait: The Hostilities and Their Aftermath* (Cambridge International Documents Series, vol 3; Cambridge: Grotius Publications Ltd, 1993)

—— (ed), *Regional Peace-Keeping and International Enforcement: The Liberian Crisis* (Cambridge International Document Series; Cambridge: Cambridge University Press, 1994)

Weller, Marc, *The Crisis in Kosovo, 1989–1999: From the Dissolution of Yugoslavia to Rambouillet and the Outbreak of Hostilities* (International Documents and Analysis vol 1; Linton: Book Systems Plus, 1999)

Westlake, John, *International Law* (2nd edn; Cambridge: Cambridge University Press, 1910)

Weston, Burns H, 'Security Council Resolution 678 and Persian Gulf Decision Making: Precarious Legitimacy' (1991) 85 *AJIL* 516

Wharton, Francis (ed), *A Digest of the International Law of the United States* (2nd edn; Washington, DC: Govt Printing Office, 1887)

Wheaton, Henry, *Elements of International Law* (1st edn; Philadelphia: Carey Lea & Blanchard, 1836)

—— *Elements of International Law* ([1866] Richard Henry Dana Jr (ed); Classics of International Law; 8th edn; Oxford: Clarendon Press, 1936)

White, N D, *The United Nations and the Maintenance of International Peace and Security* (Manchester: Manchester University Press, 1990)

Whiteman, Marjorie M, *Digest of International Law* (Washington, DC: US Govt Printing Office, 1963–73)

Wildman, Richard, *Institutes of International Law* (London: William Benning, 1849)

Wilson, George Grafton, *Handbook of International Law* (2nd edn; St Paul: West, 1927)

Winfield, P H, 'The History of Intervention in International Law' (1922) 3 *British YBIL* 130

Wippman, David, 'Defending Democracy Through Foreign Intervention' (1997) 19 *Houston JIL* 659

—— 'Pro-Democratic Intervention by Invitation', in Gregory H Fox and Brad R Roth (eds), *Democratic Governance and International Law* (Cambridge: Cambridge University Press, 2000) 293

Wolff, Christian, *Jus gentium methodo scientifica pertractatum* ([1764] Classics of International Law; Drake trans; Oxford: Clarendon Press, 1934)

Wolfke, Karol, *Custom in Present International Law* (2nd edn; Dordrecht: Martinus Nijhoff, 1993)

Woodhouse, C M, *The Battle of Navarino* (London: Hodder & Stoughton, 1965)

Woods, James L, 'US Government Decisionmaking Processes During Humanitarian Operations in Somalia', in Walter Clarke and Jeffrey Herbst (eds), *Learning from Somalia: The Lessons of Armed Humanitarian Intervention* (Boulder: Westview, 1997) 151

Woodward, Bob, *The Commanders* (London: Simon & Schuster, 1991)

Woodward, E L, and Rohan Butler (eds), *Documents on British Foreign Policy 1919–1939* (London: HMSO, 1949)

Woolsey, Theodore D, *Introduction to the Study of International Law* (4th edn; London: Sampson, Low, Marston, Low & Searle, 1875)

Woolsey, Theodore Salisbury, *America's Foreign Policy* (New York: Century, 1898)

Wright, Quincy, 'Intervention, 1956' (1957) 51 *AJIL* 257

Zöckler, Markus, 'Germany in Collective Security Systems—Anything Goes?' (1995) 6 *European JIL* 274

Zouche, Richard, *Juris et judicii fecialis, sive, juris inter gentes, et quaestionum de eodem explicatio* ([1650] Classics of International Law; Brierly trans; Washington, DC: Carnegie Institute, 1911)

# Index

*Note*: Cases, Treaties, and UN Resolutions are listed in the tables at the start of the volume.